POWER IN THE PACIFIC

DINGMAN, Roger. Power in the Pacific: the origins of naval arms limitation, 1914–1922. Chicago, 1976. 318p map bibl index 75-36402. 19.00 ISBN 0-226-15331-2. C.I.P.

Dingman (University of Southern California) takes as a point of departure the thesis that "Arms limitation is above all else, a political process"; this thesis is a timely proposition in the year 1977. He ably supports his point with extensive research in British, American, and Japanese archives; in fact his is the first English study to use the Japanese sources. Harding's desire to lead, Britain's longing to pursue a middle way and preserve coalition, Japan's wish to restructure the politics of national defense, all led to arms limitation and took precedence over technology, strategic concepts, moralism, etc. Dingman shows the interplay of domestic and defense politics as the Sprouts did for the American Navy (Harold and M. Sprout, *Toward a new order of sea power,* 1943), but widens the view to three navies. A list of statesmen mentioned, footnotes, and bibliography. Comparative history at its best, this book is highly recommended for the undergraduate library.

Roger Dingman

POWER IN THE PACIFIC

114971

The Origins of Naval Arms Limitation, 1914–1922

The University of Chicago Press/Chicago and London

The University of Chicago Press,
Chicago 60637
The University of Chicago Press,
Ltd., London

**Library of Congress Cataloging in
Publication Data**

Dingman, Roger.
  Power in the Pacific.

  Bibliography: p.
  Includes index.
  1. Disarmament—History.
2. United States. Navy—History.
3. Great Britain. Navy—History.
4. Japan. Navy—History. I. Title.
JX1974.D465   327'.172   75–36402
ISBN 0–226–15331–2

ROGER DINGMAN served as an officer
in the U.S. Navy in Japan from 1960 to
1962 and is now associate professor of
history at the University of Southern
California. He is the coeditor of Kindai
Nihon no taigai taido (Modern Japan's
Attitude toward the World).

For My Parents

Contents

Illustrations

Preface

This is a book about arms control. It attempts to answer a single question: Why did statesmen and admirals a half century ago limit the size of their navies by international agreement?

My search for an answer to that question has been long and indirect. I began it in my doctoral dissertation, an examination of American and Japanese naval policies between 1918 and 1921. As a fledgling diplomatic historian, I posed the question that others before me had raised: How did two powers on the verge of naval rivalry and diplomatic antagonism so suddenly reverse course toward naval limitation and international cooperation? In searching for an answer in Tokyo, I found, to my surprise, that I had to turn away from international politics per se and look into the fascinating but shadowy world of domestic politics.

But that, I sensed, was not sufficient. As thoughtful readers reminded me, I had left out the third power in Pacific naval affairs, Great Britain. Moreover, the documents and books I had read repeated a puzzling phrase, "the lessons of the war." I realized that I had to go back beyond 1918 to get the full story. In 1969 grants from the Harvard American East Asian Relations Committee and the American Philosophical Society enabled me to do so. I discovered new materials in Tokyo and archival riches beyond belief in London. The latter, especially the Lloyd George papers, convinced me that I had been on the wrong track. My story, in essence, dealt not with diplomacy but with a very special aspect of domestic politics—what is termed "the politics of national defense" in this book.

Three experiences over the past few years have deepened my under-standing of that politics. Participation in the Faculty Seminar on Bureau-cratic Politics at the John F. Kennedy Institute of Politics at Harvard alerted me to the influence of organizations on men and policies. Membership in the California Arms Control and Foreign Policy Seminar exposed me to the methodology and perspectives of those concerned with contemporary arms limitation. From them I gained the awareness that arms control is not so much an event as a process. Finally, in studying twentieth-century political leaders with students at Harvard and the University of Southern California, I came to understand that the perspec-tives and needs of individual leaders vitally affected that process.

The result, this book, is thus very different from my original expecta-tions. While it does explain a basic change in one aspect of the international political system, it is not a diplomatic history. It is not naval history. It is, above all else, a study in comparative history. It demon-strates that politics *within* the capitals of the three major naval nations, far more than international relationships among them, determined the charac-ter and assured the success of the first strategic arms limitation agree-ment in modern times. The story is one of change, of change brought about by war and campaigns against it, by men of high principle and of selfish motive, by their struggles to master bureaucratic organizations and their acceptance of economic, political, and strategic realities.

My narrative has three parts. In Part I, I analyze the forces that produced competitive naval expansion in the years before World War I and describe that conflict's impact on them. In London war shattered political alliances and strained the bonds of confidence between statesmen and admirals to the breaking point. In Tokyo it strengthened them. War bred a heady nationalism in Washington that inspired both unprecedented naval expan-sion and fresh thought about naval limitation. Part II describes the failure of initial efforts to make those new thoughts political realities. Chapter five shows how their imposition of arms limitation on the vanquished made the victors wary of its implications for their own mutual relation-ships. The next three chapters probe the differing domestic and bureau-cratic pressures and psychological responses to "the lessons of the war" that crushed all initiatives for naval limitation by international agreement. Part III analyzes the dramatic reversal of circumstances that led to the summoning of the Washington Conference of 1921–22. Domestic political pressures in Washington brought Warren G. Harding to the realization that he would have to take the lead in seeking an arms control agreement. In London similar forces conspired to frustrate the development of new naval policies. The very life of the Japanese government came to depend on the character and probable fate of naval limitation proposals. The final chapter reveals how differing domestic political needs shaped the behavior and set limits to the achievements of the statesmen and admirals who concluded the Washington naval limitation agreements of 1922.

Throughout the book I have used the normal Japanese name sequence. That is, the surname precedes the personal name.

Over the years since I began the doctoral dissertation which has metamorphosed into this book, I have benefited from the intellectual guidance, financial support, and personal assistance of the individuals and institutions listed below. To them, and to those others whose names a chronically bad memory may have caused me to overlook, I express heartfelt thanks.

Dr. Dean Allard, Naval History Division; Professor Albert M. Craig, Harvard University; Professor Robert Dallek, University of California, Los Angeles; Professor Hosoya Chihiro, Hitotsubashi University; Professor Akira Iriye, University of Chicago; Professor Ernest R. May, Harvard University; Professor Arthur Marder, University of California, Irvine; Professor Ian Nish, London School of Economics and Political Science; Professor Edwin O. Reischauer, Harvard University; Captain Sanematsu Yuzuru, Imperial Japanese Navy; Admiral Suekuni Masao, Imperial Japanese Navy; Takagi Kiyoko, Tokyo; Captain Tominaga Kengo, Imperial Japanese Navy; Professor Tsunoda Jun, Kokugakuin University, Tokyo; American-East Asian Policy Studies Committee, Harvard University; American Philosophical Society; California Arms Control and Foreign Policy Seminar; Fulbright-Hays Foreign Studies Program; Hoover Institution, Stanford University; Inter-University Center for Japanese Studies, Tokyo; the staffs of the Alderman Library, University of Virginia, Charlottesville; the Bancroft Library, University of California, Berkeley; Beaverbrook Library, London; British Library (formerly the British Museum), London; Detroit Public Library; *Gaikō Shiryōkan*, Tokyo; Hoover Institution Library; Houghton Library, Harvard College Library; Office of War History Library, Japan Defense Agency; Japan Ministry of Foreign Affairs Library, Tokyo; Library of Congress, Washington, D.C.; Massachusetts Historical Society, Boston; National Archives, Washington, D.C.; National Diet Library, Tokyo; Naval History Division, Department of the Navy, Washington, D.C.; Naval War College Library, Newport, Rhode Island; Ohio Historical Society, Columbus; Public Record Office, London; Franklin D. Roosevelt Library, Hyde Park, New York; University Research Library, University of California, Los Angeles; University of Southern California Library; Lt. Comdr. and Mrs. Paul R. Chatelier, United States Navy; Mr. Enamoto Jūji; Miss Hirota Noriko; Dr. and Mrs. Daniel S. Hirshfield; Commander Sekino Hideo, Imperial Japanese Navy; Rev. and Mrs. Joseph Tatnall, and Mr. Eugene Williams.

I am also indebted to the following for permission to use unpublished and copyright material: Mr. Henry Borden; Controller, Her Britannic Majesty's Stationery Office; Director, the Bancroft Library, University of California, Berkeley; Director, Burton Historical Collection; Detroit Public Library; Director, Gaikō Shiryōkan, Tokyo; Director, National Diet Library, Tokyo; Director, Office of War History, Tokyo; Mrs. William T. Gossett; Houghton Library, Harvard University; Hon. Henry Cabot Lodge, Jr.; Trustees of the Beaverbrook Foundation; Trustees of the National Maritime Museum, Greenwich; Yale University Library; University of Virginia Library; and Mrs. L. Metcalfe Walling. In some cases, I have not been able to trace if and where rights over material are reserved. To those whose permission I ought to have secured but have not, I offer my belated apologies.

Finally, a special word of thanks goes to my wife, Linda, for her help in so many ways and to my four children, Charles, Margaret, Zachary, and Andrew, for their patience in listening to so much about so many navies.

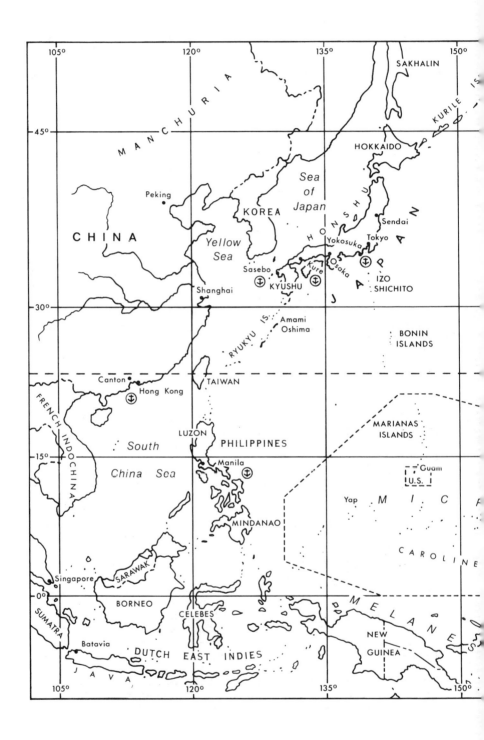

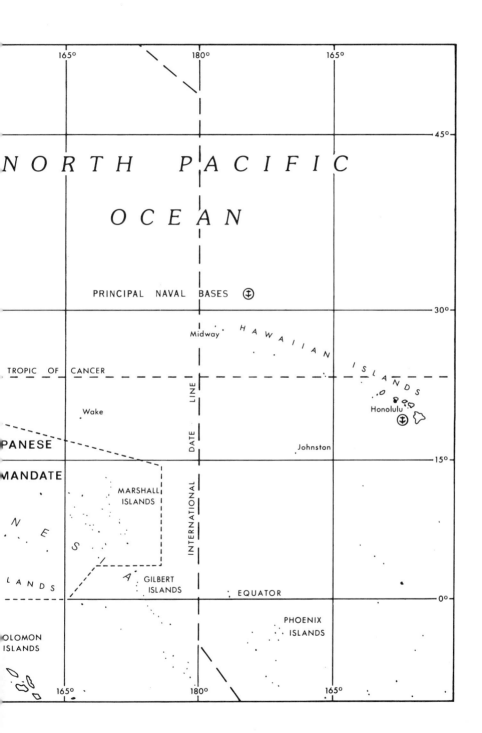

165° 180° 165°

45°

NORTH PACIFIC

OCEAN

PRINCIPAL NAVAL BASES ⊕

30°

Midway *H A W A I I A N*

I S L A N D S

TROPIC OF CANCER

Honolulu ⊕

DATE LINE

Wake

PANESE

Johnston

15°

MANDATE

MARSHALL
ISLANDS

INTERNATIONAL

N

E

S

L A N D S

A GILBERT
ISLANDS

EQUATOR

0°

PHOENIX
ISLANDS

OLOMON
ISLANDS

165° 180° 165°

1

The Storm, 1914–1918

Twilight of an Era

1 In the twilight of peace in 1914 there glimmered a sense of certainty that World War I extinguished forever. The life of the individual or the nation could, as always, be struck down by the unpredictable. But men of many sorts—politicians and journalists, clergymen and professors—shared the faith that life could be rendered progressively less unpredictable. They dreamed of order, of prosperity, and of an end to organized violence. They shared the age-old hope that man could put an end to war. Their faith touched the core of their being and gave meaning to their very existence.

On the eve of Armageddon, men were bitterly divided on how to attain their common goal. For some the realities of the present represented progress toward the desired future. A worldwide system of alliances, they argued, soothed great power antagonisms and thus increased the prospects for continued peace. That system promised stability in international relations even though it de-

3

manded continuous increases in armaments. Among them, the battleship was the most important weapon, the recognized standard of naval power which rendered clear and predictable the capabilities and perhaps even the intentions of great powers. Thus even competitive arms expansion might, in the long run, contribute to the maintenance of peace.

Other men rejected such arguments. For them the alliance system defined frightening prospects of conflict. It clarified but also intensified international antagonisms. The arms competition it spawned devoured individual nations' resources and distorted national priorities. Beyond this, they insisted, the battleship was an empty symbol of national pride. Arms expansion fostered a culture of violence—one that would inexorably lead men to individual death, national self-destruction, and international conflict.

But opponents and advocates of arms expansion agreed on one key point. International and domestic political systems were inextricably linked. They provided regularity, perhaps even predictability, to the politics of national defense. Admirals commanded ships and men—and made plans for getting more of both. Diplomats seconded their claims to strengthen the alliances that they had negotiated. Opponents of arms expansion attacked the arguments of both in press, pulpit, and parliament. But in the end politicians and bureaucrats provided more money for naval defense. This was the pattern that had repeated itself in world capitals for a decade and more.

How did this order of sea power develop? What sustained it? Was it likely to change?

In 1914 men believed that international naval relationships had grown out of the European alliance system. A decade earlier, in 1904, five of the six leading naval powers were linked to it. The two most powerful naval nations, Great Britain and Germany, were the poles around which the other powers revolved. Imperial Germany maintained the ties Bismarck had developed with Austria-Hungary and Italy. Kaiser Wilhelm II and his chief naval advisor, Grand Admiral Alfred von Tirpitz, broke with the past when they determined to build a great navy. They believed Germany must possess a fleet sufficient to deter an attack by Great Britain, the most formidable of their adversaries and the world's leading maritime power. Beginning in 1898, Berlin devoted more and more marks to successive naval construction programs.[1]

German naval expansion was one factor that led other powers to coalesce around Great Britain after 1904. London had already broken the tradition of splendid isolation two years earlier by signing an alliance with Japan. The Anglo-Japanese alliance was originally directed against Imperial Russia. It provided for naval cooperation which enhanced Japan's power and prestige in East Asia and, in 1904, permitted Britain to reduce her naval commitments in the China seas. Ships were brought home to meet the challenge posed by Germany. For the first time, the Royal Navy drew up plans for battle with the kaiser's fleet. In 1904, too, British statesmen ended Anglo-French colonial antagonisms and negotiated the entente cordiale. Three years later agreements between London and St. Petersburg completed the cluster of powers around Great Britain.[2]

Formation of the two alliance systems and mounting tension between them influenced the policies of all the naval powers. While American and Japanese statesmen and admirals did not consider their nations parties to European disputes, they did look upon British and German building programs as a barometer of international tension and a gauge of their own naval security. Britain's introduction of the all big gun battleship, H.M.S. *Dreadnought*, in

Chart 1

Naval expenditure as a percentage of total national expenditure, 1907–14

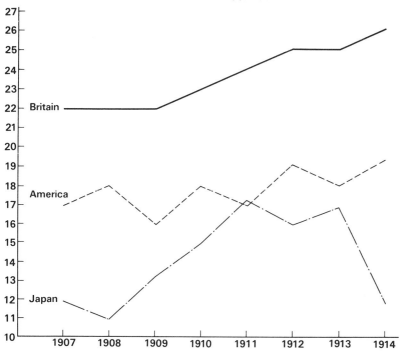

Based on: U.S. Department of Commerce, *Historical Statistics of the United States* (Washington, 1960); B. R. Mitchell, *Abstract of British Historical Statistics* (Cambridge, 1962); Kaigun daijin kanbō, *Kaigun gunbi enkaku: furoku*, chart 8, 2d ed. (Tokyo, 1970).

1906 demonstrated the unity of the international naval system. It intensified Anglo-German naval competition. But it also convinced statesmen and admirals in non-European capitals that they would have to match this naval advance if they were to remain secure upon the seas. The United States, even though it stood apart from the European alliance systems, determined to build more and better battleships. In Tokyo, Navy Ministry experts concluded that they must have a fleet of sixteen modern capital ships. On both sides of the North Sea, naval expansionists disavowed hostile intentions yet argued that they must match one another's fleet increases. All came to the conclusion that the international system demanded constant fleet growth. As chart one indicates, America, Britain, and Japan, like other major naval powers, spent more and more pounds, yen, and dollars on battleships and during the seven years prior to World War I devoted an increasing proportion of their budgets to naval defense.[3]

These statistics mirrored international tensions and reflected their impact on naval building programs. But they also echoed domestic political debates over naval policy in Washington, Tokyo, and London. Nowhere were the politics of naval defense more intense, the battle lines more clearly drawn, the strengths of friends and foes of naval growth more nearly equal than in Britain. The forces that favored an ever stronger navy were formidable. The Royal Navy itself stood first among them. Imaginative leadership and professional confidence gave the service political power. Admiral Sir John Fisher embodied both. When he became First Sea Lord in 1904, the *Daily Express* cartooned Nelson climbing back up on his column at the sight of Fisher entering the Admiralty. The caption read: "If Jacky Fisher's taking the job there's no need for me." Fisher fought to reform the service, won funds to build an all dreadnought fleet, and constantly "educated" politicians to the navy's needs. When he retired, Winston Churchill assumed the mantle of naval leadership as First Lord of the Admiralty. Although his style differed from the old admiral's, the young politician was no less effective. If Fisher "won" by hurling invective at his enemies and mastering the politics of Whitehall and London society, Churchill triumphed through eloquence and dramatic gestures such as flying in naval aircraft.[4]

The navy was also powerful because its officers were confident of its role, certain of its enemy, and convinced of the superiority of its weaponry. The admirals believed certain "truths" of sea power, most of them drawn from the writings of the American naval historian, Alfred Thayer Mahan. Mahan defined their mission: to secure and retain "command of the sea." He made clear the role and responsibilities of a navy: it existed to protect the nation's commerce in peace and annihilate its enemy's fleet in war.[5]

By 1914 British admirals had no doubt that Germany was that enemy. Berlin's repeated fleet increases threatened to destabilize the balance of naval power. A tacit Anglo-American entente quieted any fears about the security of the western Atlantic, and the Anglo-Japanese alliance permitted reduction of units in the western Pacific to the bare minimum. The Anglo-French entente dictated concentration of capital ships in the North Sea. Strategic conversations between London and Paris in 1912 reduced Britain's naval presence and responsibility in the Mediterranean. They made it clear that the Royal Navy's primary objectives in war would be to check the German High Seas Fleet, blockade German commerce, and prevent German attacks on expeditionary forces crossing the Channel. In the North Sea, the admirals agreed, the decisive engagement with the enemy would come.[6]

Admirals were certain that the capital ship would be the decisive weapon in that great battle. Recent history "proved" that either the heavily armored battleship or newer, faster, and more lightly protected battle cruisers would assure victory. At Tsushima in 1905 two parallel lines of battleships had hurled destruction at one another until the Russian fleet was destroyed. Tradition and political necessity reinforced faith in the battleship. From 1889 onward, Britain had defined naval security in terms of a "Two Power Standard," that is, maintenance of strength greater than that of the next two ranking naval powers. While admirals and statesmen often differed over the precise terms of the standard and at times felt it desirable to keep it vague, they agreed that the battleship was the best measure of naval security. Few men within the navy were ready to challenge that proposition. Naval aviation was yet in its infancy; aviators succeeded in dropping torpedoes for the first time in 1914. A few submarine enthusiasts insisted that the day of the battleship had passed. Fisher himself recognized the submarine's potential, but neither he, ranking Admiralty officials, nor politicians were prepared to admit that undersea vessels would revolutionize naval warfare.[7]

One other factor spurred the admirals to action in London's politics of national defense. They feared Britain's sea supremacy was being threatened as much or more at home as in Berlin. As Fisher saw it, a cabal of generals and professional civil servants sought to "turn us into a Continental Power when God made us an island." His fears were not without foundation. Anglo-French military conversations portended a shift in national strategy. If an army went to the Continent, it, rather than the fleet, might lay claim to being the nation's first line of defense. The War Office might well get a bigger share of the defense budget. To counter this threat, the admirals dragged their feet when the Committee of Imperial Defense discussed the implications of the French connection and championed the battleship all the more vigorously.[8]

Over the years, the Admiralty built strong ties in Whitehall, Westminster, and Fleet Street to buttress its case for naval growth. Its strongest ally within the bureaucracy was the Foreign Office. This might seem ironic, for it was Sir Edward Grey, the foreign secretary, who deepened the commitment to France and thereby strengthened the War Office's claim to more pounds, shillings, and pence. Yet Grey and his senior colleagues regarded the navy as vital to their diplomacy. Naval power helped hold alliances together. Limited naval technological change figured in the renegotiation of the Anglo-Japanese alliance in 1907, and the coordination of naval plans proved vital in 1912–1914 discussions with the French. Diplomats knew, too, that naval power provided creditability to the empire's commitments and stability to the entire international political system. To seek naval limitation in a system which premised expansion, Grey reminded Churchill in May 1914, would be to create "intolerable" uncertainties.[9]

Other bureaucratic and social factors reinforced the bonds between diplomats and admirals. Foreign Office officials may have been cool to naval limitation talks with Berlin because they felt that those within the cabinet who favored them were amateurs, if not interlopers, in their field of professional competence. They were certainly more drawn socially to admirals than to arms control advocates. Professional diplomats and sailors tended to come from the upper strata of society, while the foes of naval building came from more humble origins. Their value systems also coincided, in that admirals and diplomats sought to preserve order and stability. Nonconformist arms limitation advocates, by contrast, were passionate advocates of change.[10]

The forces behind naval expansion were also strong in Parliament. During the decade between his arrival at Admiralty House and the outbreak of war, Fisher fought skillfully and tirelessly to build friendships in Westminster. Over the years the combination that supported naval growth became a strong one. Unionist members of parliament, although in the minority, formed its nucleus. These Tories supported a strong navy by habit; in their eyes naval preeminence was inseparable from national survival. They were joined by an important element of the ruling Liberal party. These so-called imperialists were men who had supported prosecution of the Boer War when other Liberals opposed it. They thought the navy a necessity and regarded its growth as a kind of insurance against international disaster. Until the very eve of war, Irish M.P.'s formed another, if less predictable, element within the pro-naval coalition.[11]

Finally, vigorous and widespread support from Fleet Street strengthened the forces behind naval growth. The fact that Tory and Liberal editors alike championed the navy was no accident. Fisher wooed them with all the wit and cunning at his command. His most important allies were Liberals—C. P. Scott of the *Manchester Guardian* and A. G. Gardiner of the *Daily News*. Timely, useful leaks and reasoned argument brought them into the naval camp. Fisher argued that the navy was the Liberals' surest defense against a large, undemocratic army. He promised more naval defense at less cost, and when this became impossible blamed Berlin for Britain's increased naval estimates. Most importantly, Fisher appealed to editors and through them to millions of readers with the argument that the navy could and would guarantee national security. His message got through. As C. P. Scott put it, "The number of our ships as against German ships is what everybody talks about and the only thing the public understands."[12]

Those who opposed such arguments enjoyed few of their proponents' advantages. The friends of naval limitation were not led by men with the dramatic flair of Churchill, the cunning of Fisher, or the shrewdness of Grey. They were older, quieter, more genteel politicians—men who lacked the political skill and newsworthy qualities of their opponents. They, too, presided over a coalition. It included a wide variety of men with different motives, interests, and approaches to arms limitation. Some were pacifists—either from nonconformist religious conviction or from the belief that capitalist elites provoked unnatural antagonisms among Europe's working classes. Some were shippers and traders who held fast to the nineteenth-century liberal view of armaments as "waste." More battleships meant more taxation and deprived business of monies that ought to have been invested in commercial enterprises, the true source of British greatness. Still others were nationalistic idealists. These men, even after the failure of the 1907 Hague Conference, wanted Britain to take the lead in arranging arms limitation by international agreement.[13]

Time worked both for and against these friends of arms control. With the passage of the years, their arguments grew in sophistication. It was not just that battleships were wicked. They were a poor investment. The behemoths of the sea cost too much to build, quickly became obsolete, and in the long run consumed a fortune for maintenance. Those who wanted to build more were not evil men, but simply blind ones. They failed to see how huge construction contracts profited industrial monopolists and tightened the grip of conservative politicians on the poor. Beyond this, naval building distorted the vision of Britain's leaders. They had not seen that continued, competitive construction provoked Berlin to respond in kind. Surely, the advocates of naval limitation insisted, creative statesmen could find a scheme to halt "this 'crazy' competition" which their opposites in the Wilhelmstrasse could accept.[14]

But the years also sapped the strength of those who fought for naval limitation. The elections of 1910 greatly weakened their power in Parliament. Labor strength declined, and the influence of radical "economists" within the Liberal party dropped. Indeed leaders of the arms limitation movement were forced to take refuge in extra-parliamentary organizations such as the National Liberal Federation. The failure of repeated overtures to Berlin also hurt. Opponents were quick to argue that Germany simply was not interested in a naval limitation agreement. Economic developments also worked to the disadvantage of arms control advocates. In hard times unemployed workers broke with Labor leaders to seek income in building warships. More generally, after 1909 the economy seemed to be developing so as to permit Britons to have *both* guns and butter, rather than one or the other as arms control advocates insisted.[15]

The most subtle and important factor that worked against those who favored naval limitation, however, was political. Opponents portrayed them as purists, as naive radicals whose enthusiasm threatened to rend the fabric of peace and shatter the balance of political forces at home. Yet in fact their values predisposed them to compromise. As one of their slogans had it, "moderation breeds moderation." No one knew and used that truth more effectively than the prime minister, Herbert Henry Asquith. Over the years he had preserved the uneasy coalition of "economists" and "imperialists" within the Liberal party. He had opposed indiscriminate naval expansion and acquiesced in attempts at arms limitation. There was no naval increase in 1907, the year of the Hague Conference; and Asquith tolerated overtures to Berlin by David Lloyd George in 1908 and Viscount Haldane in 1912. The prime minister pretended neutrality between friends and foes of naval expansion. But at the critical moments, he sided with the former. In 1909 he rejected Lloyd George's arguments for economizing, backed a major fleet expansion program, and promised social welfare measures as well. Asquith obviously felt that Britain could have both guns and butter. His task was to manage the annual battle of the budget so as to assure moderate naval growth and harmony within his party.[16]

Asquith's skill and finesse doomed arms control advocates to frustration and failure. His handling of the last great prewar debate over naval estimates demonstrated that fact. Late in 1913, Churchill presented estimates which alarmed parliamentary opponents of naval expansion and shocked members of the cabinet. Petitions flooded Number 10 Downing Street; protest meetings were held in the City of London; editorial writers excoriated Churchill. The cabinet, however, adjourned for the Christmas holidays without reaching a decision on the naval budget. Then, on New Year's Day 1914, David Lloyd George, chancellor of the exchequer and the second most powerful man in the cabinet, published an attack on Churchill and his estimates.

For nearly a month thereafter Lloyd George and Churchill fought one another. Junior members of the cabinet who opposed the estimates resigned in protest. Asquith struggled to restore harmony within his inner cabinet. Finally, after Lloyd George had voiced all of the anti-expansionist arguments, he came to the conclusion that further resistance was politically dangerous. Further debate would destroy the cabinet, split the Liberal party, and, in all probability, ruin his own career. Asquith, Lloyd George, and Churchill then agreed on a compromise which preserved domestic political stability. They approved the largest naval estimates in British history.[17]

The outcome of this debate suggested that naval expansion was endemic to British politics. That was also the case in Washington, where the politics of naval defense had become as stable and predictable as those of London. American naval policy developed out of presidential passion, professional ambition, and congressional regularity. President Theodore Roosevelt, a naval enthusiast since the days of his service as assistant secretary of the navy, thought of the fleet as a symbol of national power and a stimulant to national unity. In 1908–1909, he sent the "Great White Fleet" around the world, in part to test its battle readiness, in part to bolster Republican popularity on the West Coast where many people feared a Japanese invasion. Year after year he championed fleet increases, Republican congresses voted the necessary funds, and the public approved what was done.[18]

Senior naval officers seconded Roosevelt's passionate appeals. They had not the leadership, bureaucratic alliances, or political sophistication of their British opposites. Admiral George Dewey, hero of the Battle of Manila Bay and chairman of the navy's General Board, was no Fisher. He embodied the nineteenth-century view that naval officers should steer clear of all politics. Younger officers, like Bradley Fiske, championed reforms to assure better command and control of the fleet; they also sought more effective civil-military-naval coordination in the shaping of national policy. But persistent interservice frictions and diplomats' deafness to all appeals for collaboration doomed their efforts to failure. Finally, the admirals lacked the kinds of friendships with politicians on Capitol Hill and editors that so strengthened the Royal Navy.[19]

Nonetheless, American naval officers were important in the politics of national defense in presenting a nonprovocative, "expert" case for naval growth. Beginning in 1903, the General Board advocated expansion until the fleet should consist of forty-eight new battleships. These vessels, the admirals explained, were needed to keep pace with British, German, and Japanese increases. The capital ship, moreover, was *the* measure of naval security. Innovators within the service were quick to second this argument. In 1912, Lieutenant Chester W. Nimitz wrote a prizewinning essay in which he argued that the submarine was a kind of underwater destroyer, a specialized craft that could serve as coast defender and as scout in capital ship engagements. Fledgling aviators simply described their machines as aids to the fleet.[20]

These arguments reflected both the admirals' sense of how the budgetary game was played and the inherent weaknesses of their own strategic thought. The General Board did want to wrest second place in world naval standings from Germany and padded its requests so as to leave room for harmless congressional cuts. But its proposals did not flow from clear strategic perspectives or careful war plans. To be sure, General Board annual reports spoke of two possible antagonists—Germany and Japan. A few staff officers had drawn up war plans for dealing with either. But in practice, as Rear Admiral Fiske subsequently recalled, the U.S. Navy looked east and south—and feared a German advance. American naval strategists worried most about the Caribbean. In that unstable region, the United States had to assert "command of the seas" and protect its commerce. Consequently the fleet was concentrated, except for the years of its circumnavigation of the globe, in the western Atlantic and Caribbean. Thoughts about war in the western Pacific, by comparison, were vague. The admirals as yet had no adequate mid-Pacific base at Hawaii. They could not agree with army spokesmen on the location and character of defenses for the Philippines and Guam. They had only the haziest notions about how to fight Japan. At best, planners thought of moving the fleet across the Pacific to defeat Japan in her home waters. At worst, they realized they lacked the logistical capability to do so. Consequently the admirals thought and worried most about "Black" (Germany) and only occasionally about "Orange" (Japan).[21]

The admirals' political opponents were quick to point out the weaknesses in their case. The foes of naval expansion, most of them Democrats from the South and Middle West, taunted the naval leaders with being unimaginative. Their scheme to build forty-eight battleships was nothing more than a ploy to get and name one for each state. Expensive capital ships were defenseless against cheap torpedoes. One staunch "little-navy" Democrat exclaimed that "from a common-sense business standpoint . . . I doubt the wisdom or expediency of the construction of any more battleships of the Dreadnought type."[22]

Other arguments heard in Washington were variations on those made in London. The missionary tradition of American foreign policy strengthened the moral argument against continued naval construction. The Republic, one Minnesota Democrat proclaimed, should not show to the world "a great Navy strutting and posing, with its cruel guns, bellowing a message of brutality and death to mankind in this civilized age." He and advocates of international arbitration agreed that America should demonstrate that "the way to prepare for peace is to be peaceful." "Economists" concurred. Washington should not waste the nation's almost limitless human, natural, and financial resources by spending one dollar out of every five on the navy. America's power was commercial, not naval—"the power which makes for peace and [which] is much more effective when invested in productive enterprises." As it was, only profiteers and "the armaments trust" benefited from continued naval construction.[23]

These arguments filled the columns of newspapers, magazines, and the *Congressional Record*, but with the exception of fiscal year 1912, when congressional Democrats approved only one battleship, they had little effect. Lethargic William Howard Taft made naval expansion "normal." Carrying out what he termed the "dearest wish" of Theodore Roosevelt, he called for the construction of two battleships annually until the Panama Canal was completed. His able secretary of the navy, George von Lengerke Meyer, put funds for these ships in the regular rather than special category of the naval budget. Administration requests nicely halved the General Board's usual proposal for four capital ships. Meyer justified them as insurance for peace. Regular, planned, long-term expansion would meet immediate needs in both Atlantic and Pacific and preserve America's standing among the world's great naval powers. Arguments of this sort took precedence even over the president's desire for a balanced budget. Thus, except in fiscal 1912, the Taft administration made the "increase of the navy" by two capital ships per year the norm.[24]

Even in years when Democrats controlled both Congress and the White House, "little-navy" men made little headway. None sat in the seats of power. Tennessee's Lemuel Padgett, the House Naval Affairs Committee chairman, abandoned his "little-navy" faith to back moderate naval growth. Senator Ben Tillman of South Carolina, his counterpart in the upper house, eagerly sought funds for the Charleston naval base. From 1913 onward, when Woodrow Wilson occupied the White House, demands of party loyalty took precedence over individual beliefs about naval needs. The president, never a naval enthusiast, needed more than Southern votes to get major domestic reforms approved on Capitol Hill. He was not willing to disrupt his party over one or two battleships.[25]

Instead, Wilson left naval matters to his loyal and shrewd secretary of the navy, Josephus Daniels of North Carolina. On the surface this string-tied Progressive seemed extraordinarily naïve. His order banning alcohol from navy wardrooms infuriated officers and made him the butt of cartoonists' jokes. But behind Daniels's Pollyanna-like smile lurked a keen mind and a razor-sharp political sense. Like Asquith, Daniels held to the center in naval policy debates. He had many ties with leaders of the peace movement and frequently lashed out against the so-called armaments trust. These gestures pleased little-navy Democrats. But the secretary of the navy also supported moderate expansion. In 1913, just like his Republican predecessor, Daniels received General Board recommendations for four new battleships, cut them to two, and then defended the result as "conservative progress" before congressional committees.[26]

The colorful North Carolinian spoke of a golden mean midway between competitive naval expansion and arms limitation by international agreement. In 1913 he expressed agreement in principle with a resolution offered by Representative Walter L. Hensley of Missouri urging the president to seek a holiday in naval building. But Daniels accepted President Wilson's and Secretary of State William Jennings Bryan's judgments that such proposals were impractical in international political terms. He then steered the naval budget through congressional waters so as to assure "increase of the navy" once again.[27]

Japanese statesmen and admirals might well have envied Daniels for the ease with which he won congressional approval of the naval budget. They, too, sought strategic security and domestic political stability through regular fleet expansion. But by 1914 that goal had become elusive. It had not always been so. The architects of the Meiji Constitution had tried to insulate national defense from partisan politics in two ways. First, the constitution made the emperor personally responsible for national security and the service ministers his retainers. Admirals and generals, unlike the other cabinet members, enjoyed the right of direct access to the sovereign. Service ministers, by tradition general or flag officers on active duty, were not subordinate to a civilian minister. They combined professional leadership and service advocacy, functions allotted to two different individuals in Britain and the United States, in one person. This, inevitably, made admirals and generals powerful figures in domestic politics. A second key constitutional provision greatly weakened the legislature's power over national defense. The Diet had to approve service budgets. But if, for any reason, it failed to do so, the army and navy might spend at the preceding year's level. This, at least on paper, significantly weakened parliamentary checks on naval spending.[28]

Powerful admirals and generals took advantage of these constitutional provisions. Admiral Yamamoto Gombei, prime minister in 1914, was just such a leader. Rightly deemed the father of the modern Japanese navy, he gave subordinates a sense of pride and feeling of unity. Yamamoto built his career on organizational skill, political finesse, and fleet expansion. A Satsuma man, he used clan loyalties yet broke the Satsuma monopoly on flag rank. He modernized and increased the fleet. At the turn of the century, Yamamoto fought to make the navy the bureaucratic equal of the army. He then got successive cabinets and Diets to approve naval expansion budgets and used the Anglo-Japanese alliance to remedy technological weaknesses in the fleet. His influence was so strong that he was called the "pope of the navy" and the greatest naval leader in modern Japanese history.[29]

When the admiral stepped down as navy minister, he could rest assured that his service would remain united. Officers were disciples of Admiral Mahan. His writings, translated for popular consumption, became required reading at the Naval Academy and Naval War College. They inspired leading strategic thinkers such as Rear Admiral Akiyama Saneyuki. Tsushima was another force for unity. The great Japanese naval victory there confirmed officers' faith in the supremacy of the battleship. It also gave coherence to the admirals' strategic perspective. Any future war would resemble the great Russo-Japanese conflict just concluded. The enemy would advance, his forces weakening as they moved further from home bases. Units of the

Imperial Navy would lure him into waters close to the home islands. Then the main body of battleships would annihilate the enemy fleet, assuring victory once again.[30]

Visions of this sort fed the admirals' desires for more and better ships. In 1907 they met with generals and politicians to define force levels and strategic priorities. All agreed that Japan should possess strength sufficient to defend her empire alone; Tokyo should not rely on London for assistance. The army would eventually consist of twenty-five divisions, and the navy would expand until it had sixteen capital ships—the so-called "eight-eight fleet." But beyond this the lines of agreement blurred. The army labeled Russia its most probable enemy, but the navy did not include St. Petersburg on its list of possible adversaries. The admirals worried about the United States; the generals did not. Neither service made specific plans for operations in the war which the other envisaged. The prime minister promised to secure funds for arms expansion but postponed full implementation of programs until the economy had completely recovered from the recent war.[31]

This was enough to assure relative harmony on matters of national defense over the succeeding four years. While there was no formal agreement on respective services' shares of the budget, the figures for each preserved a rough parity until 1911. Diet members approved long-term fleet expansion programs and voted credits for them each year. Their willingness to do so reflected party leaders' caution. Rising politicians were far more interested in issues like railroad expansion and education that might strengthen their local power bases. They also realized that they must strike bargains with elder statesmen, admirals, generals, and bureaucrats if they were to survive in the complex interelite struggle for power.[32]

Outspoken opponents of naval expansion were few indeed. Some leaders of the Osaka business community made the classic "economist" arguments against bigger naval budgets. They argued that Japan was the weakest of the great powers. The empire had seriously strained its resources in the recent war and ought to create a sound financial-industrial complex before building more battleships. Other foes of arms expansion were isolated individuals, set apart by prolonged residence in Britain or America or by faith in the Christian message of peace. Even the most influential advocate of arms limitation, Ozaki Yukio, found it difficult not to compromise disarmament for personal power. He eventually became minister of justice in a cabinet that promised continued naval growth.[33]

That government came to power at the end of a three-year-long crisis that shattered domestic political harmony on defense matters. In 1911, army and navy leaders demanded new expansion programs. Their demands and factional rivalries within the dominant Chōshū clique forced the general who served as prime minister to resign. Admiral Yamamoto succeeded him. But the great naval leader destroyed what little harmony remained by proposing naval expansion without corresponding increases in the size of the army. This infuriated Chōshū leaders, and early in 1914 they seized the opportunity to ruin the Yamamoto cabinet. A scandal over naval contracts made with the German firm of Siemens and Company developed, and demonstrators demanded that the admiral resign. Although he was not personally involved in the corruption, Yamamoto did so. But even though the new ministry that came to power promised to increase the size of the fleet, stability in the politics of national defense would not return. The increase of the navy had become a key issue in the struggle for power in Tokyo.[34]

Vast expanses of ocean separated Tokyo, Washington, and London. There were, to be sure, differences in the style and intensity of the politics of naval defense in each city. But statesmen and admirals, expansionists and arms control advocates, despite differences of nationality, were in fact quite similar. All recognized that they lived within an order shaped by the international political alliances that had developed. All were influenced more by the Anglo-German naval antagonism than by specific frictions between Washington, London, and Tokyo. One American spoke for all when he explained: "We must go on building if the others do; if the others stop building, we can stop building when we have reached the safe point."[35] The arguments heard in each capital for and against the battleship as the best means of defining that "safe point" resembled one another.

But an unspoken assumption—the desire for order abroad and harmony at home—brought Britons, Americans, and Japanese closest together. What mattered most to each was stability in the domestic politics of national defense. British and American leaders hoped to continue, their Japanese opposites to restore, bureaucratic routines, political alliances, and habits of thought that had emerged during the preceding decade. Arms control advocates, on the other hand, challenged the existing order in hopes of establishing a new stability.

Thus in the twilight of peace in 1914, naval expansion continued. Berlin built. London survived a ferocious debate that brought forth the largest naval estimates in history. In Washington, Secretary Daniels's golden mean prevailed. Far across the Pacific, not even naval scandal and political infighting stopped the engines of expansion.

These facts suggest one conclusion. Change would occur only if some massive shock struck the entire, interlocking system of naval, political, and international relationships.

2 That shock—the prerequisite for change—began in August 1914. It first appeared on the horizon as nothing more than a Balkan summer squall. But in a very short time it blew up to a storm of hurricane strength— a storm that would extinguish the light of peace for four long years. The storm touched men in every major world capital. They had different reasons for becoming caught up in it, but their purposes were similar. Each group of statesmen, admirals, and generals hoped to annihilate its enemies. They plunged into battle, exposing themselves to perils unforeseen, to winds of change they could not control. The Great War of 1914–1918 buffeted them all; it destroyed much more than fleets and armies, cities and factories. The conflict and the men who waged it put an end to an era. Wilhelmian Germany, "Liberal England," Meiji Japan, and "Isolated America" all perished in the storm. So, too, did the structures men believed guaranteed peace—alliances, proud navies, invincible armies. In their pursuit of victory, men, perhaps inadvertently, disrupted and destroyed institutions, relationships, and the ideas that had given stability to the prewar world. They put an end to the old politics of national defense.

Nowhere was the change, the agony born of prolonged exposure to the storm, the departure from the old order, clearer than in London. On August 4, 1914, Winston Churchill paced anxiously to and fro in his rooms at the Admiralty. He glanced at the hands of the clock, eager for them to reach eleven. At that moment the uncertainties of the preceding four weeks would end. Diplomatic parlays and cabinet councils over, Britain and Germany would go to war. The fleet mobilized, Churchill had no doubt that it would meet the tests of Armageddon triumphantly. He stepped to the window as the clock struck the hour. From below came the lusty voice of the crowd confidently singing "God Save the King."[1]

Four years later, on the eleventh day at the eleventh hour, men and women sang the same anthem. But their mood was very different. The tone at St. Paul's was one of relief, of thanksgiving that the war had finally ended. At Admiralty House and aboard the flagship of the Grand Fleet, however, bitterness filled the air. Admirals suspected statesmen and suffered pangs of self-doubt. "The Fleet, my Fleet, is broken-hearted . . . All suffering from a feeling of something far greater than disappointment, depressed beyond measure," wrote Admiral Sir David Beatty, its commander in chief. The Royal Navy, that finely honed instrument set for quick victory in 1914, had by 1918 become sullen, hypersensitive to criticism, and apprehensive about its future.[2] Britain's trident had been tarnished. Men who had once grasped it so confidently—Herbert Henry Asquith, Winston Churchill, and Jackie Fisher—had fallen from power. Other men sat in their places. These statesmen were not bound by ties of loyalty to Liberalism, and they did not share inner cabinet comradery. They no longer revered the mystique of sea power, and they doubted admirals' premises, procedures, and policies.

How had all this come to pass?

Contemporaries found that question puzzling, painful, perhaps unanswerable. In retrospect, however, the pattern of events that suggests a solution to the puzzle stands out clearly. War prompted men to set aside the norms of prewar politics. All were willing to make sacrifices in pursuit of victory. But when the naval triumphs they had been conditioned to expect did not come speedily and regularly, a prolonged crisis in civil-naval relations developed. Statesmen and admirals tried to resolve it with men, money, and machinery. But their quarrels weakened the navy's leadership, strained public confidence in the fleet, and eventually brought decisive changes to the politics of naval defense.

In 1914 Britons set aside the norms of peacetime politics without realizing that they might never return. Men momentarily caught up in the passion of patriotism acted on the assumption that the war would be short. Great battles would be fought on the continent. Britain would subsidize and supplement her allies' ground forces, then play the trump card of naval power. Some politicians even thought of the struggle as a welcome diversion from the perils of Ireland and labor unrest. It was easy, then, to abandon the routines of peacetime politics.

The order of parliamentary life was the first casualty of battle. By January 1915, 184 M.P.'s had left their seats in Westminster for the fields of France or the decks of the fleet. Those who remained jettisoned the old rules of budgetary politics. Men who had balked at Lloyd George's budget in June 1914 now readily approved huge votes of credit for war operations. One could not be parsimonious in the pursuit of victory. No one realized after the first vote was taken that it would be followed by twenty-four others, appropriating a total of 8,742 million pounds. Few men perceived that the costs of war operations would increase and overtake those of naval construction. And who could have predicted that war would constrict parliamentary debate until approval of naval estimates became a pro forma gesture?[3]

The House of Commons did not abandon its power of the purse, but war greatly diminished its influence. Conflict demanded decisions for action. The cabinet might discuss them, but no one dared debate them openly at Westminster. Criticism of the government had to be muted and retrospective. Opponents of war and arms expansion fell silent. Norman Angell, author of *The Great Illusion*, a widely read attack on war as economic waste, decided to "lie doggo." C. P. Scott counseled parliamentary opponents of the war to remain inactive. Those who had fought against prewar naval expansion budgets did not speak out against wartime votes of credit. Yet one cabinet minister complained that M.P.'s were "a nuisance in time of war."[4]

His remark betrayed political leaders' mixed feelings. Politicians felt the urge to pursue party advantage yet guiltily checked it. They did not declare a truce on all politics but agreed not to contest by-elections. Animosities continued, but war demanded that they be suppressed or at the very least softened. This was hard to do. Arthur Balfour, a former prime minister, managed it but told fellow Conservatives that he felt strange, even if obliged, to sit with Liberals on the Committee of National Defense. Churchill proposed a different solution: coalition. But the prime minister, a more cautious and skillful parliamentary politician, rejected the idea.[5]

Instead, Asquith tried to hold power for himself, placate Parliament, and please the press. He used the war emergency to caulk what had been a very leaky cabinet. The flow of information from Whitehall to Westminster, and even to Fleet Street, dried up. The public was so parched for news of war operations, however, that the press lords demanded more and more information. Asquith gave it to them, but only after his government worked out a scheme for controlled censorship with Fleet Street. This altered the system of political communication. As Parliament's importance declined, the newspapers became the primary means of conveying information to the public and for criticizing the government.[6]

In this changed setting, men were much more concerned with fleet operations than with naval expansion. At first Asquith left the navy to Churchill and the admirals. The first lord had improvised a small War Staff Advisory Group to plan and oversee fleet operations. Far to the north, off the Scottish coast, the Grand Fleet under its new, hand-picked commander, Vice Admiral Sir John Jellicoe, prowled, waiting for the enemy to sortie for the decisive battle. But as the days passed, that battle did not occur. Instead a different kind of war confronted Churchill and his colleagues. German submarines cruised the North Sea, posing a potential threat to the Grand Fleet in its poorly defended Scottish lairs. German mines sank cruisers, and German torpedoes bagged other prizes. In the far seas, the Mediterranean, and even the North Atlantic, German cruiser-raiders threatened the empire's far-flung lines of commerce and communication. In this kind of war progress was slow, disappointment sudden, criticism certain.[7]

Churchill and Asquith tried to silence those who complained with command changes. To quiet those who blamed the German-born first sea lord, Prince Louis of Battenburg, for fleet failures, Churchill with Asquith's blessing sacked him. He then brought tough, peppery, seventy-five-year-old Jackie Fisher back to the Admiralty as first sea lord. This was a triumph for Fisher and a political coup of the first order. Fleet Street praised Fisher as a second Nelson, and critics fell silent. More importantly, Fisher within the government was far less likely to cause trouble. His talents could be used rather than lent to the opposition.[8]

For a short time this "solution" to the problems of wartime naval operations worked. Fisher quenched the public's demand for revenge after an inferior German squadron all but destroyed British forces off the coast of Chile. He and Churchill took battle cruisers from the Grand Fleet and ordered them to the South Atlantic. There they sent the German squadron to the bottom off the Falkland Islands. This victory and the removal of German cruisers and commerce from the seas revived confidence in the navy. When Lloyd George expressed fears that German raiders might shell east coast towns, Sir Maurice Hankey, secretary to the Committee of Imperial Defence, laughed. The very day that calamity occurred, the prime minister snorted that the Germans were wrong in thinking the war would be decided on land: "It will be decided on the seas." The cabinet then authorized a huge auxiliary ship construction program.[9]

But building, prime ministerial confidence, and occasional victories could not conceal an essential failure. Prewar strategic calculations had not proven true—at least, not yet. The British Expeditionary Force on the continent had bogged down. Lloyd George charged that soldiers were "wantonly sacrificed because those in authority do not know how to make the best use of them." By mid-January 1915 doubts about the navy resurfaced. The engagement at Dogger Bank was nothing more than a brief encounter, not the great battle the admirals had hoped it would be. The fleet, the nation's "first line of defense," apparently could neither force the enemy into decisive action nor command the North Sea. It did not stop zeppelin raiders from bombing Dover. With these events fresh in their minds, statesmen began to ask questions they had previously left to generals and admirals. Would different strategies bring victory more quickly? How should Britain's immense naval power be used? Was it really necessary to concentrate so much of it in the North Sea? Throughout 1915, and well beyond it, these questions were discussed, with devastating effect on those who made naval policy.[10]

Churchill and Fisher, already uneasy in tandem harness, found it difficult to agree on a common answer to them. Beatty feared that "They cannot work together, they cannot both run the show." Fisher began to feel that he simply could not keep pace with a man nearly forty years his junior—a dynamo who out-talked him, dominated, and interfered in everything. The admiral and the first lord longed for a spectacular, decisive naval operation. Fisher talked of seizing control of the North Sea, then attacking the enemy in the Baltic or elsewhere. But he had no enthusiasm for Churchill's plans to take a North Sea island, use it as a destroyer and submarine base, and then wreak havoc on German ships. Fisher and younger Admiralty operational planners saw just too many tactical problems in the first lord's ideas. But the old admiral objected obliquely with a fantastic scheme: Britain should send three quarters of a million men to occupy Holland. The War Council did not find this idea appealing, but Fisher at least persuaded Balfour and Lloyd George that Churchill's scheme was too risky. Asquith then struck a "compromise": the cabinet approved the first lord's ideas "in principle."[11]

There matters stood when a cable from the admiral commanding in the eastern Mediterranean arrived. He proposed an independent naval attack to force the Straits. This idea momentarily captured Churchill's enthusiasm and Fisher's support. On January 13, 1915, the cabinet approved it as part of a compromise grand strategy. Two more divisions would go to France. The navy would plan and carry out the Dardanelles bombardment, then proceed up the Straits to Constantinople. The Admiralty would also continue planning for North Sea operations. If none of the proposed campaigns succeeded by late spring, the cabinet would then consider "other theatres," that is, the Balkans offensive which Lloyd George favored.[12]

Fisher temporarily accepted this compromise, then in an "orgy of discontent" objected to it. The Grand Fleet needed battle cruisers and small craft that might otherwise go to the Dardanelles. An independent naval operation there or on Churchill's North Sea island just wouldn't work; the army would have to join in. H.M.S. *Queen Elizabeth*, the newest battle cruiser in the fleet, should not, as he himself had suggested earlier, test her guns against Turkish forts. Behind all of these objections lay Fisher's unwillingness to break with prewar strategy. The old admiral threatened resignation, demanded that his objections be circulated to the cabinet, and in a private meeting tried to persuade the prime minister of their truth. But he could not convince him.

Asquith was as prone to compromise on matters of wartime strategy as he had been on those of peacetime politics. Would the admiral go along with the Dardanelles scheme if Churchill postponed his North Sea island campaign? Fisher refused to answer that question clearly, and when the War Council began to discuss it, he stalked out of the room. Lord Kitchener, secretary of state for war, brought him back. Asquith, Balfour, and Grey then pressed for an affirmative conclusion on the Dardanelles operation. They got it. The War Council, as if to soothe the admiral's defeat, then authorized the construction of two specially designed cruisers for North Sea operations.[13]

From that moment onward the Dardanelles operation was plagued with difficulties. Lord Kitchener extended only grudging promises of army cooperation. Five days after fleet operations began, the admiral commanding resigned, complaining that his task was impossible. His successor compounded Admiralty problems. He tried to invest the Straits, failed, and then disregarded orders to try again. He would not move without army support. Fisher concurred; Churchill, virtually alone at Admiralty House, disagreed. They waited. By the time troops finally arrived, it was too late. Their ground offensive stalled. Then the enemy torpedoed an old battleship at the Dardanelles and sent 570 sailors to their death. This was too much for Fisher. He thought Churchill ought to withdraw the *Queen Elizabeth* before she, too, met disaster. The first lord agreed, but the prime minister did not. Rather than evacuate in apparent defeat, the cabinet committed Fisher and Churchill to send reinforcements to the Straits.[14]

By mid-May 1915, however, the Dardanelles became much more than an operational fiasco. Admiral Fisher awoke on May 15 to find that Churchill intended to send two of the newest submarines along with reinforcements to the Dardanelles. This infuriated the admiral, and before breakfast he resigned and announced that he was leaving for Scotland. This challenge to Churchill backfired. Two days later, despite rumors that the German fleet had sortied, he refused to return to the Admiralty. This angered Asquith and set the junior sea lords against Fisher. The whole affair brought the prime minister to the decision that Lloyd George and Andrew Bonar Law had pressed on him for some time. Asquith decided to create a coalition government. Perhaps this gesture would quiet critics of the Dardanelles disaster, the stalemate on the Western Front, and the deficiencies in munitions production.[15]

The new government might be only a "flustered evasion of the problem of organization for war," but its formation was an event of great significance in

London's defense politics. In the first place, the navy lost two of its most determined and skillful advocates. Conservatives demanded that Churchill leave the Admiralty before they entered the government. Asquith acquiesced, and named Balfour to succeed him. Only with great difficulty did the former first lord retain the very junior post of chancellor of the duchy of Lancaster. In the words of his biographer, "the ebullient politician, confident of his powers, exuberant in manner, certain of a distinguished future, optimistic in his assessment of men and events [became] ... a broken figure, unsure of his career, pessimistic about the outcome of the war, lacking faith in the country's leaders." Fisher fell from power forever. He refused to serve under Balfour, then demanded virtual freedom from civilian control as the price for returning to Admiralty House. Asquith would not pay it, and the competent but docile Sir Henry Jackson succeeded Fisher.[16]

The nightmare of prewar years had become reality. Naval issues contributed to the permanent disruption of the Liberal party. To be sure, Liberals kept the key posts in Asquith's coalition government. But personal relations within the party were shattered. Lloyd George vented his pent-up hostility toward Churchill. The first lord's fall was "the Nemesis of the man who has fought for this war for years." Churchill felt that old friends had abandoned him to his enemies. He later defied Asquith by delivering a speech in which he defended his stewardship at the Admiralty. He resisted hasty retreat from the Dardanelles. Most importantly, Churchill set out to prove the correctness of his arguments about the campaign. He demanded and got a parliamentary investigation of the Dardanelles operation that would haunt those who met at Downing Street for the next two years.[17]

The greatest losses of 1915, however, were psychological. The navy had not won a spectacular victory, even in a secondary theater of war. Its failure and the ensuing political crisis shattered the prewar pattern of civil-naval relations. Fisher was no longer a demigod. When Churchill later proposed that Jackie return to the Admiralty, no one took him seriously. Neither Asquith nor his successors would trust men as dynamic or dangerous at Admiralty House again. Lloyd George explained this point to the press magnate, George Riddell, some time later. The Dardanelles showed, he said, that no politician could rely upon the behavior or expertise of naval and military "experts." Admirals harbored similar misgivings. As Jellicoe confided to Fisher, "after the Dardanelles business I mistrust everyone who in any way supported the early policy of that monument." Trust, indeed, was the greatest casualty of 1915.[18]

Little more than a year after Churchill and Fisher left the Admiralty, a second great naval crisis hit London. The single major fleet engagement of the war strained civil-naval relations, weakened public confidence in the navy, and rendered questionable the assumptions that statesmen, admirals, and ordinary citizens had shared for a decade. Winston Churchill summarized those ideas nicely when he later wrote

> Everything had been lavished upon the drawing out of a line of batteries of such preponderance and in such an order that the German battle fleet would be blasted and shattered *for certain* in a very short space of time.... Unless some entirely unforeseen factor intervened or some incalculable accident occurred, there was no reason to doubt that thirty minutes' firing within ten thousand yards between two parallel lines of battle would achieve a complete victory.

On the night of May 31, 1916, the climax of years of planning and months of waiting appeared to be at hand. The Admiralty flashed startling news to the Commander in chief of the Grand Fleet: the enemy fleet was about to sortie from its bases. While rumors of impending battle were whispered across Asquith's dinner table, Jellicoe and his second in command, Admiral David Beatty, positioned their ships. They moved swiftly and stealthily, hoping to lure the Germans into an iron-jawed trap.[19]

But the battle did not follow the pattern Jellicoe projected in his battle orders or the scenario armchair strategists fantasized. First, British and German battle cruisers dueled. Admiral Beatty lost two ships but drew the German battleships into position opposite Jellicoe's main body. For a moment, all went as planned. The dreadnoughts hurled destruction at one another. This, however, did not bring "complete victory." Instead, the Germans broke contact, and Jellicoe pursued them. Then in a maneuver which occasioned decades of professional controversy, he gave up the chase. Beatty, however, signaled "follow me," hoping to force a second engagement. Neither Jellicoe nor commanders of other ships fast enough to catch the Germans responded. Jellicoe ordered his exhausted men and ships back to their bases, while remnants of the German High Seas Fleet fled to theirs. What was to have been the most decisive battle thus came to an uncertain end.[20]

The battle over, the doubts began. A crisis of confidence hit the Asquith cabinet, then struck the navy, and finally burst in full fury in the press. Jellicoe's initial battle report was devastating. It matter-of-factly listed British losses: ten, perhaps as many as sixteen, capital ships. It claimed the enemy had lost two capital ships, two cruisers, and numerous destroyers. News of this sort "shattered" the prime minister's daughter. The usually imperturbable cabinet secretary, Sir Maurice Hankey, recorded in his diary that Jutland was "a bitter disappointment ... One's confidence [is] shaken." So, too, was the myth of Royal Naval invincibility. On the morning of June 3 every major newspaper, with the exception of the Conservative *Morning Post* and Asquith's *Westminster Gazette*, called the battle results unsatisfactory. The *Times'* headline, "Great Naval Battle Heavy Losses," expressed the national mood. Churchill hurried to Admiralty House to write a more favorable account of the battle for publication. At Walton Heath, Lloyd George dropped his golf clubs, railed against Admiralty incompetence, and hastened back to London to face the storm.[21]

During the next week the government made gestures in the hope of calming it. The Admiralty published yet another report which made the battle seem less a disaster. But this failed to quiet uneasiness within the cabinet. Doubts became anger and grief when Asquith's colleagues learned that Lord Kitchener had drowned after an enemy mine struck the cruiser *Hampshire*. Asquith responded by fending off Lloyd George's demands for a full discussion of Jutland. Balfour then read Admiral Beatty's account of the battle. But this was not enough. All realized that the enemy had struck a strong blow against British naval prestige. Why else did they think it necessary to rush messages of reassurance about Jutland to Paris and St. Petersburg? What other than a sense of naval insecurity could have prompted Bonar Law's suggestion to Balfour: Would it not be wise to ask Britain's Far Eastern ally, Japan, to send battleships to replace those lost at Jutland? The first lord testily rejected such advice. The navy was not so crippled that it needed support in home waters from a distant Asian ally.[22]

While politicians tried to ride out the storm, admirals reflected bitterly on what had—and had not—occurred. The psychological burden of incomplete victory was more than they could bear. Jellicoe, although deluged with public praise, suffered terribly. He had not repeated Nelson's triumph at Trafalgar. Subordinates offered tactical reasons for the battle's outcome. Something, a vague something, was wrong with British shooting. Then, too, the Germans had zeppelins. And there was the weather. But down deep this could not "explain" Jutland. Beatty spoke of the battle as "a veritable nightmare of an afternoon" and confided to Jellicoe that "my heart aches with thinking about" how the navy was deprived of the victory it deserved. Condolences, however, were not enough. Jellicoe and Beatty both had doubts: Had they done the right thing? Could tactics have been different? Need losses have been so great? As they pondered these questions, the two admirals drifted apart. By late June Jellicoe completed his official report of the battle. Beatty, convinced that Jellicoe had not given him proper support in the fight and worried about criticisms of his own tactics, submitted a separate account. This incident drove a wedge of distrust between the two men that poisoned their relations for years. Indeed, not even a ceremonial reunion of the two admirals' forces in July 1916 restored their friendship and fleet harmony.[23]

By midsummer it became clear that explanations and gestures could not clear away the smoke of doubt that hung over Jutland. Lord Riddell cajoled Fleet Street colleagues into softening their judgments on the battle, and Jellicoe's report got good press reports. But that did not convince those who knew the Royal Navy. John Leyland and H. W. Wilson ridiculed "eulogists who pretend that all is well" and charged that admirals on both sides of the North Sea had fabulously overestimated the other's losses. Fisher began to think that Beatty had wrecked Jellicoe's chances for victory. Churchill publicly insisted that Jutland was a victory but privately implied to Jellicoe that it could have been at least the equal of Trafalgar. Those who had criticized naval expansion before the war were now more certain than ever that they were right. As the Socialist *New Statesmen* put it, the navalists were hoisted on their own petard. They had defined victory as annihilation of the enemy's fleet. "Anything less than that is at best a partial failure; and we doubt whether the Navy itself will ever call the Battle of Jutland a British victory."[24]

Jutland and the Dardanelles left statesmen and admirals ill-prepared to deal with the third great naval operational crisis of the war. By the autumn of 1916 men recognized that Jutland was a turning point in the conflict. Grand Fleet admirals were correct in claiming that the High Seas Fleet would never sortie again. But they were not ready for the new German naval challenge: renewed submarine attacks on British merchantmen and daring destroyer raids on transports ferrying troops to the Continent. Balfour admitted that he "could not see, and [he] thought Sir John Jellicoe would not see any means of coping with this new menace." Churchill charged that the navy had lost the initiative in the war, and more than a few journalists agreed. Sir Maurice Hankey came to the same conclusion. The navy, he said, provided passive defense, but it could not impose a blockade that would force Berlin to surrender. The chancellor of the exchequer deepened the sense of crisis with a chilling financial report: If the conflict did not end soon, Britain and her allies would "become entirely dependent on the good will of the President of the U.S.A. for their power to continue the war." Lloyd George, now secretary of state for war, could not sleep. He talked of resignation and complained that his colleagues had "made a muddle of the whole war."[25]

The government responded to this crisis as it had to those of the past—with a change of faces. Balfour brought Jellicoe to London to find new ways of dealing with enemy submarines. The Grand Fleet commander and Admiralty officials agreed to create a special submarine division. Jellicoe then explained his ideas to the cabinet, and Balfour skillfully interpreted them to get permission to arm merchantmen. This quieted some critics and gave Asquith the opportunity of inviting Jellicoe to become first sea lord. The admiral hesitated. He knew Fisher opposed his coming to London. But he was tempted, perhaps by the thought that he could consolidate his power [of the navy] by naming his brother-in-law commander in chief of the Grand Fleet. Finally Jellicoe agreed. Asquith named Beatty to succeed him. The press cautiously approved these changes. The *Times* said that Jellicoe would be "an immense advantage to the Admiralty, and to the whole conduct of the war."[26]

Changes in naval command were not enough. Frustrated in his attempts to control the War Office and infuriated by the generals' refusal to abandon plans for a spring offensive, Lloyd George demanded that Asquith change the entire system of command for war. Bonar Law began to listen to Tory critics who charged that the coalition was ineffective, and once joined Lloyd George and demanded the establishment of a small, all-powerful War Committee, Asquith's fate was sealed. For two days, from December 5 to 7, 1916, the prime minister fought for survival. But when the battle was over, David Lloyd George emerged prime minister of a coalition government determined to win victory.[27]

The new prime minister was a very different kind of leader from Asquith. He was not a member of the ruling elite by virtue of birth or education. He had fought his way up from the outside to the pinnacle of power on the inside. The very day he became prime minister, his mistress wrote with great relish that "all these great Tories . . . who a few years ago would not have shaken hands with him [were] . . . now waiting to be granted an audience of the little Welsh attorney!" Many thought Lloyd George little more than a cunning opportunist. Lord D'Abernon described him as "a grand man to go tiger hunting with, were it not for the possibility that, at the critical moment of the chase, he may conceive of the tiger as the underdog and go over to his side!" At the opposite end of the political spectrum, Lord Keynes taunted Lloyd George by saying, "Who shall paint the chameleon? Who can tether the broomstick?" But the great economist did Lloyd George a disservice. He may not have been a man of great principle, but he was a doer.[28]

In war, that was a great virtue. Frances Stevenson, his mistress and secretary, explained how Lloyd George used power to attain success:

> He is indefatigable in his efforts, probing every source from which he may gain information which may be of some use to him, scrutinising every difficulty which might present itself, and adopting flanking movements, so to speak, when a frontal attack is not likely to prove successful, 'roping in' persons whose influence is likely to prove helpful or whose opinion counts . . . seeking out those who are 'on the fence' and whose opposition would be dangerous, and then talking them round, using all the arts of which he is a past master . . . His patience in overcoming obstacles, and in returning again and again to their attack with undiminished cheerfulness and confidence, his tirelessness in examining and arranging for details, above all his complete self-effacement in his desire that the idea which he has conceived . . . shall not fall to the ground and escape fulfillment, all these characteristics indicate the real greatness of the man.

Unlike Asquith, the new prime minister was not so much a master compromiser as a productive activist. Once he knew "when he has hit upon the right idea, when his plan is the one which ought to be followed," Lloyd George was difficult to stop.[29]

At least insofar as the navy was concerned, the prime minister had yet to find that "right idea." He had shattered political barriers of the past in creating a cabinet that was much more a genuine coalition than Asquith's. He tightened the system of war direction and called for a "knock-out blow" to end the war. But, for all his earlier doubts about the admirals, Lloyd George was not about to interfere at Admiralty House. His choice of a first lord made that clear. At the last moment, Balfour, Churchill, and Fisher rejected, he named the fiery Ulster Tory, Sir Edward Carson, first lord. Carson had a sharp tongue which he would use as the navy's advocate at Westminster. But he was unlikely to cause trouble at Whitehall. The new first lord stood in awe of the admirals and told them that his only qualification for office was the fact that "I am very much at sea."[30]

For a few weeks things seemed to go well. Jellicoe brought some of the Grand Fleet's "best brains" with him to devise antisubmarine measures. But the admiral made a fateful choice. He retained the chief of the Admiralty War Staff and the director of the Operations Division, men who opposed convoying merchantmen. He also launched a campaign to search and destroy U-boats and fought for more materiel. The War Cabinet gave him guns to arm merchantmen and authorized their use as decoys to draw submarines to the surface for destruction. Jellicoe revised the building program, giving antisubmarine warfare vessels priority over capital ships. He commandeered steel to build them while Carson tried to improve the production of mines. The admiral also swallowed service pride and asked the War Cabinet for Japanese assistance in the Mediterranean and South African waters. These measures had some effect. Fewer armed than unarmed merchantmen were lost, and British men-of-war did fight successful engagements against the U-boats.[31]

Lloyd George turned a deaf ear to those who argued that these measures were not enough. Jackie Fisher's pleas for a naval offensive did not appeal to him. The arguments, pro and con, for convoying merchantmen, were not convincing. Perhaps, he mused to George Riddell, the only real answer to the naval crisis was some inventive genius who would produce the ultimate antisubmarine weapon. In the meantime, the prime minister favored measures to compensate for shipping losses over new schemes for naval warfare. He appointed a shipping controller to end labor disputes that delayed construction of new merchantmen. He proposed giving a food controller real power over agricultural prices and wages to stimulate domestic food production. Lloyd George even considered cutting imports drastically and ending the Australian wheat convoy.[32]

Not until events and his own cabinet colleagues forced his hand did Lloyd George intervene in Admiralty affairs. By the end of April 1917 neither Jellicoe's operations nor the prime minister's compensatory schemes had checked the submarine menace. Once again, from many quarters, Lloyd

George heard that convoying was the best answer. Young Turks at the Admiralty argued for it and organizational reforms to make it effective. Carson became worried, and suggested that Lloyd George sound out Beatty. The admiral bombarded him with complaints against the Admiralty. On April 19, President Wilson's naval liaison officer in London, Rear Admiral William S. Sims, expressed support for convoying. The following day the War Cabinet—in the prime minister's absence—concluded that a sweeping review of antisubmarine measures was necessary. Admiral Jellicoe gloomily said that the war at sea might be lost before July when American naval power would begin to be effective. Finally, on April 25, 1917, the War Cabinet (in what Churchill later called a "menace" to professional control of fleet operations) directed intervention. The prime minister was to go to Admiralty House to see what could be done to bring about vigorous, successful antisubmarine operations.[33]

Five days passed before he did so. In the meantime, the bureaucratic tide within the Admiralty changed to favor convoying. On April 27 Jellicoe laconically approved what he had long opposed, so that when Lloyd George came, the issue was no longer a matter of dispute. The prime minister had a pleasant visit and subsequently acted with the tact of an Asquith. On May 2 he told the War Cabinet that organizational reforms suggested by Admiralty young Turks should be implemented. He also proposed to compensate for shipping losses by naming Eric Geddes, a civilian, temporary vice admiral and admiralty controller responsible for all shipbuilding. To soothe Carson and Jellicoe's ruffled feelings about this invasion of their domain, Lloyd George sought approval to build Jellicoe's "unsinkable" ships. He also promised to end the Salonika expedition which the admiral opposed. After the War Cabinet approved Geddes's appointment, the prime minister confidently claimed that these changes in personnel and procedures would double the output of desperately needed merchantmen.[34]

But Lloyd George was prematurely optimistic if he supposed that the solution to the naval crisis had been found. Eric Geddes, able railway manager and organizer of troop transportation, could not singlehandedly change the Admiralty. Carson and Jellicoe remained wary of innovation. The first lord stood by the admiral in resisting Naval Staff changes and rejecting army proposals for an assault against enemy submarine bases in Belgium. Jellicoe's caution infuriated General Douglas Haig. He eagerly listened to naval young Turks, complained to Geddes, and persuaded Lloyd George at least to consider changes in Admiralty leadership. Alfred Lord Milner, a member of the War Cabinet, was more direct. Geddes should replace Carson. Jellicoe should be succeeded by a man possessed of "courage and knowledge of men and an intimate acquaintance with the best men in the service and a determination to bring them on and put them into their right places regardless of seniority and red tape."[35]

The prime minister acted on those suggestions with considerable caution. Within the War Cabinet, Curzon, Bonar Law, and Shipping Controller Maclay wanted to oust Carson. Hankey confirmed the existence of "obstructionism" at Admiralty House, and once again Lloyd George talked with Beatty. He then informed the king of his intention to make Geddes, a "first rate administrator," first lord and cannily suggested to Carson that he move up to membership in the War Cabinet. But the Ulsterman resisted, and Lloyd George waited. Perhaps it would be best to remove Jellicoe as well. Finally, on July 17, 1917, he eased Carson out of Admiralty House and determined to force a new Naval Staff and Board upon Jellicoe. Three days later Geddes was formally installed as first lord.[36]

These half measures promised both change and conflict. Geddes readily took command. He fought off interference by Churchill, now minister of munitions, and tried to improve the Admiralty's public image. The navy, he told the press, was to be bent to his will in pursuit of victory. The canny Scot treated the Admiralty as if it were a decrepit business firm. He put his own men in key positions; his cousin replaced him as controller. His personal private secretaries dredged information up from the depths of each department and took over the task of writing daily operational progress reports for the War Cabinet. Geddes cultivated cordial relations with the new secretary to the admiralty, Sir Oswyn Murray, a professional civil servant who had no longstanding loyalties to department heads. He shrewdly drew the Naval Staff in on plans for its reformation and created a Training Division to act as watchdog over various departments.[37]

Geddes then began to circumscribe the power of the first sea lord. His personal secretary took control of the Board of Admiralty agenda and recorded its decisions. Two subcommittees which predecided virtually everything to come before the full Board were created. Geddes brought in the young Turks' favorite, Admiral Roslyn Wester Wemyss, as deputy first sea lord and established a Plans Division which diminished the power of the director of operations. The final step went beyond that. The first lord secured an Order in Council which made control of naval operations his, rather than the full Board's, responsibility. Geddes the civilian had entered and taken command in the admirals' most hallowed sphere of competence.[38]

These changes paved the way for still more in operations and construction. The new first lord recognized the necessity of close cooperation with the Americans. He welcomed proposals from Washington, strongly seconded by Admiral Beatty and young Turk Captain H. H. Richmond, to lay what became the Northern Mine Barrage. He urged the Americans to modify their building program to provide more antisubmarine craft. His own reconstituted Board completely revised building priorities. It decided to build antisubmarine submarines, then concentrated scarce steel resources for the superdreadnought H.M.S. *Hood*, and finally agreed to postpone work on that last capital ship in the building program.[39]

Geddes's actions temporarily quieted critics outside the navy but fueled controversy within it. Admiral Jellicoe grew more suspicious daily. He felt that "the politicians here have been very busy intriguing against myself and the Admiralty for some time." He resisted Geddes's organizational reforms and Lloyd George's efforts to change the Board of Admiralty. He resented Admiral Sir Roslyn Wester Wemyss's presence. He felt that new, younger men were selling out to the politicians in agreeing to the establishment of a separate Royal Air Force. Previous first lords and first sea lords had opposed this, but now Geddes, Wemyss, and even Beatty cautiously approved it.[40]

In this climate, operational failure became the spark that would ignite civil-naval conflict. In October 1917, a convoy from Norway was lost. Geddes then met with his two predecessors and Lloyd George and demanded Jellicoe's head. But the prime minister, then hunting those of generals responsible for failures on the Continent, was not about to take on the admirals at the same time. He assuaged Geddes's feelings and convinced him that it was his duty to work with Jellicoe. In December, however, when another convoy was lost, the spark ignited. Geddes demanded that Beatty conduct an investigation and insisted that Admiral Reginald Bacon, commander of the Dover patrol and a Jellicoe protégé, be sacked. The admirals were divided on what to do. Jellicoe at first raised objections, then veered toward compromise. That was not good enough for Geddes. The two men argued before the full Board of Admiralty. Then the first lord went to Lloyd George with a question: He was a square peg in a round hole at Admiralty House; could he not return to transport work on the Continent?[41]

This shrewd formulation of the issue forced Lloyd George to choose between Geddes and Jellicoe. Neither he nor the War Cabinet hesitated in giving an answer. Geddes, the civilian manager, was far more valuable than Jellicoe in the politics of war. If the first lord thought it necessary, Jellicoe would go. Given the green light, Geddes acted with dispatch that angered the Jellicoe family for generations and wounded the pride of the naval service. He quickly got Wemyss to agree to succeed Jellicoe, secured the senior admiral's resignation on Christmas eve, and got the king's assent the next day. Then he went to Scotland where he won Beatty's concurrence. Returning to London, he swiftly scotched some of the junior sea lords' schemes to stand by their old chief.[42]

What followed demonstrated how war had changed the politics of naval defense. Jellicoe stood quite alone. Virtually none of the major dailies or weeklies protested his departure. Within the cabinet, no one attacked Lloyd George. Outside, Jackie Fisher made no public complaint at the fate of his old protégé. Jellicoe's overtures to the old Liberal leaders of 1914—Asquith, Walter Runciman, and Reginald McKenna—came to nothing. Even Jellicoe's most ardent defender, Sir Edward Carson, proved powerless. He protested that Geddes had acted in bad faith toward Jellicoe. Lloyd George let Balfour answer the Ulsterman. Balfour denied Carson's charges, insisted that

Jellicoe was overly tired and lacking in the "offensive spirit," and argued that he should have stepped down sooner. Carson, already at odds with Lloyd George over Ireland and military management of the war, then resigned. But his departure failed to ignite sparks of controversy. Not even the fiery Ulsterman could get press and parliament to support Jellicoe against Geddes and Lloyd George.[43]

Thus a kind of harmony in naval affairs came to prevail. Operations remained routine rather than spectacular. The Grand Fleet behemoths languished in their Scottish harbors, while ever increasing numbers of destroyers and submarines fought the battles that mattered. Convoy, transport, and mining in concert with the Americans—not preparation for the decisive battle—occupied the fleet. The young Turks, even when they got their chance to influence Admiralty planning, failed to come up with a major naval offensive. The quarrels over the building program all but disappeared once admirals realized that vessels to protect merchantmen were more urgently needed than battleships. Thus, in 1918 the Royal Navy found itself fighting in a manner unimaginable four years earlier: trying to keep the sea lanes open, contain the enemy, and outlast his will to seek victory in the land war.[44]

But changes on land were perhaps more significant that those at sea. The war imposed a new pattern of civil-naval relations on London. In the new calculations of power, the admirals counted for much less than they had in the years before the war. The Royal Naval officer corps was no longer one. Its more prestigious leaders, with the possible exception of David Beatty, had fallen from power and public esteem. Critics of the navy could be found in Westminster, Whitehall, and Fleet Street. No admiral, moreover, could fight them with the constituencies that had supported fleet expansion before 1914, for the demands, tensions, and failures of wartime operations had shattered old friendships and political alliances. No one, finally, could claim possession of the expert knowledge that would assure security and quick victory. The Dardanelles fiasco, the indecisive encounter at Jutland, and the new terrors of submarine warfare severely weakened faith in the admirals' competence.

The admirals' decline spelled the statesmen's rise. Civilians had taken on new roles. The prime minister was not merely the architect of budgetary compromise, as he had been in 1914. Instead, as Lloyd George demonstrated in the sacking of Jellicoe, he was the court of last resort, the ultimate source of political support, for subordinates committed to changing the navy. The first lord was no longer parliamentary advocate for the fleet, but a powerful administrator more interested in Admiralty House than in the House of Commons. Eric Geddes, unlike his predecessors, was not as concerned with maintaining sound relations with the admirals as he was with assuring effective, efficient management of the naval war. To attain that goal he had reached down into the naval bureaucracy to disrupt routines, displace subordinates, and test new ideas.

Those outside the corridors of power in Whitehall seemed disposed to accept these changes. But were they permanent? Did they portend basic shifts in the politics of national defense, or were they merely temporary wartime phenomena? In January 1918, Lloyd George hinted at an ambiguous answer to these questions. In an address which won the "unanimous . . . approbation" of the British public, he voiced the intention of establishing "some international organization to limit the burden of armaments and diminish the probability of war."[45] But he said nothing of the political or diplomatic means by which such a goal might be attained. The notion of arms limitation had not fallen victim to the war. But what would be its fate in the new atmosphere of civil-naval politics in London?

No one, not even the prime minister, could resolve these questions in 1918. The answers would have to wait until the storm of war had passed, and until men saw its effects on Washington and Tokyo.

3 On February 3, 1916, in St. Louis, Missouri, President Woodrow Wilson in a moment of impassioned oratory called upon his fellow Americans to build "incomparably the greatest navy in the world." The crowd thundered applause. But the president, in a quieter moment, changed the official text of his address. He would build "incomparably the most adequate navy in the world."[1] The change was an important one, conditioned in part by Wilson's estimate of the balance of forces in Washington's politics of national defense. But it also had a broader significance, more fundamental, perhaps, than the president himself realized. The difference between "the greatest" and the "most adequate" was not simply numerical, but qualitative and functional. The latter phrase raised questions of purpose: Was the United States Navy to stabilize its position within the existing system of international naval politics, to dominate it, or perhaps to become the means of transcending it?

That question surfaced time and again in Washington during the years of the Great War. There the atmosphere differed from that in London. In Europe the war was a storm that destroyed personal relationships, political structures, and policy premises. But on the western edge of the Atlantic it was a tempest—one whose winds shifted in contradictory directions. At one moment they created waves of support for naval expansion. First the threat of war, then participation in it built a consensus on fleet increases unequaled in American history. At another moment the winds cleared the skies, unfolding before men's eyes the vision of a new international order in which armaments would be limited. That vision would change the way in which statesmen and admirals thought about naval needs. To understand that shift, and indeed the war's broader impact on Washington's politics of naval defense, it is necessary to analyze the forces which fostered expansion and those which favored limitation.

Statesmen and admirals were slow to feel the winds of change that war brought. Ex-president Theodore Roosevelt might warn that "giants . . . engaged in a death wrestle . . . are certain to trample on whomever gets in the way." Eastern Republicans might second his demand for preparedness, that is, immediate increases in American military and naval strength. But the Wilson administration felt no compulsion to abandon past policy norms. While the General Board wanted a navy second to none, late in 1914 it asked for four new battleships in the coming year's budget—precisely the number proposed in years past. Secretary Daniels sliced the admirals' request to the "normal" two. While this recommendation wound its way through congressional committees, those worried by the war turned to command problems. They succeeded in creating a chief of naval operations and a modified war staff—probably the most significant institutional change within the Navy Department in the preceding seventy-five years. Congress then approved a naval bill virtually indistinguishable from the administration's original proposal.[2]

By the time President Wilson signed it, many Americans sensed that the European War threatened their security and demanded preparedness for the vigorous defense of their sovereignty. In March 1915 the British Cabinet determined to enforce a blockade against Germany. This portended Anglo-American conflict over neutral maritime rights. Berlin refused to abandon submarine warfare. But it was the sinking of the *Lusitania* on May 7, 1915, with the loss of 128 American lives, that brought home the message of danger to the American people. Wilson's special emissary to Berlin and London, Colonel Edward M. House, realized that his peacemaking efforts were fruitless and urged defense of the national honor even at the risk of war. President Wilson, sensing "an apparent surge of nationalism," concluded that he could not follow the milder courses suggested by Secretary of State Bryan. He demanded that Germany cease surprise attacks on passenger ships. But his critics deprecated mere exchanges of diplomatic notes and demanded immediate preparations for possible conflict. The more ardent among them insisted that the navy was in such a state as to be "not only a disgrace but a serious danger."[3]

While there were hints of an administration response to this charge as early as May, the president did not concern himself with naval matters until the dog days of July had passed. Wilson had only the most general notions of what was needed. He lacked the knowledge of things naval and the love of the sea that possessed ex-president Theodore Roosevelt and Assistant Secretary of the Navy Franklin Roosevelt. He felt no compulsion to match the strength of European combatants but was guided simply by the feeling that the nation required him to lead it toward the right kind and degree of naval preparedness. And in the summer of 1915, the president was ready to rely upon the counsel of his civilian and professional advisors as to specific naval needs.[4]

Secretary Daniels sought the General Board's advice early in July 1915, and by the end of the month the admirals presented a fleet construction program of unprecedented size and cost. They recommended building four battleships, four battlecruisers, six scout cruisers, twenty-eight destroyers, thirty-seven submarines, and various smaller craft. In addition, they sought an 11,000 man personnel increase and a special five million dollar appropriation for naval aviation. They projected that 286 million dollars would be needed to complete the program. Their proposals broke sharply with the past in cost, but not in basic strategic or technological assumptions. The admirals did not think of the program as preparation for possible belligerency in the European war. Instead they felt it would give them a navy "ultimately equal to the most powerful maintained by any other nation" by 1925. Such a fleet would enable them to meet the strategic danger of conflict with the victor in the present war or a possible German-Russo-Japanese alliance in the future. The General Board was so enchanted by the hope of attaining long-defined standards of capital ship strength that it refused to modify designs of proposed submarines to match those of the German U-boats. Chief of Naval Operations William S. Benson insisted that capital ships requiring years to build should be laid down first, on the ground that they would deter all possible future enemies.[5]

The president, meanwhile, maneuvered between Republican preparedness chauvinists and pacifistic little-navy Democrats. He let Secretary Daniels manage the admirals while he wooed the chairmen of House and Senate naval affairs committees. Wilson got House Speaker Champ Clark to endorse naval and military expansion. He failed to win over Claude Kitchin, an archenemy of such programs in the House, and dismissed as unavoidable former Secretary of State Bryan's opposition. But the president did pledge Republican congressional leaders to nonpartisanship on national defense matters.

Wilson and Daniels then tried to strike a balance between General Board long-range concerns and immediate public fears. They chose less expensive Board recommendations on capital ship building and increased the number of submarines sought from 67 to 100. As presented in December 1915, the administration program called for the construction of 185 ships over the next five years. This, clearly, was a break with the past.[6]

In their testimony before congressional committees, however, administration spokesmen argued that they were not abandoning the moral and strategic premises of past naval programs. The admirals insisted that the United States was simply catching up with other world powers—moving up from a poor fourth to a healthy second place among the navies of the world. They conceded that the proposed program would bring the U.S. Navy very close to the strength of the Royal Navy. But Admirals Charles J. Badger and Austin M. Knight denied that this meant Anglo-American friction. There were long-standing bonds of friendship between the two nations, and it would be some time before Britain had resources free to match the American increases. Secretary Daniels tackled opponents from another quarter. He had already proposed construction of a model, government-owned armor plant to quiet those who charged that only the "arms trust" profited from naval expansion. Now he confronted arms control advocates directly. To build was not to abandon disarmament but rather to prepare for postwar arms control talks. Daniels put the case bluntly to Representative Hensley, leader of the prewar arms control forces. America should tell the other naval powers that "We have a program which is the minimum, and if you intend to keep this big navy building we can keep on increasing it more rapidly than any other nation in the world, because we are the richest country in the world." He categorically insisted that the United States would fare better in arms control talks if it had a large naval building program.[7]

Daniels's words betrayed a subtle but significant shift in the Wilson administration's assumptions. Defense, not economy, was the paramount issue, and massive naval building best demonstrated Washington's ability to provide it. But President Wilson, embroiled in the controversy over army expansion, left it to the legislators to realize that fact. Nonintervention very nearly proved disastrous. The House Naval Affairs Committee reported out a one year naval program that gave priority to destroyers and submarines rather than to the battleships admirals wanted. This infuriated Republicans who then put forward their own proposals and came within six votes of getting full House approval for them. Daniels lobbied intensely to help defeat this measure, and the Senate could have been expected to support a long-term building program. But if it was to succeed, presidential leadership would be necessary.[8]

Wilson came to that conclusion for a variety of reasons. Those closest to the president warned him that the prestige of his office depended on passage of a major naval expansion bill. He had already compromised on army programs.

To back down on the navy as well would make him seem weak to the citizens of New York, New Jersey, and Connecticut—states whose congressmen sided with Republicans in the House vote and whose ballots would be vital to his own reelection. Others insisted that a big naval program would demonstrate America's strength and determination to defend her maritime rights. Secretary of State Robert Lansing had long insisted that Wilson show his strength to Berlin and to the American people. Colonel House agreed—for different reasons. Naval building would "enormously strengthen your hand" in seeking a negotiated end to the European war. It might eventually serve the "league to enforce peace" which Wilson had endorsed in May and written into the Democratic platform in June. Confessing his faith in battleships as symbols of national power, the colonel then hinted that a bigger navy might even help Wilson deal with the Japanese and Latin Americans.[9]

However reasonable these arguments may have been, one senses that they were not the compelling ones. Wilson was an intuitive, independent thinker, a man whose precise motives were often opaque even to those closest to him. To make a decision he had to be certain within himself that he was absolutely right. But, as Patrick Devlin has noted, Wilson also sought throughout his career a favorable conjunction of the right and the expedient. While any reconstruction of his motives must be tentative, Wilson's words throughout the preparedness controversy suggest what weighed most heavily on his mind. The president felt that the world was changing. America must fulfill her mission in it and possess force, if necessary, to accomplish it. In October 1915, he told the Navy Department's civilian advisors that America was a nation that "knows and loves its mission in the world and knows that it must command the respect of the world." By late January 1916, Wilson sensed that the world "is on fire and there is tinder everywhere." Six months later the president informed a Detroit audience that war had changed America's economic position. The nation was no longer independent of foreign trade but dependent upon it for continued prosperity. Only a few days before this he told West Point graduates that "mankind is going to know that when America speaks she means what she says." Whether to protect her commerce, defend the national honor, or lessen the risk of future conflict, the president agreed in July 1916 that there must be sustained, major increases in American naval power.[10]

But this is not to say that Woodrow Wilson accepted the premises that underlay competitive naval arms expansion. It is true that his actions in the final moments of the legislative battle over naval expansion were critical. The Senate had passed a three-year comprehensive naval program by a 71 to 8 margin, yet House Democrats continued to balk at anything other than a one-year authorization. Wilson twice talked with House Naval Affairs Committee Chairman Padgett of Tennessee before the opposition collapsed, and the House by a margin of more than five to one passed the Senate bill. But

Wilson was reluctant to intervene in what he termed "an eleventh hour performance." Moreover, upon signing the final bill, which provided for 588 million dollars for the construction of 157 ships over a three-year period, his enthusiasm ran simply to calling the Naval Act "a very remarkable measure." One senses that even in this final moment of political victory Wilson thought simply in terms of having met the immediate political crises of preparedness both at home and abroad.[11]

Wilson's modest remarks suggested that the 1916 Naval Act by no means answered all the questions his call for "the most adequate" navy had raised. Supporters and critics alike were correct in regarding passage of the naval bill as a milestone in American defense policy. American admirals for the first time had an ongoing expansion program, something with a bureaucratic life of its own, to defend. In their eyes it was a means of reaching second, if not first, place in the existing naval system. Secondly, the administration in 1916 abandoned the old golden mean logic for a massive increase that shattered past standards. Budget statistics showed that in 1916 more than one out of every five dollars spent by the federal government would go to the navy. This increase paralleled increments abroad but was more significant in that it came before belligerency brought massive jumps in all federal expenditures. In 1916, too, the Wilson administration cut across the old divisions between economists and big-navy men. Eastern Republicans, Progressives, and Democrats favored an increase in the navy. Their coalition was held together not by the bill's provision authorizing the president to call an arms limitation conference once the war was over, but by the conviction that national security demanded immediate, massive naval expansion.[12]

During the next year American entry and participation in the war fueled the forces of expansion still further. The mere prospect of belligerency fed the notion that what was just approved would not be enough. While the president made his last efforts at mediation and Berlin decided on unlimited submarine warfare, the mood in Washington changed. General Board admirals read the first reports of Jutland and concluded that the fleet needed five battle cruisers and numerous screening vessels beyond those just authorized. Congressmen read reports of shipping losses in the submarine war and demanded protection. Republicans, and then Speaker Champ Clark, urged the Navy Department to speed work on ships in the 1916 program. Senator Miles Poindexter introduced a bill that provided for the immediate laying down of one hundred submarines. House Naval Affairs Committee Chairman Lemuel Padgett then countered with an even more significant proposal: Congress should give the president $150 million to build vessels at his discretion. Secretary Daniels cut the number of subs from one hundred to twenty believing that that was the limit of current building capacity. But old disarmament advocates went no further than offering a weak resolution which reaffirmed the principle of settlement of disputes by arbitration. A mere twenty-three congressmen dared to vote against the naval bill, and they suffered editorial excoriation far stronger than that heaped on opponents of preparedness a year earlier.[13]

Once the United States became a belligerent, a wave of patriotism washed away the old norms of naval budgetary politics. In May 1917, Senator Claude Swanson of Virginia told Secretary Daniels that he could, in effect, write his own ticket on naval needs. Later in the year Congress broke the usual appropriations cycle with War Urgent Deficiency Appropriations Bills that gave President Wilson still more discretion to build ships for wartime purposes. Behind these votes lay radically new assumptions about America's needs and capacities. If, as the *New York Times* claimed, the immediate need was "making a Great Navy," it was inconceivable that "with the rich resources of this country" the nation could not build both the capital ships authorized in 1916 and antisubmarine craft for war use. Indeed "our navy may turn out to be, when it is completed, not the second but the first in the world." The old limits, the old lines of political cleavage, the old reluctance to expand appeared to vanish in the new war atmosphere.[14]

The shift from peacetime preparations to wartime operations also stimulated desires for fleet expansion beyond immediate combat needs. Washington found it difficult to make the choices that war demanded, but the agonies of decision were far fewer than those London experienced. The critical issues that divided the navy concerned priorities in expansion, not operations or preparations for them. Josephus Daniels expressed a wish that probably crossed many a mind when he lamented a few days after the vote for war, "O for more destroyers! I wish we could trade the money in dreadnoughts for destroyers already built." His admirals were divided on that proposition, torn between the obligation to meet immediate needs of war and the responsibility to assure long-term naval security. In London, Admiral Sims had few doubts as to which was the more important. He peppered Wilson and Daniels with cables that insisted that the Admiralty was doing everything possible to meet the submarine menace. America could help by producing and dispatching more and more destroyers to fight the German U-boats. By early summer, younger officers in the Office of Operations came to share Sims's point of view. They argued that immediate needs should take precedence over future problems; more destroyers and fewer dreadnoughts should be rushed to completion.[15]

Chief of Naval Operations Benson and senior admirals on the General Board doubted this argument. In February 1917 Benson ranked aiding Britain in the current war third, development of "the full military and naval strength of the United States as fast as possible" first among naval priorities. Benson doubted Britain's ability to survive the U-boat onslaught, and he feared possible Anglo-American commercial rivalry in the future. The General Board had its doubts about London's staying power, too. But senior admirals were also disturbed by intelligence reports from Tokyo which raised questions about Japanese loyalty to the anti-German coalition. America might yet have to fight Germany alone or a German-Japanese combination. Given these concerns, it was hardly surprising that the Board urged Secretary Daniels to build even more capital ships than those authorized in 1916.[16]

Daniels and Wilson were deaf to the senior admirals' arguments. They concurred that immediate needs must take priority in the naval building program. To engineer that change, Wilson proposed to bypass rather than confront bastions of conservative opinion within the navy. The General Board, he advised, should be "tactfully but altogether relegated to the function of advice upon large questions of general policy, judiciously selected." Admiral Benson, "too prudent, too unimaginative," would be "associated in counsel" but surrounded by younger, more imaginative officers. These changes were skillfully managed. Later in the year Wilson honored Benson by sending him on a mission to London with Colonel House, and Daniels did come to rely more and more on bright young officers like Captain William V. Pratt. The secretary then took the decision to give destroyers priority over battleships in new building programs and authorized the use of scarce steel and shipbuilding ways for merchant ship construction. But as a consequence, Daniels and Wilson stimulated desires within the navy for more battleship building.[17]

As Wilson presided over the shift from peace to war, he himself became much more conscious of the potential diplomatic uses of naval power. Civilian advisors anxious to resolve the quarrel over building priorities were partly responsible for this change. Assistant Secretary of the Navy Franklin D. Roosevelt suggested that Washington get an option on some British capital ships in return for sending destroyers across the Atlantic. Colonel House broached this idea again in mid-May, when Arthur Balfour came to Washington. According to the foreign secretary's messages to London, Britain and the United States might conclude a secret naval alliance. The War Cabinet rejected this suggestion, and Balfour left Washington offering hazily only "some assurances" as to the future. In July quite a different suggestion wafted back across the Atlantic. If the United States slowed work on capital ships to build more antisubmarine craft now, might not Britain, America, and Japan, as well as other members of the anti-German coalition, pledge mutual assistance against any aggressor that might threaten Washington within four years of the war's conclusion? Colonel House spurned this offer and continued to prefer some kind of bilateral arrangement between Washington and London.[18]

But Woodrow Wilson was cool to all of these suggestions. He suspected that London might later demand support for its war aims in return for any alliance. In July 1917 he made that point clear to Sir William Wiseman and emphasized the American tradition of playing a "lone hand." The 1916 building program was not a card to be taken from it. As Wilson told Wiseman, it "probably would be undesirable" to try to persuade Congress to reverse naval construction legislation. Behind these tactful words lay presidential doubts about the prowess of the Royal Navy and determination to use the American fleet to win victory. Wilson still had negative thoughts about British naval power left over from the long conflict over neutral rights. But cobelligerency impressed him with the "failure of the British Admiralty to use Great Britain's great naval superiority in an effective way." Late in the summer he appeared ready to believe that the United States Navy could succeed where the Royal Navy had failed. In a rare appearance as commander-in-chief, he told Atlantic Fleet officers of the need for American innovation and leadership in the war.[19]

Wilson fought for that leadership and believed that it could be used to change the behavior of his British ally. During the summer of 1917, Admiral Mayo, commander-in-chief of the Atlantic Fleet, begged to be allowed to go to London to coordinate Anglo-American fleet cooperation. But the president refused to let him until London agreed to a formal naval conference. Wilson would not supply ships he felt would be sacrificed by a faulty British naval strategy. He held out—and won his point. A conference was arranged before four coal-burning battleships were dispatched to join the Grand Fleet. Moreover, in late October 1917, Wilson was sufficiently convinced of American naval prowess to warm to proposals to increase Admiral Sims's staff and use it as a lever to force change upon the Royal Navy.[20]

Insofar as the public was concerned, the navy more than fulfilled the mandate the president had given it. To be sure, there were apparent slip-ups. Submarine raids along east coast shipping routes sent waves of alarm up and down the Atlantic seaboard. But these were mere ripples in comparison with the criticisms that battered the Admiralty for its inability to prevent coastal raids or draw the High Seas Fleet into battle. Moreover, the navy looked efficient and innovative in the public eye. American destroyers took up station on antisubmarine patrols. American vessels convoyed thousands of troops and millions of tons of equipment to the European battleground. American experts promoted advances in mining techniques, aerial spotting, and land gunfire support. American inventive genius, in the person of Thomas Edison and Henry Ford, mass-produced new types of antisubmarine vessels. Secretary Daniels, an old journalist, saw to it that the press reported these triumphs. Participation in the war thus brightened, rather than tarnished, the navy's public image.[21]

The impact of these war-induced changes on long-term naval policy began to reveal itself in 1918. By that time the admirals had long since lost unity and clarity of strategic perspective. The tide of war had turned against the old German hypothetical enemy, and revolution had sapped the strength of Imperial Russia. These new uncertainties led General Board officers to fear postwar conflict with an "anti-democratic" alliance of Germany, Russia, and Japan. Chief of Naval Operations Benson worried more about the British. Indeed, in February 1918 the admiral was even prepared to look favorably upon Japanese advances in Siberia. These would soften Pacific tensions and enable the navy to concentrate on the more serious potential menace in the Atlantic. Admiral Sims's staff in London had yet another view: the real danger was an Anglo-Japanese combination. But Sims in London and his friend Captain Pratt in Washington came to precisely the opposite conclusion. Security and peace depended on continued close Anglo-American cooperation. The two greatest sea powers together had more than enough strength to overcome possible difficulties with Japan.[22]

In spite of their differing assessments of the threat to American naval security, the admirals agreed on the need for more capital ship construction. General Board officers, even though they admitted the "utter futility" of trying to attain parity with Britain or a possible Japanese-German combination by 1920, had unsuccessfully sought five new battleships late in 1917. Undaunted by this failure, they wanted to use wartime congressional and public support to obtain twenty-eight capital ships beyond those authorized in the 1916 program. Their case rested on a new standard of naval strength, devised by Admiral Sims's staff, which committed the United States to reach for first place in the international naval system. The navy was to be

a self-contained organization designed to exercise, in the Pacific, a commanding superiority of naval power, and, in the Atlantic, a defensive superiority of naval power against all potential enemies who may seek to extend their spheres of influence over, or to impose their sovereignty on, any portion of the American continent or Islands contiguous thereto, not now in their possession or who may unjustly interfere with our international rights or our trade expansion.

To attain that rank, Washington would have to complete the 1916 program and go on to build a "two-ocean" navy.[23]

The debate over naval appropriations in the spring of 1918 suggested that these hopes for naval preeminence might not prove entirely vain. In February, Josephus Daniels told the National Press Club that the time was at hand when the United States would possess, in Wilson's phrase, "incomparably the greatest navy in the world." He praised Henry Ford, pacifist turned manufacturer of submarine chasers. On Capitol Hill war nationalism fueled the determination to attain preeminence on the seas. Members of the House Naval Affairs Committee wrote into the appropriations bill a provision urging resumption of work on ships of the 1916 program. Senate Republicans made the mandate clearer: the navy must commence work on all ships authorized in the 1916 program no later than July 1, 1919. Senator France of

Maryland, who on the eve of war had urged Wilson not to declare it, would require the navy to build the world's biggest battleship. Both Houses passed the naval appropriations bill without debate on these provisions in an enthusiastic *viva voce* vote. Josephus Daniels then claimed, as President Wilson signed the bill, that he welcomed and had inspired this mandate to achieve the preeminence which renewed capital ship construction would assure.[24]

On the surface it appeared that the friends of naval expansion had completely routed their foes. But just as the war had strengthened the forces of expansion, so, too, had it modified the ideas and political posture of those who favored arms limitation. That shift began early in the war when the movement to establish an international peacekeeping organization gathered strength. Hamilton Holt, editor of the *Independent* and strong supporter of what became the League to Enforce Peace, was one of the first to consider its potential impact on arms policies. Its very title suggested the direction in which his and other men's thoughts were moving. Holt argued that the purposes of armed force in an internationally organized postwar future would be different. Armies and navies would not be instruments of aggression, evil by their very nature and hence subject to limitation, but rather potential tools for good. Armed force might indeed be necessary to make concerted efforts at peace preservation effective.[25]

Others in the peace movement who hoped to see an international organization established were not prepared to go as far as Holt in modifying their prewar views on armaments. Pacifists suspected a league possessed of armed force and demanded abolition of standing armies and navies as the first step toward permanent peace. Former Secretary of State Bryan championed their point of view in a widely publicized 1917 debate with former president William Howard Taft. Early in 1918, Navy Secretary Daniels swung over to Holt's point of view. In his annual report released in December 1917 Daniels argued that American naval power so vital to victory in war might eventually guarantee peace. By forming an "international police of the sea," America and other nations might be able to reduce the size of their respective navies. The secretary was impressed with this new, collective approach to naval arms limitation, and he repeated the idea in an article he contributed to the League to Enforce Peace and in an address before its "Win the War for Permanent Peace" convention at Philadelphia.[26]

Daniels spoke as he did, secure in the thought that he was simply elaborating on President Wilson's own ideas. Wilson had long since endorsed the creation of a postwar international organization and had proclaimed the war a crusade to make the world "safe for democracy." By the end of 1917 neither Russian revolutionists nor war-weary Western Europeans were prepared to continue fighting for so vague an objective. Lenin appealed to all belligerents to set forth their war aims as he himself meditated on a separate peace with Germany. Wilson seized this opportunity to proclaim America's intention to transcend the old order of international politics. With Colonel House's counsel, he drafted his scheme for the future, set forth in the famous Fourteen Points address of January 8, 1918.[27]

Three of the fourteen concerned the navy. Points two and four dealt with naval issues often discussed in the past. Neither was included in the memorandum prepared by the Inquiry, a body of experts Wilson had authorized to examine peacemaking problems. House claimed that those points reflected Liberal opinion in London, but they also resonated with Woodrow Wilson's personal feelings. Point two called for "Freedom of the Seas" but implied that it might be limited by "international action for the enforcement of international covenants." Point four, "perhaps the most Wilsonian of the Fourteen Points," called for arms control by international agreement. "Adequate guarantees [were to be] given and taken that national armaments will be reduced to the lowest point consistent with domestic safety." But Woodrow Wilson reserved his most important point for last. The fourteenth point proposed "a general association of nations" strong enough to guarantee the political independence and territorial integrity of member nations.[28]

This speech proclaimed Wilson's determination to create a new international order. But it also laid the foundations for new political alliances on naval questions in Washington. Men began to subordinate particular views on naval expansion or limitation to more general attitudes toward international organization. Nationalistic advocates of preparedness like Theodore Roosevelt and Senator Henry Cabot Lodge scoffed at Wilson's dreams. Progressive, potentially isolationist Idaho Senator William E. Borah, who had previously voted for naval expansion, insisted that America's future international responsibilities did not extend beyond the Western Hemisphere. Wilson's words mesmerized other progressives and attracted one-time doubters. William Jennings Bryan, for one, warmed up to the League to Enforce Peace and admitted that the Fourteen Points met the "requirements of today."[29]

For the time being these differences between friends and foes of international organization, no less than those between advocates and opponents of naval expansion, might remain hidden in the fog of wartime patriotism. But foreign observers in Tokyo and London were puzzled and worried by them. Did the president's words portend new naval policies, or were they simply a pall to cloak his determination to command the mightiest navy in the world? At the Admiralty, Sir Eric Geddes probed for an answer to this question by suggesting to Franklin D. Roosevelt that perhaps Washington might modify its 1916 program. He made the point once again to visiting members of the House Naval Affairs Committee. America might "sacrifice a national aspiration, namely to upbuild your battleship fleet," and at the very least postpone completion of the 1916 ships. Geddes spoke the rhetoric of wartime urgency, but his audience thought in longer range terms. Representative Padgett, who had required presidential pressure to push the 1916 program through the House, now resented Geddes's remarks and reported them to Secretary Daniels. The navy secretary harbored similar feelings and forwarded Padgett's report to Wilson. Displeased at the implications of Geddes's remarks, and leery as always of any talk of the capital ship balance of the future, the president directed that upcoming Anglo-American naval conversations be limited to topics of immediate wartime cooperation.[30]

Those talks suggested how much war had modified American naval thinking. By the time Sir Eric came to Washington, he, his staff, and the Foreign Office thought better of raising sensitive questions about the future Anglo-American naval balance. Instead, the first lord tried to get the president to clarify the naval implications of his Fourteen Points. But Wilson disappointed Geddes. He spoke vaguely about members of an association of nations using their naval force against aggressors. He did not clarify his understanding of the meaning or limits of freedom of the seas. Significantly, neither Wilson nor Geddes discussed the fourth point, arms limitation. Geddes thus reported to Lloyd George that Wilson had only hazy notions about the shape of the naval future.[31]

But in fact Wilson's thoughts were not as vague as Geddes had imagined. As his handling of the naval budget for the coming year suggested, the president was well aware of mixed feelings that belligerency had stirred on Capitol Hill. Consequently, when Secretary Daniels came to discuss recommendations for the naval budget, Wilson hit upon an interim policy that provided for both expansion and limitation. The president rejected General Board recommendations for massive new construction as unwise and incompatible with disarmament discussions that might come about if current negotiations with Germany led to peace. Instead, he advised putting a second three-year program nearly identical to that of 1916 before Congress. This nationalistic gesture would soften the cries of chauvinist Republicans opposed to a negotiated peace and eager to seize control of Congress in the impending elections. But it would also strengthen and appeal to the forces of internationalism. A second fleet expansion program, put forward at the end of a war that had exhausted other nations' resources, would symbolize Washington's power to predominate in any international system. It could also serve as a diplomatic goad to force others to accept Wilson's particular vision of the future. The president made that point clear only two days after he took the decision for a second naval expansion program. Worried about "selfish" British attitudes, he said he needed "as many weapons as my pockets will hold so as to compel justice."[32]

The president's remarks made one point clear. America's position in the international naval system, no less than the attitudes and alliances that shaped her domestic politics of national defense, had changed between 1914 and 1918. In the last prewar year, Wilson and Daniels resolved naval problems primarily in domestic political terms; they promoted measured expansion as the golden mean. But by 1916 the domestic demand for preparedness and the threat of belligerency forced the administration to think in international terms. President Wilson supported both the notion of a universal league for peace and the largest naval expansion program in American history. In so doing, he shattered the old lines of division between economists and big-navy men. He also made clear America's ability to disrupt the old order of seapower.

But despite this legislative triumph, and despite the further increases in naval strength that followed Washington's entry into the war, the American naval future in 1918 was by no means clear. Statesmen and admirals might agree that the nation needed "incomparably the most adequate navy in the world." But what was "adequate"? Admirals sensed that the word demanded continued naval expansion, but they were far more uncertain of its purpose and character than they had been in 1914. Legislators agreed that the 1916 program was in some sense adequate. Yet as the debates in the spring of 1918 suggested, radically different understandings of the term lay hidden in their consensus. President Wilson himself had a mixed understanding of his own words. His decision for a second expansion program hinted that "adequate" had to be defined both in domestic political terms and in terms of the new and different international climate that would emerge from the war.

Thus as the war tempest passed over Washington, crosswinds of nationalism and internationalism buffeted American naval policy. Until peace warmed the atmosphere, clouds of unanswered questions would remain.

4 Tokyo: From Conflict to Compromise

On October 15, 1918, the day before Woodrow Wilson and Josephus Daniels decided upon a second American naval expansion program, Navy Minister Admiral Katō Tomosaburō sent Prime Minister Hara Kei a most unusual memorandum. In it he outlined the navy's needs for the future: seven hundred fifty million yen over a seven year period to build four battleships, four battle cruisers, and numerous smaller craft. This much would give the navy the minimum strength necessary to national security—a fleet whose nucleus was eight battleships and eight battle cruisers. The very size of the admiral's request was remarkable. But what was striking, indeed unprecedented, was his willingness to drop plans to build two cruisers immediately and to postpone beginning work on the other ships he sought until the following year.[1]

Katō's memorandum symbolized the paradoxical changes that war brought to Tokyo. The shifts of premise, perspective, and procedure resembled yet differed from those

48

that occurred in Washington and London. While war divided and embittered the Royal Navy, it helped unite and soothe the Imperial Japanese Navy. If the conflict stimulated nationalism which demanded that Washington transcend the old political and naval order, it fed a nationalism in Tokyo which sought first security and harmony within any domestic and international political system. And if war raised questions in both Western capitals about the future of competitive arms expansion as a means of preserving national security, it seemed to confirm Japanese policymakers' faith in the wisdom of building bigger and better battleships.

How was it that the Great War affected Tokyo so differently from Washington and London? And why did Japanese political leaders support arms expansion when their Anglo-Saxon counterparts began to consider arms limitation?

Men in London and Washington had few doubts about the outcome of the conflict brewing in Europe. But Japanese observers found it difficult to read the barometer of change. Some felt the war presented a golden opportunity to stabilize the empire's position in East Asia and consolidate relationships with the other great powers. Others vaguely sensed the force of the storm that destroyed so much in London and changed a great deal in Washington. But from the moment Japan declared war against Germany, statesmen and admirals were inclined to rely upon favorable forecasts. War for them was an external crisis which might be used to bring harmony to politics in general and stability to the politics of national defense in particular.

Their reading followed in part from the very instability and violence that threatened prewar political order in Tokyo. In August 1914, the Japanese political world was still suffering from the aftershocks of Admiral Yamamoto Gombei's fall from power. His demise came, at least in part, because the admiral was unable to bring stability to the politics of national defense. Yamamoto asked for a major naval expansion program without endorsing a similar army growth plan, and in doing so broke an unwritten rule of Japanese politics. This, together with scandals in naval construction, gave his Chōshū political opponents the opportunity to pull him from power and install their own candidate, Ōkuma Shigenobu, and old political party leader turned senior statesman, as prime minister. Aware of the fate of his three immediate predecessors, Ōkuma determined to restore order, interservice harmony, and stability to Japanese political life.[2]

He had scarcely begun his work when the war in Europe broke out. Ōkuma and his foreign minister, Katō Kōmei, seized it as an unprecedented opportunity. Katō, long an admirer of Great Britain, saw in the Anglo-Japanese Alliance a chance to cement ties with London and an opportunity to improve Japan's East Asian position. He and a majority of the cabinet wanted to drive Germany from her position in Shantung and the Pacific islands. Quick victories would please both armed services and improve

Japan's overall strategic security. Katō and Ōkuma may also have been moved by a desire to lay to rest the influence of elder statesmen like Marshal Yamagata and Marquis Matsukata on foreign policy decision making.[3]

But the decision for war had precisely the opposite effect. What was to unite at home and consolidate abroad brought further domestic disagreement and major international uncertainties. Marshal Yamagata had serious reservations about the decision for belligerency, and Admiral Yamamoto, his great rival, was equally incensed at the way it was taken. Katō Kōmei found himself tangled in an unseemly dispute with Britain over the extent of Japanese operations that strained, rather than strengthened, the ties between Tokyo and London. Early in 1915, tensions created by the war destroyed his China policy. When both Britain and America protested the so-called twenty-one demands, Ōkuma's government was shaken. The elder statesmen felt Katō had acted rashly, when in fact he probably had done little more than amalgamate various conflicting proposals from different sectors of the bureaucracy. In any case, he had to go. But with Katō went any real hopes of harmony on broad foreign policy matters. The Twenty-one Demands instead became a symbol of disunity among the elites concerned with foreign policy and an example of diplomatic opportunity lost.[4]

Increasing disagreement over foreign policy questions fed the natural desire of statesmen and admirals for harmony on matters of national defense. The latter, during the first fifteen months of the war, had little choice but to cooperate. Ōkuma's navy minister, Admiral Yashiro Rokurō, was both eccentric and weak. Katō Kōmei had helped pick him up from far down the seniority list and had convinced him that duty demanded that he accept a cabinet post. Yashiro was not in the navy mainstream, and he sidestepped the usual consultations with service elders in reaching the decision to become navy minister. Indeed this eccentric, noted for playing his flute on deck on moonlit nights at sea, stood so low in service esteem that his vice minister thought serving under him would be fatal to his future career. Yashiro carried out the unenviable task of removing his predecessors, Admirals Yamamoto and Saitō, from the active duty list. Ōkuma may have regarded this action as punishment for those who pursued individual service advantage at the expense of broader political harmony. To many, it smacked of revenge wreaked upon navy leaders by Chōshū clan adherents. But Yashiro justified it as a step necessary to restore the navy's public image and strengthen ties with others in the governing elite.[5]

A step of this sort might well have divided and embittered the Imperial Japanese Navy, just as war split the Royal Navy. But war opportunities and the emergence of new leaders brought quite different results. The war was a balm to many of the wounds the navy suffered in Tokyo's political battles. The fleet carried out highly successful operations, easily transporting troops to invest Tsingtao and demonstrating its innovative skill by using aircraft in combat operations for the first time. Admirals who might otherwise have remained in the capital sulking at their opponents' misdeeds, scattered to command various task forces. One seized German islands north of the equator. Another chased German capital ships to the Chile coast and eventual destruction by the Royal Navy. Yet another took on patrol duties in the South China Sea and Australasian waters in place of British forces. These operations were demanding of professional skill and were scattered enough to prevent the emergence of personality conflicts and command problems like those that plagued London. Moreover, in fulfilling goals of greater regional power and improved cooperation with Great Britain, they pleased professional diplomats like Foreign Minister Katō Kōmei.[6]

Successful operations at sea set the scene for even more favorable developments in Tokyo. In August 1915, Navy Minister Yashiro fell from grace along with his friend, Katō Kōmei. Two men anxious to preserve intraservice harmony and establish stability in extraservice relations took command of the navy. One, Admiral Shimamura Hayao, became chief of the Naval General Staff. Shimamura was the archtypal staff officer, a former attaché in London and Rome, a visitor to the United States, and a reformer of naval education. He had also commanded a battleship and served as aide to Admiral Tōgō in the latter part of the Russo-Japanese War. He was portly, jovial, fluent in English, and brilliant. Indeed early in 1915 foreign observers had felt that he was the real power within the navy.[7]

The other was a man of quite a different cut. Admiral Katō Tomosaburō, who succeeded Yashiro Rokuro as navy minister, was thin to the point of appearing frail. He had a formidable personality. Service rumor held that he never cracked a joke, and many a subordinate had withered before the sarcasm he used to annihilate those who would question his judgment. But Katō too, was brilliant. He stood second only to Admiral Shimamura when both graduated from Etajima, the Japanese Naval Academy. Former British instructors there years later recalled his brilliance for Japanese visitors in London. His pedigree and connections made him the naval administrator-politician par excellence. He had served Admiral Yamamoto as chief of the powerful Military Affairs Bureau at the turn of the century, worked under Admiral Saitō as vice minister after the Russo-Japanese War, and stood by Admiral Tōgō's side as chief of staff during the early part of that conflict. Katō had the political advantage of not being a Satsuma clansman and yet having good personal relations with Satsuma leaders.[8]

Katō and Shimamura were life-long rivals, but in 1915 they put aside personal feelings to pursue larger goals. Fleet expansion ranked foremost among them. Growth was the mortar which held the Navy Ministry together. It helped unite those within and strengthened all against the attacks of enemies without. Expansion as the primary naval goal came readily to both Shimamura and Katō. The head of the Naval General Staff had grown up in the service as reporter and analyst of foreign building programs, and Katō was midwife at the birth of the eight-eight fleet plan in 1906. Indeed, less than a month after he came to office, Katō, as if to demonstrate the continuity of naval leadership, demanded that Prime Minister Ōkuma commit his government to continued fleet growth. He refused, as had Yashiro Rokurō, to abandon construction of three battleships on the ways and repeated his predecessor's argument that four more should be built as the first step in attaining eight-eight excellence.[9]

But Admiral Katō pursued fleet expansion quite differently than did his predecessors. In 1914 he had brought about the collapse of a would-be cabinet, whose leaders could not promise Diet approval of naval expansion, by refusing to serve as its navy minister. But this raw use of political power had little appeal to Katō a year later. Rumor held that he had made approval of more naval building a condition of his service as navy minister. If he did, Katō certainly chose a mild, cooperative way of pursuing his goal of fleet expansion. In contrast to the generals who loudly demanded authorization of two more divisions, Admiral Katō took a "low posture." He rarely spoke on nonnaval matters in cabinet meetings. He worked to foster a spirit of cooperation with party leaders in the Diet. He retained Vice Minister Suzuki Kantarō, Yashiro's appointee, to cultivate the legislative friendships he had developed. In his own testimony before Diet committees, he was brief and to the point. Katō gave the impression that the increases in fleet construction he sought were moderate and indeed natural in a world at war. Naval journalists were courted and put to the service of expansion. They trumpeted the navy's war triumphs, insisted that the fleet was more than ever the first line of defense, and denied that growth meant enmity to a particular power.[10]

By autumn of 1916 Katō's cooperative approach paid handsome dividends. Despite intervening party political crises, Ōkuma made good his pledge to fund construction of battleships already on the ways. He went on to net approval of funds for four more capital ships in the winter of 1915–1916. Cooperation with political leaders was so much the order of the day that Admiral Katō scarcely blinked when Ōkuma fell from power. His own skill in winning approval of fleet expansion programs and the navy's sea successes had softened feelings about the events of 1914 that had dishonored the navy's leadership and threatened its internal harmony. Indeed, there was not a murmur of opposition to Katō's decision to serve in a cabinet headed by Terauchi Masatake, a Chōshū general and protégé of Admiral Yamamoto's old enemy, Field Marshal Yamagata Aritomo. Cooperation in what navy leaders hoped would be a stable political order conducive to fleet expansion was the order of the day.[11]

Civilian leaders were willing to go along with Admirals Shimamura and Katō for many of the same reasons that led their counterparts in Washington and London to back naval expansion. In the immediate flush of belligerency in the autumn of 1914, they had readily authorized ten new destroyers for the fleet. As the war continued they felt that the Imperial Navy could expand without major international complications. Prime Minister Ōkuma was willing to use the "American threat" in private arm twisting on behalf of naval growth. But in backing the eight-four fleet program, he, like Woodrow Wilson, felt that expansion need not mean Japanese-American conflict or increased tension with any nation. Growth, as the Americans themselves demonstrated in 1916, was simply endemic in the international system.[12]

Until late 1917 civilian leaders did not feel economic constraints against building a bigger navy. War wrought changes in Japan like those it brought to the United States, even if on a smaller scale. Domestic industry boomed as the empire supplied arms and goods to erstwhile enemy Russia and ally Britain alike. In 1915 the balance of international accounts tipped in Japan's favor for the first time in years. The nation was on its way to becoming international creditor rather than debtor, and specie reserves of 360 million at war's beginning were spiraling upward to nearly 1.6 billion by 1918. In these prosperous times politicians and even finance ministry bureaucrats found funds for naval and military expansion. They raided bond sinking funds and manipulated other accounts to avoid the political stigma of seeking new taxation.[13]

But the most compelling motive for expansion was political. Prime Minister Ōkuma and his opponents alike felt that they must master the politics of national defense if they were to hold the reins of personal power for long. If fleet and army expansion brought political stability to Tokyo, they were well worth the price. Ōkuma sought stability, however, on his own terms. Years of experience in Tokyo's politico-bureaucratic wars made him anxious to remove national defense from the larger political arena. He first proposed to do this by creating a Council of National Defense, composed of the two service ministers, chiefs of the respective general staffs, himself, and his foreign and finance ministers. Ōkuma hoped that private discussions within this group would lead to consensus on balanced expansion for both services. His government would then fare better in seeking Diet approval of budgets for a bigger navy and army.[14]

The prime minister seriously underestimated the strength of opposition to this plan. Bureaucratic rivalries were far too strong to vanish at the desire of a mere prime minister. Foreign Minister Katō Kōmei reportedly doubted the need and wisdom of army requests for two additional divisions, yet supported naval expansion. Successive finance ministers grimaced at the costs of expansion. One felt that the council was little more than a stage for ritual combat between his ministry and the two services. Ōkuma's hope that private discussions would calm interservice tensions also proved ephemeral. Army and navy leaders continued to find it difficult to agree on their respective share of the budgetary pie. Even when they did reach a tenuous compromise,

Finance Ministry representatives might stalk out of the council in disagreement over how to provide them. But the key flaw in the Council of National Defense idea was Ōkuma's own political weakness. Lacking a clear Diet majority for the first year of his prime ministry, he could not promise bureaucratic contenders certain legislative approval of the compromises hammered out in the council. To remedy this weakness, Ōkuma dissolved the Diet in December 1914 and called elections. But even after his followers triumphed in a corruption-ridden campaign, the prime minister had considerable difficulty in forcing expansion budgets for both services through the Diet.[15]

In the late spring of 1916, Ōkuma sought stability and a measure of arms control in another way. Through secret intermediaries he approached opposition party leaders with proposals to limit and depoliticize debate on national defense matters. Diet leaders would promise not to attack expansion programs already authorized. In addition, they were to set some kind of norm in monetary terms, such as a specified percentage of the national budget, for arms expansion. For a period of about two weeks, it appeared as if a compromise of this sort might be worked out. But Ōkuma miscalculated the intentions of former Foreign Minister Katō Kōmei, still the leading light within the Dōshikai party. Isolated and opposed to his former cabinet colleagues, Katō held fast to the idea of party responsibility in government. He balked at giving any pledge restraining freedom of debate. Katō also may have sensed a larger truth—the fact that arms expansion was too central to the entire political process for any politician to foreswear using it to his own advantage.[16]

Katō Kōmei made the point bluntly, but his great rival, Hara Kei, president of the opposition Seiyūkai party, exploited it brilliantly. Between 1914 and 1918, Hara made the national defense issue, called "the politicians' shoals" by journalist wags, the ladder to the prime ministry. Hara was an extraordinary individual, perhaps the greatest of modern Japanese politicians. His career, like that of David Lloyd George, was already a bundle of contradictions. He had come from the poor Northeastern part of Honshu to Tokyo and rose to prominence by way of journalism, a stint as zaibatsu executive, and second-level positions in the Foreign and Commerce Ministries. Although he came from a distinguished family, he styled himself a commoner in a political world ruled by titled politicians, admirals, and generals. He proclaimed himself the champion of party government, yet the briefest glance at his record showed that he had risen by touching base with the dominant, nonparty elites that struggled to govern Japan. As vice minister of foreign affairs, for example, he mastered the intricacies of bureaucratic life and strengthened his ties with the dominant clique of professional diplomats educated at Tokyo University. He had served as home minister in Yamamoto Gombei's cabinet and had many ties to Satsuma clansmen in politics. Once

Yamamoto's government fell, he kept up ties with the old admiral and at the same time courted favor with his great antagonist, Field Marshal Yamagata of Chōshū. Even in his personal life, Hara had something of Lloyd George's flair. He put aside a wife of many years to live with a courtesan in a beautiful villa overlooking the sea.[17]

Unlike Lloyd George, Hara was far from eloquent, but he shared with the British prime minister a taste for behind-the-scenes legislative manipulation. He thrived amid Tokyo's politics of factional maneuver. Hara was an exceptionally good listener, and what he heard in 1914 and 1915 told him that outright opposition to arms expansion or trying to side with one service against the other was unwise. But Diet members of his own Seiyūkai party felt differently as 1914 turned to 1915. They determined to keep up ties with the Satsuma clique by opposing army increases and backing navy expansion. However, they pushed this measure through the lower house of the Diet by only seven votes. Their weakness signaled to Prime Minister Ōkuma the opportunity for elections which decimated Seiyūkai strength. Hara Kei's party thus proved unable to block joint army-navy expansion later in the year.[18]

This defeat may have stung Hara Kei into the realization that his own ambitions could not be fulfilled by party strength alone. Throughout 1916 and 1917 he maneuvered carefully to avoid coming to grief on "the politicians' shoals." Early in 1916 he visited Sasebo and Kure, both major naval ports, and spoke of the need to expand shipbuilding facilities. His party made "the perfection of national defense" one of its four major platform planks. But Hara left to others the advocacy of naval building and, unlike Katō Kōmei, refused to block overtly Ōkuma's proposed truce on national defense matters. He kept up ties with Satsuma's Admiral Yamamoto, but was even more careful to cultivate good relations with Chōshū's Marshal Yamagata. When he spoke, it was more often than not on behalf of politically profitable and less sensitive issues like improved education and railway expansion. His calculated ambiguity toward the government of General Terauchi Masatake forced another election in the spring of 1917, and this time the Seiyūkai triumphed handsomely.[19]

When at the close of that year the budgetary cycle brought arms expansion to the fore once again, Hara played his political hand brilliantly. He determined to make Prime Minister Terauchi and Marshal Yamagata recognize that his party's support was vital to political stability and arms expansion. National Defense Council bargaining produced a budget that horrified Finance Ministry officials. The navy was to receive three billion yen to begin work on two additional battle cruisers—the so-called eight-six fleet. The army sought five billion for an eighteen year expansion program. National defense was the single largest item in the budget. To provide necessary funds, the government would have to violate earlier pledges not to raid bond sinking funds—or raise new taxes. Some politicians, including those close to the prime minister himself, felt that the army's requests were unrealistic and unwise. But War Minister Oshima staunchly defended them, just as Admiral Katō defended the requests of the navy. Both men came to Hara to explain their proposals. With his large bloc of Diet votes he obviously was the man to convince.[20]

But their arguments were, for the most part, unnecessary. Hara Kei was not interested in the absolutes of national security or even in the supposed financial problems that arms expansion would create. On the contrary, he wanted to resolve yet another budget battle to his own advantage. Instinct told him that tampering with service budget proposals was a risky business. Sound political intelligence proved that Terauchi might try to maneuver tax increase proposals in such a way as to create a coalition that could best the Seiyūkai in the Diet. Consequently Hara wrung from Terauchi's agents the promise that the Seiyūkai might rewrite tax proposals to safeguard its interests. In return he convinced his party's leaders not to attack the inadequacies and distortions of government arms expansion programs. The result was easy passage of tax increases for arms expansion and express thanks from the prime minister to Hara for preventing a major political battle over them. Hara Kei had become the key to success in Tokyo's politics of national defense.[21]

Hara might well have brought stability to that politics had not larger, war-related events intervened. Down through the last weeks of 1917, Terauchi had been remarkably successful in holding the war at arm's length. He had established a Foreign Affairs Advisory Council to define foreign policy consenses, and its members agreed on the broad goals of wartime policy: the empire should assert and stabilize its position of leadership in East Asia and, at the same time, preserve and improve relations with her allies and associates in the European War. Diplomats pursued both goals by means of alliances with the European imperial powers, climaxing their success with a Russo-Japanese agreement on China shortly before Terauchi came to office. Thereafter, in response to pressures from within the army and from ultranationalist groups, Terauchi opened his government's coffers to buy stability and influence in Republican China. To satisfy those who feared involvement in Chinese affairs, Terauchi agreed to improve relations with the Great Powers. While the army declined to send troops to Europe, Admiral Katō agreed early in 1917 to send cruisers and destroyers to aid England at the hour of maximum submarine peril. Later in the year former Foreign Minister Ishii Kikujirō went to Washington to quiet lingering American suspicions of Japan's continental intentions. He returned late in the year with an ambiguous agreement which many read as American recognition of Japanese hegemony in Northeast Asia.[22]

But in January 1918, just as Woodrow Wilson enunciated his vision of a new world order, this balance crumbled, and with it went the sense of remoteness from the European War. Admirals, generals, and politicians were shocked by revolutionary Russia's talk of a separate peace with Germany. When revolutionary unrest broke out in Vladivostok early in January, they began to fear that the security and stability within the existing international order they had long sought might vanish. Whether or not to intervene in Siberia became the most pressing issue. For six months top policymakers debated within the Foreign Affairs Advisory Council over the wisdom, feasibility, and mode of intervention. Their discussions ranged over three questions. First, did disorder in Siberia and a separate German-Russian peace threaten the empire's security? On this point there was no agreement. Second, if Japan were to act, had she resources enough to restore order? Here, too, there were violent disagreements. Army staffers insisted that they were up to the task, while Marshal Yamagata, Hara Kei, and professional diplomats had their doubts. Finally, if Japan lacked the strength to act alone, ought she to respond favorably to European and eventually American proposals for cooperative action? This was the real sticking point. When Terauchi's foreign minister, Motono Ichirō, was tempted to act alone, he fell from power. His successor, Gotō Shinpei, a strong nationalist of the Theodore Roosevelt variety, pulled and hauled his colleagues together behind a patchwork compromise in late June 1918. Leaving virtually all of the larger implications of the issue unresolved, Foreign Affairs Advisory Council members agreed to send a limited force to Siberia in conjunction with European and American troops.[23]

The prospect of intervention in Siberia thus gravely weakened the consensus underlying Tokyo's foreign policies. But it did far more than that. Revolutionary turmoil in Siberia brought the war close to Japan for the first time. It focused educated public opinion on questions of security and international status rather than ideas of a new world order. In March 1918 the journal *Taiyō* published a symposium of opinion leaders' views on war aims. Their replies revealed considerable fears for Japan's international position, and evinced more than a few suspicions of American and British intentions. The war, several authors claimed, was a struggle for respective national advantage and no amount of Wilsonian or Leninist rhetoric could hide that fact. By April the Siberian question had become so central that the same journal devoted an entire issue to it. In this climate of opinion, little wonder that army leaders saw a golden opportunity. Early in June they agreed to push for a new definition of strategic priorities and force levels to meet the Siberian threat and to improve their own position in future budgetary battles.[24]

From the naval point of view, this was a dangerous development. Any definition of probable postwar conditions during the European War would be foolish. Admiral Shimamura made this point to General Uehara Yūsaku, chief of the Army General Staff, when he raised the question of strategic plans revision two years earlier. On that occasion the admiral argued that European conditions were uncertain and that it would be better to await the full results of war before making formal changes in Japan's strategic posture. Jutland had just taken place, and although the Imperial Navy had observers with the Grand Fleet, the battle's consequences were far from clear. By 1918 the entire international naval order had been blurred by war. The United States had passed its 1916 Naval Act, and if all of its ships were completed, the Pacific balance would tip decidedly against Japan. But the war emergency had pressed America into destroyer construction, just as it had slowed Britain's plans to build four superdreadnoughts of the H.M.S. *Hood* class. Admiral Katō spoke the truth when he told Diet questioners early in 1918 that it would be best to await clarification of the international naval situation before making further expansion decisions.[25]

Admirals Katō and Shimamura also recognized dangers to intraservice harmony in army overtures for strategic redefinitions. Both continued to think in terms of the prewar balance of naval power, despite the fact that observers like strategist Admiral Akiyama Saneyuki had come back from Europe convinced that the war demanded new definitions of naval strength. A nation like Japan had to have not only a fleet strong enough to deter would-be intruders in the western Pacific, not only high morale and national spirit to compensate for her inability to match invaders' larger naval forces, but also a firm resource base. Akiyama and other Japanese observers pounded home the message that the Empire needed to find resources and build industries which would give it the staying power necessary in modern warfare.[26]

Shimamura and Katō drew one conclusion from these arguments— caution must be the watchword. Shimamura, much like Admiral Benson, wanted to concentrate the fleet in home waters. When Katō finally persuaded him to acquiesce in sending destroyers and cruisers to European waters, Shimamura insisted that the navy ought to be compensated with needed shipbuilding materials after the war. Admiral Katō was equally cautious. Japan was weak relative to the Anglo-Saxon giants. She might improve her strategic position through occupying the German islands in the North Pacific. They might be held permanently, as a kind of strategic screen blocking American access to Philippine bases or, as the admiral's secretary argued early in the war, be used as bargaining counters to be traded for some kind of Pacific island nonfortification agreement. By 1917 war developments made the navy minister's sense of weakness and desire for cooperation with the United States even stonger. He endorsed orders directing Admiral Takeshita Isamu, the naval representative who accompanied Ambassador Ishii to Washington, to offer naval cooperation in the eastern Pacific and to raise tactfully the question of Japan's need for American steel exports. Early in 1918, when the steel embargo began to take its toll on Japanese shipbuilding and the Americans proved rough bargainers over exceptions to it, Katō had all the more reason to tread warily. It was not surprising that he sided with Hara Kei against an independent expedition to Siberia.[27]

Less senior naval officers on the general staff read the preliminary lessons of war quite differently and struck a different balance of costs and risks involved in preemptive action in Siberia. Japan might have to continue to exist in a multipolar naval order, but she could greatly improve her position by action on the Asian mainland. Rear Admiral Abo and Captain Kiyokawa of the general staff set down their arguments for immediate action early in January 1918. They argued that the threat of a German advance eastward was real. They bristled at the insult to Japan's regional naval hegemony posed by American and British cruisers speeding toward Vladivostok. Putting the issue in much broader terms, they feared that the United States, already advancing into Japan's sphere from the south via the Philippines, would now close the circle of containment by way of the Aleutians and Siberia. But the key point in their case was resources. Immediate action in Siberia would give the empire riches enough to improve significantly her overall standing in the hierarchy of great powers. Rear Admiral Yoshida Sojirō's arguments for immediate Sino-Japanese naval and military cooperation agreements simply seconded their case.[28]

Senior admirals may have detected threats to service unity and Japan's international position in these arguments. Too great an emphasis on resource needs might weaken the hold of the eight-eight fleet on professional imaginations. But whatever the internal dangers, those looming outside the service were far greater. In the shadow of the Siberian crisis interservice discussions of strategic priorities were bound to produce disagreement. The army would insist upon making Russia the prime hypothetical enemy, a choice which naval leaders had rejected a decade and more earlier. Moreover the strong likelihood was that the generals would use the Siberian peril to inflate their demands for new divisions and claim the lion's share of the budget. But by mid-June 1918, Admirals Katō and Shimamura did not have the political strength to resist army pressures. A Chōshū general was prime minister, and his foreign minister urged revision of strategic plans. The Foreign Affairs Advisory Council had agreed on Siberian intervention, and Hara Kei seemed unwilling to challenge the decision. The politico-bureaucratic balance had shifted markedly against naval interests.[29]

In part to sweeten the bitter pill, Marshal Yamagata put together an enticing memorandum on force levels. While he continued to feel that Japan must exist within a balanced international system, he argued that the empire should set strategic priorities now to fortify her East Asian position. Security lay in extending the hand of friendship and protection to China against Western inroads. It demanded that the empire gain access to resources vital to national defense. To this end, a great reordering of national defense programs ought to allow both army and navy to grow. The old marshal argued that the navy ought to be strong enough to assure the safe transport of troops to the Asian mainland—a traditional definition of naval needs in army eyes. But he added that the fleet also should be strong enough to dominate East Asian waters at least as far south as the Taiwan straits and perhaps even to Singapore.[30]

This last provision was the carrot that accompanied the stick of bureaucratic-political reality. Katō and Shimamura used it to their own advantage. If the navy was to command the farther seas, then it needed more strength. If the army was to have twenty-five divisions in peace and forty in war, then the fleet ought to consist of twenty-four capital ships, not merely of the sixteen of the eight-eight program. This kind of numerical interservice trade-off sealed the bargain. Despite its broader political distastefulness, Prime Minister Terauchi, the full Board of Field Marshals and Fleet Admirals, and finally the army and navy ministers approved the new definition of strategic needs.[31]

Scarcely a month passed before it became obvious that the bargain sealed late in June 1918 was hollow and the politics of national defense as unstable as ever. The army not only launched its Siberian expedition, but escalated troop levels there far beyond the numbers agreed upon in the Foreign Affairs Advisory Council. Neither service did anything to bridge the gap between quite different assessments of strategic priorities or develop sound operational plans. Army staffers busy with Siberia had no time to consider what the navy's insistence on naming the United States probable enemy number one meant. Their promise to provide a division and a half for an attack on the Philippines meant nothing. Naval staff planners did nothing to follow up the decision to name America their service's prime hypothetical foe. They had not decided whether or not the former German North Pacific islands ought to be included in Japan's defense perimeter. They talked of invading the Philippines in discussions with army opposites but did nothing to develop specific ship construction programs or amphibious landing plans necessary to a successful attack.[32]

The final proof that certain and orderly naval arms expansion was as remote as ever came in mid-September 1918. By that time a much larger crisis had enveloped official Tokyo. Riots against spiraling rice prices had exploded throughout the home islands. Prime Minister Terauchi, ill and exhausted, seemed unable to act decisively—whether to deal with the underlying economic problem, to restore public confidence through some gesture, or to control the burgeoning Siberian expedition. He tottered on the brink of resignation while his army colleagues considered the possibility of using troops to quell the disturbances. Amid these alarming circumstances, Admiral Shimamura and General Uehara were summoned to the Imperial

Palace. In their audience with Emperor Taishō national defense plans and army expansion schemes were discussed. The strong probability is that the two service chiefs were told their growth programs were simply impractical.[33]

The dangers that disrupted the already tenuous agreement between army and navy proved to be Hara Kei's great opportunity. The rice riots and Siberian problem were clearly beyond General Terauchi. When the elder statesmen met to consider the situation, they had little difficulty in agreeing that Hara Kei must succeed the ailing Chōshū prime minister. Hara's past record of cooperation and consultation temporarily put to rest Marshal Yamagata's fears of his being a purely partisan leader. Amid the crisis provoked by the rice riots, Hara the commoner as prime minister might evoke national unity. Indeed, when Hara moved into the prime ministerial villa at Nagata-chō, newspapers proclaimed the advent of a new era in the empire's political life. And no one, not even Hara's most bitter opponents, could deny that his bureaucratic expertise and political shrewdness promised sound management, if not solution, of the problems confronting the nation.[34]

The national defense issue ranked near the top of the list, but Hara was convinced it was not as dangerous as his predecessors' followers whispered to him. His judgment may have rested on selfconfidence born of his handling of the expansion program earlier in the year. But it coincided with developments within the army that worked to his advantage. Hara chose the vice chief of the General Staff, General Tanaka Giichi, as war minister. Tanaka, a Yamagata protégé, told Hara he would not insist upon approval of the army's draft budget as a condition for joining the cabinet. On October 11, he indicated willingness to put aside plans for army expansion in the face of the current domestic turmoil and expressed his personal desire to pull back from the Siberian adventure. His arguments probably reflected a shrewd assessment of the overall political situation. But they also had roots in broader trends of thought within the army. General staff officers were unhappy at Terauchi's leadership, and the more perspicacious among them sensed that raw interservice rivalry for defense funds hurt the nation. As General Ugaki Kazushige put it, the European war demonstrated the folly of relying solely on land or sea power. The successful nation must have both—and the resources to back army and navy alike.[35]

Four days later, on October 15, 1918, Admiral Katō offered to drop plans for building two new cruisers. He defended the decision as a response to the immediate economic and social crisis. But the admiral may have sensed that Hara's accession to the prime ministry afforded an opportunity to escape the unpalatable interservice agreements of the summer and establish a new stability in the politics of national defense. That thought certainly haunted one of his cabinet colleagues, Finance Minister Takahashi Korekiyo. On October 18, he raised the question directly with Hara. Big service expansion programs meant more raids on the bond sinking fund or unpopular new taxes. The rivalry between army and navy for a piece of the budgetary pie was unseemly. Now, amid social turmoil at home, increased military demands were certain to alienate the public even more than in the past.[36]

Hara listened quietly to his finance minister's exposition of the classic bureaucratic arguments against more money for the services. Then he told him what to do. Takahashi was to prepare an interim budget for the coming year without major increases for arms expansion. This would avoid undesirable Diet struggles over tax increases and postpone defense issues until the following year. By that time the European war might well be over and sentiment for arms limitation might have increased. But Hara refused to abandon the notion of arms expansion as an integral part of national defense policy. He reminded Takahashi that the Seiyūkai was pledged to attain "the perfection of national defense." The finance minister would have to find funds for later increases in army and navy budgets. Hara, clearly, was making the same kind of choice in October that he had made earlier in the year. He would postpone the difficulties and uncertainties implicit in arms expansion to reap the political benefits of solid relations with the armed services.[37]

This point and more emerged from conversations between Takahashi, Tanaka, and Admiral Katō during the next week. The three readily agreed upon a stopgap budget for the coming year. They sketched long-range expansion plans which the Finance Ministry would seek to fund. The navy would build its eight-eight fleet; the army would increase division strength and modernize its equipment. Hara had his cabinet colleagues agree that in the light of

> the present condition of the Empire and developments in the world's great powers, it is necessary to formulate a policy for the perfection of national defense and to keep it in harmony with finances which . . . are at an unfortunate level. The army and navy, simultaneously formulating major programs for the period from fiscal 1920 onward, desire their implementation. Should increased resources for this prove necessary, plans for increased taxes, government revenues, and public securities must be developed and carried out.

There, clearly, was the political commitment to expansion.[38]

But General Tanaka added something more. He proposed and his cabinet colleagues agreed on a sliding scale for alloting scarce funds to the two services. In the immediate postwar years, the navy would receive the larger share. But as it approached completion of the eight-eight fleet program in 1927, the army's portion would increase. This notion seemed to promise stability in the politics of arms expansion. But the general qualified that commitment in a memorandum circulated to army colleagues and not revealed to the cabinet. In it he argued that an end to the fighting in Europe, technological change, and probable arms control efforts would sweep away the navy's expansion plans long before they became budgetary realities.[39]

Hara Kei probably knew nothing of Tanaka's memorandum. In the last cabinet meeting devoted to service budget requests, he proposed that the terms of the compromise between the services, Finance Ministry, and himself be kept secret. Government spokesmen would simply plead immediate financial stringencies to push through the budget drawn up. Unspoken but implicit in his words was the last, vital element in the compromise. Hara in effect promised that he would marshal Seiyūkai votes behind unchanged service budget requests now and in the future. He would pass safely over the "politicians' shoals" and bring the stability that had eluded his predecessors to Tokyo's system of national defense.[40]

As the Great War drew to its close, then, Tokyo chose a course of action far different from that of Britain or the United States. Japan's statesmen, admirals, and generals agreed on continued arms expansion primarily for domestic political reasons. They agreed that the procedures and premises of naval policy should be stabilized. Indeed, stability, security within the existing international order, was their common goal. Hara, Katō, and Tanaka could not comprehend fully or manage all the uncertainties in that broader order. What was uncertain—peace possibilities, naval weapons developments, and even arms control—they would postpone. But what was manageable, essential, they would seize. It was this desire for domestic political stability, bureaucratic harmony, and indeed for personal power that carried them to the compromises of October 1918. The choice, given their assumptions and experiences, could have been no other.

But that choice left one major question unanswered. Could governmental stability dependent on arms expansion survive the storm of war? The European conflict had all but destroyed the old order of sea power. The war had driven Imperial Germany from the Pacific, shattered Britain's prewar politics of national defense, and brought major uncertainties to American naval policy. When the storm passed, and peace once again prevailed, could the balance of power among the three major naval nations—and indeed that within each—remain unchanged for long?

2

The Dangerous Drift, 1919–1920

The Fourth Point and the Fourth Power

5 In October 1918 the storm of war suddenly began to lose force. Peace feelers and then a coup d'etat in Germany sent currents of warmth rushing across the Atlantic. In a matter of weeks world politics shifted dramatically. The war ended in an armistice. War leaders became statesmen, concerned anew with balances of power at home and abroad. Admirals turned from the sea to the land, from battle charts and construction schedules to schemes for peace, the handiwork of politicians and bureaucrats. Plans for treatment of the vanquished and designs for order among the victors would occupy the thoughts and energies of statesmen and admirals in Washington, London, Paris, and Tokyo for nearly a year.

But the passage from war to peace was not to be easy. The long struggle had disrupted the old order—set aside patterns of thought and action. By its very length the war had forced men to think about the future, about the peace they would create. Some dreamed with Woodrow Wilson of a millennium, a new order of politics which would strike down forever the fears that divided man against man and set nation against nation. Disarmament was essential to that vision. Others thought in more conservative terms. They hoped to piece back together the order shattered and shaken by the long war. They wanted to restore the strength of their navies, perhaps revise the rules for their use, and most certainly restrain the power of their onetime enemies. Admirals and statesmen were to be found in both camps, each in his own way committed to peace, security, and order.

Whatever their thoughts, those who framed policies in world capitals found it difficult to make them reality. The world of 1914 had vanished. The international system had been shaken to its very foundations. Three European empires—Germany, Austria-Hungary, and Russia—writhed in revolution. Britain, France, Italy, and their lesser allies had poured men and resources into the struggle until they themselves faced sweeping economic, political, and perhaps social, change. The powers on the horizon—America to the west, Japan to the east—loomed as the more resourceful players on the world stage.

But the young and the old, the vigorous and the exhausted, faced common problems, common questions. Three of those questions dealt directly with naval armaments, with President Wilson's fourth point—arms limitation—and with the fourth naval power, Germany. The first was deceptively direct: Would arms limitation become a fundamental part of the postwar world order as the American president hoped? The second was more subtle and perhaps even more complex: What would become of the fourth power, Germany, and its seapower in the new international order? The third question was the most difficult of all: Would it be possible for the three victorious naval powers to strike some sort of balance among themselves? For nine months after peace feelers broke the ice, through armistice talks, preparations for a general peace conference, and finally negotiations at Paris, America, Britain, and Japan were to struggle with these questions. In the process they laid the foundations for a new international system and learned a great deal about arms limitation.

In October 1918, and indeed throughout the next nine months, the initiative in dealing with these questions lay in Washington. Woodrow Wilson answered the first peace feelers from Vienna and Berlin. He rejoiced that America's enemies sought to make his Fourteen Points the basis of a negotiated settlement. But Wilson sensed that allies abroad and opponents at home might make it very difficult to render his vision of a new world order political reality. From East Asia came alarming signs that Japan harbored imperialist designs. Tokyo poured troops into Siberia far in excess of the numbers Washington thought it had agreed upon. Suspicions born of the knowledge of secret wartime agreements among America's associates rose from the past, to trouble the president. The possibility of Anglo-American friction was never very far from Wilson's thoughts. The president was troubled by rumors of British commercial designs on Latin America and disturbed by Sir Eric Geddes's remarks about the United States' acknowledgment of Britain's preeminence on the seas. Wilson's comments were ambiguous at best. In one breath he told Sir William Wiseman that aspects of his second point most likely to trouble Anglo-American relations—those dealing with blockade, maritime law, and submarine warfare—might best be left until after a peace conference. But in another, he insisted that Britain accept his principle of freedom of the seas.[1]

Obstacles at home loomed even larger than those abroad. Leading Republicans had already disassociated themselves from the notion of an international peacekeeping organization, as presented in the president's fourteenth point. Theodore Roosevelt and Henry Cabot Lodge objected vigorously to the mere thought of a negotiated peace with Berlin. Republicans smelled victory and revenge against Wilson in the congressional elections which would occur in November 1918. The president recognized the political force behind their objections. But opposition both at home and among political leaders in London and Paris provoked Wilson's determination to resist—and overcome. Once Berlin replied to his second, stiff peace note, Wilson authorized Colonel House and Admiral Benson, already in London, to meet with the British and the French to work out a prearmistice agreement based on his Fourteen Points.[2]

By the time House and Benson reached London, a mood of uncertainty and division had gripped Whitehall. Allied military and naval men had already met in Paris to explore possible armistice terms, and a meeting of the full Supreme War Council was set for the end of October. These negotiations, and with them the possibility of an end to the long war, upset London's political timetable. Lloyd George had just launched plans for an early election, one which he hoped would render permanent the wartime coalition and give him a clear mandate to lead the empire toward peace.[3] But now the basic question of war or peace—and with it a host of potentially divisive foreign and naval policy issues—demanded his attention. Ought Britain to settle for a negotiated peace? What should the naval and military terms of an armistice be? And how should London regard Washington's insistence that the Fourteen Points form the basis of any settlement?

Admiral Sir Roslyn Wester-Wemyss, the first sea lord, brought the armistice question to the cabinet table first. The idea of demanding the surrender of sixty German submarines as proof of good faith for an armistice had come up in preliminary naval talks at Paris. But Wemyss found that service opinion rapidly escalated to demand terms equivalent to those of a final settlement. Admiralty voices demanded surrender of the full German fleet, evacuation of Heligoland and other North Sea islands, and abandonment of German colonies. Old Jackie Fisher agreed with these terms and with the help of Cabinet Secretary Hankey got his ideas before the cabinet. Then, on October 21, 1918, Trafalgar Day, Admiral Sir David Beatty, commander in chief of the Grand Fleet, clinched the Admiralty case. He told the cabinet that these preliminary terms had to give Britain the equivalent of full victory at sea. Germany must yield her submarines and the heart of the High Seas Fleet so as to be unable to resume the war. Behind these stiff demands lay the admirals' unspoken assumption that the war must end on terms which would preserve Britain's naval preeminence: the fourth power must be rendered navally impotent.[4]

Arguments about the military and naval terms of an armistice gave Lloyd George the opportunity to maneuver his colleagues into agreement on the issue of a negotiated peace. He agreed with Admiral Wemyss's logic: the "great principle" of an armistice should be to take what one expected to keep in the final peace. But was Berlin likely to accept terms which amounted to "abject surrender"? Lord Milner put the case differently: If London demanded all of Berlin's submarines, then Washington would insist on an end to the blockade. Milner's argument convinced Bonar Law, leader of the Unionist Party and an early supporter of the Admiralty point of view, that perhaps the proposed naval terms were too harsh. Lloyd George then got Sir Douglas Haig to express army fears about Admiralty terms. Evading a clear-cut decision, he referred the question to a joint army-navy study committee, asking that it set forth minimum armistice terms. Four days after that group completed its work, Lloyd George put the question bluntly to his colleagues: Were they willing to continue fighting for the Admiralty's proposed terms? In the absence of affirmative replies, he was free to conclude that the time had come to seek a negotiated peace.[5]

That answer came slowly because London was far from agreement on the meaning and implications of Woodrow Wilson's Fourteen Points. The most troublesome of them was not the fourth point, arms limitation, but the second, freedom of the seas. Admiral Wemyss argued that freedom of the seas was inconsistent with the very existence of a powerful navy. Spurning the counsel of young Turks within the Admiralty who thought such outright opposition to Wilson's concept logically unsound and politically tactless, he insisted that Britain must retain the freedom to control the trade of neutrals and enemies. Without such freedom, she could not hope to remain first upon the seas. At first Lloyd George seemed to go along with this argument. He mocked Wilson, calling him a combination of old Lord Bryce and the general secretary of the Y.M.C.A. with his schemes for a league of nations. He said the Germans would interpret freedom of the seas to their own advantage, just as they had in talks with Colonel House in 1915. The prime minister even spurned Balfour's suggestion that Wilson might be open to compromise on the issue. Instead, as the long cabinet meetings drew to a close, the colleagues agreed to send Washington a cable stating that "the British Government could not accept the doctrine of Freedom of the Seas." But the prime minister held the door ajar for another choice: perhaps all should reconsider whether Britain should continue to fight.[6]

Overnight the prime minister changed his position, but not his principles. When the cabinet reconvened, he opened with the suggestion that it might be better to make the British position clear in the coming Paris talks rather than send a blunt cable to Washington. Austen Chamberlain and Lord Curzon objected. Chamberlain insisted that limiting sea power without touching land armaments was unfair. Lloyd George agreed. "Public opinion in this country would never stand any faltering on the question (of freedom of the seas)." But wouldn't it be more tactful, Lloyd George suggested, to make the point in negotiations? Sir Eric Geddes, fresh from Wilson's study, then tried to defuse the underlying issue. Although the president was "rather bitten with the effectiveness of sea power," Geddes felt he meant no challenge to Britain's supremacy. Wilson's recent call for a second three-year building program was probably to get ships for a league navy, Geddes postulated, and the same motive made him unwilling simply to destroy the German fleet. Lord Reading saw in the league link a way out of the dilemma: perhaps Lloyd George ought to insist that Britain could accept freedom of the seas only after a league of nations became effective.

Lord Reading's view opened the way for one of the prime minister's deft evasions. Of course, his own view was that "we should challenge the doctrine of the Freedom of the Seas altogether." But he personally preferred to go to Paris, state Britain's objections to it, and agree to talk about it later. Chamberlain protested, but this time Bonar Law and Balfour favored caution. The continental allies did fear Britain's sea might, and perhaps the coming talks would show whether or not they might side with Washington against London. But further discussion brought more basic issues to the surface. Lord Reading felt that the moment had arrived to make a "good peace." Questions of sea power, he implied, ought not to obscure the larger realities of world power. At present Britain and America controlled the world situation. But with each passing day, Washington grew stronger. Moreover, "there were ... important influences in the United States which were getting the idea that America should dictate the conditions [of peace]." On this sobering note—a reminder of how war had changed the international power dynamic—the cabinet went on to give Lloyd George the freedom he sought.[7] He would, if possible, end the war, soothe Anglo-American relations, and avoid commitments that might limit Britain's traditional sea supremacy.

During the next week's discussions at the Supreme War Council, Lloyd George taxed his skills to the utmost in pursuit of these goals. He played a brilliant, if devious, game. At first he hinted to Colonel House that compromise on freedom of the seas was possible. Britain would voice her objections, then agree to discuss the principle later. Then, in what may have been either an attempt to test American firmness on the subject or a cover for eventual compromise to Unionist cabinet colleagues, he reversed himself. That afternoon, after French Premier Clemenceau objected to freedom of the seas, Lloyd George insisted that it would denude Britain of the blockade weapon. No English prime minister could even discuss the subject. This switch incensed Colonel House and convinced him that Lloyd George was trying to torpedo the Fourteen Points as a whole. Privately he threatened naval and mercantile competition and publication of Anglo-American differences. The Texan then cabled Wilson for instructions. The president replied with a stern threat of separate peace, but House declined to disclose it. Instead he hesitated and tried to persuade the British to yield on freedom of the seas.[8]

House failed. The most ardent pro-Americans in the prime minister's entourage rejected his arguments. Lloyd George himself spoke of spending whatever might be needed to maintain Britain's sea supremacy. Then House gave ground on the blockade; a timely cable from Washington disavowed any desire to end it. This quieted one of the cabinet's qualms and gave Lloyd George a much needed quid pro quo. When on November 3, at the afternoon meeting of the Supreme War Council Clemenceau sided with the Americans, Lloyd George reverted to his original compromise position. House, jubilant in the belief that he had forced Lloyd George to back down and eager to bolster his stock with the president, then reported victory to Wilson. London could not accept a German interpretation of the second point, House said, but Lloyd George would be "perfectly willing and ready to discuss it with you." In fact the prime minister had deftly maneuvered toward peace and better Anglo-American relations.[9]

Lloyd George also triumphed in the battle over the fate of the enemy's fleet. An ugly difference of opinion divided Americans and Britons in the Allied Naval Council. Admiral Wemyss wanted Germany to surrender virtually all her naval forces upon conclusion of an armistice. This, as he had argued in London, would demonstrate the Royal Navy's victory. Admiral Benson objected, arguing that the Germans would not accept such harsh terms. Benson feared Wemyss's demands foreshadowed destruction of the "balance wheel" of European naval power. Consequently he argued that the disposition of the High Seas Fleet should not augment the naval strength of any European nation. This deadlock forced the issue to the civilian negotiators' table. There Lloyd George, Balfour, and House shunted aside the larger issues that divided the admirals. Rather than worry about the impact of the fourth naval power's defeat on the two or three remaining maritime giants, they proposed to intern the nucleus of the High Seas Fleet in neutral ports. Submarines were to be surrendered. The statesmen concluded successful prearmistice negotiations on that note of compromise, despite the admirals' grumblings.[10]

A week later Germany signed an armistice that ended the long war. But the conclusion of one struggle marked the commencement of another, one that continued until formal peace negotiations opened in Paris two months later. Statesmen and admirals wanted to preserve amity born of wartime cooperation among Washington, London, and Tokyo, and they agreed on the need to constrain Berlin. But could they create a postwar international political and naval system without crossing swords with one another? Could they endorse Wilson's vision of the future and yet preserve individual national security? Would it be possible to agree on what the president's points—especially fourteen, two, and four—really meant? or would preparing for peace disrupt relationships and destroy the premises on which they rested with the same vengeance as the waging of war?

The man who championed the new order was least troubled by these questions. Wilson was elated but suspicious, magnanimous but aggressive when the war ended. House warned of Lloyd George's toughness as a negotiator and doubted his full acceptance of the president's principles. Admiral Benson was even more certain that Britain sought only her own national and naval advantage in the talks to come. But despite these doubts, Wilson set about preparing for his unprecedented journey to Europe for the peace conference. This left precious little time for the navy. Indeed Wilson and Daniels held fast to the course they had charted in mid-October and attempted to steady discussions of naval affairs along routine routes. The navy secretary defended arms expansion in congressional testimony late in November, and Wilson automatically endorsed the second three-year building program in his December message to Congress. The congressional cycle of hearings and debate would give him ample time to resolve larger international, political, and naval uncertainties.[11]

As he prepared for the peace conference, Wilson's thoughts about international organization and arms control were still quite vague. The president had priorities and principles, not specific programs. He had often said that arms limitation might follow the establishment of an international organization. But when Navy Department experts produced an elaborate scheme for a League Navy—one that provided arms limitation and promised international stability with a force that gave Britain and America parity with one another and all other powers equality with their combined strength—Wilson scoffed at the idea. A detailed scheme of this sort, he said, was "only another form of militaristic propaganda," no better than individual nations' abuse of armed force. Perhaps as a matter of principle, perhaps from awareness of how bitterly the notion of using force to preserve peace divided American internationalists, Wilson rejected arms control of this sort. Instead larger imponderables—whether or not the European powers would accept his peace program—occupied the president's thoughts.[12]

The same question ranked first on London's agenda. But until mid-December 1918 domestic politics shunted it aside. Lloyd George and his colleagues triumphed in the so-called "khaki" election, and only after the reconstruction of the cabinet was complete could the Imperial War Cabinet turn to peace conference preparations. By that time several individuals and groups had publicly championed international organization. The Union of Democratic Control, perhaps the most important among them, had endorsed the Fourteen Points. Within the war cabinet the time was at hand for serious discussion of a peace program. From the very outset opinion was split along two lines. Prime Minister "Billy" Hughes of Australia, representing one side, railed against Wilson and all his works, insisted on annexing German colonies, and demanded *résistance à l'outrance* to freedom of the seas. Borden of Canada and Smuts of South Africa argued the opposite side of the case. Borden postponed the issue by suggesting that it be referred to the Admiralty and Crown Law Officers for further study. Smuts addressed the larger issue: Britain must accept Wilson's league, recognize American naval preeminence in the Pacific, and incline toward Washington rather than Paris in shaping the postwar world. By December 20, it became clear that Hughes stood alone in his desire to resist Wilson. Four days later, on Christmas eve, London made another critical decision: the empire should not oppose a league of nations and would tie arms limitation to it.[13]

But members of the Imperial War Cabinet had only the vaguest notions of how to achieve arms limitation. Ardent League of Nations supporters like Lord Robert Cecil and General Smuts felt that arms control was the test of league effectiveness. Bonar Law, the senior Tory partner in the coalition cabinet, agreed that the public demand for arms control was real. Lloyd George summed up the apparent consensus on behalf of Wilson's point four: "If the League of Nations did not include some provision for disarmament, it would be regarded as a sham ... There would be the greatest disappointment among the people." But ought arms control to touch Britain's sea power? Admiral Wemyss had already answered the question of freedom of the seas with a resounding "No!", and friends and foes of the League of Nations concept had reservations about arms control for the navy. Bonar Law suggested that Britain had everything to gain from an agreement that would leave her naval superiority untouched and yet force the French to reduce their armies. Lloyd George seized upon this suggestion to propose a strategy for arms limitation: perhaps London should impose arms control first on Berlin, setting limits on permanent armed forces and prohibiting conscription. This might bring the French around. But shrewdly, the prime minister said nothing about the navy.[14]

The issue of arms control had to wait until Lloyd George actually met Woodrow Wilson. That meeting came on December 26 after careful planning by both sides. The two men chipped away at their accumulated suspicions of each other and reached general agreement on how to manage arms limitation negotiations. Wilson was vague and inclined to postpone detailed conversations on freedom of the seas until a league had been established. He held firm to the principles of his fourth point, but readily concurred that detailed arms limitation discussions were beyond the scope of the coming conference. The president accepted, too, Lloyd George's proposal that the victors should first impose arms control on Germany in order to soften French resistance to the idea. As in the War Cabinet discussions, the two men were treating arms control in general and avoiding the more sensitive naval aspects of the question. But this meeting was sufficient to convince Lloyd George that Britain and America "were, in the main ... in agreement." He reassured the Imperial War Cabinet that when and if Wilson proved obdurate, he would compromise but not sacrifice what was vital to the empire's interest. Implicit, but unspoken once again, was the notion that the supremacy of the Royal Navy was just such a vital concern.[15]

Tokyo was half the globe away from London and Washington, yet her statesmen and admirals were far from disinterested in developments in Europe. Peace came suddenly, stimulating anxiety and caution alike. Japanese diplomats in Europe were instructed to avoid the final armistice negotiations and felt unready for the coming peace conference. Naval representatives came to regret their absence at initial discussions of naval peace terms, and Katō Tomosaburō subsequently directed them to keep a sharp eye out for the empire's interests. There was little concern at the fate of Germany, the fourth power; for the Foreign Ministry had long since prepared a detailed case for her exclusion from the Pacific. But as in London, President Wilson's Fourteen Points raised new issues which the bureaucracy simply had not anticipated. To be sure, there was a general consensus on maintaining harmony with the Anglo-Saxons. The long Siberian debate had convinced Prime Minister Hara and Marshal Yamagata that Britain and America would remain the two strongest world powers. Hara and Yamagata knew something of the differences that divided Americans and Britons. Yet caution, and perhaps confidence born of successful maneuvering in domestic politics, inclined Hara in his more sanguine moments to think that Japan, at least in East Asia, might play the role of broker between the two.[16]

Once the Foreign Affairs Advisory Council turned to discuss Wilson's peace program, however, it became obvious that contradictions ran all through the apparent consensus on peace proposals. The League of Nations sparked contradictory reactions. Foreign Ministry bureaucrats conceded that they knew little of its details and advised caution, even if Japan accepted the idea in principle. As discussions proceeded, a sharp split emerged in official and public debates. Intellectuals and journalists, ranking army officials, Itō Miyoji in the Foreign Affairs Advisory Council and Prince Konoe without, feared that the proposed organization might turn out to be a mere cover for Anglo-Saxon domination. But Makino Nobuaki, Hara Kei's choice for Japan's senior working negotiator in the coming peace talks, insisted that Tokyo ought to embrace the idea wholeheartedly and help write rules for the international organization. Wilson's second point pulled Tokyo's decision-makers in contradictory directions, too. Foreign Ministry officials routinely advised following Britain on the matter. Admiral Katō termed freedom of the seas "a double-edged sword." Intellectually he leaned toward the American position, but practically he was satisfied to champion the need to dominate the seas surrounding Japan and accept the diplomats' muddy suggestion to follow Britain. The fourth point fared no better. Everyone was for disarmament in principle. But Admiral Katō did not want arms limitation if it meant that the Pacific would become an American lake, and diplomats doubted that the powers could agree quickly on any standards for arms control.[17]

Consequently the final instructions drawn up for those going to the Paris peace talks were imprecise. Tokyo had reservations about the league, about freedom of the seas, and about arms limitation. Yet her representatives had been instructed not to oppose Wilson's principles but to adjust to "developments at the conference." Hara Kei, like Lloyd George, was being cautious. Having just concluded a compromise on national defense, he was wary of quarrels over peace terms that might, as they had in the past, destroy a cabinet. He avoided choosing among those who backed cooperation with the Anglo-Saxons as a matter of habit, those who accepted it as a power-political necessity, and those who opposed it as a stigma of inferiority. Instead, in personal instructions to Makino Nobuaki, he simply directed that the delegates cooperate with the Anglo-Saxon powers.[18]

Hara's caution mirrored that of political leaders everywhere during the first postwar months. In the transition from war to peace, they faced imponderables both at home and abroad. No one knew for certain how strong countercurrents of nationalism and internationalism ran in public opinion. What statesmen could be certain that his conscious acts could calm the instability created by war and revolution? These uncertainties set limits to the achievements of statesmen and admirals during the six months of negotiations at Paris in 1919. They made it difficult to be precise about arms limitation in the League of Nations Covenant. They complicated the endeavor to set limits to German sea power and made impossible agreement on a balance of naval strength among the naval powers.

Drafting the principles of a new world order, the League of Nations Covenant, showed just how difficult arms limitation could be. The issue that Tokyo feared might divide Britain and America—freedom of the seas, or limitation of naval power by restraints on its use—was the first to be settled. Wilson and Lloyd George had already agreed to postpone talks on this touchy subject, and the president's first Paris draft of a league covenant made no mention of it. The fact that Wilson avoided mentioning freedom of the seas may have reflected the views of Colonel House and David Hunter Miller, the drafting expert. They knew the issue provoked London's sensibilities and felt that once the league was established the issue would diminish in importance. Their naval counterparts, Admiral Benson and his staff in Paris, concurred for quite different reasons. They argued that artificial legal restraints on the use of sea power were inconsistent with its very existence and were certain to be ineffective.[19]

Admiral Wemyss could not have agreed more. But Balfour, the foreign secretary, and his nephew Lord Robert Cecil, the chief British draftsman for the league covenant, and Lloyd George revived the issue. Cecil wrote Lloyd George's idea of banning conscription as the first step toward disarmament into his January 8, 1919 draft of the covenant. General Bliss and David Hunter Miller thought this unfair: Why limit armies but leave sea power untouched? Secretary of State Robert Lansing insisted that any covenant guarantee the maintenance of America's maritime rights. Wilson thus accepted the conscription ban and added supplementary pledges to respect freedom of the seas in his second draft covenant of January 20. There it remained until January 31—a sticking point between the Anglo-Saxon powers. The Admiralty adamantly resisted Cecil's blandishments for a compromise, and the French refused to abandon conscription. Thus when Miller met with his British opposite for final draft covenant revisions, the second point was dropped. President Wilson did not like the result, but in the interests of preserving Anglo-American unity on a draft and getting the other nations' approval of it, he abandoned freedom of the seas.[20]

The French were also indirectly responsible for the death of another approach to arms limitation. Woodrow Wilson had already scotched the notion of creating a multinational league navy that would both limit individual nations' forces and regulate their respective sizes. Admiral Benson would have none of the idea, and Admiral Wemyss insisted that Royal Navy operations at the behest of an international organization would be unconstitutional. But men like Lord Robert Cecil and Sir Eustace Percy of the Foreign Office responded differently. Cecil, still worried about how a league could make its pronouncements effective, and Percy, in deference to what he presumed American feelings were, proposed a definition of respective national naval strengths that kept alive the notion of a multilateral force. But the French sealed the fate of this idea with their enthusiasm for a league army. Wilson would have no part of that, and the final draft covenant thus excluded another approach to arms limitation.[21]

General Smuts proposed two other major means of arms limitation. In contrast to most British proponents of international organization, he did not feel that disarmament would follow automatically once a league had been established. It would be necessary to regulate competitive arms expansion by nationalizing arms production, prohibiting the arms trade, and abolishing conscription. These ideas were by no means new to London, and despite doubts within the Admiralty, they appeared in both American and British drafts for a league covenant. They remained in the final version presented to the other powers. But others, especially the Japanese and the French, had ample reason to chip away at their meaning. In Tokyo, General Tanaka used the American drafting experts' arguments on freedom of the seas to oppose the abolition of conscription: it was not fair to limit land but not sea power. In Paris the French and smaller European powers bore the brunt of negotiating a compromise that would endorse the desirability of ending conscription. They also successfully opposed banning private manufacture of arms and international arms trade. Clearly, the weaker nations in the international system were not going to accept production controls or nonproliferation agreements that worked to their disadvantage.[22]

Smuts's second major proposal was more significant—and controversial. The South African felt that the powers might accept the principle that the League of Nations had the power to define fair standards for national armaments. His proposal coincided with President Wilson's thoughts, and the result was article eight of the draft covenant. It recognized the right of all nations to maintain arms consistent with "domestic safety." This phrase sent shivers up and down the spines of professional military and naval men everywhere. It was hardly consistent with Admiral Benson's mood or thoughts. While he and his staff were not opposed to a league per se, they had become increasingly worried about the prospect of Anglo-American rivalry within it. Such a rivalry would demand arms expansion beyond the strict terms of the draft article. The Admiralty had long since expressed its opposition to any "mechanical scheme of limitation of naval armaments." Put bluntly, "the Admiralty cannot agree to any proposals for the reduction of armaments the effect of which would be to take away from them and to place in the hands of some international tribunal the responsibility of determining what naval force is required for the protection of the Empire." Admiralty representatives in Paris protested the wording of the draft article, and Admiral Takeshita, the ranking Japanese naval officer at Paris, immediately cabled his objections to Tokyo.[23]

In Japan Admiral Katō and General Tanaka joined in opposing the draft arms limitation proposal, and Hara Kei appointed a special subcommittee to study the constitutional questions it raised. Tokyo then proposed a compromise—rewording the draft so as to permit arms consistent with "national" safety. In Paris the French argued that different geographical circumstances for each power had to be taken into account in determining armaments. They led a successful fight to change the article. But even in a modified and softened form, the idea of League of Nations involvement in national decision-making processes alarmed the Admiralty. The Board protested that its constitutional prerogatives were being threatened, and the new first lord, Walter Long, sent the cabinet a memorandum insisting that they be protected. Long insisted that unanimity of League Council decisions concerning arms limitation should be guaranteed. The Paris negotiators did take cognizance of this concern in the final league covenant. But they also left open the door to all that the admirals and generals had protested about by creating a permanent advisory commission on military and naval matters that would have the authority to consider arms limitation.[24]

The many compromises on arms limitation in the league covenant made one point clear: the victorious powers were still far from agreement on the meaning and implications of Wilson's fourth point. Within the British Empire Delegation, Admiralty representatives protested the final version of article eight, and Long was careful to forward the Admiralty's reservations to the War Cabinet. Sir Robert Borden of Canada brushed off these doubts by asserting that article eight was an exercise in futility. Cecil, ardent league supporter though he was, looked toward bilateral negotiations outside the league as the more likely avenue toward arms limitation. Admiral Takeshita, who knew that Benson's staff wanted parity with the Royal Navy, recommended a policy of caution first, then studious preparation for possible later arms limitation efforts. Even Wilson, late in the conference, did not hesitate to put off suggestions for arms limitation talks.[25]

If they were cautious about the implications of League Covenant provisions on arms limitation for themselves, the victors were eager to apply them—and more—to their recent enemy. But in trying to determine the fate of German colonies, attempting to set the size of German naval defenses, and banishing German submarines from the seas, they discovered that arms limitation was a difficult, sensitive issue. Those who would impose limits on the fourth naval power differed over the means and degree of doing so. Admirals feared that constraints on Berlin might somehow affect their own freedom of action in Tokyo, London, and Washington. Both they and civilian political leaders began to sense that severely limiting German naval expansion might very well effect unwanted, potentially dangerous changes in relations among the remaining three major naval nations.

This last point became clear in the first issue with which they dealt, the disposition of Germany's colonies. Americans, Britons, and Japanese generally agreed that Berlin should not recover those of greatest potential naval significance, the Pacific islands. In Tokyo, Admiral Katō wanted to keep those north of the equator in full sovereignty. Foreign Ministry bureaucrats agreed, partly in response to widespread public expectations that the islands would be a kind of reward for participation in the European war, and partly from the conviction that wartime agreements with London already assured their retention. In London Admiralty spokesmen and Tory members of the coalition wanted to strip Germany of all potential submarine and air bases. The only point of disagreement was whether or not the islands should be annexed. Australian Prime Minister Hughes, who thought of those south of the equator as a barrier against Japanese expansion, insisted on annexation.

Those more sensitive to Wilson's appeal doubted the wisdom or feasibility of such a move. Washington's agreement on dispossession was riddled by doubts at its consequences. The president's advisors accepted his fifth point: no power should unconditionally annex the islands. But what were the alternatives? General Board officers had pointed out the desirability of acquiring all of the Marianas and perhaps the Marshalls and Carolines as well. Admiral Benson and his Paris staff, more worried about Britain's monopolization of strategic positions, felt that if Tokyo promised not to fortify the islands Japan might possess them. Their civilian counterparts argued that the islands, if unfortified, might be held by some power under league supervision.[26]

Long before Wilson had considered these alternatives, Lloyd George had brought the issue to a head. The prime minister painted the alternatives as annexation, internationalization, or control by a league of nations. He preferred the last alternative, at least insofar as territories conquered by British arms were concerned. But Lloyd George let Australian Prime Minister Hughes and Baron Makino make the case for annexation of the Pacific islands. Colonel House suspected that Lloyd George raised the colonial issue to test Wilson's mettle on the larger league of nations issue. But in fact the prime minister was simply trying to maneuver Hughes into a compromise. On January 28, 1919, he urged the Australian to accept it in the form of a "class C" mandate, which provided virtual sovereignty over the islands. The hot-tempered Hughes refused and went on to enrage Wilson in subsequent debates, but Lloyd George had suggested the essential compromise.[27]

Wilson was loath to accept it, for he wanted to avoid the appearance of "distributing the spoils" before the league covenant had been completed. He also harbored doubts, born of the Siberian intervention episode, of Tokyo's trustworthiness as holder of a mandate for islands north of the equator. Baron Makino and his naval advisor, however, warmed to Lloyd George's suggestion. The diplomat recommended that Tokyo not risk isolation by insisting on outright annexation; the terms of a class C mandate amounted to virtual sovereignty, anyway. Admiral Takeshita, the senior Japanese naval representative at Paris, considered annexation the more desirable choice but began to think application of the mandate principle to the former German islands inevitable. He was willing to compromise, provided Tokyo was assured of receiving the mandate. He also saw potential strategic advantage in the nonfortification principle for all mandates. If the Americans tried to apply it to these islands, Tokyo might counter with demands that they stop work on, or raze, naval facilities on Guam. Perhaps in this way the kind of limitation on strategic bases that Yamakawa Tadao, formerly secretary of the Navy Ministry and now an advisor to the Paris delegation, had earlier suggested might be achieved.[28]

These developments in Paris forced Tokyo to make a significant decision.

Important figures in the Navy Ministry had circulated reports which scoffed at the feasibility of Wilson's league and doubted his sincerity on arms limitation. Various nationalist groups had also demanded the Pacific islands in full sovereignty. But Hara Kei and Katō Tomosaburō rejected these arguments. Hara, perhaps in deference to Makino's judgment, perhaps in response to anticolonial arguments put forward by intellectuals and journalists, favored accepting the mandate principle. Admiral Katō seconded him strongly. Reversing earlier arguments about the islands' value, he told the Foreign Affairs Advisory Council that the empire need not possess them in absolute sovereignty. The navy had not intended to fortify them and did not fear Wilson's nonfortification principle. Even if nonfortification were subsequently applied, Japan could, in case of war, quickly develop the necessary bases. This was enough to enable Hara to persuade his colleagues to instruct Makino to accept the mandate scheme—provided Japan was assured the mandatory power.[29]

Months passed before Tokyo got that assurance. Wilson adamantly resisted distribution of mandates for the Pacific islands until April. He recognized their strategic value athwart the navy's lines of communication to the Philippines. He was impressed, too, by arguments about the commercial value of the cable island of Yap. But Wilson knew that Lloyd George could not jettison wartime pledges made to the Japanese; nor was he likely to disregard completely the feelings of the Australians. Total resistance to the Japanese, whose good will Wilson had already strained by not writing race equality into the League Covenant and by resisting Tokyo's case for the disposition of Shantung, was equally impossible. Thus on April 21, the president tentatively agreed that Japan should receive the mandate for islands north of the equator. Two weeks later he offered no objections to making that designation formal. But for two months more the negotiators haggled over the details of mandates. Finally in early July, after Wilson had departed for Washington, Colonel House wrote nonfortification into the terms of the mandate. Wilson had gotten this guarantee against changes in the Pacific naval balance, but in the process Admiral Takeshita's hopes for Japanese-American agreement on mutual limitation of strategic bases, an important form of arms control, evanesced.[30]

Setting permanent limits to German naval power and sweeping enemy submarines from the seas forced statesmen and admirals to face still more difficult questions about arms limitation. As in the case of colonial dispossession, there was broad consensus on the need to contain German seapower. Wilson and Lloyd George had already agreed to disarm Germany as the first step toward broader arms limitation. Virtually all their associates concurred—at least on the first premise. Bonar Law insisted that the Anglo-German naval rivalry must not continue in postwar Europe. Admiral Wemyss argued that the German challenge so recently overcome could not be allowed to rise again. Beatty tried to make that point clear with a dramatic surrender ceremony for German ships interned in British ports. Tokyo, having pushed German sea power from the Pacific, was inclined to regard Berlin's permanent naval status as an essentially European matter. Navy Ministry spokesmen felt it would be unwise to quarrel with the allies over the fate of the German fleet. Insofar as Washington was concerned, only Admiral Benson raised serious objections. He feared England's rise in Germany's decline. Setting permanent limits on German naval power would entangle the United States in a European system of containment, one which, he added, was bound to demand increases in American armaments. Benson's arguments destroyed unanimity in the committee drafting naval terms of peace. But they proved politically fruitless. Other members of the American delegation wanted to set the final naval terms of peace quickly and opposed Benson's sending a personal appeal to President Wilson.[31]

The chief of naval operations' objections notwithstanding, the admirals went on to consider how they might limit German naval power permanently. They stumbled into a measure of agreement on the techniques of naval limitation without knowing that their civilian masters thought of Germany as the test case for future efforts at arms control. The British, most directly concerned about the European naval balance, took the initiative in designing permanent controls. Originally the Admiralty thought simply of dispossessing Germany of all naval power. But in preparing for the negotiations, Admiralty planners came to the conclusion that arms limitation in general and naval terms of peace might be compartmentalized. They damned all "arbitrary and artificial standards of relative strength" and excised words commending the general principle of arms limitation by international agreement. Yet at Paris Admiral G. P. W. Hope proposed to leave Germany a fleet whose nucleus would be six battleships, an equal number of light cruisers, and twelve each of submarines and gunboats. He went on to suggest limits on German naval personnel and the establishment of a permanent Allied supervisory commission to insure German adherence to limits on naval construction. This last point incensed Admiral Benson, and discord among the admirals left the final choice to civilians on the Supreme War Council. There the decision was made to impose kinds of limitations which the Admiralty had earlier called impractical: restrictions on the numbers and tonnage of individual ships, personnel limits, and prohibition of conscription. The final result cast doubt on admirals' objections to the practicality of arms limitation and left Germany with what President Wilson called a "third-rate navy."[32]

According to the terms worked out by the admirals, the German navy was not to have submarines, but other fleets would. This curious, limited attempt at controls on the development and use of the most terrifying innovation in the recent war reflected the admirals' very ambivalent attitudes toward the U-boat. Admiral Benson, despite his objections to limiting German naval strength permanently, wanted to ban the submarine. His Paris staff felt that the navy would always be constrained by the American public's moral revulsion against the weapon and argued that Britain and Japan might agree in order to save themselves from a repetition of submarine attacks on their seaborne commerce. But Admiral Sims, the General Board, and submarine advocates disagreed. They insisted that it was technically impossible to limit any ship type. Furthermore, they felt that the United States should not abandon a weapon which might prove quite useful in a trans-Pacific war.[33]

Similar arguments divided London and Tokyo. Admiral Wemyss favored prohibiting submarine warfare in general and, at the time of the prearmistice negotiations, made a strong case for depriving Germany of her U-boat power. War Cabinet members shared his general feeling that Britain ought not to have to face the threat of another submarine crisis. But once peace preparations began in earnest, there was little agreement. Within the Admiralty, Wemyss's subordinates split over whether limitation by prohibiting submarine construction was technically feasible. They also questioned whether other powers would be likely to agree to a general submarine prohibition. Nonetheless, the Admiralty's final preconference position paper favored exploring the possibility of sub prohibition. Tokyo was cautious and opportunistic. While official navy spokesmen insisted that the capital ship was and would continue to be supreme, Admiral Katō knew the value of the submarine. He instructed navy representatives in London to claim seven German U-boats as reward for Japan's part in the antisubmarine campaign. Yet he and general staff planners probably were also aware that the submarine might someday threaten the island empire's commerce and the navy's command of its surrounding seas.[34]

This mix of professional motives, together with statesmen's broader concerns, boded ill for anything beyond minimal agreement on the fate of German submarines. The admirals were able to agree on extending the time each victor nation might exhibit and study surrendered German U-boats. Moreover their preliminary draft naval terms left Germany with ten coast-defense submarines. But civilian statesmen, mindful of the immense public outcry against the submarine, struck them from the final terms. Germany was forbidden to construct or use U-boats. But the victors did not impose restraints on their own use of the submarine. The admirals ran aground on solid French opposition to submarine abolition; and Admiral Takeshita tactfully informed Benson and Wemyss that Japan could not yield the "weapon of the weak." In subsequent discussions the admirals rejected operational restraints on the submarine. More importantly, neither Wilson nor Lloyd George abandoned their tentative agreement that disarmament had best wait on the establishment of the League of Nations. Consequently the submarine was denied to the fourth naval power but not prohibited to the other three.[35]

The outcome of these attempts to limit German naval power suggested a cynical conclusion: Arms control was fine so long as it was not self-denying. That thought recurred to statesmen and admirals as they wrestled with the question posed by Germany's disappearance as a naval power: Could they agree on a new naval balance which would neither disturb their present relationships nor promote future competition in naval expansion? The question presented itself most directly when negotiators considered the fate of Germany's capital ship fleet. On this issue, the positions of admirals and statesmen were reversed. Naval experts wanted to dispose of the German behemoths as painlessly as possible. Neither Benson nor Wemyss thought his fleet would gain anything by possessing them, and both wanted to keep the ships from lesser European powers. The Japanese were ready to go along with this way of thinking. Only in moments when he feared the Anglo-Saxons would bow before French and Italian demands for a share of the High Seas Fleet did Admiral Takeshita suggest that Tokyo might have to acquire two or three German dreadnoughts. It was hardly surprising, then, that draft naval terms of peace provided for the sinking of all interned German ships.[36]

Political leaders, however, found it difficult to accept this proposal. They worried not so much about the international consequences of Germany's naval demise as about its domestic political effects. In Washington, Republican senators Lodge, Borah, and Harding objected to outright destruction of the German capital ships. President Wilson late in December 1918 agreed that destruction would be "silly." Navy Secretary Daniels was pulled in two directions. On the one hand his idealism commended destruction. On the other, political savvy said destroying an entire navy while fighting Congress for funds to build up one's own was foolish. Similar difficulties plagued London. The Board of Admiralty urged Walter Long to destroy the German ships and resume work on battle cruisers. But the old Tory recognized the incongruity of the request. His dilemma was at least partially resolved by the cabinet decision, made final in mid-March, not to seek parliamentary approval of any new naval construction in the coming fiscal year.[37]

That decision was rendered somewhat easier by developments in Paris. During the first week of March the question of the German fleet's fate threatened to drive Britain and America apart. Benson's suspicions of Britain mounted, and even Colonel House feared that the Anglo-Saxons would be pitted one against the other if Lloyd George did not stand firm against French and Italian demands for a share of the German fleet. The British prime minister agreed in principle but for domestic political reasons was unwilling to take the lead. Nothing was resolved at the formal meeting of the Supreme War Council on March 6, but the following morning House, Lloyd George, and French Prime Minister Clemenceau hit on what seemed a reasonable compromise: the three leading naval powers would destroy their shares of German booty, but France and Italy might keep theirs. President Wilson repeated his opposition to destruction that same day, and upon his return approved deleting clauses requiring it from the draft naval terms. The admirals then began their tortuous search for a formula apportioning the ships, and Lloyd George expressed the view that London and Washington must agree not to rival each other in naval building. For the moment, statesmen and admirals seemed to agree on preserving the present international naval balance.[38]

But subsequent developments at Paris suggested that they were far from agreement on what that balance ought to be. The admirals found it difficult to work out plans for distribution of the German fleet. Only the enemy's scuttling of his own ships at Scapa Flow laid the question of destruction or distribution to rest. Admiral Wemyss was so vexed by the problem that he called the sinking "a real blessing . . . [one that] eases us out of an enormous amount of difficulties." But before Scapa, Anglo-American naval tensions strained almost to the breaking point. They did so, in part, because the admirals were frustrated in trying to reconcile individual service goals with the diplomatic realities of Paris. Admiral Benson grew more angry with each passing day. He had long since abandoned the idea of a league of nations navy, and the battle over the German High Seas Fleet convinced him that Great Britain was out for worldwide maritime domination. His passion overcame the calm of Admiral Sims and Captain Pratt, men who peered into the future and saw Anglo-American naval cooperation as the keystone of peace and international naval stability. Indeed, by early April Benson endorsed staff memoranda that described Britain and Japan as rivals and called for resumed capital ship construction.[39]

The quarrel over the German fleet and the pressure of domestic and intraservice politics pulled Admiral Wemyss in the same direction. By early April he and Long had come a long way from the axioms that Admiralty planners had hoped to write into the peace. Early in the year the assumption common to Britain's statesmen and admirals alike was that Anglo-American harmony and British naval preeminence were consistent. For all his disputes with Benson, Wemyss continued to hope for long-term Anglo-American agreement. In Paris, Captain Cyril T. M. Fuller, his senior representative, squelched subordinates who hypothesized future difficulties with the Americans. The first lord, moreover, had circulated to the cabinet Rear Admiral Grant's powerful arguments for Anglo-American cooperation as the fundamental premise of British foreign and naval policy. But by the spring Long and Wemyss began to have their doubts about Anglo-American agreement. They lost the battle for immediate resumption of capital ship construction.

In parliamentary replies to his speech on naval estimates, Long heard worries about the American building program and sensed threats to British naval supremacy. He and Wemyss began to hope for a very special kind of arms limitation agreement—one that would end the American 1916 building program, permit a smaller fleet and reduced budget, and ensure Britain's traditional sea supremacy. [40]

These motives brought Wemyss and Long across the Channel and set the stage for what Josephus Daniels later termed the "sea battle of Paris." This was definitely an unexpected engagement. Daniels had come to Europe more or less on a junket. Troubled by his chief of naval operations' Anglophobia, the navy secretary was stunned into silence when, on March 29, Wemyss and Benson battled one another. The British admiral mistakenly concluded that Daniels cared little for naval parity with Britain and labeled Benson the real enemy. The American admiral demanded equality with the Royal Navy, but Wemyss suggested that Washington would do better to recognize Britain's permanent naval superiority. Wemyss momentarily softened the antagonism by proposing that the two navies agree to patrol separate seas. But then he provoked the Americans by pointing out that the sixteen-inch gun dreadnoughts of their 1916 building program were hardly necessary for such tasks. Daniels became quite worried when Wemyss insisted that Britain could not take part in any league of nations "which did not leave her in a satisfactory position as regards her Navy." The British admiral was so upset by this encounter that he suggested to Lloyd George that naval questions might be resolved more easily if he and Benson were kept apart. [41]

Daniels left this meeting deeply worried and turned to Colonel House for advice. The Texan bore the navy secretary no love and distrusted him as a negotiator, but his suspicions of Lloyd George ran still deeper. House thought the British prime minister was trying to blackmail Wilson into naval inferiority in return for accepting revisions in the League Covenant that recognized the Monroe Doctrine. He was correct. Lloyd George did seek an agreement that would limit American naval building. But Daniels, at House's suggestion, resisted this ploy and said Washington could go no further than pledging not to build ships after completion of those in the 1916 program. He then said President Wilson would have to decide matters of this sort and escaped to vacation in Rome. [42]

When Daniels returned a week later, feelings had hardened on both sides. Wemyss, convinced that he could do no good, prepared to go home. Long urged Lloyd George to fight for naval supremacy and sent him statistics which Long interpreted to mean the imminent end of Britain's capital ship superiority over the Americans. Benson, angry and desperate in defense of the parity principle, had gone so far as to try to exclude Daniels from any further talks with the British. House had forwarded Benson's arguments to the president, now ill, angry, and firm. Wilson was convinced that the colonel's suspicions were fact: Lloyd George was playing diplomatic poker with the naval issue. The president directed Daniels to tell the British that nothing could be discussed until the broader question of the League of Nations was resolved. The navy secretary then met Walter Long and told him that only the president and the prime minister could resolve the naval quarrel. Newspapers the same day headlined that Wilson had ordered the *George Washington* prepared for his immediate departure.[43]

The circle of conflict might well have closed had not Robert Cecil stepped in. He told Lloyd George that linking the naval and league issues would only provoke Wilson's stubborn resistance. When Long reported his last conversation with Daniels, the prime minister seized the opportunity presented by Cecil's concern and authorized him to probe American intentions further through House. Cecil suavely put his case before the Texan. Naval rivalry was no foundation for a successful league. Britain did need a large navy, and Britons unquestioningly supported the tradition of sea supremacy. Admirals might disagree, but couldn't statesmen do better? House responded warmly. He held back an angry letter blaming Lloyd George for blocking progress on the final league covenant through the naval issue. Instead, with Wilson's approval, House sent Cecil a letter in which he reaffirmed America's intention to avoid competitive naval arms expansion. The United States stood ready to abandon or modify its second three-year program of 1918 and would be willing to confer with London on future construction plans.[44]

This note of compromise whetted Lloyd George's curiosity. He had Cecil ask House if Washington would consult London before resuming any major naval construction—including ships in the 1916 program. Cecil told the colonel that such restraint was "very vital to us, both from a national and political point of view." But the Texan was as evasive on this point as Woodrow Wilson had been in 1917 and 1918. He said that Congress, not the president, would have to authorize any change in the 1916 program but did not rule out that possibility. Instead he simply said that Washington had no stomach for competitive naval arms expansion and might, after the establishment of the league, work out definite strength ratios with London. That was enough to convince the British they could go no further. The same evening Cecil dropped all opposition to Wilson's Monroe Doctrine amendment to the draft league covenant. The "sea battle of Paris" was over.[45]

In its wake, some things were clear and others uncertain. When presidents and prime ministers signed the League Covenant and the treaty of peace at Versailles' Hall of Mirrors, they accepted the essential elements of Woodrow Wilson's design for a new world order. Arms limitation, despite the many compromises made at Paris, was an intergral part of that order. Admiral Takeshita, originally skeptical toward the idea, recognized that fact when he cabled that Tokyo had best prepare for arms control talks soon to come.[46] The belief that disarmament and the demise of German naval power were compatible with good relations among Washington, Tokyo, and London was also an essential element in the new order. Wilson, Lloyd George, and Hara had each compromised particular national aspirations in the interests of harmony—Wilson, clear-cut assurance of freedom of the seas; Lloyd George, certain naval supremacy; and Hara, undisputed title to Germany's Pacific islands. All did so in the belief that continued cooperation was essential to peace and security.

But there were limits to that cooperation. Statesmen at Paris who hoped for harmony and accepted arms limitation by international agreement in principle had only begun their quest for a new naval and international political order. Their effort to control German naval power suggested that conscious restriction of arms expansion was technically feasible, but it also revealed a certain reluctance to apply the same standards to oneself as to other powers. The Anglo-American differences over the fate of the German fleet further demonstrated that London, Washington, and Tokyo were by no means in full agreement on each other's position in some new naval hierarchy. Most importantly, no group of statesmen and admirals was yet ready to consider the impact of arms limitation on particular expansion programs. The negotiators at Paris silenced the German engines of expansion, but what about their own—Washington's 1916 program, London's *Hood* battleship plans, and Tokyo's eight-eight fleet scheme? In London, Josephus Daniels finessed questions about American expansion in his speeches; in Washington he avoided discussing the issue. Walter Long, torn between doubts that the Americans could equal the Royal Navy and the belief that Britons feared loss of sea supremacy to them, postponed parliamentary consideration of naval growth. In Tokyo, Admiral Katō put off Diet discussion of future expansion plans while his subordinates pondered contradictory clues from Paris as to Anglo-Saxon intentions.[47]

Thus as the negotiations at Paris drew to a close, the naval future was unclear. Whether or not the idea of arms limitation became reality would depend on how statesmen and admirals assessed its power in their respective politics of national defense.

6 September 13, 1919, was a day of celebration in Seattle, Washington. The city played host to two distinguished visitors, Woodrow Wilson and Josephus Daniels. They came on different yet related errands. Wilson had come west, to the homeland of those who opposed him bitterly on the Versailles treaties and League of Nations, to defend and explain his handiwork at Paris. Daniels came from the opposite direction. He had taken nearly a month's leave of humid Washington to go to the tropic climes of Hawaii and the Pacific Coast's summer coolness. His mission was to dedicate the huge drydock at Pearl Harbor and drum up support for the construction of more naval bases on the Pacific coast. At Seattle, the two men's purposes fused into one. Enthusiastic crowds showered Wilson with confetti and thundered applause at his speeches on behalf of the League. They joined him, too, in reviewing the fleet Daniels had assembled in Puget Sound. On that occasion the navy secretary stood by Wilson's side, smiling, proud of the service he guided, inspired by Wilson's vision of a new world order. For the moment, neither man thought it inconsistent to be championing a new order in international affairs and American naval greatness in the same breath.[1]

The Seattle review symbolized Democratic hopes for the naval future: the League would become reality, the tensions that fed competitive naval expansion would loosen, and the chances for an international agreement to limit navies would improve. America would possess a powerful, efficient, and economical fleet, just as Daniels told audiences on his Pacific tour. It would be defensive, with half its capital ships on either coast and its cruisers deployed to protect American commerce. To realize the dream, the navy secretary argued, the navy must have both a League of Nations and bases on the Pacific coast.[2]

But by the time he and the president parted at Seattle, obstacles to the realization of their dreams had already begun to appear. Politicians mired in debate over Wilson's peace program were becoming less interested in naval matters. Admirals were falling into bureaucratic and professional quarrels that would all but destroy their political effectiveness. And before the year was out there would develop a civil-naval controversy destined to shatter the consensus that had helped make expansion the golden mean of prewar years. But for the moment, the implications of these developments lay hidden in the future. Daniels returned to Washington to face the usual problems of developing and defending a naval budget. Wilson headed south to California, where he would defend his peace program in the homeland of one of its bitterest enemies, Senator Hiram Johnson.

Wilson's battle was the more significant. His fight for the treaty and League of Nations had long since enveloped all who would influence American naval policy. Wilson and Daniels had linked League and navy late in 1918 when they called for a second three-year building program. Daniels endorsed it and predicted speedy resumption of work on capital ships in the 1916 program in his *Annual Report*. But when he went before Congress to defend naval building, the secretary was shocked to discover a new and strange combination of opponents. In the House, onetime Republican preparedness advocates clamored for demobilization and economy. In the Senate, even big-navy men like Henry Cabot Lodge balked at Wilson's proposals for a second expansion program. Daniels did use the president's prestige to hold little-navy Southern Democrats in the House in line. They approved a second building program but made massive cuts in the naval budget, proposed delaying work on ships of the 1916 program, and authorized Wilson to stop work on the new expansion plan if an international peace-keeping organization came into being.[3]

Pyrrhic victory in this skirmish portended full scale retreat in the next battle. In May 1919 Republicans anxious to destroy Wilson's League forced upon him a special session of the Congress that would be under their control. By the time it convened, Daniels had tacked before winds of serious opposition to continued naval expansion. He privately decided not to seek funds for anything new other than naval aviation, then explained to congressmen that the imminent prospect for realization of a League of Nations made the second three-year expansion program unnecessary. Then, in a political faux pas, he reported his impressions of British naval intentions in such a way that newspapers headlined his willingness to cease all construction. When rumors of opposition to so hasty a retreat from past administration policies floated back from Paris, the navy secretary quickly shifted his position to defend appropriations for renewed work on ships of the 1916 program.[4]

Despite appearances to the contrary, Republicans were even more divided on naval policy than Democrats. In the House, they were united in their support for economy and in their opposition to naval construction. Eager to cut taxes, they pared down Daniels's request for additional naval aviation funds, slashed two hundred million dollars from his proposed budget, and after a brief debate approved the naval bill. Senate Republicans, clinging to a precarious two-vote control of the upper house, were neither as disciplined nor as united as their House colleagues. They had just survived a bitter progressive-conservative battle over the distribution of committee chairmanships. That fight embittered big-navy champion Miles Poindexter of Washington and left the colorless C. S. Page of Vermont chairman of the Naval Affairs Committee. Henry Cabot Lodge, majority leader, chairman of the Foreign Relations Committee, and Wilson's inveterate foe on the League issue, was the real manager of naval legislation. Lodge needed the support of every Republican to oppose Wilson's League, but those most devoted to opposition were bitterly divided on naval matters. Robert LaFollette of Wisconsin and George Norris of Nebraska had opposed naval expansion before 1917. Frank Brandegee of Connecticut and Miles Poindexter of Washington, on the other hand, were big-navy men. Cantankerous Progressive nationalists like Hiram Johnson of California and William Borah of Idaho had uneven records on arms expansion. The Idahoan threw consistency to the winds when he argued that the League would force giant naval budgets on America and lamented its failure to regulate British seapower. Given this intraparty division, Senator Poindexter confidently predicted no change in or beyond the 1916 program.[5]

He was right. Senate Republicans restored funds of naval aviation, left the 1916 building program untouched, and joined in bipartisan determination to ignore protests on behalf of arms limitation that came from both sides of the aisle. Leaders of both parties then pushed the final bill through the House and sent it to Wilson for his approval. Four days after he returned from Paris, the president signed the naval bill without fanfare. Thereafter he strained every muscle, every nerve, on behalf of the League. For the next five weeks he tried every ploy he knew to soften Senate opposition to League and treaty. He even broke precedent to meet with the Foreign Relations Committee at the White House in the League's defense. When this proved fruitless, he decided, against the advice of his physician and political counselors, to take his case to the people. The navy and arms limitation could await the final verdict on his League. Indeed, during his 8,000 mile journey through twenty-three states, the president scarcely mentioned disarmament. When he did so, it was simply to contrast the horrors of prewar arms competition with the stability and peace that might follow establishment of his League.[6]

Republicans rarely spoke of arms limitation. Their anti-League campaign increased friction with the other two major naval powers. They baited Britain with criticisms of London's Irish policies and attacks on covenant provisions that gave the British Empire six votes in the League Council. They provoked Japanese anger by condemning treaty terms concerning the Chinese province of Shantung. By the time Wilson and Daniels reached Seattle, Republicans had agreed on forty amendments and four reservations to the proposed treaty. Their consensus on what was wrong with Wilson's League included the "collective security" of article ten, insufficient protection of the Monroe Doctrine, inadequate provisions for withdrawal, and too little protection of matters solely of domestic concern. Significantly, when Senator Lodge added another ten reservations, only one dealt with arms limitation. It merely required congressional approval of any League measures for arms control and freed the United States from them in time of war or invasion.[7]

Republicans and Democrats who voted for the naval bill in June 1919 expected the moratorium on naval issues to be limited. But the politics of the League of Nations extended it far beyond their wildest imaginings. Paralysis gripped the Democrats. Exhausted by his long tour, Woodrow Wilson collapsed and had to cancel his last speeches. A week after he returned to Washington, the president suffered a stroke that left him partially paralyzed. But he was strong and determined enough to marshal Democratic votes against Republican reservations and to insure Senate defeat of the League and treaty as modified by those reservations. Wilson had not the strength, however, to guide Daniels in making the naval budget or to preside over the cabinet. Without his leadership the cabinet splintered in indecision and delay on innumerable issues. Daniels shrewdly hid behind admirals' disagreements over what kind of new building was necessary and offered no new program. Instead, he sought funds for ships of the 1916 program and for politically profitable bases on the Pacific Coast.[8]

The first defeat of the treaty shook the Republican party to its very foundations. Reservationists joined Democrats to urge reconsideration of the treaty. Irreconcilables refused to compromise. For three solid months Henry Cabot Lodge struggled to hold the two elements together. He briefly toyed with the idea of making a League with reservations acceptable by tying it to a resolution calling for a disarmament conference. But Borah, Johnson, and other irreconcilables were so adamant that he did not dare bring the proposal to a vote. When Lodge did agree to reconsideration of the treaty, Washington buzzed with rumors that Progressive Republican irreconcilables would bolt their party in the coming presidential contest. But Wilson's loyal Democrats saved the day. On March 19, 1920, they provided the key votes that defeated treaty and League with reservations and preserved precarious amity among Republicans.[9]

The fight over League and treaty slammed the door shut on hopes for an Anglo-American agreement to limit naval competition. Viscount Grey personified those hopes. Coached by Colonel House and blessed by Lloyd George, he came to Washington hoping to ease frictions over Ireland, the terms of the League Covenant, and naval construction. He might well have failed in any event, for Lloyd George wanted not merely pledges against competition but mutual reductions in existing building programs—that is, the 1916 program. But the League fight, Wilson's illness, and maladroit preparations for Grey's journey kept him from even raising the naval issue. Indeed, he inadvertently worsened chances for Anglo-American harmony by siding with reservationists. This made him persona non grata to Wilson and alienated him from Progressive Republican irreconcilables. Before ending his futile mission, Grey reported that Washington was not ready for naval arms limitation by international agreement.[10]

The treaty fight also effectively ended hopes for substantive change in American naval policy. The fears and divisions it raised would not disappear quickly. Wilson had tied League and navy together and would not loosen the bond. He insisted that the League would be his party's major issue in the coming campaign. Republicans were similarly constrained by the presidential contest. Anxious for unity and victory, they buried divisions on naval policy and covered over differences on League and treaty.[11] Respective ties of party loyalty thus prevented the reemergence of the prewar combination of Southern and Middle Western little-navy Democrats and Progressive Republicans. Although mavericks in either group might occasionally champion stopping work on ships in the 1916 program and seeking arms control agreements, they were powerless.

The paralysis that gripped the politicians was bound to affect the admirals. Fearing its effects on naval policy, and increasingly divided over the materiel and strategic lessons of the war, they drifted into increasingly bitter and politically debilitating debates. Their discussions of capital ships, aviation, and submarines bared some of the forces that were pulling the naval service apart from within. The most sensitive issues before the admirals in the spring of 1919 concerned the capital ships of the 1916 building program. Should the navy build both battleships and battle cruisers as originally planned, drop or redesign the latter, or perhaps build a composite new type?

Two war-related developments made it difficult if not impossible to answer these questions. The first problem was organizational. In 1916, when the ships were authorized, decisions about their characteristics flowed from the technical bureaus through the General Board to the secretary of the navy. Daniels did not interfere with the conclusions of the General Board. But by 1919 war operations had diminished the General Board's importance and spawned powerful competitors: the London Planning Section under Admiral Sims, and the Planning Committee within Admiral Benson's Operations Department. Each had its own views on the battleship versus battle cruiser question, as did the staff of the commander-in-chief of the Atlantic fleet. By March 1919, all spoke discordantly, although Assistant Secretary Franklin D. Roosevelt heard in the chorus notes of agreement on building both types.[12]

The second difficulty was broadly international. In 1916 the commander-in-chief of the Atlantic fleet argued that the standards for deciding such questions were clear: "In building types of ships that will have to contend against similar types of ships of a possible enemy, our policy should be to insure that we will have a greater offence, a greater defence, and greater speed than the enemy." In practice this meant matching the latest innovation to come out of the Anglo-German naval competition. But by 1919, this standard was blurred by war developments and postwar uncertainties. Britain had begun work on H.M.S. *Hood*, a superdreadnought 15,000 tons larger than the preceding class of British battleships and seven knots faster than any American ship of the 1916 program. The submarine crisis had forced London to stop work on ships of the *Hood* class, and in the spring of 1919 no one was certain what would become of them. Secretary Daniels took experts from the technical bureaus with him across the Atlantic to survey admirals' judgment there. But upon their return, they reported that the French and Italians were undecided about matching the *Hood*, yet they implied that Admiralty officials wanted to trick Washington into building ships inferior to the new superdreadnought. Interestingly enough, Admiral Sims, the man closest to the Admiralty, and the last American admiral to think of Britain as a possible enemy, reversed his views late in 1918 to insist that the U.S. Navy match the *Hood*.[13]

Given these uncertainties, political rather than professional considerations decided the issue. Secretary Daniels brought his wrangling subordinates together late in May, just before he was to defend the 1916 program against its congressional critics. Frightened by their cries for economy, the admirals agreed to push for rapid completion of the 1916 battleships already laid down. Seeking congressional approval and more funds to equal the *Hood* seemed just too risky, and they hid their differences of opinion by reporting that subsequent capital ship designs would wait on "future developments in battleship construction." Battle cruisers met a similar fate. In some cases little more than keels had been laid down. The Jutland controversy had just resurfaced in Britain with the publication of Admiral Jellicoe's memoirs. It raised serious questions about battle cruiser design. Because so little had

been done on them, redesign and delay would have been far less costly for
battle cruisers than for the battleships. But the navy's senior officers,
fearing their onetime friends on Capitol Hill, decided to do little more than
increase armor on these ships. Important questions about the adequacy of
the 1916 capital ships, the heart of America's postwar naval defenses, thus
went unanswered. [14]

The determination to protect what the navy already had made innovators
appear to be the enemies of the naval service. The admirals agreed on the
need for more and better airplanes, aircraft carriers, and submarines but
found it difficult to concur on specific building recommendations. During
the war years their views on naval aviation had shifted subtly. The naval air
service had grown, acquitted itself well in Europe, and achieved organizational status with the establishment of a directorship of naval aviation. The
General Board dropped its earlier opposition to carriers and by 1918 was
arguing that future capital ship engagements would be preceded by air
combat. But in the uncertain climate of the winter of 1918–19, Secretary
Daniels found it easy to put aside the Board's pleas for carrier authorizations
and order instead a study of the long-range aviation needs of the navy. [15]

That study, commencing with General Board hearings in the spring of
1919, revealed striking unity on the need for aircraft carriers. Influenced by
tradition and habit, General Board admirals felt that the navy ought to have
the best designed carrier as rapidly as possible, even though it might be
necessary to first convert a merchant or collier for immediate use. They
drowned out the voices of naval aviators just back from Europe who
cautioned against slavishly following the British model and who perhaps saw
the carrier as a threat to their hopes for more funds, the best possible
aircraft, and more experience with existing seaplanes operating from
battleships or cruisers. By late summer, the Board urged Daniels to build at
least seven carriers in any new construction program. Veterans of the
wartime Operations Department championed the carrier, and their successors in the Plans Division insisted that the need for carriers was second to
none in any building program. Indeed, they had worked out a preliminary
scenario of how carriers would be used in a Pacific war. [16]

Once again, however, larger considerations intruded to make innovation
seem threatening and divisive. On the one hand, Congress seemed unlikely to
approve any new building program. On the other, General "Billy" Mitchell's
campaign to create a separate air force alarmed senior admirals and made
them anxious for rapid development of naval aviation. Indeed the navy's fear
of losing all aviation rescued Captain T. T. Craven, director of naval aviation,
from the position of impotence to which Admiral Benson had consigned him.
Craven became Secretary Daniels's right-hand man in the fight against a
separate air service. Frustrated at congressional attempts to cut naval
aviation funds and worried by Mitchell's maneuvers, he offered the very

suggestion that senior admirals rejected in the capital ships controversy: Why not modify one of the scout cruisers of the 1916 program to serve as a fast aircraft carrier?[17]

By the time the General Board gave its answer, naval aviators had, in a sense, joined the enemy. They had bombed surface craft for the first time and were fighting for the chance to try their skills against old battleships of the former German fleet. The General Board, nonetheless, longed for fleet aircraft carriers and began to discuss their characteristics. Captain Craven had bolstered his case for converting a cruiser into a carrier by reminding the Plans Division of the importance of airpower in a war against Japan. But the senior officers within the Navy Department were not about to touch ships of the 1916 program. They stressed the need for cruisers and feared to open the Pandora's box of congressional reconsideration of the existing program. Admiral Sims, now president of the Naval War College, favored Craven's suggestion. But Secretary Daniels, a lame duck by late 1920, had neither the will nor the energy to intervene in the admirals' dispute. Thus once again agreement in ideal terms bred frustration and division in reality.[18]

Postwar discussions of the submarine were equally acrimonious. The 1916 program provided for a standard coast defense submarine, three experimental larger types, and nine "fleet" submarines that were to serve as the underwater eyes of the capital ship. With the war emergency work stopped on the latter two types and all available resources were devoured for coast defense submarines. When Navy Department officials discussed subs, they were interested in their rapid production and possible use against other submarines. Peace suddenly reversed their concerns. Secretary Daniels suspended submarine construction in anticipation of their possible abolition. Admiral Benson concurred. Submarines, until the admirals at Paris recognized that abolition was improbable, simply fought to keep their part of the fleet alive.[19]

By the autumn of 1919 submariners were ready to take the bureaucratic offensive. Captain Thomas C. Hart, formerly commander of the tiny Philippine sub flotilla and now director of the submarine section in Operations, did not have the power of his colleague in aviation. But he argued, and the war planners agreed, that six of the nine fleet boats in the 1916 program ought to be modified into long-range, Pacific cruiser submarines. Anxious for a more scientific building program, the war planners told the chief of naval operations that boats of this type would be needed as commerce raiders or blockaders in a trans-Pacific campaign.[20]

When the issue came before the General Board, however, it exploded into something far more divisive than the submariners had imagined. The admirals did not even discuss the issue in terms of having to go before a parsimonious congress to seek approval for change. Instead, General Board officers read the proposal as a challenge to their bureaucratic authority. Hart and the war planners argued too vigorously, leading old one-eyed Admiral Albert Winterhalter to retort that the Board's, and not their conception of strategy would have to govern all decisions on ships' characteristics. Beyond this, the submariners' arguments threatened to pull apart the very standards that the board had used for decades. To modify the fleet boats was in fact to render them capable of independent operations that submariners like Hart believed would preclude the need for costly battleship engagements.[21]

In good bureaucratic fashion the senior admirals proposed a paper compromise: the ships in the 1916 program would not be touched, but two experimental boats would be included in a new expansion program. Since no one believed Congress likely to fund such a plan, the issue simply festered on without resolution. Angry and frustrated, Hart left the Navy Department late in 1920. His successor made the submarine issue even more explosive. In fighting to extend the time that the United States might keep former German U-boats, he charged that Navy Department technical bureaus wanted to be rid of them so as to hide their superiority to American subs. Angry charges were traded back and forth on this point, but the admirals did nothing to the boats of the 1916 program.[22]

Changing strategic perspectives compounded the internal differences brought on by these debates on specific weapons. The defeat of Germany shattered the vague but widespread consensus that the Atlantic and Caribbean were the prime theaters of naval warfare. Admirals, their views shaped largely by immediate war and postwar experiences, found it impossible to agree on the magnitude or location of threats to naval security. Their differences became apparent before 1919 was very old. Admiral Sims and his London Planning Staff, for example, detected troublesome signs of Anglo-American friction, but regarded cooperation with Britain as the key to future peace and security. Captain Pratt of Operations, responsible for cooperation with London, agreed with Sims. He also discounted rumors of malignant Japanese aspirations on the Asian mainland and possible Japanese-German collaboration. The General Board, on the other hand, listed both Britain and Japan as potential rivals for naval greatness, but its senior officers were pulled by habit and experience to define security in Atlantic terms. In their view, capital ship strength sufficient to defend the United States against Britain would be more than enough to overwhelm Japan in the far Pacific. Chief of Naval Operations Benson concurred in this opinion, for quite different reasons. His negotiating difficulties in Paris convinced him and converted his staff to the view that Britain's aspirations for worldwide naval hegemony posed the greatest possible threat to American naval supremacy. Stronger, historically more aggressive in trade and naval competition, Britain was the enemy whose strength America should match.[23]

Benson created the unit within the Navy Department that forced these differences of strategic perspective to the surface. The Plans Division of

Operations brought together the most experienced, intelligent, and aggressive of the navy's junior staff officers. Collectively they sought to transform the Navy Department's internal decision-making processes. Rather than rely upon the whims of Congress or the particular twists of bureaucratic politicking within the department, they intended to draw policy conclusions from scientific assessments of the strategic problems confronting the United States. Within weeks of their coming together, these new war planners concluded that Japan was their most probable hypothetical foe and that the Pacific would be the prime arena of strategic concern. In part this evaluation flowed from their immediate superiors' and associates' prior concern with Pacific problems. In part it reflected their sound judgment that Secretary Daniels's plans for dividing the fleet and improving Pacific bases would demand careful strategic thought. Intelligence reports also made it clear that East Asia brimmed with possible conflicts and unresolved problems. Finally, even though all recognized that the United States faced a two-ocean threat, the Pacific challenge, certain to be much more a naval war than the Atlantic conflict just concluded, was inherently more interesting to Navy planners.[24]

By the autumn of 1919, the War Plans Division had written what the assistant chief of naval operations termed the first "real" plan for a Pacific campaign. It rested on several assumptions, some highly dubious, others quite accurate. Foremost was the argument that China would remain the principal source of antagonism between the United States and Japan. This thought was hardly new, but current information from an extremely narrow intelligence base, the bias of numerous China hands who offered "expert" counsel, and the raging Senate controversy over Shantung made it seem logical. American planners also intuitively perceived the concerns of their Japanese opposites. If Japan were to strengthen her resource base for possible conflict with America, she would have to exploit China. But this would take time. Although any number of eventualities might tip the delicate balance between liberals and militarists in Tokyo in favor of the latter, the strong probability was that Japan had her sights set on future rather than immediate conflict with America.[25]

The planners assumed that their Japanese opposites would wage a defensive campaign. After seizing Guam and Manila Bay, the Japanese fleet would concentrate in home waters and send cruisers and commerce raiders out to sever American lines of communication. To counter this, the U.S. Navy would wage a three-staged campaign. First, it would secure bases and control of the eastern Pacific. Then, reinforced by auxiliary ship and logistic buildups, the fleet would seize bases in the former German north Pacific islands and move on to recapture Guam and the Philippines. Thereafter the war would be one of close blockade and eventual economic strangulation of the Japanese Empire. These ideas were not new, but the conclusions the war planners drew from them were startling. They argued that decisions on future building programs should flow from the specific needs of this projected campaign. In October

1919, this meant a radical reversal of existing priorities and programs. Bases, in particular a well-fortified one at Guam, rather than battleships would become the prime deterrent to conflict. There would be no need to continue capital ship construction, but a very real need to build critical cruiser and other auxiliary types. In the long run, moreover, aircraft carriers and a large sub flotilla would solve the problems of naval warfare in the western Pacific.[26]

The plan showered sparks into the dry tinder of the naval profession. Naval War College officers studied the Pacific problem and reached the same conclusions as Captain Harry Yarnell of the Plans Division. Admiral Sims, however, had opposed division of the fleet and held fast to the belief that the total size, not the location of the fleet would deter Japan. Captain Pratt, writing from the U.S.S. *New York*, accepted the idea of a three-staged Pacific naval campaign but challenged its underlying diplomatic assumptions. Japan was not the hostile, suspicious empire that war gamers imagined. "In the age of the Anglo-Saxon," he wrote, "where he sets his hand and seal other nations step aside." Unity of the Anglo-Saxon group would contain Japan, and even if war came, diplomatic maneuvering with China rather than a climactic sea battle or war of attrition might ultimately defeat the Nipponese. General Board officers regarded the plan as a challenge to their authority and asked Daniels to keep the planners out of their bailiwick. But the plan captivated the new chief of naval operations, Rear Admiral Robert W. Coontz. In a Pacific war plan he saw what the chief of the Plans Division insisted would eventually convince Congress to authorize a new naval building program.[27]

Coontz, a soft-spoken Missourian, was alarmed by quarrels over weapons and differences of strategic perspective within the navy. He feared that if the admirals disagreed so violently with one another, the politicians would make decisions for them. To prevent this, Coontz, sounding a theme advanced by his senior assistant early in 1919, proposed to define "the navy point of view." Admirals would go before Congress "all of one decided opinion." This would make it impossible for politicians to rule by exploiting their differences of opinion. But given the fact that Secretary Daniels had already put the radically different General Board and planners' proposals before Congress, Coontz ruefully admitted in March 1920 that it was "too late this year" for full unity. For the remainder of the year, however, he fought vigorously to create the unity essential for the success of any naval expansion proposals.[28]

But the admiral and his strategic planner allies faced formidable obstacles in their plan for unity. Their effort to build consensus around Pacific war plans in general and the fortification of Guam in particular revealed just how serious the divisions were. First, within the navy, professional judgments varied widely. While the general outlines of the war plan did not provoke major opposition, the idea of fortifying Guam did. The General Board suspected planners' motives in the war plan, and at Secretary Daniels' direction, drew up its own schedule of base needs and priorities. Guam was low on the list. It could not, in the senior admirals' view, replace the battle fleet. It ought not to come before far greater needs at Hawaii. Moreover, even if fortified, it could not be defended for long. Admiral Sims at the Naval War College concurred in this last judgment, and the naval constructors whom Daniels appointed to survey Pacific base needs urged fortification of the eastern Pacific before making a leap to the western.[29]

Secondly, interservice agreement on war plans and Pacific bases remained paper-thin. Navy planners imbued with missionary zeal had first urged broad political-military collaboration in developing war strategies. By December 1919, aided by army desires to revive the Joint Board, the two services had agreed upon what later became known as War Plan Orange. But much in the same fashion as their Japanese counterparts in 1918, the admirals and generals found it difficult to agree on how to implement plans. They battled one another over their respective responsibilities in Hawaii. Navy planners also found it difficult to make speedy progress on increasing even a temporary marine garrison at Guam. By midsummer, admirals and generals had drawn up general principles that named Hawaii the major Pacific base and spoke of giving second priority to creating subsidiary bases at Guam and in the Philippines. But even this degree of interservice agreement meant little in the absence of State Department endorsement of the political and diplomatic assumptions behind the war plans. The State Department spurned planners' initiatives for collaboration in 1919, and while Secretary Daniels mentioned the gist of navy planners' ideas to President Wilson and Secretary of State Lansing, no formal consultations ensued. Indeed, after Wilson summarily dismissed Lansing for supposedly unauthorized collaboration with cabinet members during the period of the president's illness, it seemed extremely unlikely that either his successor or any of his one-time subordinates would respond favorably to navy pleas for interdepartmental cooperation.[30]

Finally and most importantly, Coontz failed to win over Secretary Daniels. The North Carolinian was not certain that Japan was the most likely enemy. When his testimony in executive session of the Senate Naval Affairs Committee on the strategic implications of Japan's occupation of former German islands was leaked to the *Washington Post*, he denied any hostility toward Japan. In the spring of 1920, Daniels was willing to seek funds for bases at San Francisco Bay, but not for Guam. The legislators refused to vote monies for either and rejected the strategic planners' program to round out the fleet. Daniels lamented Congress' failure to fund Pacific bases, yet at the same time did little to resolve continuing intraservice differences over the issue. When in the final weeks of his tenure as secretary of the navy he finally initialled the Pacific war plan, he noted that it would be valid "unless a guaranteed international agreement makes it unnecessary."[31]

Daniels's private doubts and the admirals' own differences over Pacific bases, strategic plans, and weapons were bound to weaken the navy politically, but these factors paled when compared to the effects of the actions of one of the navy's greatest figures, Rear Admiral William S. Sims. President of the Naval War College in 1919, Sims came to believe that scientific reform and greater professional influence in policymaking could be achieved only through a direct challenge to Secretary Daniels. The thought must have come easily, for Sims's anger had been growing steadily since 1917. Throughout the war he railed at Daniels's and Benson's management of the Navy Department. Sims wanted, yet did not get, a place on the American peace delegation to Paris. Furious at this slight, appalled by Daniels's "League of Nations or the world's largest navy" rhetoric, and alarmed by the secretary's decision to divide the fleet, he even spurned Daniels's offer to bring Mrs. Sims to London for a visit. Late in 1919 the issue of war medals pushed Sims over the edge. Angry at a supposed slight to his London staff in the distribution of medals, he declined speaking invitations in New York, refused to wear other decorations, and rejected his own award.[32]

Josephus Daniels quite rightly smelled politics in the admiral's behavior. Worried about the League of Nations, President Wilson's illness, and Democratic prospects in the coming election, Daniels at first claimed that Sims was just jealous. Then he shrewdly agreed to reconvene the board that had recommended decorations so that it might hear Sims's arguments. But medals had ceased to interest the admiral. His anger mounting day by day, he finally published a full-scale attack on Daniels, charging that the navy had been unready for war. Sims held that the Navy Department had rejected professionally sound recommendations for wartime ship, personnel, and operational needs. Errors had occurred because the Department was slipshod rather than scientific in making policies. Sims justified his charges as an attempt to make certain that the navy would learn and profit from the lessons of the war. The admiral then charged in a New York City speech that Daniels improperly muzzled admirals in peacetime. When Republican partisans published charges that Daniels and Assistant Secretary Franklin D. Roosevelt had resorted to immoral means to trap homosexuals at the Newport Naval Base during the war, the stage was set for a civil-naval donneybrook.[33]

Sims was moved to make his charges partly because he thought that a great naval controversy like those of pre-1914 Britain would awaken politicians and public to the navy's postwar needs. But he had seriously miscalculated political realities. Late in December of 1919 Senators Page, Lodge, and Poindexter pressed for joint congressional investigation of Sims's initial charges, but Republican Thomas S. Butler, chairman of the House Naval Affairs Committee, rejected the idea. Democratic Senator Thomas J. Walsh of Montana then took up Daniels's defense and introduced a resolution to censure Sims. Senator Lodge pulled fellow Republicans in line to defeat the measure, but party loyalty was not strong enough to get the full-scale congressional investigation Sims wanted of the naval conduct of the war. Senator Borah of Idaho cast the deciding vote against a congressional investigation. Indeed, the intraparty split was so strong and the need for party cooperation on the still-pending League of Nations issue so great, that a week passed before the senators agreed on a compromise Senate subcommittee investigation of Sims's most recent charges.[34]

Sims hoped to unite fellow admirals behind his arguments for greater professional control of the Navy Department's policymaking machinery. In preparing for what he privately called a political trial, Sims welcomed the support of two old Daniels adversaries, retired admirals Bradley Fiske and William Fullam. Fiske, like Sims, was an innovator and tough bureaucratic fighter who had just published an account of his debates with Daniels. Fullam sought support for the navy from Republican senators and wrote spirited articles in its defense for the *New York Tribune*. But others —Rear Admiral Twining, Sims's chief aide in London during the war, Captain Yarnell of the Plans Division, and Captain Craven, the director of Naval Aviation—shied away from the fight. The man most clearly caught in the crossfire, Captain William V. Pratt, wartime "brain" of the Operations Department and a close friend of Sims's, viewed the controversy with foreboding. He confided to his wife that Sims "is both right and wrong." The investigation "won't do Daniels any good, neither will it the Navy, unless they can get rid of Daniels, which I fear is impossible."[35]

Admiral Sims hoped to demonstrate through the errors of the past the needs of the future. But his temper and flare for vivid language ran away with him, exposing his political motivations. Captain Pratt then tactfully but decisively disproved Sims's charges. He showed that the navy had had contingency plans for war, but that the war's unusual qualities—the lack of repeated major fleet engagements and the magnitude of the submarine threat—rendered them obsolete. In testimony that Daniels labeled "ninety percent correct," Pratt showed how these circumstances, rather than errors of judgment, slowed the navy's mobilization for war. Thereafter, Sims's arguments for scientific decisionmaking and greater authority for naval professionals simply fell apart. Senator Frederick Hale, chairman of the subcommittee and no match for Daniels, prodded various admirals into testimony which revealed the absence of professional agreement on standards and procedures for policymaking.[36]

By May 1920, Daniels was ready to close the hearings with a spectacular demonstration of political shrewdness. During the course of testimony, Sims's charges were described as an "abortive attempt" to discredit the navy's real achievements during the war, and Sims himself was said to be disobedient, lacking in vision, Anglophilic, greedy for honors, and deluded in the notion that a "Prussian," professional system of policymaking was appropriate for the American navy. Thirteen full days of such testimony was sufficient to bury Sims politically and made everyone involved eager to end the investigation. The admiral admitted that "with all due respect ... I am tired of appearing before the committee," and Democrat Key Pittman of Nevada quipped that everyone was "buoyed up with hopes ... that this was going to end."[37]

The senator's remark expressed a larger truth. Sims had failed, and he knew it. He merely exposed the navy's divisions and, by the exposition, rendered them deeper. Politicians and the press did not respond as he had expected. Even pro-navy journals like the *New York Times* headlined the investigation as a series of personal clashes among admirals. The *Times* was also careful to print anguished British reactions at the exposure of wartime clashes between Washington and London. Even before this, Sims's image, and perhaps with it that of the naval profession, was tarnished in the public eye. Rollin Kirby of the *New York World* captured the public mood with a cartoon of Sims trying to shoot holes in the navy's war record. He captioned it "Something the Enemy Never Did." Late in April, Representative Butler told Daniels that Republicans had tired of the investigation. When the investigation closed the *New York Times* let it die without editorial comment. Politicians were glad of the death. Franklin D. Roosevelt, after a public speech that deeply wounded Daniels, patched up their relationship and won nomination as vice president at the Democratic Convention. Outgoing President Woodrow Wilson counseled Daniels not to make Sims a political martyr. The navy secretary, rather than banish the admiral to sea, left him at the Naval War College to brood on his sins. Republicans were bruised by the whole affair. They stopped the hearings barely two weeks before their national convention was to open. In a gesture that humored Republican Progressives like Senator Borah, whose support was critical to victory in the fall, Senator Lodge got an indefinite postponement of publication of the investigating subcommittee hearings. Sims, onetime naval aide to Theodore Roosevelt, was as politically dead as the president whom he had served.[38]

Sims's initiative for change collapsed just as Congress completed its work on the naval appropriation bill. Leaders of both houses, facing presidential conventions in a matter of weeks, compromised on a policy of no change. The Senate spurned both House economizers' efforts to cut funds for the 1916 building program and admirals' attempts to go beyond it. Major appropriations for Pacific bases—anywhere—vanished, and a hasty agreement to split the difference kept funds for naval aviation at approximately the level of past years. As Senator Poindexter had predicted in 1919 and as Admiral Sims bitterly admitted a year later, fundamental shifts in American naval policy—either for expansion or limitation—would have to await the coming of a new administration.[39]

The fate of the naval bill spelled the failure of the admirals' initiatives for expansion and change in the politics of national defense. In later years they would look back and blame shortsighted statesmen and penurious congresses for naval weakness. But in fact far more complex realities stalled the engines of postwar American naval expansion. The postwar navy had lost whatever unity it enjoyed before 1914. General Board admirals could not champion expansion to attain material excellence because they were as yet unsure of the lessons of the war. Admiral Coontz could not unite fellow officers on a Pacific-first building program, let alone persuade generals, diplomats, and congressmen of its necessity. Admiral Sims let pride and ambition push him into a political initiative that poisoned civilian-naval relations and tarnished the admirals' reputations. All of this weakened those who advocated growth toward eventual naval preeminence.

But if the forces of expansion were divided and embittered, those that might have championed arms limitation were weaker still. Wilson's leadership for disarmament collapsed with his health. Strained beyond the limits of endurance by his campaign for the League of Nations, he had neither energy nor will to prevent splintering within executive departments and defections within his own party. Josephus Daniels had all he could do to hold congressional Democrats together on behalf of their common achievement of 1916. Republicans were still worse off. Their absorption in the League fight obscured their differences on naval matters and rendered initiatives for naval change futile and dangerous. Their hopes of capturing the White House in 1920 made "compromise," that is, continuation of the 1916 building program, acceptable.

Thus the American initiative for change in the international naval system faltered. Dreams of arms limitation by international agreement floated away, and the reality of Washington's 1916 challenge to the old naval order remained. The dangerous drift had begun.

Beatty, Lloyd George, and the Lessons of the War

On a gray November day in 1918, Sir Oswyn Murray, permanent secretary to the Admiralty, penned a short memorandum to the first lord, Sir Eric Geddes. Murray was worried about the future of the Royal Navy. Before the war the Admiralty had championed a two-power standard against the German navy in the political wars of Whitehall and Westminster. Now, with the war over and the bulk of the German fleet interned at Scapa, a decision had to be made about what the new standard was to be. Murray tactfully suggested that this question ought to be resolved quickly. The first lord drafted a negative reply: the old prewar budgetary battles were unlikely to recur in March, and any real definition of postwar naval standards would have to await the outcome of the peace conference; there would be time for change, reform, and response to new conditions. Nine months later, Lord Riddell, press baron and friend of the prime minister, wondered if that moment had not already passed. He found Lloyd

George weary, the ministries riddled with waste and inefficiency, and the sense of drift at Whitehall pervasive. "The Government," he complained, "have no grip on the administration." This led him to wonder if Lloyd George, the great mobilizer and spender in war, could succeed as the manager of reform and retrenchment in peace. For the moment, Riddell had no answer.[1]

Murray, Geddes, and Riddell each in his own way raised the central questions before the makers of postwar British naval policy: Could Great Britain preserve naval preeminence and simultaneously adjust to new realities in the postwar world? Did naval greatness require expansion programs or fresh initiatives for naval limitation? And if statesmen agreed on the means for reducing navies, could they also effect their will on the national defense bureaucracies? For nearly two years David Lloyd George and David Beatty wrestled with these questions. Their debates resulted in a paradox: London sought arms limitation yet simultaneously decided to authorize new capital ship construction.

This contradictory course reflected the mixed hopes and conflicting political currents of postwar London. Britons no less than Americans wanted both to protect the new peace and to restore prewar domestic political and social stability, but the tasks before them were staggering, and notions of how to go about them varied. Situations both at home and abroad made the world of 1919 vastly different from that of 1914. In India and the Middle East nationalist sparks threatened to consume the empire. Europe's continuing disorder demanded numerous summit conferences. The menace of Bolshevism loomed large in Russia. Britain had troops there, and whether or not to extricate them troubled the Lloyd George government throughout 1919.[2]

The world at home was just as fluid, uncertain, and troublesome. While the 1918 election had given Lloyd George's coalition an apparently indefinite lease on life, and "Coalie Libs" and coupon-holding Unionists occupied most of the seats at Westminster, M.P.'s were a hard-faced, sullen, unpredictable lot. Irish members, who had held the balance of power in the House of Commons before the war, now sat in defiance in Dublin in their own parliament. The seemingly insoluble, eternal war between Celt and Anglo-Saxon promised disorder of an intolerable magnitude. Only the fear of even more alarming uncertainties in Britain proper stayed the hands of those who would wage war against the Irish. Labor unrest was greater than at any time before the war. Workers whom Lloyd George had harnessed to the war effort now struck so often as to make Churchill, secretary of state for war and air, consider calling out troops against them. Lloyd George, however, hoped that "reconstruction"—better health care, housing, and terms of employment—would remedy such cancerous social unrest.[3]

The nature of the national defense problem and its politics had also changed. Men sought ways to reduce the navy to peacetime dimensions rather than means of expansion and war preparation. Churchill embodied the new bureaucratic and political order. Restless under Lloyd George, prone to intervene in naval affairs, and anxious to become the first minister of defense, Churchill had changed radically since 1914. Then he had fought for a bigger naval budget; now he championed army needs and a naval limitation agreement with Washington. His defense of intervention in Russia infuriated Lloyd George, and his visions of Middle Eastern empire were dismissed as "hot air, aeroplanes, and Arabs." But Churchill's impact on defense budgets was unmistakeable. His vigorous defense of postwar operations and the war had reversed the prewar balance of service accounts: the better than two to one budgetary superiority enjoyed by the navy in 1914 now belonged to the army.[4]

In this atmosphere of social unrest and bureaucratic division, it was hardly surprising that men tried several methods simultaneously to solve a particular problem. By the late summer of 1919, Lloyd George had taken various steps to control the politics of national defense and reduce the size of the Royal Navy. He strengthened control of the Admiralty by removing possible sources of opposition there. When Walter Long became first lord early in 1919, Long had in effect acknowledged that the prime minister could be his own first lord. Admiral Wemyss learned that truth during the prearmistice negotiations and simply resigned himself to it. Even Beatty, first as commander in chief of the Grand Fleet and then as first sea lord, recognized civilian ascendancy. Thanks to an enlarged personal staff and the loyalty and ambitions of the shrewd cabinet secretary, Sir Maurice Hankey, Lloyd George had considerably more influence in the politics of national defense than had his prewar predecessors.[5]

Hankey envisaged reviving the Committee of Imperial Defence (C.I.D.) to shape postwar defense policies, but Lloyd George preferred another instrument. In August 1919 he established the Cabinet Finance Committee, an exclusively civilian group which was to influence policies through budgetary control. The shift from War Cabinet to finance committee mirrored the shift in London's priorities: pounds sterling, not naval tonnage or weights of shell, were what mattered. Lloyd George also implemented reforms designed to restore "Treasury control" abandoned during the war. Treasury men were to go to every ministry in search of economies, and each ministry was to send officers to the Treasury to develop retrenchment programs. The brilliant Warren Fisher headed a whole new department at the Exchequer to assure treasury control. The Treasury's senior civil servant became the head of the entire civil service bureaucracy. Finally, the prime minister acquired more eyes and ears through his power to appoint permanent secretaries in all departments.[6]

While civilians sought better control of the defense bureaucracies, admirals struggled with the "most extraordinarily difficult" tasks of developing postwar policy norms. In March 1919 Admiral Wemyss felt that the transition from war to peace would take months and admitted that "our difficulties at the Admiralty are much greater than they were before the Armistice." Indeed they were. Wemyss and Long stopped work on three sister ships to H.M.S. *Hood* and sought agreement on peacetime budget, personnel, and force levels. By mid-June the Admiralty envisaged a peacetime fleet composed of twenty-one capital ships manned by 140,000 men. A much larger fleet would temporarily be concentrated in home waters—to save money rather than to deter an enemy. Maintaining this amount of naval power would cost 170 million pounds for the 1919 fiscal year, a sum far in excess of the previous peacetime naval budget. Walter Long justified this expense in axiomatic terms: there was no specific enemy, and the possibility of Anglo-American differences over Ireland's provoking hostilities was remote; yet the fleet must, as always, show the flag and defend commerce. In short, Long felt that the Royal Navy must preserve its preeminence because it always had been preeminent.[7]

Arguments of this sort were bound to provoke opposition. The chancellor of the exchequer, Austen Chamberlain, discounted Long's vague fears of the Americans and insisted that 110 million pounds be pared from the naval estimates to help reduce a projected deficit of nearly a quarter billion pounds. Indeed, Chamberlain argued that the former sum should become the standard annual total for all defense estimates. The acting cabinet secretary, Thomas Jones, raised different objections and delayed further cabinet discussions of the naval estimates. Even though Long's proposals did not call for new naval building, Jones discerned in them Long's fears about the prospect of Anglo-American rivalry. "Are we now," he rhetorically asked Hankey, "to start building against America?"[8]

The cabinet secretary was quick to reply with a resounding "No!" but he was uncertain how to translate that feeling into policy. While Hankey thought war with the United States improbable, he could not exclude the possibility that "a truculent overbearing and anti-British President" might mount "unbearable pressure" against Britain. Thus he advised Lloyd George to keep the fleet at least as large as that of the United States. Since American enmity would never stand as a parliamentary defense of naval estimates, Hankey suggested a two-power standard—one that excluded the United States. Yet at the same time, disliking such deception and the risk of competition, he hoped it would be possible to negotiate mutual reductions with the major naval nations.[9]

Even though he was not privy to Hankey's views, Walter Long sensed that he must bend before the opposition his proposals had stirred. He quashed the sea lords' efforts to fight Chamberlain and decided to seek only 70 million pounds, the amount projected in interim estimates. To demonstrate its concern for economy, the Admiralty would postpone any final decision on postwar standards until the report of its Postwar Questions Committee was in hand and set up a special Committee on Naval Expenditure. Parliamentary approval of a final budget might then come in the fall.[10]

If Long was willing to procrastinate in the face of strong parliamentary criticism of his proposed budget, Viscount Grey was not. The former foreign secretary, warming to Colonel House's suggestion that America and Britain should reach a naval understanding, urged a positive, clearly new naval policy on Lloyd George. Grey reminded the prime minister that he—Lloyd George—had opposed competition with the United States before the war. Now after that exhausting struggle, Grey insisted, Britain was certain to lose any race with the Americans. He thought the government should base naval estimates on a purely European standard, renounce all pretensions to "purely British supremacy" in the western Atlantic and Pacific, and declare that "we leave the United States programme out of account as a rival or enemy in framing our own." Grey argued that British restraint would deflect American naval concerns to the Pacific and deflate naval jingoism at home. The opposite course would only provoke the Americans into building a two-ocean navy, one that would end Britain's sea supremacy. The old Liberal then demanded that more naval budget cuts, cessation of all construction, and a public abjuration of rivalry with America precede his going to Washington on special mission.[11]

Lloyd George was not about to take so bold an initiative as Grey proposed. Instead, blending elements of what Chamberlain, Long, Hankey, and the former foreign secretary had said, he emphasized the domestic imperatives of national defense policy. The government, the prime minister said, must restore public confidence by reversing an adverse balance of trade, putting an end to strikes, and increasing workers' productivity; and the armed services should prepare statements of their needs for the next five to ten years rather than fight over specific estimates. Significantly, Lloyd George let stand the proviso that the Admiralty was to take American naval policies into account in projecting its needs.[12]

While Long and his Admiralty colleagues scurried to develop the required budgetary data, the Cabinet Finance Committee, at its very first meeting, decided that the cabinet must take the initiative to force budget cuts on individual departments. Lloyd George was simply to tell Long to stop all new construction and to cut the number of ships in commission to "at least the prewar standard." To counter possible fears that such a cut would mean surrendering sea supremacy, the government would seek agreement on arms limitation with Washington as Grey had proposed. But even if agreement should not prove possible, the navy would still cut its estimates to 60 million, the army and air force to a total of 75 million. Reductions would be made on the assumption that war was unlikely for the next ten years and with the understanding that the services' maximum responsibility consisted in preserving order in the United Kingdom, India, and all British territories.

Finally, in an indirect blow to the battleship fleet, the committee directed that the services should make maximum use of airpower and mechanical devices to reduce manpower needs.[13]

The Admiralty naturally objected to this effort to impose arms control by limiting force levels and budgets. The admirals teasingly asked whether or not the government intended to preserve British supremacy on the seas. In their view, "the only Navy for which we need have regard ... is the Navy of the United States of America." The admirals felt that Japan was beneath notice, and disarmament beyond the vague phrases of article eight of the League Covenant was to be discouraged. Rather than provide the projections that the cabinet had asked for, the Board once again protested that further cuts would prevent showing the flag in defense of empire and commerce.[14]

The Board's evasions had little impact on the prime minister. Lloyd George said he hoped war would not recur in his lifetime—but would not plan on it. While he was concerned for empire, he was "astounded" by the "great" strength of feeling about the nation's overall financial position. Thus on August 15 he got the full cabinet to accept the Finance Committee's earlier decisions on national defense estimates. Four days later, the same group gave final approval for Grey's seeking agreement on mutual naval reductions in Washington.[15]

The pattern by which these decisions were taken and pursued tells more about the nature of postwar British naval policy than does their substance. On the surface it appeared that London had defined broad national policies: cutting defense estimates at home and seeking protection against competition expansion abroad so as to free resources to rebuild prewar strength in world markets. But in fact the Lloyd George government had set guidelines without making the political commitments necessary to enforce them. The prime minister did not, as Grey had demanded, abjure rivalry with the American navy in any of his speeches before the House of Commons, nor did he give real support to the agents of Treasury control who insisted that the Admiralty was the most resistant of all bureaucracies to retrenchment. Lloyd George also failed to nip Admiralty evasions of Finance Committee directives in the bud. The Board did agree to stop all construction that could not be completed by October 1, 1919, and did make further cuts in immediate estimates. But before the year was out, the Admiralty sought supplementary credits from Parliament. Despite cabinet injunctions to the contrary, the admirals interpreted the phrase "prewar standards" to mean inclusion of American strength in determining Britain's naval needs. The persistence of such evasion suggested that statesmen and admirals were as yet far from agreement on a postwar naval policy.[16]

Their differences left the door open to initiatives designed to preserve naval supremacy through new capital ship construction. Admiral Beatty, who succeeded Wemyss as first sea lord in November 1919, led the campaign for such a policy. Beatty, despite his image as the young, dashing admiral, was a complex man. Married to the daughter of Chicago department store magnate Marshall Field, he was financially and temperamentally independent. In the spring of 1919 this "greatest figure in the Navy today" refused to chair Admiralty committees and to wear his many decorations. He longed to succeed Wemyss and to come to Admiralty House as commander of both the Naval Staff and the fleet. But when it became clear that this was politically impossible, the admiral reversed himself. He accepted the imperatives of financial retrenchment and fleet reduction and seemed ready to work with the politicians on the navy's behalf. Beatty expressed his dual sense of responsibility in his dress: at cabinets he appeared in morning coat and striped pants, black satin tie and pearl stickpin; at Admiralty Board meetings he wore full dress uniform.[17]

Beatty was a man with a mission. Fearing that the Royal Navy might not triumph over those domestic forces assailing its supremacy, he had spoken out on the lessons of the war and the need for a definite naval policy. He reminded Britons that "the prosperity and interests" of their empire "depended on a free passage of the sea today and tomorrow just as much as it did yesterday and the day before." While he admitted the possibility of arms limitation by international agreement, Beatty insisted that Britain would still have to remain first upon the seas. Keeping her there would be his personal responsibility. "You would not have me," he later told his wife, "go down to history as the First Sea Lord . . . who made so bad a struggle that our rulers gave up the heritage of command of the sea which we have held for over three hundred years."[18]

Struggle, indeed, is what Beatty faced. By the time he came to the Admiralty, his colleagues on the board had fought for nearly a month over preliminary estimates for the coming year. They wanted to preserve naval supremacy without antagonizing the United States and to avoid treasury control, but the method for doing so occasioned bitter debate. Beatty steered clear of Board discussions until after the first of 1920. By that time the case for resuming capital ship construction had grown stronger. The Grey mission to Washington had ended in failure, and there were signs of Anglo-American friction everywhere. Amidst "a latent trade jealousy; a fear for threatened maritime supremacy; a dread of competition in naval armaments; and a heavy realization of the legacy of financial and economic disadvantages which the war has bequeathed," Beatty, the Board, and Long agreed to put the case for building battleships before the cabinet. Contradicting Grey, they claimed that the Americans had introduced estimates calling for three capital ships beyond the 1916 program. They argued that while London could accept "an Alliance or Entente with the United States based on equality in Naval Material," without such an alliance Britain must somehow maintain a one-power standard "in a way that will not prejudice our relations with the U.S.A., nor lay us open to the charge of entering into building competition with them."[19]

But making the case and fighting for it were two different matters. Neither Beatty nor Long gave new construction first priority in his budget request. More concerned about guaranteeing the size and personnel of the postwar fleet, they cut estimates to nearly half the size of the preceding year's, agreed to accept further reductions if necessary, and decided not to seek new construction authorizations. Long, perhaps inadvertently, won a battle against Treasury control by padding the estimates with funds for massive fuel oil depots spotted throughout the empire. When the Cabinet Finance Committee pressed for cuts in capital ship construction, the first lord sacrificed capital ships and got Bonar Law to hold the line on the number of battleships to be kept in commission. The budget battle thus ended in a draw. The Finance Committee promised to review the size of the permanent fleet before considering the next year's estimates, and Long warned that in the absence of an arms limitation agreement, Britain would have to resume capital ship construction within a year.[20]

This compromise on construction survived cabinet and parliamentary debate for two reasons. First, other problems absorbed the energies of civilian leaders. Lloyd George was too busy—with strikes, the Irish problem, negotiations with the Continental allies, and most importantly with efforts to create a "center" party that would make his coalition leadership permanent —to think much about naval affairs. Hankey's pleas to revive the C.I.D. and to appoint a subcommittee of admirals to study naval limitation thus fell on deaf ears. Secondly, when the naval estimates were announced in mid-March 1920, the prospects for agreement with Washington seemed bleaker than ever. Long spoke just two days before the Senate's final rejection of Wilson's peace settlement. The new ambassador in Washington, Sir Auckland Geddes, felt that the deadlock between president and Senate left the United States without effective government. He subsequently reported that Secretary of State Bainbridge Colby felt naval limitation negotiations would be impossible for the remainder of the Wilson administration.[21]

The compromises and indecision buried in the naval estimates of 1920 were intolerable to a man like Beatty. Drifting along without resolving differences was dangerous to his leadership and, as he saw it, to the welfare of service, nation, and empire. Beatty felt he must mobilize fellow sailors, Fleet Street journalists, M.P.'s, and cabinet ministers on behalf of new naval construction. The admiral had little difficulty in getting the navy behind him. Unlike the leaders of the U.S. Navy, he was a national hero with a colorful personality and strong tongue that could match that of the politicians. His first lord, unlike Josephus Daniels, believed in naval supremacy with an almost religious fervor. Beatty also exercised tighter control over his subordinates than Admiral Coontz did over his. Aviators as yet had little strength within the service, and submariners, fighting for the very existence of their weapon in the wake of attempts to ban it, had been banished to Portsmouth. Most importantly, by the autumn of 1920 Beatty had replaced the squabbling junior sea lords, who had cramped his style in the previous year, with officers more amenable to his personal leadership.[22]

By July 1920 Beatty and his colleagues had built a new, stronger case for resuming capital ship construction. Intelligence estimates claimed that the U.S. Navy had more men than the Royal Navy and predicted that the United States would attain a one capital ship margin of superiority by 1925. Beatty's assistant chief of the Naval Staff, Rear Admiral A. E. Chatfield, insisted that H.M.S. *Hood*, as had *Dreadnought*, created a new standard of naval strength. While Britain had only one such ship, America and Japan would have twenty-three and fourteen, respectively. Unlike the American war planners, Chatfield did not develop strategic arguments for more building. He made no mention of the United States and simply pointed to the logistical difficulties of trying to send a fleet to deal with the Japanese in "Eastern waters." Chatfield's arguments provided Beatty with a way out of the dilemmas that had surfaced in 1919. Beatty argued that new construction was necessary solely for technical reasons; it need not signal competition with America. Thus he urged Long to seek authorization to lay down eight capital ships during the next two years. The first lord, certain that Washington would not abandon the ships of its 1916 program, was impressed enough to order preliminary cost studies, forward Beatty's arguments to the cabinet, and declare his intention to give contractors "confidential warning" that the government might require their services.[23]

When the Board of Admiralty met in autumn to put finishing touches on its defense of proposed estimates, Long was sanguine about getting funds for new battleships. Strong arguments pitched toward naval efficiency and the security of empire, together with "united action here," would overcome the cabinet's reluctance to provide the 84 million pounds Beatty's proposed program would cost. Long's memorandum to the cabinet, as finally agreed upon by the Board, discarded Chatfield's argument that more building could be justified as "normal replacement policy." It insisted that the retention of first place in naval power was vital to the continued existence of Britain's empire and the preservation of its diplomatic influence. Long wrote that "omitting the United States from our calculations" would be sheer folly, for other nations most certainly would compare American and British naval strength. Hence, he concluded, the navy must have, at the very least, "approximate equality" with the United States Navy.[24]

This request for new naval construction was shot through with logical inconsistencies and potential political pitfalls, but it so soothed Beatty's pride and ambition that it blinded him to its shortcomings. With Long ill, the admiral assumed the responsibility for defending the proposed estimates.

When the Cabinet Finance Committee discussed them, it demanded further cuts in the overall budget, but the Board of Admiralty agreed to accept more cuts only if the Beatty building program were authorized. The first sea lord then took the daring step of making public his call for starting four capital ships and an experimental submarine and completing cruisers, destroyers, and aircraft carriers already laid down.[25]

Beatty appeared to have succeeded where Admiral Coontz had failed, for he had united his colleagues behind a single building program. But late in 1920 Jutland, which the admiral had called "the great tragedy in history," became the subject of a controversy that shattered service unity, tarnished the Admiralty's public image, and threatened Beatty's capital ship program. The fight over the great battle began in February 1919, when Admiral Jellicoe published his memoirs. Critics disputed his account of Jutland, and Admiral Wemyss quickly moved to establish a special Admiralty committee, chaired by Captain J. E. T. Harper, to prepare an official study of the battle. The establishment of the committee temporarily frustrated young Turks who wanted to use Jutland to force scientific reforms upon the Admiralty; they could not garner significant parliamentary support. In March 1919 Long further dampened potential controversy over Jutland by indicating that the Admiralty was considering publication of Harper's study when it was completed.[26]

When the captain finished his work in October 1919 it soon became apparent that his study would revive quarrels harmful to naval unity. Harper concluded that an inferior number of German battle cruisers had inflicted severe damage on Beatty's battle cruisers and qualified his tactical judgments by admitting that the precise positions of ships involved was difficult to establish. Wemyss did not seek publication of the Harper account in his last days as first sea lord, and left it for Beatty to review. The new first sea lord insisted that Harper had erred in charting ships' positions and ordered him to make changes. Long temporarily countermanded this order, but in May 1920, Beatty persuaded him to allow reconsideration of the Harper Report, first by the sea lords alone and then in consultation with Harper. The first lord then brought his subordinates around to proposing the changes he sought in charting and adding an explanatory preface. But when Long invited Admiral Jellicoe to read the revised version, Jellicoe was incensed; he considered the revisions an attack on his professional honor and reputation. Only Long's promise that nothing would be published until the admiral was satisfied with the final text mollified Jellicoe.[27]

Long then announced that publication of the Harper Report would be delayed. The publishers of Sir Julian Corbett's history of the naval war wanted to get his account of Jutland before the public first, and Long used this pretext to hide naval disunity. This incensed young Turk naval reformers and their parliamentary friends. Carlyon Bellairs, M.P., had already published *The Battle of Jutland: The Sowing and the Reaping,* a scathing anti-Jellicoe account of the battle. An anonymous navy reformer then used the columns of the *Times* to attack Corbett's impartiality. Naval critic Arthur Pollen went on to insist that Jutland was the result of prewar failures in naval education and demanded a court martial investigate the great battle. Pollen's demand prompted Jellicoe to demand immediate publication of the Harper Report and Captain Harper to insist that anything released should state that he was not responsible for the changes Beatty had made. But most damaging of all was the editorial criticism the Admiralty suffered. The *Times* thundered its opposition to Long's decision to delay publication, and the Northcliffe press charged that "the Admiralty itself is on trial."[28]

Lloyd George drew cheers from the House of Commons when he insisted the Admiralty would censor nothing and proposed it publish all documents pertaining to Jutland. But Admiral Beatty doubted the wisdom of that course. He summoned young Turk Captain Richmond for counsel but rejected his argument that full publication risked nothing because the battle tactics of Jutland were obsolete. Beatty sensed that "it would be impossible to get money for battleships if this campaign continues," yet he determined to withhold publication of the Grand Fleet Battle Orders of 1914—the very document which had become the crux of the debate among retired officers, armchair strategists, and naval journalists. The first sea lord then agreed to publish the so-called Jutland dispatches, withhold the Harper Report, and establish yet another committee to study Jutland.[29]

This decision was a political blunder of the first order. Admiral Wemyss, furious at Admiralty's handling of the Harper Report, charged that Long had lied in public about it. The *Times* damned Lloyd George for not publishing everything and agreed with Richmond that Jutland's tactics were indeed obsolete. The Northcliffe press attacked the Admiralty's "official blundering" as no less dangerous in 1920 than it had been in 1916. And even the Conservative *Spectator*, traditionally friendly to the navy, concluded that Jutland could not by any standard be rated a British victory.[30]

The Jutland controversy over the elements of naval strength affected the Royal Navy far more deeply than similar questions did the United States Navy. Those who regarded the great battle as proof positive of certain lessons of the war revived prewar controversies and attacked Beatty's building program. Commodore S.S. Hall, who had commanded submarines during the war, charged that his boats and aircraft had already rendered capital ships obsolete. War, he said, had proven them useless against enemy sub and airplane bases. Rear Admiral Sir Percy Scott, who had proclaimed the superiority of the submarine on the eve of Armageddon, now insisted that the war had proven him correct. Over and over he sarcastically asked, "What is the use of a battleship?"[31]

Men like Hall and Scott had had few listeners in 1914, but in the wake of the Jutland controversy, their claims attracted considerable support. The *Times* serialized Hall's arguments and for months printed a daily column of debate on them. Editorially damning "Our Obsolescent Navy," it agreed that whether or not the battleship provided security was open to question. The *Times* denounced Beatty's attempt "to rush the Cabinet and the country into a machine-made programme of capital ships." Instead, the *Times* proposed, the government ought to establish a special investigatory committee to answer the questions that Scott and Hall had raised.[32]

Other journals of various political persuasions agreed with the *Times*. The Labor *New Statesman* concluded that " 'command of the seas' in the old sense" had gone forever. The Conservative *Spectator* condemned the expense and futility of a naval race with the United States. *The Nation* voiced radical Liberals' suspicion that the admirals were trying to burden taxpayers with expensive submarines and aircraft as well as battleships and concluded that "There is no case for any naval building whatever." Even the navy's prewar champion, the *Manchester Guardian*, doubted the wisdom of putting all Britain's budgetary eggs in a single battleship basket. Would it not be better to reorganize the Naval Staff to get "a decisive opinion" on the proper mix of naval weaponry?[33]

Comments like those presented in the *Guardian* suggested that naval policy had become an issue which demanded prime ministerial attention. Austen Chamberlain, fearful of "a grave trade depression" and furious at rising naval estimates, urged Lloyd George to use the Cabinet Finance Committee to force retrenchment on the services. When the committee met early in December 1920, Chamberlain insisted that if defense estimates were not brought under control, the government would have to cut funds for education, umemployment compensation, and pensions. Hankey, on the other hand, was intrigued by the argument that London's mere announcement of a capital ship inquiry would lead Washington and Tokyo to postpone their building programs.[34]

The prime minister, however, was not about to choose between guns and butter or to take diplomatic initiatives—at least, not yet. He proposed that in his budget speech Chamberlain should say that the government would not resume capital ship construction until it had investigated the worth of the ships; but that at the same time the government would reaffirm Britain's determination to retain sea supremacy. This compromise easily won committee and full cabinet approval. It also proved to be good parliamentary strategy. In "an adroit apology," Lloyd George had pledged both economy and a capital ship investigation. His remarks held parliamentary supporters in line and handily defeated a motion to set an absolute limit on government expenditure.[35]

The scene of battle then shifted to the C.I.D., where Beatty and Lloyd George confronted one another. The admiral, perhaps blinded by the *Times'* suggestion that he chair the investigating committee, had originally welcomed the investigation as an aid to his building program. But now he correctly perceived it as a threat. Pressing for quick resumption of battleship building, he snapped that the Admiralty was already well aware of the lessons of the war. When this argument got nowhere, the admiral complained of C.I.D. interference in Admiralty affairs to ailing Walter Long. The first lord then ill-advisedly wrote Lloyd George threatening resignation.[36]

The prime minister, however, was not to be persuaded by such arguments. He doubted Beatty's claim that the moment for agreement with Washington had passed. Shortly after the American elections, Lloyd George told American Ambassador John W. Davis that Britain did not want a navy larger than America's, nor did she wish to compete with the United States in naval building. Davis mentioned the possibility of private conversations on the subject, and by mid-December new signs of possible agreement had appeared. Lloyd George clearly rejected Beatty's logic and psychology when, as Grey had urged earlier, he publicly appealed to Washington to stop its 1916 program and denied any intention of rivaling America in naval building. The prime minister reminded Parliament that "Arming on a great scale in any quarter of the world must mean the starting of a competition that will beggar all nations and bring us all to the disaster that navies are intended to provide against." In the privacy of the C.I.D., Lloyd George attacked Beatty's logic directly: Britain was enormously in America's debt and, as Bonar Law agreed, could never win a war against her. Lloyd George got Beatty to admit that Anglo-American naval rivalry would only serve the interests of Japan. Finally, he argued that "sea supremacy" did not simply mean equality with the next power in numbers of capital ships. In other words, as Lloyd George confided to Lord Riddell, now was not the time to resume building battleships.[37]

If this was so, then what was the purpose of the C.I.D. investigation? Lloyd George wanted to give the committee a very broad mandate and suggested it might explore ways of sharing control of the seas with the Americans. Churchill objected, insisting that to help clear the air of charges of government mismanagement of naval affairs, the committee should simply hear and report the views of naval officers and their critics on the capital ship question. That, at the very least, is what Lloyd George wanted. Hankey suspected that the prime minister intended "to be able to prove that the capital ship is doomed, which would be very convenient politically." The thought may have been present in Lloyd George's mind, but if it was, he was cautious in implementing it. He probably hoped an investigation would, at the very least, buy time and clarify the relative strengths of champions of traditional sea supremacy and advocates of naval retrenchment. His careful balancing of both groups on the investigating subcommittee suggested that this was so.[38]

Admiral Beatty regarded the subcommittee's deliberations as "a political trial." Marshaling veterans of the wartime Grand Fleet or Admiralty, he set out to prove that his reading of the lessons of the war and his building program were correct. The veterans' testimony reaffirmed the axioms that guided the admiral's generation of Royal Naval officers. Vice Admiral Brock insisted that the battleship remained the world standard of naval power, regardless of possible enemies; it was the symbol that united the empire. Rear Admiral Roger Keyes spoke in similar tones, and anti-submarine warfare experts insisted that destroyers remained superior to subs. Rear Admiral Chatfield, insisting that each new advance in naval weaponry begot a counter-weapon, circulated copies of the Admiralty Postwar Questions Committee's ponderous but axiomatic defense of the battleship to support his case. To all of this Beatty, even though a member of the panel hearing evidence, added his own insistent claim for the immediate resumption of capital ship construction.[39]

These arguments elicited surprisingly strong rebuttals from an unexpected quarter. It was not Rear Admiral Hall or Air Marshall Trenchard, men who had insisted that the day of the capital ship had passed, but Captain H. H. Richmond who relentlessly attacked the logic of Beatty's case. Unlike Admiral Sims's supporters in the United States, Richmond felt the future importance of submarines and aircraft was still too unclear to determine policy. But the old notion of absolute command of the seas had died. If that phrase meant anything, it referred to the totality of naval power-fleet, bases, and geographic position. Richmond insisted that Britain was clearly superior to any other power in the latter two categories. He went on to argue that in battle with the United States the numerical equality in capital ships that Beatty championed would not suffice. Richmond sided with Beatty's arch-enemies, men of the Exchequer, when he held that "the whole of our strength depends upon the restoration of our credit and also the development of our trade." These old Liberal staples and not a capital ship fleet, Richmond maintained, were what held empires together. Consequently, as he put it, 1921 was a year not for renewed capital ship construction but rather for research and reflection upon the strategic lessons of the war.[40]

By late January 1921, when the subcommittee completed its hearings, Beatty must have felt that he had lost the battle. True, Churchill insisted that the champions of aircraft and submarines had not proven the battleship obsolete. But Sir Eric Geddes strongly seconded the Jutland critics, arguing that because the battleship had not defeated the enemy on that occasion Britain had had to endure the submarine crisis. Bonar Law was even more hostile. He termed command of the seas "a lovely phrase" and doubted that any power would possess it in the future "in the sense that we had it" in the past. Rejecting Beatty's complaint that the government had not provided adequate strategic guidelines, he angrily snapped that "the Government are not going to decide to fight America!" In the end, only Long, too ill to take an active part in Beatty's defense, and Churchill stood by the admiral. Bonar Law quashed Churchill's suggestion that the subcommittee make policy recommendations. A full month then passed before its final report was submitted.[41]

But the admiral had won at least a partial victory in the annual fight over naval estimates: he staved off Treasury attacks as planned. The junior sea lords rejected specific cuts apart from construction which Exchequer budgeteers sought. Long defended sea supremacy, urged the Capital Ships Sub-committee not to put economy above it, and heeded Beatty's pleas not to resign. But victory came at a great price. Early in February Lloyd George insisted that Long step down. When naval estimates were of such obvious importance, the prime minister said, it was "indefensible" to leave the Admiralty bereft of civilian leadership. Bonar Law readily agreed, and Long, regretfully and not without a last plea for preserving Britain's sea supremacy, left the government.[42]

Lloyd George then effected cabinet changes that worked to Beatty's disadvantage: he pushed Churchill from the War Office to the Colonial Office and named Lord Lee of Fareham Long's successor at the Admiralty. Lee was clearly a second-rank figure. Sitting in Lords, he commanded no following similar to Long's among Conservatives. He came to the Admiralty on Lloyd George's terms. He was to enforce retrenchment and to regard the question of resuming naval construction as "sub judice," that is, not to be championed à la Long. Lee, who had once defended the two-power standard, now confessed opposition to "the present Admiralty case" of preparing for war with America. Such a contest would be financially impossible and ruinous to Anglo-Saxon civilizations. Instead, Lee felt that "our only hope for the future is to come to an immediate understanding, as regards armaments, with both America and Japan." But he was not prepared to say whether or not "we should strengthen our hand, for the purposes of discussion and bargaining, by adopting 'building programmes.'"[43]

That doubt afforded Beatty the opportunity to win the new first lord over to his bargaining strategy. Lee agreed to slash estimates by nearly ten million, cutting them to just under 83 million pounds. But this figure included 2.5 million for four replacement capital ships. On February 28, 1921, the very day the Capital Ships Subcommittee agreed to disagree on the testimony it had heard, the new first lord initialled a memorandum that frankly acknowledged the motivation that the board had earlier cut out of its defense for renewed capital ship building. He argued that new construction was essential to naval morale. Then, balancing his request for building in the manner of Josephus Daniels five years earlier, Lee added that talks with other powers might lead to arms limitation.[44]

Lee's memorandum provoked bitter debate within the Cabinet Finance Committee. In response to his claim that building was necessary and diplomatically nonprovocative, Treasury spokesmen retorted that the Admiralty must accept the risk of war's unlikelihood and cut its budget still

further. Bonar Law objected that the Admiralty had no real knowledge of
what the ships proposed would ultimately cost. But these were not the
arguments that appealed to Lloyd George. Politics, abroad and at home,
were what concerned him.[45]

He had ample reason to avoid making fundamental choices about postwar
naval policy. The direction of imperial and diplomatic currents was as yet
unclear. Dominion prime ministers would discuss Britain's relations with
America and Japan when they came to London in June. The American
situation was uncertain. Ambassador Geddes returned in January with
impressions of America's immense resources and worries about anti-British
feelings. The prime minister himself fumed at nationalistic overtones he
heard in recordings of president-elect Harding's speeches. But the greatest
uncertainty of all concerned politics at home. The relative strength of
economizers and champions of sea supremacy was as yet unclear. Even more
significantly, Bonar Law expressed doubts about the permanency of the
coalition. Under these circumstances it seemed best to follow a course which
offended no one and evaded real decision. Little wonder, then, that late in
January press reports made it clear that nothing would be done about the
recommendations of the Capital Ships Committee until after the Imperial
Conference in June.[46]

This news portended yet another bureaucratic compromise on the naval
budget. The Cabinet Finance Committee rejected the argument that estimates should make no provision for new construction. It also spurned the
counsel of those who insisted that including any funds for expansion
amounted to a decision to compete with Washington. Instead, the committee
agreed that Lee should include 2.5 million pounds for new construction but
make further cuts in other parts of the estimates. This, the new first lord
argued, would "make it quite clear that the Government were empowered by
Parliament to build capital ships if the American government insisted on
extending or accelerating the shipbuilding program." The very same day the
Subcommittee on the Question of the Capital Ship agreed to disagree about
the wisdom of renewed battleship building. The group decided to submit two
separate assessments of the expert testimony it had heard.[47]

These evasive decisions suggested that the questions Murray, Geddes, and
Riddell had raised two years earlier were still unanswered. There was no new
definite standard of British naval security, no return to normal peacetime
procedures, no decisive leadership by David Lloyd George. The outcome of
the struggle between Beatty and Lloyd George was as yet unclear. The first
sea lord had succeeded in keeping alive the possibility of new construction—
despite the harm that the Jutland controversy brought upon his service. The
prime minister had sought naval limitation at home by administrative and
budgetary means, abroad, through overtures to Washington. But neither he
nor his colleagues had taken any real political risks. Cabinet members

preferred compromise time and again, despite their personal certainty that the old faith in capital ship supremacy had gone. Thus they simultaneously endorsed naval limitation and determined to fund more battleships.

The actions of Britain's statesmen and admirals might, in retrospect, seem illogical. But to at least one insightful contemporary, they were not. Far from London's budgetary battles, in Paris Arthur Balfour cautioned fellow Tory Bonar Law that there had to be a middle way between "eternal competition ... with the U.S.A. and continued acquiescence in a policy which would put us in third place among Naval Powers." The latter course, "merits apart ... would permanently damage the prestige of all the statesmen responsible for it." Bonar Law hastily reassured Balfour that everyone, "including the P.M.," shared his feelings.[48] Put in another way, it might be said that British political leaders were chary of taking any risks on naval policy. Until larger events clarified popular and parliamentary feelings about it and rendered more certain American and Japanese intentions, the contradictions and questions in British naval policy would remain unresolved.

The Eight-Eight Fleet Attained

8 On July 29, 1920, the forty-third session of the Imperial Diet came to an end. The night before its formal closing ceremony, Prime Minister Hara Kei recorded a self-congratulatory note in his diary. The legislators had passed his budget and brought the national defense problem to "complete resolution." That is, they had authorized an unprecedented 398,811,538 yen for the navy, funds that would get the eight-eight fleet expansion program underway.[1] In his moment of pride, Hara seemed to have overlooked one very important fact: at a time when Washington simply agreed to continue its existing program and London drifted toward a new one, Tokyo took a giant step toward a major new expansion program. The empire, it appeared, was moving in a direction quite contrary to that of the other major naval powers.

Within a few months foreign observers would note this difference and draw strong conclusions from it. In their dictionary "expansion" in Japanese translated to "aggression" in English. But their translation and assumptions about the motive forces behind Japanese naval expansion were erroneous. While Tokyo's perspective on international political conditions differed from Washington's and London's, that perspective was not the determining factor in Japanese naval policy. On the contrary, postwar naval expansion was the product of essentially domestic political forces. These forces were conservative and resembled similar ones at work in both the American and British capitals. The eight-eight fleet program was not a radical attempt to create a new order of sea power in the Pacific but a conservative, bureaucratically generated scheme. It commanded Hara's support for reasons of domestic, bureaucratic politics. Its object was not so much to enhance national security as to stabilize the domestic politics of national defense. Indeed the program rested on the assumption, held by Japanese statesmen and admirals as well as by their British and American counterparts, that naval policy could be shaped to meet national needs without creating international friction.

When one analyzes the eight-eight expansion program, one cannot overlook its resemblance to the dreams of American and British admirals. The scheme looked very much like General Board pronouncements on long-range postwar needs or Admiralty estimates—before the admirals took stock of immediate political and financial realities. The eight-eight program appealed to every constituency within the Japanese navy. An amalgam of conservative bureaucratic routine and innovative lessons of the war, it offered something to everyone and, with a few exceptions, deprived no one. The plan's basic structure and scheme for allocation of resources were conservative. Expansion was not purchased at the cost of other naval needs; it claimed 57 percent of total naval funds, precisely the proportion of 1918 and only one percent less than in the last peacetime year. The program restored a semblance of balance between capital ship and auxiliary craft needs. The four battleships and four battle cruisers to be built would take little more than half the total projected expenditure and amount to 8 percent of the 103 ships to be built. These figures did not differ radically from those of 1916. Submarines came to 20 percent of the total number of ships to be built, just as they had in 1916 and 1911.

But the eight-eight plan was also handsomely innovative. It projected a diversification of types unimaginable in prewar days and well beyond the reach of David Beatty or Robert Coontz. Twelve cruisers, five gunboats, thirty-two destroyers, twenty-eight submarines, two aircraft carriers, six fuel oil tankers, and numerous other types were included among the 103 ships to be built. The plan promised a major jump in expenditures for naval aviation. In 1916, the first year in which funds were sought for aviation construction, such funds claimed a mere .002 percent of the total building program budget. In the eight-eight program this figure rose to nearly .3 percent and, if the cost of carriers were included, nearly 3 percent of the total construction budget. The eight-eight scheme also prefigured a major shift in the balance between ship construction and shore facilities expansion funds. The latter sum skyrocketed from its normal 8 percent to nearly 20 percent of the total naval construction budget in the first post eight-eight fleet budget year. Old and new goals alike seemed realizable, for the total naval budget had more than doubled since the last prewar year and had risen from 12 to 31 percent of total national expenditures.[2]

These figures provide an important clue to how the eight-eight program took shape. They suggest that intraservice considerations far more than international ones determined the shape and size of Japan's postwar naval program. Early in 1919, when staff officers within the Naval General Staff and Navy Ministry began detailed preparation of the eight-eight scheme, the Japanese navy was in a unique position. It had escaped the disruption that war brought to the American and British navies. Instead of emergency expansion followed by enforced contraction, the Imperial Navy had grown steadily. By 1919 the number of men on active duty had risen by about 25 percent over the 1914 figure, a paltry increase in comparison with the wartime enlargements of American and British personnel figures. Moreover, the Japanese figure continued to rise while corresponding personnel statistics abroad curved downward.[3]

Secondly, unlike their counterparts in Washington and London, the two major naval leaders, Chief of the General Staff Shimamura Hayao and Navy Minister Katō Tomasaburō, had strengthened the machinery for naval expansion. Personnel shifts in top-level posts within the General Staff were minimal. In the Navy Ministry, Rear Admiral Ide Kenji, a champion of the submarine, headed the powerful Naval Affairs Bureau from late 1916 through the summer of 1920; he left that post only to become Katō Tomosaburō's vice-minister. The navy minister quietly but effectively put back together the pieces of the once-powerful Fleet Construction Bureau, split after the scandals of 1914. Only two officers headed it between 1916 and 1920, and both had been long associated with expansion programs. Moreover, when the bureau's integrity was reestablished, it had expanded to include special sections for submarines and aviation.[4]

While it is highly unlikely that there were not differences of opinion within this group of naval leaders, available evidence suggests that Tokyo's admirals were far more in agreement with one another than their British or American counterparts. In the spring of 1919 they shared the view that Japan's international naval position had worsened during the war. The admirals felt that this was due, in part, to systemic changes in the international naval situation. It was clear that Germany had been destroyed as an effective Pacific power. Her demise also meant the disappearance of the prewar standard against which naval excellence had been measured. The two remaining great naval powers had significantly increased their capital ship and submarine strength during the war, and their projected expansion programs promised to create an even greater gap between their individual strength and Japan's naval power.[5]

Beyond this, a general consensus on the lessons of the war prevailed. Quite unlike their British counterparts, Japanese strategists admitted that the terms of modern warfare had turned against them. As early as 1916, Rear Admiral Akiyama Saneyuki had pointed to the need for economic self-sufficiency as the key to victory in protracted war. Other naval observers sent to Europe during the conflict and immediately thereafter came to the same conclusion. National defense could not be termed adequate if measured in naval hardware alone. Industrial capacity was critical. So, too, was the ability to mobilize and maintain the support of the mass of the people. A preliminary Naval General Staff study on the reasons for German defeat completed in April 1919, laid special stress on the importance of mass support. Indeed, in the light of the number and character of Japanese naval missions to Germany in 1919 and the repeated Naval General Staff studies of the causes of her defeat, it is no exaggeration to say that the admirals feared that Germany's fate might someday be their own.[6]

These general apprehensions were magnified by specific lessons drawn from the admirals' own experience. The war in Europe had disrupted the flow of new weapons to Japan. British-built destroyers, German turbines, French diesel-powered subs, and Italian submarines failed to arrive. On top of this, skilled Japanese shipwrights and constructors left naval yards for more profitable private shipbuilding firms. Navy Ministry relations with these firms, difficult at best, became even more strained. The flow of foreign steel for naval construction dried up when the Americans imposed an embargo on shipbuilding steel exports. Finally, war developments made it clear that oil, not coal, was the naval fuel of the future. Here again Japan lagged behind the other powers in acquiring all oil-burning ships. The empire was poor in oil resources. The navy was locked in combat with other potential users for what little petroleum there was to be had at home. Worse still was the fact that by 1919 the navy depended, and for the foreseeable future would continue to depend, on British and American firms for its fuel oil supplies.[7]

If these general lessons were clear, their immediate strategic implications and the intentions of other major naval powers were not. Despite the interservice strategic revisions of 1918, there is no evidence to suggest major changes in naval strategic planning by early 1919. In 1918 army and navy staff planners had talked of invading the Philippines, but no sign of specific plans that might influence naval construction decisions has been found in surviving naval records. During the war years those close to Navy Minister Katō spoke of acquiring bases in Borneo, and in 1919 naval publicists wrote of commanding the entire Asian Pacific littoral. Katō Tomosaburō perceived the need to patrol the South China Sea, but the admiral retreated from any real commitment to defend islands that would be mandated to Japan and instead concerned himself with assuring the security of the Sea of Japan. Indeed, at least insofar as surviving evidence would suggest, Tokyo's strategic planners in the spring and early summer of 1919 were not thinking of a dramatic new war strategy which would make major building program demands. Instead, quite unlike their American counterparts, they sought more ships to carry out a defensive strategy designed before the war.[8]

Their own basic plans unchanged, naval strategic planners had little evidence to suggest that their American and British counterparts' basic intentions had changed. From Tokyo's vantage point it seemed likely that Washington and London would continue to expand, or at the very least, modernize their capital ship-centered fleets when peace was finally concluded. Japanese naval observers were impressed by the financial strain the war had imposed on Britain, yet seemingly despite it, the Royal Navy had begun work on H.M.S. *Hood* and planned three sister ships to her. Furthermore, early in 1919 Admiral Jellicoe visited Australia and New Zealand to survey future British naval needs in the Pacific. American intentions were clouded by President Wilson's talk of disarmament and simultaneous pursuit of arms expansion. The Tokyo press reported Secretary Daniels's campaign for a second three-year building program in great detail. Consular reporters chronicled progress on development of Pearl Harbor naval facilities, and later in the spring the Navy Ministry received reports on congressional surveys of additional Pacific coast base sites. In the Diet Admiral Katō used uncertainty about foreign naval plans to defend his own relatively modest requests; but he was also convinced that the Americans would, at the very least, modernize and continue to build capital ships in their 1916 program.[9]

This uncertainty about precise Anglo-American intentions added to the weight of internal bureaucratic and domestic political considerations in designing the eight-eight expansion program. The force of tradition, the emotional tug of the eight-eight slogan, and Admiral Shimamura's earlier repeated emphases on capital ship needs all demanded more battleship building. The 1918 interservice agreement on force levels projected twenty-four ships, and the national defense compromise gave the navy priority in expansion. If the navy were to hold its own with the army in the bureaucratic politics of force level definition, it had to get authorization to begin more battleships. Since the ways were full of previously authorized capital craft, it would be impossible to commence work on them immediately. But, much in the fashion of American General Board officers, Navy Ministry officials considered it essential to secure funds for new battleships. At the same time, they recognized in the promises of October 1918, an opportunity to catch up with foreign advances in submarine and aviation technology. As presented to the cabinet, the eight-eight scheme sought funds for submarine and aviation schools; it also paid the cost of bringing French and British aviators to Japan as flight instructors. Eight-eight funds would allow the navy to build a one thousand ton submarine, slightly larger than American wartime coast defense boats; construct an aircraft carrier; and more than double the number of aviation squadrons by 1927. Thus the proposed expansion program, designed within the navy, met its various internal and domestic political needs.[10]

By early June 1919, Navy Ministry planners had agreed on the essentials of the eight-eight program and drawn up preliminary cost estimates. Admiral Katō presented the estimates to Finance Minister Takahashi and Prime Minister Hara. He told the prime minister that due to price increases in materials and labor the total costs of the seven-year expansion scheme would approach two billion yen. But Katō also said that he would make every effort to keep annual expenditures for the plan in line with projected government revenues. Hara made no specific comments on the program, but simply said that he would have to take Katō's proposals under advisement.[11]

Hara's reply, however vague, by no means suggested that he opposed naval expansion. On the contrary, he had deepened his commitment to it during the months following the national defense compromise of October 1918. The Seiyūkai retained "the perfection of national defense" as one of its four major party planks, and the chief opposition party, the Keneseikai, ranked that point third on its list of sixteen objectives. During the Diet session of 1918–1919, Hara, Finance Minister Takahashi, and Admiral Katō defended relatively modest naval budget requests by indicating that expansion would follow once domestic economic conditions had stabilized and the results of the Paris peace conference were known. Indeed, Admiral Katō replied to eager champions of expansion by arguing that projected American programs did not demand an immediate Japanese response. All of these factors contributed to a major domestic political achievement for Prime Minister Hara—virtually effortless passage of the government's proposed budget.[12]

The prime minister had every reason to believe that naval expansion would be expensive but not impossible. During the war years Japan had enjoyed unparalled prosperity and had improved her international financial position enormously. Hara shared Admiral Katō's hope that peace would lower administrative, labor, and raw materials costs so as to render naval expansion less costly. As late as May 1919, the prime minister was sufficiently confident in these projected developments to tell Finance Minister Takahashi that he hoped to avoid tax increases contemplated in the national defense compromise of 1918 and yet present a realistic, financially honest budget for the coming year.[13]

During the spring and summer of 1919, Hara, like the admirals, had little reason to think expansion inconsistent with major foreign policy goals. A few weeks after his conversation with Katō Tomasaburō about naval expansion, the prime minister talked with elder statesman Yamagata Aritomo about Japan's position in the international political system. Hara continued to believe that the empire operated within limits broadly defined by the Great Powers and that only two of these powers, the United States and Great Britain, were of primary importance to Japan. Hara had earlier suggested that the old Anglo-Japanese alliance might best be broadened into some kind of tripartite arrangement, but on this occasion he pointed out that Japan might well play the balancer's role between Britain and America in East Asia. To achieve that end it would be essential for Japan to possess naval power commensurate with that the other two powers could bring to bear in the western Pacific. Expanding the fleet to compensate for Anglo-Saxon wartime increases and to improve the empire's ability to use the newest submarine and air weapons hardly seemed unreasonable.[14]

But while Hara talked of playing the balancer's role, disorder and instability in East Asia threatened to bring Japan into conflict with Britain and America. In April rebellion erupted in Korea, stirring the sympathies of Anglo-Saxon missionaries. In May Chinese students renewed revolutionary turmoil and triggered an anti-Japanese boycott; yet by early fall Hara faced the necessity of propping up the shaky Peking regime, a procedure that promised further domestic turmoil in China and more friction with Washington. During the summer, discussion over the Shantung question arising during the American debate over the peace treaty caused friction in Japanese-American relations. On top of that, Siberian uncertainties continued to trouble Washington and Tokyo. War Minister Tanaka Giichi argued for spending more to send troops there at the very time Foreign Minister Uchida and American Ambassador Morris failed to resolve antagonisms created by the earlier intervention.[15]

Despite these problems and the international political frictions they generated, Hara apparently felt he could manage East Asian difficulties and naval expansion without creating further suspicions of Japanese militarism. The old journalist and diplomat missed no opportunity to reassure London and Washington. He reminded the British chargé d'affaires that the Anglo-Japanese alliance was central to his foreign policy. He gave interviews to American missionary leaders, journalists, and politicians. Hara sent Captain Yamanashi Katsunoshin, an aide to Katō Tomosaburō, to Korea to salve British feelings and later named former Navy Minister Saitō Makoto, a man noted for good relations with the Anglo-Saxons, governor general. In May 1919, War Minister Tanaka held a reception for Americans of importance in Tokyo to dispel impressions that the empire harbored aggressive intentions in Siberia and China. As he later expressed it in an American magazine, Hara felt it would be possible to reconcile national needs with new international conditions. By September 1919 he had evidence that the latter would accommodate arms expansion: Baron Makino, back from the Paris

Peace Conference, told the prime minister that while Western leaders had written disarmament into the League of Nations Covenant they did not think it likely to be achieved soon.[16]

All of these factors may have made arms expansion appear feasible, even necessary, and at the very least not incompatible with postwar international conditions. But by the autumn of 1919, the importance of international factors paled compared to the domestic political significance of arms expansion. For various reasons the ability to achieve expansion had become critical to Hara's leadership as prime minister. On the other hand, expansion may have appeared to him as a prerequisite for continued navy support in domestic politics. Admiral Katō had followed Hara's foreign policy leadership in the spring and accepted compromise on the mandates and League of Nations Covenant issues. He had not sided with army defenders of Japan's position on Shantung and was a natural bureaucratic ally against army demands for more troops and monies for Siberia.[17] On the other hand, Hara may have thought arms expansion a means of buying off those within the army; weapons modernization and expansion might well compensate for withdrawals from advanced positions on the Asian mainland.

Beyond these bureaucratic arguments, Hara could see even broader political advantages to be gained from expansion. By the last quarter of 1919, he had not achieved the domestic economic stability and political tranquility which he had promised before his selection as prime minister. The government had proven itself unable to solve key economic problems. A year after the rice riots, it was faced with the unpleasant possibility of having to subsidize rice imports. Despite all the talk in 1918 of orderly decline in wages and prices, when peace came inflation continued unabated. The Japanese economy was still extraordinarily prosperous, yet recurrent strikes and labor organizing disputes shattered industrial order. These economic uncertainties troubled elder statesman Yamagata and fed rumors that the Hara government did not have long to live. But from the prime minister's point of view, such rumors made it all the more important to remove the potentially disruptive national defense issue from the forefront of domestic politics. Insofar as his bureaucratic rivals were concerned, success in defense would compensate for failures in economics. Insofar as his Seiyūkai party followers were concerned, successful management of defense would open prospects for concentration on the politically far more attractive issues of education, railway expansion, and government aid to industry.[18]

Thus Hara had good reason to give political considerations priority over economic factors when budget negotiations began late in September 1919. The classic bureaucratic stalemate had developed at the sub-cabinet level. Navy representatives wanted approximately 102 million yen for expansion during the coming year. Army spokesmen put forward a fourteen-year expansion plan whose annual costs exceeded the 10 million yen per year scheme developed in 1918. The Finance Ministry opposed both. Treasury officials argued that navy estimates were unrealistic; it would cost 173 million yen to build capital ships alone in the coming year, and no more than two should be authorized. Hara did not immediately join the budget melee but instead reemphasized his commitment to measured expansion for both services. On October 3, he persuaded the cabinet to give national defense needs first priority in budget development. Then, in an effort to soften elder statesman Yamagata's attacks on his finance minister, Hara sent Takahashi to Odawara. There the financier showed the old marshal rough outlines of proposed budgets that confirmed Hara's commitment to arms expansion.[19]

The prime minister then negotiated changes in both services' proposals which reaffirmed that commitment yet saved funds. While detailed information on the trading process is extremely sketchy, contemporary and retrospective sources reveal its general character. Hara cut the army fourteen year expansion plan to an eight year scheme. Under this plan annual expenditures would increase, but War Minister Tanaka was persuaded to postpone them until fiscal year 1921. Admiral Katō accepted cuts, too. Newspapers reported that submarine construction was reduced from seventy-five to twenty-eight boats, destroyer strength from eighty-two to sixty-four ships, and various special service types from thirty to eighteen. Hara made no attempt to tamper with the critical capital ship proposals, but Katō did agree to increase spending on shore facilities likely to engage the services of private industry. The cabinet reviewed these decisions on October 28 and gave its formal sanction to the proposed national defense expansion budget on November 3. The same day Navy Minister Katō joined his fellow admirals for a banquet at the Imperial Palace that must have resembled a victory celebration. The eight-eight fleet program had moved one step closer to realization.[20]

From this point onward Prime Minister Hara managed the financial and political preparations for the coming Diet with an eye to his personal political success. He simply ignored Finance Minister Takahashi's qualms about arms expansion amid financial uncertainties. Hara told the finance minister that he wished to avoid full-scale debate on major tax reforms that might bring in the revenue needed for national defense. Hara realized that debate might divide the Seiyūkai, and that it would certainly alienate the small but important Kokumintō led by Foreign Affairs Advisory Councillor Inukai Ki. Thus Hara and Takahashi devised a politically safe revenue budget that used all the devices of their predecessors and opponents. They drew on the surplus in the preceding year's revenues; they tapped the bond-sinking fund. They proposed increases in the sake and income taxes which resembled those the Seiyūkai had accepted two years earlier. By mid-December 1919 their scheme easily won cabinet approval and the emperor's sanction.[21]

The prime minister then consolidated his forces in preparation for Diet debates on the proposed budget. Once again, he sent Takahashi to Odawara to reassure elder statesman Yamagata. Hara traveled to Osaka to seek business leaders' support for his economic policies, then suppressed debate among cabinet colleagues on inflation-fighting measures. He also succeeded in putting off a discussion of troop increases in Siberia that would have pitted War Minister Tanaka Giichi against Admiral Katō and Finance Minister Takahashi. The prime minister called for absolute cabinet solidarity—and let reporters know of cuts already made in the services' budgets. Admiral Katō then appeared before Seiyūkai party directors to defend his requests in detail, and Takahashi published rosy international trade and revenue statistics for the preceding year. Finally, on January 22, 1920, Hara told the reconvened Diet that arms expansion was necessary and compatible with international harmony. After reaffirming the empire's commitment to the League of Nations and denying any aggressive intentions toward China and Siberia, the prime minister asserted that "the system of our national defense is intended for no purpose of aggression . . . in the light of actual experience gained in the field of the European War just ended we can hardly allow it to remain in its present condition."[22]

Hara's words suggested that he expected Diet approval of arms expansion as a matter of course. Press commentary, the response of his legislative opponents, and the behavior of his own party adherents justified that assumption. For months, leading newspapers had endorsed naval expansion. The *Jiji* lamented the absence of a sufficient number of modern dreadnoughts at the grand imperial review of the fleet held in October; a month later it readily endorsed the eight-eight fleet program and argued that "it cannot be helped if it inflates [government] expenditure." At about the same time, the *Japan Advertiser* printed excerpts from Jackie Fisher's *Memoirs* that strongly endorsed innovation in naval weaponry and fuels, and Tokyo learned more details of Jellicoe's proposals to London for increasing Britain's Pacific naval strength. Editorials written after the national defense budget was published did not attack expansion itself but simply questioned the wisdom of measures proposed to fund it. The same was true of opposition party leaders: they attacked the financial realism of the budget and asked only nettling questions about naval issues. But Admiral Katō easily fielded the latter while Hara overcame Seiyūkai leaders' qualms about tax increases. The prime minister simply insisted on increases as a matter of party discipline. Then, while his partisans formed a special committee to study taxation, Hara negotiated with his opponents. On February 12, 1920, he succeeded in getting approval of his proposed budget which included both naval expansion funds and increases in income and sake taxes.[23]

Hara was emboldened by this triumph to deal forcefully with his political enemies. The opposition made expansion of suffrage, rather than the budget, its principal cause. The choice came naturally, for in February 1920 "democracy" loomed large in Tokyo. Workers rioted and began a prolonged strike at the Yawata Steel Works, the major domestic supplier of naval needs. On February 11, demonstrators demanding suffrage reform coiled around the Imperial Palace and Hara's official residence. Three days later, just after the lower house passed the budget, the Diet exploded in bitter debate over the suffrage question. Hara firmly rejected suffrage expansion and decided to destroy those who agitated for it by dissolving the Diet and calling national elections. The cabinet concurred in his decision on February 19, and a week later the prime minister secured formal dissolution of the Diet—without first getting its final approval for the eight-eight fleet expansion program.[24]

The decision to dissolve the Diet was a political masterstroke, one that demonstrated Hara's leadership and routed his enemies. The prime minister had used the challenge of democracy both to strengthen service ministers' loyalty and dependence upon him and to increase his party's majority in the legislature. Hara had acted boldly by seeking dissolution before approval of national defense programs, against the advice of elder statesman Yamagata. The prime minister had won Admiral Katō's active cooperation, for the navy minister persuaded Admiral Shimamura of the Naval General Staff to accept delay in Diet approval of naval expansion and then volunteered to get War Minister Tanaka's concurrence for Hara. Tanaka, perhaps even more sensitive than Katō to the necessity of strong public support in the new era of "total war," readily agreed with the admiral's argument that insisting on immediate passage of expansion program legislation would harm both services' political interest. The prime minister then staged a campaign whose outcome was clear long before the votes were counted. His Seiyūkai had revised electoral districts to its advantage and honed its campaign machinery for victory. The party's triumph was impressive. As a result of the May 1920 elections, Hara's Seiyūkai gained a nearly two to one majority over all other parties combined. Completing his success, Hara then consolidated his alliance with the important Kenkyūkai faction in the House of Peers by naming one of its leaders minister of justice.[25]

This political strength became all the more important in the light of adverse economic and diplomatic developments in the spring of 1920. While Hara campaigned, the Japanese economy plunged into depression. Finance Minister Takahashi tried to stave off the collapse that financial experts had long predicted with interim assistance to banks and industry, but by early May his efforts had failed. Major banks closed their doors. Prices on commodity and stock exchanges plummeted. The balance of trade suddenly and drastically turned against Japan. On top of this economic crisis, trouble exploded in Siberia. Tokyo had announced its intention to withdraw troops there, but in March 1920, Bolshevik partisans slaughtered one hundred twenty-two Japanese soldiers and citizens at Nikolaevsk. When details of the massacre became public in June, Hara faced a major crisis. Nationalists demanded retaliation and the resignation of Tanaka and Katō for their failure to provide adequate protection for Japanese nationals. Liberals and pacifists renewed their campaign for complete withdrawal from Siberia. The cabinet split. War Minister Tanaka demanded a major punitive expedition. Katō Tomasaburō, well aware of the immense economic and diplomatic costs of earlier intervention in Siberia, wanted only a measured response. Hara fought desperately to prevent the break-up of his government on the Siberian issue. He persuaded Tanaka to stay on as war minister and agreed to an open-ended, costly, punitive occupation of Northern Sakhalin and portions of the Siberian coast. This decision, certain to provoke new Anglo-American suspicions of Japanese militarism, demonstrated once again that in determining policy Hara put domestic political imperatives ahead of international political aspirations.[26]

These adverse developments in Siberia simply reinforced all the arguments for arms expansion proposed in the preceding autumn. Hara might have used the Meiji Constitution to evade seeking big service budget increases in the special Diet session planned for the summer, since the constitution provided that only emergency requests beyond the preceding year's expenditures should be proposed. Long-term expansion, much of it not scheduled to begin for several years, could hardly be deemed an emergency need. But Hara's political prestige was now, more than ever, dependent on arms expansion. As the prime minister's opponents later charged, Admiral Katō and General Tanaka had materially contributed to Seiyūkai victory by agreeing to Diet dissolution. Moreover, the prime minister apparently believed that he could offset the negative international effects of expansion by careful diplomacy. Hara pushed for agreement with American financier Thomas Lamont in a multinational China consortium plan born in Washington. The prime minister stressed the empire's Pacific intentions in an April 1920 article for a special issue on Japan in *The Outlook*. He welcomed two groups of important visiting American businessmen to Tokyo. Thus his decision to approve individual ministry budget requests was hardly surprising for the coming Diet and won cabinet approval on May 21, 1920—even though the requests included both services' expansion programs.[27]

Little over a month later, on June 29, 1920, the forty-third Diet was formally summoned—to approve the eight-eight fleet budget. But that night dynamite destroyed the gates to the lower house chamber. The explosion prefigured Hara's difficulties in getting quick approval of arms expansion legislation and demonstrated that the political mood was quite different from what it had been earlier in the year. In presession party meetings, Kokumintō leader Inukai Ki came out against naval and military expansion programs and once the session began Kenseikai leaders followed suit. These leaders attacked Tanaka and Katō for supporting supposedly unconstitutional Diet dissolution and argued that arms expansion was not an emergency need. Editors and journalists took up these arguments and added that while the press did not oppose arms expansion in principle they felt that it should be postponed until financial stability was restored. To the fourth estate, a time of economic decline hardly seemed the moment to seek income tax increases.[28]

Hara moved with his usual skill in surmounting these criticisms. While he appeared to bow before Seiyūkai desires, in fact he maneuvered his followers as shrewdly as ever. The prime minister agreed to let party leaders write revisions in the revenue sections of the budget, but such changes had to be coordinated with Finance Minister Takahashi and given final approval by the cabinet. The legislators did make minor changes in the tax proposals, and Katō Tomosaburō readily concurred in them. Then Hara united his party behind them, pushed the tax proposals through the lower house, and on July 15, before galleries jammed with spectators, secured lower house approval of the full budget. He simply repeated these tactics in dealing with the House of Peers. Finally, on July 27, 1920, amid an uproar created by charges of corruption against cabinet members, the lower house accepted revisions proposed by the House of Peers and gave final approval to the budget. Thus, as July drew to a close, Hara achieved success with service budgets just as he had promised Katō Tomosaburō and Tanaka Giichi he would nearly two years earlier. The foundations for postwar arms expansion appeared to be securely laid.[29]

While Hara and Katō fought for the eight-eight fleet in Tokyo, New York City officials feted officers of the Imperial Naval squadron making a good will visit to America. Neither Washington nor London was troubled by Tokyo's simultaneous expression of friendship and approval of naval expansion. American Ambassador Roland Morris blamed a temporary upsurge of anti-Americanism on military leaders' desires to inflate their budgets. American journals and newspapers scarcely noticed passage of the eight-eight fleet legislation. The *New York Times* simply commented on the unusual frankness of those who opposed it. The situation in London was no different.[30] The apparent lack of concern there and in Washington reflected an important but unspoken assumption about the immediate postwar international naval system: naval policy was essentially an internal affair. Whether budgets would increase, stabilize, or reduce the size of individual navies depended on how statesmen and admirals assessed their respective domestic political needs and opportunities. Domestic political circumstances shaped their decisions far more than had international considerations.

The Japanese political system was neither British parliamentary democracy nor American federal republicanism, but in many respects Japanese leaders thought and acted like their Western counterparts. Admirals who sought bigger budgets and larger fleets had not modified their basic assumptions about the role of naval power in international politics. Rear Admiral Satō Tetsutarō defended naval expansion in August 1920 with the same logic he had used in 1913. "Our armament may be sufficient," he wrote, "if it is just strong enough to make America think it impossible to wage an unjust war against Japan, or even if she did, that she must expect very serious loss. . . . The object of armament is to maintain national dignity against foreign nations."[31] These sentiments were precisely those which Katō Tomosaburō had expressed in the Diet over the preceding two years. In essence, they were no different from the arguments of Admiralty or General Board.

But Japanese admirals' understanding of their needs and of the means of achieving them had changed enormously. The eight-eight program was far more diversified than prewar expansion schemes; it sought more kinds of ships, paid greater attention to aviation needs, and put new emphasis on the development of shore facilities. Admiral Katō had changed his tactics in the fight for expansion: in 1914 he had wrecked a would-be cabinet that could not promise fleet growth; in 1920 he helped prolong the life of the Hara regime so as to attain it. Unlike his Anglo-Saxon opposites, Katō pursued budget increases through cooperation and compromise rather than through frontal politico-bureaucratic conflict.

Admiral Katō's actions testified to the achievement of Hara Kei. The prime minister had done more than acquire power. He had taken major steps to transform national politics generally and the politics of national defense in particular. Hara had entered an extremely dangerous area of civil-military conflict and through creative management of arms expansion made himself the key broker-stabilizer. He did so in ways which consistently put immediate domestic political needs before long-range ideals and diplomatic aspirations. This is not to say that Hara was atavistic or blind to the international risks that arms expansion prompted by domestic needs might eventually require. He simply trusted that such risks could be reduced by cautious, friendly diplomacy. Thus as "transitional bureaucrat"[32] and party leader, and above all as political realist, Hara fought for naval arms expansion. He did so secure in the conviction that he and his government would be stronger because of it.

In retrospect, the end product of Hara's choices, the eight-eight expansion program of 1920, appears strikingly different from British and American programs for the same year. Yet all three plans reflected dynamics of domestic politics that gave the immediate postwar naval system its peculiar character. Until some new factor—some new development in the politics of national defense of one or more of the major naval nations, or some change in the system as a whole—appeared, the chances for arms limitation by international agreement would be few indeed.

3

The New Course, 1921–1922

9 During the first two postwar years, American, British, and Japanese naval policies drifted along, each in their own way. Statesmen and admirals in the three nations defended arms expansion or continuation of existing programs for particular bureaucratic and domestic political reasons. They felt that their choices would not disturb international political relations or upset the international naval system. Indeed, those who sensed that the three major maritime powers were drifting along a course that might end in a dangerous collision were few and outside the circles of power. In November 1920, hopes for disarmament were slight. Even though the League of Nations was scheduled to discuss the problem a month later, few people expected much to come of its deliberations. With Washington outside the League, Geneva hardly seemed the site for successful Anglo-American-Japanese talks on arms limitation. Yet little more than six months later, expectations and calculations had changed dramatically. Statesmen and admirals struggled to stop the drift in their naval policies and chart a definite course toward an international agreement on arms limitation. High hopes for the summoning and success of an arms control conference at Washington replaced the low expectations of six months earlier. An issue that in November 1920 fell far down on political leaders' lists of priorities demanded their closest attention and highest skills a year later.

This transformation of attitudes and policies has fascinated analysts for half a century. How and why, they have asked, did arms limitation by international agreement, impossible in November 1920, become probable in November 1921? Historians have unearthed many causes for this change in attitude toward arms limitation. Economics, technology, public opinion, and diplomatic pressures all figure in their explanations and evaluations of the Washington naval limitation effort.[1] But for all the richness of their findings, they have stumbled on a key problem: How did the statesmen and admirals of fifty years ago perceive these causes and shape them into arms limitation policies? Put in another way, the question might be, How did the leaders of 1921 change the dynamic of naval policy from expansion to limitation?

The answers to this question cannot be found simply by identifying various causes and trying to determine how they ranked in the minds of individual statesmen and admirals. On the contrary, the solution to the puzzle demands that one probe deeply into the politics of leadership in Washington, London, and Tokyo. For it was politics in the most personal, aggressive, and fundamental sense of the term that shaped statesmen's and admirals' approach to arms limitation. Indeed, as the following chapters will demonstrate, political considerations, far more than economic necessity or the demands of strategy and weapons technology, determined how Washington, London, and Tokyo would revise their naval policies.

The United States offered the most dramatic example of change. There the politics of foreign policy leadership pushed naval arms limitation from near the bottom of the list of national priorities to the very top with amazing suddenness. What appeared impossible in November 1920 seemed desirable only a month later, and by November 1921 statesmen, admirals, and ordinary citizens thought a naval limitation agreement was both urgent and attainable. During the intervening year domestic political developments forced American leaders to reconsider the assumptions that had guided their naval policy throughout the preceding five years. These developments worked to make naval limitation seem critical to leaders who had previously supported naval expansion. Indeed, the politics of domestic leadership demanded American initiatives for arms control and profoundly influenced the character of American proposals for disarmament.

Until mid-December 1920, men of power in Washington agreed with Belgian Senator LaFontaine's comment on League of Nations discussions of arms limitation at Geneva. The Nobel Peace Prize winner and president of the Belgian Peace Society told reporters that with Germany, Russia, and the United States outside the League, the time was "not ripe" for arms limitation by international agreement. Weak, leaderless Democrats stunned by the magnitude of their defeat in the 1920 presidential election seemed unlikely to abandon the position Woodrow Wilson had staked out for them back in 1918. Secretary Daniels epitomized their thinking in his annual report, released early in December 1920. Desirable though naval limitation might be, Daniels wrote, America dare not seek it while she stood alone outside a working international organization. Republicans, while hardly ready to accept that proposition, had suppressed their differences over naval building and even over the League of Nations issue in order to wrest control of the White House from the Democrats.[2]

The Republican victory in November 1920 had suddenly altered the political dynamic. Having won the election by an unprecedented majority, Republicans could turn back to the issues that all knew deeply divided them. The navy was among these issues, but its importance paled when compared to problems in domestic politics—taxation, trade, and tariffs—not to mention the still explosive League of Nations question. Campaign rhetoric notwithstanding, leading Republicans realized that the League and the larger issues of terminating World War I had to be resolved if they were to govern effectively. One cartoonist captured the essence of the Republican dilemma when he portrayed President-elect Warren G. Harding standing on a doormat labeled "Republican household." In his right hand Harding held a growling dog, labeled "irreconcilables"; in his left hand, a black cat marked "pro-leaguers" hissed defiance at the dog.[3]

The president-elect might have been caught between these antagonistic elements in his own party, but he was more than a puzzled householder. To millions of Americans Warren G. Harding had become the peacemaker, a role to which he was well-suited. During the campaign this handsome, swarthy, silver-haired Ohio politician, a man who had what William Allen White called "the harlot's voice of the old-time orator," soothed a nation tired of Woodrow Wilson's incessant demands for sacrifice and principle. A veteran of the guerilla wars of Ohio politics, Harding had tried throughout his senate career to avoid antagonizing opposing elements in his party and local constituency. He carefully prepared himself as the "harmony" candidate for the Republican nomination in 1920 and succeeded in winning his party's endorsement. During the campaign he even more shrewdly harnessed California's irreconcilable Senator Hiram Johnson, a defeated rival, and Eastern internationalists like Nicholas Murray Butler to his team. To resolve the many differences that split his party, Harding promised to consult "the best minds."[4]

Politically adept though this campaign promise was, it hurt Harding's image as a leader and intensified the competition for influence in his councils. Lame duck president Woodrow Wilson reportedly quipped shortly after Harding's election, "How can he lead when he doesn't know where he wants to go?" The remark was cruel and inaccurate, for Harding sensed that he would lead—but quite differently from Wilson. The president-elect felt that "the judgment of many, rather than the will of one" was necessary to assure the success of his administration-to-be. But to seek the advice of others without appearing to be the captive of one's counsellors was not easy. For a time, Harding fled the problem by vacationing in Texas and the Caribbean, where he sunned, inspected the defenses of the Panama Canal, and avoided the public spotlight. En route home he visited Norfolk, Virginia, where he delivered a speech that seemed to confirm Democratic editors' doubts of his capacity for leadership. In glittering generalities Harding dreamed aloud of "the day when America is the most eminent of maritime nations" and asserted that "A big navy and a big merchant marine are necessary to the future of the country." He then endorsed "partial but not permanent disarmament"—without defining what that meant.[5]

The president-elect then stopped off in Washington, where he gently but definitely sought to assume the leadership of his party. He made it plain that there was no "Senatorial oligarchy" as journalists were wont to claim. He conferred with his senate colleagues and urged that they pass appropriations bills—including one for the navy—before his inauguration. Harding then returned to his Marion, Ohio, home for conferences with the "best minds." There he explained to a long-time political confidant, "I am just beginning to realize what a job I have taken over." Cabinet making would not be easy, nor would harmonizing his party. Harding noted a "general feeling of apprehension among the Republican Senators" over his remarks on the so-called oligarchy, but was confident that he "gave them the impression . . . that I had a little more good sense than some of them were willing to accredit me."[6]

His traveling over for the present, Harding began his promised meetings with "the best minds." Eastern internationalists, Midwestern irreconcilables, old Progressives and staunch conservatives, party stalwarts, halfbreeds like Herbert Hoover, and even Democrats made the pilgrimage to Marion. Their comings and goings occupied journalists for a month and more. Their chance remarks about possible cabinet nominations or the president-elect's views on a particular subject heightened the drama of presidential transition. But their presence also fostered the impression that Harding was as much the captive as the master of the forces swirling around him. While Mark Sullivan, a journalist friendly to Harding, eventually credited him with real political mastery in cabinetmaking, the pages of daily newspapers were filled with rumors of discontent over prospective cabinet nominations and predictions of conflict between the president-elect and Senate. Harding, however, took all this speculation in stride and expected that his meetings with senate colleagues in Washington would assure approval of naval and other appropriations.[7]

Harding's expectation might well have become reality had not President Wilson and Senator William E. Borah of Idaho intervened. Together, but for very different reasons, they thrust arms limitation to the center of the political arena. Wilson took the first step early in December. Intellectually consistent to the end and bitter over the defeat of his League and the outcome of the "solemn referendum" on it in 1920, he rejected appeals from Geneva to join League discussions of the arms limitation problem. Geneva's invitation, even when qualified by assurances that the United States would not be bound by conclusions of the League's permanent commission on military, naval, and air affairs, held no charms for Wilson. The president replied in terms that expressed his personal interest in disarmament but lamented the American government's refusal to join the League. Without the government's essential support, Wilson wrote, he could do nothing. A few days later, Navy Secretary Daniels repeated the point as he had stated it two years earlier: Without League membership, arms limitation would risk the security of the United States.[8]

Senator Borah bristled at this rejection of Geneva's appeal. In part to counter Democrat Thomas Walsh of Montana who proposed that the Senate ask Wilson to send a representative to the League arms control talks, Borah introduced a resolution of his own on December 14, 1920. It called upon the president to negotiate directly with Great Britain and Japan to secure a fifty percent reduction in the three greatest naval powers' construction during the next five years. Borah's motives for introducing the resolution were mixed, as was his voting record on naval matters. Back in 1916, he had endorsed reasonable preparedness and voted for the naval expansion act. Later, however, he condemned Wilson's League as an organization that would perpetuate British maritime supremacy and force the United States to maintain a huge fleet. Borah was very much a Progressive, obsessed with suspicions of the urban East and its so-called "armaments trusts." When asked about the immediate purposes of his resolution, he replied that he wanted to test the sincerity of other nations' claims. Borah was particularly troubled by former Japanese Ambassador Ishii's charge that America's continued naval building and refusal to join in the Geneva talks made prospects for arms limitation dim.[9]

Within little more than a month, however, very different motives came to command the Idaho senator's actions. His resolution both attracted support and stirred opposition. First the *Philadelphia Public Ledger*, then the *New York World* conducted polls which showed strong international interest and overwhelming congressional support for disarmament. Prominent figures— General Tasker Bliss who sat with Wilson on the American delegation at Paris and Admiral Sims who had served as his liaison officer in London—

spoke out on behalf of arms limitation. By mid-January 1921, Borah's resolution drew the support of naval innovators. Retired Admiral William F. Fullam, editor of the *New York Tribune* naval affairs column and champion of a "three plane" (air, surface, and submarine) navy bombarded the senator with his theories and urged congressional hearings on the worth of the capital ship. But old enemies like Josephus Daniels rejected Borah's proposal. The Navy Secretary turned the senator's isolationist arguments against him when he insisted that a naval limitation agreement outside the League would amount to an entangling alliance. The roles Daniels and Borah had played in the League controversy were reversed in the debate over arms limitation. Now Borah, whom Eastern newspapers such as the *New York Times* and *New York World* had depicted as a narrow, provincial nay-sayer to Wilson's grand design, appeared as the angel of peace. His badly tarnished image suddenly began to glow.[10]

The senator sensed that much more than personal prestige was at stake with the arms limitation issue. Borah considered himself the underdog in the bitter struggle for influence in the incoming Harding administration. He wrote that he was "exceedingly anxious" to interest the president-elect in arms limitation. But in fact, Borah was plagued by the fear that the seemingly lethargic, mildly conservative Harding would fall prey to the senator's own enemies within the Republican party. Borah had considerable evidence to substantiate his forebodings. Although Harding had written promising to consult Borah, he had not summoned him along with pro-League "best minds" to Marion. The two men met only briefly and unceremoniously during Harding's stopover in Washington. By contrast, Charles Evans Hughes, Herbert Hoover, and Elihu Root—all "League with reservations" men—had consulted the president-elect. Rumors of Hughes's selection as secretary of state were rife in late January and early February. For a man of Borah's temperament, it was not at all unreasonable to assume that Eastern "internationalist" Republicans had all but captured the foreign policy machinery of the incoming administration.[11]

The fate of Borah's arms control resolutions on Capitol Hill confirmed his worst fears. Senator Lodge, no friend to Borah after the League fight, chaired the Foreign Relations Committee to which the Idaho senator's first proposal was referred. Lodge delayed discussion on it, permitted crippling amendments, and then presided over its passage in emasculated form. While this took place, Borah, prompted by Admiral Fullam and perhaps inspired by the Capital Ships Committee hearings in London, introduced a second resolution. It called upon the Senate Naval Affairs Committee to study the worth of battleships and consider stopping their construction for six months. This idea not only brought staunch defenses of the capital ship by Josephus Daniels and General Board admirals but was condemned by the Senate committee. The House Naval Affairs Committee, heeding advice from elder statesmen Henry White and Elihu Root, also rejected both of Borah's proposals. When Harding urged the full House to accept the committee's judgment, Borah had "proof" that he must fight the Eastern Republican establishment, lest it control the party and the new president.[12]

Borah's maneuvers thrust fundamental questions of naval policy before the public for the first time in five years. His proposals and the debate over them filled many a newspaper column. The public, quite naturally, wanted to know just where the president-elect stood on what had become a major issue. Harding was anything but anxious to relieve such curiosity. Busy with cabinet making and prudent enough not to want to commit himself to anything definite before inauguration, Harding tried to remain aloof from the controversy. But his silence fed rumors of all sorts. Journalists anxious for copy seized upon words in Harding's newspaper, *The Marion Star*, that could be interpreted as favoring continuing naval building. One article would report that Harding was ready to call a disarmament conference almost immediately upon inauguration, while another one would proclaim that the president was opposed to any such action for another three to four years.[13]

Copy of this sort was hardly welcome to Harding. Some commentators justified his silence as natural for a man not yet in command of the machinery of government. Other, more partisan critics insisted he had no real position on arms limitation, the League of Nations, or anything else. As the *New Republic* quipped, "I may do everything, or I may do nothing, but whatever I do, it will be becoming." Late in February, when the Senate took up debate on the naval appropriations bill, Harding sensed that the "becoming" thing to do was urge passage of the bill without any Borah resolutions tacked on to it. Colleagues close to the president-elect rejected the construction-holiday proposal in the Senate Naval Affairs Committee, and Harding wrote Senator Lodge opposing it. As Harding put it, "I cannot understand the attitude of members who want to halt our program at a time when we have nothing in the way of battle cruisers to protect our commerce. I cordially favor a program of approximate disarmament, but when that day comes I want America to have the best that there is for the advance of our commerce." But Lodge, apparently, was not so certain that Harding's views, even if put to his colleagues privately, could stop Borah or representatives who were attempting to cut naval personnel authorizations to 100,000 men. Lodge feared that despite Harding's hopes, naval appropriations could not be passed before the end of the current session.[14]

The Massachusetts senator was correct. Senator Borah was determined to filibuster if necessary to force consideration of his proposals by the special session of Congress Harding was expected to call after his inauguration. Borah's plan reinforced the president-elect's determination to lead, already provoked by those who attempted to dictate cabinet appointments, and may have inspired Harding's last-minute effort to ram the naval appropriations bill through the Senate. The *New York Times* carried reports that Harding agreed with Secretary of the Navy-designate Edwin Denby's call for a navy second to none. But in the last-minute maneuvering over the bill—a debate that ran well past midnight on the very day of Harding's inauguration—Senator Lodge won out. Neither Borah, who demanded passage with his resolutions, nor Senator Poindexter, who sought "clean" approval of the bill, succeeded. Instead, the Senate, already depicted as leaderless by journalists, appeared to have rejected the leadership of the first of its members to become president.[15]

Harding probably felt dismayed but hardly defeated by these events. Borah had won a battle of sorts, using the same tactics he had employed against Wilson in 1919 to force the new Harding administration to consider his ideas. He also, perhaps inadvertently, modified the new regime's internal politics of naval decision making. Harding had quickly determined that Theodore Roosevelt, Jr., should carry on a tradition by serving as assistant secretary of the navy. The president had hoped in the early days of cabinet making to get a prestigious political figure representative of a significant body of intraparty opinion to serve as secretary of the navy. But Massachusetts Senator Weeks preferred the War Department, and Harding's popular rival of 1920, former Governor Frank Lowden of Illinois, twice refused the navy secretary's post. This left Harding, at the very moment Borah breathed defiance in the Senate, with Detroit industrialist Edwin Denby as his last-minute choice. Competent administrator though he may have been, Denby was by no means capable of bearing the political burden of leadership in naval policy. Instead, that task very definitely devolved upon the president.[16]

After March 4, 1921, Harding had every reason to believe he was equal to shaping naval policy. As president he possessed the prestige, power, and patronage that Senator Lodge felt would assure passage of naval legislation as Harding wanted it. The new Sixty-seventh Congress appeared more likely to be amenable to the president's desires. Harding had carried ten new Republican senators to office on his coattails and given his party a 172 vote margin in the House of Representatives—the largest in history. Furthermore, there was no clear evidence that disarmament was the most pressing political issue. With 3.5 million more unemployed in February 1921 than in January 1920, business sluggish, and agriculture sliding into depression, tax relief and tariff modification—anything to "get the economy going again"—loomed as more immediate issues. Even among foreign policy problems disarmament stood only fourth on a list compiled by the *New York Tribune*. Harding also lacked conclusive evidence to indicate that opinion leaders considered Borah's the only or most popular way to limit the navy. While the editors of the *Nation*, the *New York World*, the *New York Evening Post*, and

Forbes Magazine endorsed a broad public movement to stop naval building, other journals—the *New York Times* among them—supported Harding in his preinaugural rejection of Borah's proposals.[17]

The president avoided clear commitments on naval policy in his inaugural address. He had sound politico-diplomatic reasons for so doing. From the very moment of his election, Harding sensed that he must lay the divisive League of Nations issue to rest and make peace with the "best proposal on which we may hope to unite American sentiment." His conferences with the "best minds" produced no specific scheme, but what Harding heard between election and inauguration did point to a consensus on procedures and priorities. The troublesome, primarily European issues of peacemaking bequeathed to him by Wilson would have to be resolved first. Proposals to that effect were made in the Senate, and even though Harding's colleagues differed over how best to preserve the advantages of the Versailles treaties, they agreed that peace should be made speedily. Illinois Senator Medill McCormick, who went to Europe shortly after the election, reportedly as Harding's eyes and ears, concluded that the League was "dead." He insisted that "We must preserve the advantages given us by our economic position. . . . We must *declare* peace in order to be free to negotiate. We must keep on with our naval program for another year. In this way we can contrive what we want internationally and . . . secure the payments of the interest and I believe the principal of the debt due us." As McCormick saw it, continued naval expansion provided "diplomatic influence [which] at this point is inestimable."[18]

Senator Lodge agreed with McCormick's arguments, but for rather different reasons. Lodge feared that anything short of a separate European peace would open the doors for protracted debate over the League which Democrats would use to partisan advantage. Naval building, according to Lodge, was also essential to bring peace to the Pacific. In December 1920, the senator met with the wealthy publicist, vice president of the English Speaking Union, and soon to be vice president of the Navy League, William H. Gardiner. Gardiner had insisted for some time that Japan was America's long-term enemy and must be deterred. Gardiner felt that a strong fleet and courtship of Britain's Pacific dominions would prevent any Japanese aggression. Lodge, while he harbored doubts as to whether or not a democracy could pursue coercive diplomatic strategies, concurred in these ideas. In February, Lodge described a strong American navy as both deterrent and magnet in the Pacific. As he put the case to Harding, "Nobody in this country wants to go to war with Japan and there is not the slightest danger of it if Japan understands that she cannot get control of the Pacific. . . . I think we ought to endeavor to unite Australia, New Zealand, and Canada with us in an identic policy in regard to Asiatic immigration." Lodge did not make explicit what he most probably told Gardiner and journalist Frank Simonds back in December—that a strategy of this sort would force London to drop the Anglo-Japanese alliance Republicans had condemned so roundly in 1919. The senator argued that "If these great self-governing dominions want [an end of the alliance] . . ., Great Britain will yield because she cares more about her self-governing dominions than she does about anything else."[19]

Read in the light of Lodge's and McCormick's advice, the diplomatic and naval policies Harding outlined in his first address to the new Congress were hardly surprising. The president made it clear that his administration would have no part of Wilson's League. Yet in deference to his own vague feelings and the desires of Eastern internationalists, Harding expressed willingness to join an "association to promote peace." He called for a separate peace with Germany—along the lines Senator Philander C. Knox had suggested months earlier. Then Harding confronted Borah: "We are ready to cooperate with other nations to approximate disarmament," he asserted, "but merest prudence forbids that we disarm alone." Instead, Harding chose the tactic that appealed to Lloyd George at almost this same time. "The reasonable limitation of personnel . . . combined with economies of administration," the president asserted, and not precipitate abandonment of the 1916 building program, might "lift the burden of excessive outlay" for naval defense.[20]

But Harding was not simply the passive recipient of other men's advice. True, he did meet with leading senators and Secretary of State Hughes before delivering his address, although the meeting was, in all probability, much more a gesture of consultation than an appeal for advice. The issues Harding treated in his speech were simply too important to the future of his administration to be left to subordinates. Navy Secretary Denby lacked the political stature and perhaps the intellectual ability as well to formulate broad policies. Indeed, he was away in the Caribbean until shortly before Harding delivered his address. Secretary of State Hughes, despite the laudatory claims of later biographers, was not in a position to become the most important foreign policy leader within the administration. His nomination, although handily approved by the Senate, had generated considerable intraparty opposition. Hughes himself recognized that his personal hopes for some sort of American participation in a League of Nations had to give way to Harding's judgment. The president's decision for a separate peace might occasion a "wry face" from Hughes, but the secretary sensed that to challenge it would be to court disaster for the administration. The secretary of state was also by temperament much more the advocate than the innovator. Shrewd, imbued with the lawyer's caution, and given to holding himself aloof from those around him, Hughes served and identified himself with the president. In all probability, he was responsible for Harding's insistence that the Senate approve measures for a separate peace without interfering with presidential treaty-making powers.[21]

The program that Harding spelled out on April 12, 1921, taxed his leadership abilities abroad and at home. Six days later, the president clarified his priorities: naval arms limitation, however desirable, could not become the subject of formal negotiations until his administration had ended the state of war with Germany. To achieve peace would not be easy. As Hughes later explained it, his purpose was to secure all the rights promised America in the Wilsonian settlement, yet avoid all obligations dangerous in domestic political terms. To achieve that goal would demand constant, careful consultation with the president.

The administration could not follow the overtly coercive negotiating strategies which men like McCormick, Lodge, and Gardiner favored.[22] Instead, Washington tried to deal with Tokyo and London within the framework of its larger design for peace. There were those within the administration who felt that coercion was the best way to get Japan to resolve outstanding issues on American terms. Early in April Secretary Denby succumbed to his subordinates' discontent at Josephus Daniels's division of the fleet. Denby proposed to implement a strategy of deterrence by reuniting the fleet in the Pacific. Hughes seconded this idea, but Harding ruled it out as too threatening a gesture. The secretary of state also pressed Tokyo to agree to the disposition of the tiny cable island of Yap, but he postponed further discussions on the problem. He did not continue negotiations on the draft immigration agreement which Japanese Ambassador Shidehara Kijūrō and former American Ambassador Roland S. Morris had initialed. The administration was also blind and deaf to signs of willingness to negotiate a naval agreement that emanated from Tokyo in the spring of 1921.[23]

Washington mixed cooperation and coercion in Anglo-American diplomacy. Rejecting McCormick's suggestion that he use American economic power as a lever to pry diplomatic concessions from London, Harding did not ban loans to Great Britain. Moreover, he allowed American representatives to continue discussion of oustanding military and economic aspects of the peace settlement in the Supreme War Council and the Reparations Commission. While Washington had to negotiate with European nations if rights recognized in the 1919 agreements were to be included in a separate peace, cooperation of this sort evoked howls of protest on Capitol Hill. Harding responded by reminding his former colleagues that the White House made foreign policy. Hughes appealed for British assistance in persuading the Japanese to compromise on Yap. When this gentle hint was lost on London, Hughes, thinking that firm American opposition to the Anglo-Japanese alliance would convince Dominion prime ministers to abandon or emasculate the pact at the coming Imperial Conference, exploded in anger. His performance, probably a deliberate display of bad temper, was so convincing that Ambassador Auckland Geddes, a physician, reported that the secretary of state had gone mad. The Administration also paid little heed to London's expressions of interest in naval limitation, while it pursued the more immediate tasks of ending the state of war with Germany.[24]

While efforts to end the war formally were underway, Harding asserted his leadership in the domestic management of naval policy. At first he had considerable success. The new House of Representatives passed the naval appropriations bill as he wished barely two weeks after his April 12 address. The administration demonstrated its desire for economy by cutting out proposals for aircraft carriers, and House managers responded by removing Borah-like resolutions from the bill. The Republican leadership also indicated willingness to economize by approving new procedures which gave the Appropriations Committee a much larger say in the final shape of the bill. But Harding's spokesmen refused to touch the 1916 program. Arguing that foreign developments made the present inauspicious for arms control talks, they beat back efforts to slash funds for and slow work on ships authorized earlier.[25]

But in the Senate, obstacles to Harding's hopes loomed far larger. Borah's opposition to naval expansion stood as the greatest obstruction. The Idaho senator had not forgotten the events of January and February, and he introduced another resolution that would require the president to summon an arms limitation conference. This time a somewhat different mix of motives guided his actions. Borah had no doubt that the British and Japanese were eager for naval limitation. When the Senate debate began, he was quick to cite evidence of such eagerness which he felt the administration had neglected. He was also riding the crest of a wave of popularity such as he had never known. For millions he had become a new prophet, perhaps the Isaiah whom some said he resembled, preaching a crusade against merchants of death. His followers had already made Easter Sunday a national day of prayer for arms limitation and flooded Washington with appeals for disarmament. They planned to make the last week of May National Disarmament Week. Borah himself remained suspicious, suspended as it were between the fear that Harding was drifting toward entanglement in European affairs and the conviction that arms limitation was the most important issue of the future. The senator's old irreconcilable colleagues bristled at Harding's efforts to negotiate a separate peace, and Borah himself could hardly accept without question policies approved by old internationalist enemies. But for the moment Borah was, as Senator Hiram Johnson of California later put it, "the biggest figure in the Senate, by far, ... [and] at the very zenith of his career."[26]

Warren G. Harding did not see Borah in Johnson's terms and proposed to outmaneuver the Idahoan. On May 3, 1921, the president spoke out against Borah's resolution, calling it an invasion of presidential prerogative. Harding then met with various representatives who had sponsored similar initiatives in the House and succeeded in persuading all but one to stop them. Senators close to the White House then got the Naval Affairs Committee to report a bill which eliminated Borah's resolution. For a week thereafter, Harding spokesmen dueled with Borah. The Idahoan denied that his resolution invaded presidential prerogatives and insisted that the issue was economy. Without cutting naval funds, Borah demanded, how could his colleagues fulfill their promises of reduced federal expenditures? Administration defenders vigorously opposed Borah for a time, but then, after consultation with the White House, reversed their strategy.[27]

On May 17, Senator Poindexter of Washington revealed that Harding had dropped his opposition to passage of a Borah resolution. In a letter, written a few days earlier, the president appeared to leave the initiative to Congress. He repeated his opposition to unilateral disarmament, acknowledged the sincerity of arms limitation advocates, and promised negotiations "at the earliest possible day." Harding then left the Congress free to pass resolutions it deemed appropriate. But in fact the White House hoped to soften Borah's attacks through compromise. In return for accepting Senate additions to the House version of the naval bill and maintaining manpower levels, Borah was to be permitted passage of his resolution. After yet another week of debate, the Senate approved it by a 74-0 vote on May 25, 1921.[28]

This triumph for the Idaho senator altered but did not end the debate over naval arms limitation. Borah and his supporters doubted the president's good faith, and Harding fed their suspicions by opposing all efforts to stop work on ships of the 1916 building program. This presidential opposition led the *New York Times* to term passage of the Borah resolution "little more than a fine gesture." One cartoonist caught the immediate mood when he drew a $396 million naval cannonball crashing through the House and Senate and quipped, "Doesn't look like disarmament." When the Senate added $98 million to this sum and administration supporters refused to allow House consideration of the Borah resolution, the cartoonist's caption seemed true. Indeed, the Porter resolution, which called for arms control on land as well as at sea, gave Democrats a golden opportunity to attack Harding. They charged that the administration was anything but sincere in its efforts for naval arms limitation by international agreement.[29]

In fact, by his opposition to stopping work on the ships, Harding was fighting to preserve his leadership and the priorities he had defined in his April 12, 1921, speech. The president apparently believed that through his control of the House of Representatives he could checkmate Borah and those irreconcilables who would tie his hands in negotiating a separate peace. After the Porter resolution on arms limitation and Harding's plan for ending the war won House approval by a large majority, the White House appeared ready to trade House abandonment of the Porter arms measure for Senate relinquishment of the Borah resolution. But conferees on the naval bill suddenly resolved most of their differences on appropriations and agreed to let the House vote on the Borah resolution. Harding then drafted a letter which reversed his earlier position. It was "wholly desirable," he wrote House Majority Leader Frank Mondell, to have congressional opinion formally support "inquiries and negotiations ... with regard to the attitude of foreign nations on the general subject of disarmament." In plain English, this meant Harding no longer opposed House passage of the Borah resolution; indeed, it passed the very day his letter was made public.[30]

Harding's retreat before the Borah resolution was a dangerous one. The president had bowed before House economizers' desires on funds and manpower for the navy. He had accepted Borah's priorities rather than his own: the arms limitation resolution was approved before one ending the state of war with Germany. Moreover, despite efforts to protect presidential prerogatives in "declaring peace," the measure Harding signed was a compromise worked out between the two houses of Congress. These setbacks made coercive diplomacy impossible. In mid-June Secretary Hughes suddenly and warmly welcomed conversations with Ambassador Shidehara on a wide range of issues. The secretary of state also met British Ambassador Geddes, this time to express in firm but pleasant tones Washington's hope that the Imperial Conference would end the Anglo-Japanese alliance. But Lloyd George, deaf to such suggestions for reasons which will be explained later, responded by dealing Harding's leadership another blow: just as the House approved the Borah resolution, the press reported that London and Tokyo had agreed to continue their alliance.[31]

When the Imperial Conference met in London, it made another decision that proved extremely embarrassing to Washington. Lloyd George got the prime ministers to sanction suggesting a conference on East Asian, Pacific, and naval problems to the Americans. Lord Curzon, the foreign secretary, spoke with Ambassador George Harvey about the proposed conference; but Harvey, whom Harding had appointed over Hughes's objections, delayed reporting the conversation to Washington. Lloyd George then made statements which the press construed as signals of his intention to call for a conference. Hughes, whom Harding claimed had been preparing quietly for arms control talks for weeks, became alarmed at these rumors and cabled Harvey to ask if London would accept an invitation to arms limitation negotiations at Washington. In doing so Hughes had disregarded another administration priority, for Congress was still wrangling over the final details of the naval appropriations bill. When Harvey reported his earlier conversation with Curzon, Hughes hastily amended his informal invitation to include talks on both arms control and Pacific problems. Finally, in a press statement released barely in time to beat news of Lloyd George's parliamentary remarks on a conference, the State Department announced that the governments of Great Britain, Japan, France, and Italy had been asked to participate in "a conference on limitation of armament ... to be held at Washington at a mutually convenient time."[32]

The invitation to the conference ended one phase of Washington's debate on arms limitation but opened another which made even heavier demands for presidential leadership. Having failed to overcome Borah and his allies, having seen his priorities upset by congressional wrangling, and having brushed disaster in the last-minute struggle to preserve the initiative in calling a conference, Harding more than ever before needed to control the politics of arms limitation at home and the negotiations to come. Yet the president's opponents were not disposed to let him exercise such control. While journalists questioned the veracity of administration statements about events leading up to the calling of the conference, Republican senators expressed doubts about its proposed agenda. A striking coalition—Lodge, McCormick, and Borah—felt that discussing naval limitation and East Asian problems simultaneously would be a mistake. Borah, who sensed that the coming conference had replaced European peacemaking as the most significant test of administration foreign policy intentions, went so far as to say that Washington had opened "a Pandora's box" of problems by agreeing to discuss anything other than disarmament. Borah also must have felt that the conference increased his (and the entire Senate's) leverage against Harding. The Senate would have to approve any agreements negotiated at Washington. Anxious to keep up the pressure for disarmament and to remind Harding of that fact, Borah and his allies introduced resolutions late in July calling for the immediate cessation of capital ship construction.[33]

Borah's actions and congressional inaction deprived Harding of the negotiating strength his advisors had claimed for him earlier in the year. However superior the American position might be in terms of sheer economic and industrial power, the president faced strong political pressures for an arms limitation agreement. In midsummer 1921, these pressures seemed about to overwhelm him. Harding was anxious to demonstrate his leadership at home. "I find," he wrote early in July, "I cannot carry out my pre-election ideals of an Executive keeping himself aloof from Congress." But he enjoyed little success in managing his supposed followers. Sweltering in Washington's muggy heat, Harding's huge Republican majority in Congress refused to act on "must" items. The senators and representatives did not deliver the tax and tariff reforms for which Harding had called them into special session. They passed an expensive veterans' bonus bill which he was forced to veto. Indeed, by late July the Congress had become so unmanageable that administration leaders proposed a six weeks' recess. Yet it took three weeks' wrangling to get agreement even on that.[34]

Success in managing the coming conference became more and more important to the president as he faced such congressional obstinacy. But Secretary of State Hughes found it extraordinarily difficult to close the lid on the Pandora's box Senator Borah had opened. On the one hand the secretary of state recognized that the conference would have to end the Anglo-Japanese alliance—without drawing the United States into an "entangling alliance" open to senate criticism. On the other hand, he faced strong pressures from London to agree to a preliminary meeting that would put America in the thick of the intra-Imperial argument over how to end that pact. Hughes also became involved in a bitter dispute with Curzon over the invitation cables. The Japanese were hardly more amenable to Washington's leadership. While they welcomed talks on naval limitation, Tokyo's leaders were wary of discussions on East Asian problems that might be construed as condemnation of past continental policies. Hughes publicly appealed late in July for speedy and unconditional acceptance of Harding's informal invitation, but nearly a month passed before Tokyo and London, Paris and Rome accepted the president's formal invitation and an essentially American definition of the conference agenda.[35]

While Hughes fought for diplomatic leadership, Harding struggled to demonstrate domestic leadership and define a negotiating position that would assure success in the coming conference. By midsummer 1921 the president sensed that he must lead quite differently from his predecessor. Harding had read and was impressed by former Secretary of State Lansing's critique of Wilson at Paris. The president recognized that his personality differed from Wilson's and that the mood in Congress had changed greatly since 1918–19. He could not, as the fight against the Borah resolution amply demonstrated, "command" the legislators, and ought not to make himself the focal figure of the negotiations to come. Instead, Harding chose to lead in his own way—quietly, indirectly, accommodatingly. The president selected a delegation certain to meet with senate approval—even before Eastern internationalist Republicans bombarded him with nominees. He named Majority Leader Lodge, Secretary of State Hughes, party elder and former Secretary of State Elihu Root, and Democratic Minority Leader Oscar W. Underwood to the American delegation.[36]

Harding also attempted to mollify his archenemy, Senator Borah. Before the names of delegates to the conference were published, he called Borah to the White House and urged him to "come along with the administration." When the Idahoan replied that he could not, Harding retorted that the president was the leader. Borah acknowledged that fact, but insisted that he must hold true to what he conceived to be the righteous position on arms limitation and other foreign policy questions on which the two men differed. The senator left the White House apparently not embittered by his exclusion from the delegation and as certain as ever that continuing public pressure was necessary to bring about meaningful disarmament.[37]

His appeal for cooperation and reconciliation having failed, Harding determined to guide public opinion to circumscribe Borah's influence. He announced formation of a broadly representative Advisory Commission to inform delegates of public feelings. He quashed millennial expectations stirred by disarmament advocates and did not claim, à la Wilson, that God

stood firmly committed to the president's proposals. Harding rejected pleas
to proclaim a public day of prayer for the conference, yet sensed that it
would be politically unwise to oppose Vice President Coolidge's proposal for
prayers on the Capitol steps for its success. In his speeches, Harding
carefully avoided promising too much. Instead, he tried to convince his
audiences that they should look for both triumphs and compromises in the
negotiations ahead.[38]

While Harding dealt with the broader domestic politics of arms limitation,
he let subordinates shape a preliminary American negotiating position. He
did so in the confidence that internal, bureaucratic opponents of naval
limitation were weak. American admirals lacked a leader of David Beatty's
skill and stature, a man who might dare to oppose publicly limits on naval
expansion which now seemed inevitable. The General Board had tarnished
its image by taking part in anti-Borah maneuvers during the spring. Admiral
Sims, even if he had opposed arms limitation (which he did not), was
weakened by his quarrel with Secretary Daniels and recently chastened by a
reprimand for making Anglophilic remarks in London. The chief of naval
operations, Rear Admiral Coontz, regarded arms limitation efforts as
"propaganda" which threatened to snatch naval greatness from America at
the very moment capital ships authorized in 1916 were about to assure it. But
as previously pointed out, Coontz had difficulty enough in managing his
squabbling colleagues.[39]

Two other factors diminished the admirals' political strength. The first was
intangible but nonetheless significant. In midsummer 1921 reformers within
the Navy Department abandoned all efforts to reconstitute the department to
give professionals a greater say in policymaking. The wave of reform and
anger which Sims had raised a year earlier washed away in acceptance of the
reality of civilian control. To be sure, control wielded by the easygoing
Denby, or by Assistant Secretary Roosevelt, who had denounced Borah and
his followers as "pacifists and muddle-headed idiots," was gentle; but there
was no alternative to accepting it. Secondly, public confidence in the
admirals' technical judgment had reached a new low. For over a year
"quarterdeck" admirals in Washington had fought Billy Mitchell and all
those who claimed that the airplane had replaced the capital ship, yet in July
aviators successfully sunk the former German battleship *Ostfriesland* off the
North Carolina capes. Although neither admirals nor statesmen regarded
this demonstration as conclusive proof that the dreadnought era had ended,
the bombing tests did raise questions about the soundness of professional
judgment on materiel. The admirals' expert opinions against naval limitation
thus would carry little weight in administration councils or the halls of
Congress.[40]

Nevertheless, Admiral Coontz and his associates on the General Board
resisted disarmament. Together with Assistant Secretary Roosevelt they

wrote the precept that was to guide General Board discussions of arms limitation. It asked the admirals to define a "naval unit" and "equitable relativity of strength"—but with two key assumptions. First, the navy would fulfill all its traditional responsibilities: the fleet would defend commerce, protect the Monroe Doctrine, and symbolize and safeguard American sovereignty after arms limitation as before. Secondly, strategic and technical judgments rather than domestic political and economic considerations would shape the admirals' conclusions. The precept reflected the defensive mood that gripped the Navy Department and suited the temper of the General Board. Four of the Board's members had been naval advisors at the Paris Peace Conference of 1919. They regarded arms control talks on that occasion as a disaster and wanted to develop a navy negotiating position so logically constructed and shrewdly presented that no politician or diplomat could destroy it.[41]

In this half-frightened, defensive mood, the General Board found it easy to assuage differences of the past and agree on proposals that looked more like budget requests than arms limitation position papers. Preservation of the 1916 program capital ships and protection of the trans-Pacific strategic capability championed by planners from 1919 onward became the sine qua non of the admirals' proposals. None doubted that the capital ship–centered fleet was the closest one could come to defining "a naval unit." None imagined the American people ready to support war in the Pacific, but nonetheless, the admirals felt that the navy had to have parity with Great Britain and a superiority over Japan that would preclude aggression in the western Pacific. The General Board concluded that a 10-10-5 capital ship ratio among the three major naval nations was necessary—a greater margin of superiority over Japan than war planners had earlier considered necessary for a trans-Pacific campaign.[42]

The admirals also opposed deployment controls that might prevent American domination of the Pacific. In arguments consistent with the bureaucratic thrust of war planners' budget proposals over the preceding two years and more conservative General Board positions of 1919, the admirals opposed Pacific island nonfortification agreements. The General Board also found it impossible to escape the expansionist ethic of a generation. Damning Borah and all his works, they proposed that the three major naval powers reach the suggested ratio not by stopping capital ship construction but by building up to it. Such a plan would permit completion of the 1916 ships and leave the United States with the newest fleet—one "second to none."[43]

Proposals of this sort understandably shocked civilian officials who read them. The General Board admirals neglected the very imperatives of domestic politics that most concerned the Harding administration. Their "parity" gave Great Britain 32 capital ships to America's 23. This might be equality in technical "fighting power" terms, but how could one explain that to the Senate or the American people? The admirals' proposals promised few if any economies in the naval budget. That issue revived just as the General Board submitted the first portions of its recommendations. The chairman of the Democratic National Committee charged that Harding was not sincere about disarmament, and even Republicans on Capitol Hill spoke of cutting $100 million from the naval budget. Little wonder, then, that Navy Secretary Denby quickly denied that the General Board recommendations represented the considered judgment of his department.[44]

Civilians then stepped up pressures on the admirals. With Harding's express approval, Hughes sent two agents to observe General Board deliberations. The White House also loosed upon the Navy Department Budget Bureau officials who sought greater efficiency and spoke of $50 to $100 million cuts in the coming year's budget. Secretary Denby said he was not frightened by such talk, but General Board admirals sensed that more economical arms limitation proposals were in order. Their second draft scheme left all three major naval powers with fewer capital ships in commission, adjusted technical details to bring the actual comparative tonnage ratio closer to 10-10-5, and sacrificed four ships of the 1916 program. But this was not enough. Secretary Denby apparently recognized that the problem was beyond the General Board and shifted responsibility for shaping limitation proposals to a small advisory committee. Ten days later, that group, consisting of Assistant Secretary Roosevelt and Admirals Coontz and Pratt, produced three alternative plans. These plans cut varying numbers and combinations of ships from the 1916 program and displayed the cost of maintaining the resulting fleet. Denby favored the second of these plans—that which left the American capital ship fleet most nearly numerically equal to Great Britain's.[45]

But Denby and his advisors were not on the right track and were not the men to make the choice. The ultimate decision rested with President Harding. As Harding saw the situation on October 14, "it all comes down to this: We'll talk sweetly and patiently to them [the other major naval powers] at first; but if they don't agree then we'll say 'God damn you, if it's a race, then the United States is going to go to it.' " A week later he told Hughes and Denby that he wanted a plan "sufficiently drastic to prove the honesty of our intentions to the country and to place us ... in a position where, if any refusal came on the part of any European powers, Congress and the Senate would be behind the administration's plans."[46] The president, obviously, was moved first and foremost by the desire to protect his leadership. He hoped to control the domestic politics of arms limitation as he had not earlier; and if his subordinates proved unequal to the task of managing its external politics, he would at the very least protect himself and his party from the domestic political consequences of their failure.

Harding left it to Hughes to work out the details of an acceptable proposal, but the central ideas of the proposal were clearly the president's own. On October 24, the secretary of state told members of the American delegation what Harding had insisted be the essential element of any American proposal: Naval building must "stop now." Hughes got Navy Department representatives to accept it, secured Harding's express approval of it, and committed his fellow delegates to the principle. It was hardly an unfamiliar or original proposal, for Borah had demanded it since January. Hughes also overrode General Board qualms about the term of any arms limitation agreement. Doubling Borah's original suggestion, he proposed a ten year construction holiday. Searching for positive proof of administration sincerity that Harding wanted, Hughes got Denby's advisory committee to list the ships the United States, Great Britain, and Japan must scrap. This massive cut in ships afloat went beyond the admirals' proposals, met the demands of House and Budget Bureau "economizers," and corresponded to the hard lessons of postwar naval budget making: a big fleet in being meant heavy maintenance expenditures.[47]

But Hughes, like Harding, was cautious when it came to other aspects of naval arms limitation that might have to be settled through compromise in the coming negotiations. He did not spell out, as Assistant Secretary Roosevelt favored, specific ratios for France and Italy, the lesser of the five ranking naval powers. He did not call for abolition of the submarine as Wilson had two years earlier and disarmament advocates had in 1921. He equivocated on the question of strategic dominance of the Pacific. Hughes ferreted out inconsistencies in General Board proposals to raise the proposed ratio to something close to 10-10-6, thus reducing the admirals' margin of superiority. But he made no statement on deployment controls in the form of island nonfortification agreements, despite his own State Department experts' insistence that Japan would never accept the proposed ratio without them. Instead, he wrote only the bare essentials of naval arms limitation that Harding had defined—assurance of sincerity and safety from political attack at home—into the text of the proposal. Then, on the eve of the opening of the Washington Conference, he locked it away in his safe.[48]

That proposal would subsequently go down in history as Hughes's "bombshell" address to the Washington Conference delegates. When read in the domestic political context of 1921, however, it hardly seems as surprising as contemporaries and historians have considered it. The United States shaped the kind of limited arms control proposal it did primarily for domestic political reasons. To be sure, arms limitation advocates inside and outside the administration were deeply concerned about the high costs of naval construction and the frictions it caused in relations with Great Britain and Japan. But these considerations by themselves were not sufficient to energize American political leaders; they were not adequate to get Washington to assume international leadership for arms limitation. On the contrary, very mundane concerns—the desire to succeed where his predecessor had failed, the need to prove others' low estimates of his capacity wrong—impelled Warren G. Harding to try to master the domestic and international politics of arms limitation. This desire for mastery, so consistent throughout the months between November 1920 and November 1921, drew him into conflict with Senator Borah, tempted those around him to use continued naval building to achieve other diplomatic goals, and ultimately convinced him to sacrifice the construction program that had promised an American navy "second to none."

Out of Harding's desire to lead came the will to master and the conviction that naval arms limitation was an issue of the highest importance. In November 1921 Americans of all sorts agreed on that point. Only time and an understanding of political developments in London and Tokyo would tell if Britons and Japanese shared that belief.

10 In the autumn of 1921 no one in Washington could ignore naval arms limitation. The issue was central to a power struggle that engaged widespread public interest and stimulated individual political ambitions. The realization of naval limitation by international agreement came to be seen as something which would assure the "success" of the Harding administration. In London, arms limitation was viewed quite differently. Beatty and Lloyd George disagreed on the naval needs of empire and the wisdom of naval limitation by international agreement, but they did not engage in a naked struggle for power. Instead both men tried to respond to the challenge Balfour put before them. They sought a "middle way" between "eternal competition" with the United States and "abject surrender" of Britain's traditional sea supremacy.

The problem Britain confronted was by its very nature different from that facing Washington policymakers. British naval policy, as numerous historians have noted,[1] was inextricably tied to diplomatic and naval issues. A preeminent fleet, the Anglo-Japanese alliance, and solidarity of empire had in the past constituted indissoluble elements of a single political reality. To modify any one of the three was bound to affect the other two. Because the navy was a symbol, an institution with roots deep in the traditions and psychology of British political life, it was also a domestic political and bureaucratic problem. That problem could not be resolved à la Harding or Borah. Rather than trample its roots in a race for personal success, British statesmen and admirals had to protect those roots while searching for consensus.

Lloyd George carried on that search in a manner that hardly looked like leadership. Critics taunted that his England was not "happy or prosperous." They charged that he "never achieves or settles anything; but he soothes and he threatens; and either way he defers."[2] Harsh though they were, these words aptly described the prime minister's approach to the problems of naval arms limitation. For unlike Harding, Lloyd George led through evasion, inconsistency, and delay. The "Welsh wizard," bureaucratic manipulator par excellence, and seer into the hearts of ordinary Britons—the man whose talents far exceeded those of Warren Harding—simply could not seize the initiative for naval arms limitation.

To understand why the prime minister seemed unable to take control and how London prepared for the Washington conference, one must begin by considering the British domestic political milieu. In the spring of 1921 the navy was simply not a major political issue, due in part to Lee's shrewd budgeting tactics. As chart two on page 162 indicates, the percentage of national expenditure devoted to the navy had dropped dramatically since 1914. While estimates by no means met the Treasury's "normal year" standard, they were less than the sums sought in 1919 and 1920. The naval budget promised painless expansion; Lee squeezed funds for the construction of four replacement capital ships from other portions of the estimates. As the cabinet had agreed, the first lord argued that renewed building did not spell competition with the United States Navy.[3]

Division among would-be opponents was another factor lessening the importance of naval budgetary issues. Both big-navy and "economizer" resolutions were offered in the House of Commons in response to Lee's remarks. Neither resolution got anywhere, and Asquith, now leader of the "Wee Free" Liberals, spoke but a few words of criticism and championed an adequate navy. The press did not approach Lee's estimates in guns vs. butter terms, and the *Times* did not contest his claim that renewed building would not mark the beginning of Anglo-American rivalry. "Anti-waste" advocates vigorously attacked subsequent government budgetary proposals. But neither economy advocates nor old-line Liberals agreed on how best to force reductions in budgetary proposals. While Lord Robert Cecil and Labor's J. H. Thomas wanted to slash service estimates, Sir Frederick Banbury and

Chart 2   Naval expenditure as a percentage
                                              of total national expenditure,
                                              1914–1922

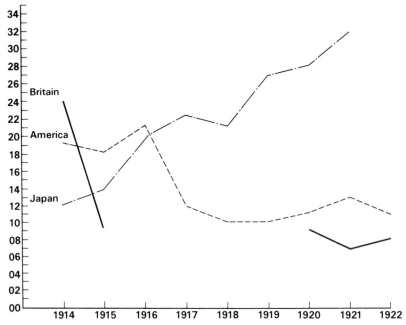

Based on: U.S. Department of Commerce, *His-*
             torical Statistics of the United States;
             B. R. Mitchell, *Abstract of Brit-*
             ish Historical Statistics; Kaigun
             daijin kanbō, *Kaigun gunbi enkaku:*
             furoku, chart 8.
             Note: Due to the use of votes of credit
             which did not differentiate between
             army and navy expenditures, the per-
             centage for Britain cannot be computed
             for the war years.
             Further data of comparable accuracy
             not available for Japan between 1921
             and 1922.

others favored reforming the entire budgetary process or setting absolute
limits on all government expenditures. In short, neither a little-navy coalition
of M.P.'s and editors as in prewar days nor a new combination of
"economists" led by a British Borah existed to make the navy a major issue.[4]

Instead, other problems occupied center stage. Throughout the spring and
early summer, a nationwide coal strike gripped Britain. Unemployment,
failures in government housing schemes, and the high costs of pensions

worried M.P.'s and ministers. But the most important issue was Ireland. The "outrages," that is, guerilla warfare, and government efforts to suppress them kept the Irish question before politicians and public. But then, suddenly, the possibility of a truce and perhaps a negotiated settlement of the Anglo-Celtic war presented itself. The opportunity to resolve this most difficult of all British political problems appealed to Lloyd George. From June through December 1921, it would indeed be "Ireland over everything" for him. But the Irish problem entailed enormous risks and imposed weighty burdens on his leadership. If he were to solve it, he would have to persuade the British public to discard the shibboleth of devolution toward home rule. Even more critically, he would have to engineer change so as not to prompt die-hard Unionists into leaving and thus destroying his coalition government.[5]

The latter task seemed all the more critical in the spring of 1921. Lloyd George's cabinet was shaken by the resignation of Bonar Law on the very day that naval estimates were presented in the House of Commons. The *Times's* parliamentary correspondent was not exaggerating when he termed Law's resignation "the most severe blow the Government and the Parliamentary Coalition had suffered since the General Election [of 1918]." A former staff member felt that Lloyd George was simply "hanging on without any particular policy or support" and predicted that the prime minister would, like Asquith, be "kicked out ignominiously." Austen Chamberlain, who succeeded Bonar Law as senior Unionist in the coalition and leader of the House of Commons, provided little strength to the government. He had neither Lloyd George's confidence nor the respect of Parliament. Moreover, his promotion left other Unionists unhappy. Churchill was particularly upset at not succeeding to the Exchequer, and by late May rumors of an anti–Lloyd George cabal were rife.[6]

Internal political instability of this sort took its toll on Lloyd George's psychological and physical resources and reinforced his natural caution. One day he was "a little worried," and then "very cross and irritable"; his doctor ordered ten days' complete rest. The prime minister swung from fatalism to defiance and back again. At one moment he felt his political influence was declining; at another he spoke of creating a new party and calling autumn elections. Busily quashing coups and forming countercabals to confound his supposed enemies, the prime minister could not regard those who sat around the conference table when naval matters were discussed as mere experts: they were pieces in the political chess game whom he hoped to move to his own advantage—or checkmate.[7]

Under these circumstances, it was hardly surprising that Lloyd George and his colleagues dealt with naval limitation gingerly. Throughout the spring the prime minister could justify evading the issue of limitation by pointing to adverse American conditions. While he himself thought in December 1920 that the new Harding administration was likely to seek an "amicable arrangement" on naval matters, reports from Washington rendered that assumption questionable. In January Ambassador Auckland Geddes was skeptical of the chances for a quick agreement; in March he was certain that Washington would deal first with broad peace-making questions; and by late April the ambassador was convinced that Hughes was tricky, unreliable, and anything but friendly. The *Times*'s Washington correspondent seconded these views. He thought it unlikely, even after Senate approval of the Borah resolution, that Harding would yield to the demand for disarmament. Lloyd George's own conversations with Senator McCormick in December and Ambassador George Harvey's remarks of April 1921 also probably signaled "go slow" on naval limitation to the prime minister.[8]

Consequently Lloyd George put off those who urged him to take the lead in seeking naval agreement with Washington. In January 1921 he rejected Canadian diplomat Loring Christie's suggestion that Ottawa sound Washington out on naval issues and the Anglo-Japanese alliance problem. Two weeks later, and again in April, the prime minister spurned the notion of approaching the Americans through Canadian intermediaries. He twice turned a deaf ear to Lee. A mere two days after presenting his estimates to Parliament, the first lord proposed that he, Lee, go to Washington and use his ties to the Roosevelt family to foster an Anglo-American naval understanding. Late in May Lee pressed his case once again. He believed that Washington "would make very great concessions on many points now in dispute, and would accept real equality of naval strength (even though it involved a curtailment of their building programmes) if we would disentangle ourselves from Japan and come to some formal—possibly tripartite—agreement for the defence of our respective and legitimate interests in the Pacific." Lloyd George listened to his first lord's words, but did not act upon them.[9]

Instead, the prime minister deferred all decisions on naval, diplomatic, and imperial issues to the forthcoming Imperial Conference. When the cabinet met on May 30 to prepare for it, Lloyd George's colleagues once again sought a middle way out of the dilemmas before them. Having promised a White Paper to explain the earlier decision to resume capital ship construction and having sanctioned an interpretation of the Anglo-Japanese alliance's terms which made the alliance due for expiration or renewal in mid-July, the ministers felt compelled to argue for definite decisions.[10]

But their discussions revealed only sharp differences of opinion. Curzon argued that the Anglo-Japanese alliance must be continued so as to constrain Japan, reassure the French, the Dutch, and the peoples of Australasia, and prevent the emergence of a Russo-German combination. He noted that the Admiralty and the War Office had endorsed its continuation and insisted that Canadian opposition to it could be overcome. The foreign secretary then added that the pact would serve to sober American naval extremists. Balfour replied that such a policy would only foster Anglo-American antagonisms. Churchill agreed. Rather than alienating the Canadians by renewing the alliance, Curzon's opponents argued, London should renew it for a short term and sponsor a Pacific conference to soften Japanese-American antagonism over China and allay Australasian fears for security. Such a move would also remove the cause of American-Japanese naval rivalry and the risks of similar Anglo-American competition. Lee insisted that Anglo-American relations were "of transcendant importance and outweighed in every way those with other Powers or any combination of Powers." He proposed that London get Washington to call a conference designed to end fears of naval competition and resolve Pacific problems. Balfour, always the discreet compromiser, suggested amalgamating these proposals so as to renew the Anglo-Japanese alliance for a short term and convene a Pacific conference.

Faced with such disagreement, Lloyd George avoided making a clear-cut choice and delayed any final decisions; he seemed to agree with everyone. In words which might have been Curzon's, the prime minister said he "liked the Japanese. The reasons they [the Japanese] gave very often for doing things were quite unintelligible, and they might have no conscience, but they ... had given unfailing support to their Allies at the International Conferences." Lloyd George favored holding a Pacific conference only after Tokyo had been assured that the alliance would not be terminated, but the prime minister's conclusions, which the cabinet accepted, were ambiguous at best. It was agreed that the Imperial Conference should propose that Harding summon a Pacific conference—after Britain had given Japan reassurances about the alliance. To soften American misgivings about it, London would confer privately with Washington and Peking before extending the alliance for another ten years. Yet for the time being, it would be renewed only on a three months' basis. Then, in a last, contradictory, and evasive instruction, the cabinet directed the War Office and Admiralty to prepare memorandums showing Japan's contribution to the recent war effort and ordered the C.I.D. to estimate the strategic situation if the alliance were ended.[11]

These very contradictory conclusions by the cabinet set the stage for Admiralty and C.I.D. review of questions of imperial defense and Pacific strategy that had troubled the navy for years. Back in June 1918 Admiral Wemyss had urged dominion prime ministers to create and finance a single imperial navy. His ideas grated on the dominion leaders' national feeling and appeared wildly impractical against the background of war. But less than a week after the armistice, Sir Joseph Cook of New Zealand asked that Admiral Jellicoe come to the Pacific to survey imperial defense needs. The former first sea lord agreed to go almost immediately, but his colleagues at Admiralty House were hardly enthusiastic about the journey. Sir Oswyn

Murray tried to get Jellicoe's instructions drawn to make it clear the admiral came at the dominions' request and not as spokesman for the Admiralty. As finally written, moreover, Jellicoe's orders left him only a very weak, advisory role. He was not expected to raise broad strategic problems—the very issues that would shape dominion leaders' assessment of their needs and obligations.[12]

From the moment Jellicoe left for the Pacific, he was set on a collision course with Wemyss. He advocated creating an extensive Indian naval defense force. In Australia he wrote recommendations which assumed that Japan was the most important enemy and called for the creation of a mixed British-Australian naval force of eight battleships and eight battle-cruisers—precisely the size longed-for by the Imperial Japanese Navy. The proposed fleet would be commanded by a British admiral based at Singapore. In New Zealand Jellicoe said he favored contributions to such a fleet rather than the establishment of a separate naval force. Suggestions of this sort prompted Admiral Wemyss on the very last day of his tenure as first sea lord to ask that Jellicoe be reprimanded and instructed not to discuss broad strategic issues at other dominion capitols. Wemyss's attitude mirrored his despair of progress in coordinating imperial naval defense. By the middle of 1919 he suspected army bureaucratic maneuvers on strategic issues and concluded that "Each dominion must decide its naval programme on its own responsibility." In more sanguine moments he hoped for exchanges of Royal Naval and dominion staff personnel. With that, the issue lapsed, buried in the personal antagonism among Wemyss, Jellicoe, and Beatty.[13]

Something more than personal quarrels among admirals accounted for Admiralty reluctance to discuss Pacific strategic questions. In 1919 Naval Staff planners recognized that Royal Naval forces in the Pacific were and in all probability would continue to be vastly inferior to those of Japan. The planners proposed development of Sydney and Singapore as major bases and of subordinate ports scattered to make it possible to run away from superior enemy forces. Early in 1920, in "a brief delphic utterance," planners indicated that the Anglo-Japanese alliance might be terminated, but at the same time hoped for "some satisfactory understanding with Japan." Indeed, they were not interested in Pacific conflict. In response to the cabinet's directive, the Naval Staff concluded that Japanese pressure combined with difficulties in Europe would be "the worst situation with which the British Empire could be faced."[14]

Until the spring of 1921 the Admiralty dealt with this potential double threat by ignoring it. When Admiral Alexander L. Duff, commander-in-chief, China Station, submitted plans for convoying merchantmen in case of war with Japan, the Admiralty filed his proposal without action. When in December 1920 the Australians asked that a conference of flag officers consider Pacific naval needs, London spurned the request. Such a rejection contradicted the rhetoric of seapower which Beatty and Long had spoken, but suited the realities of budgetary politics. While the admiral stressed the need to control Suez, and Long urged construction of fuel depots to permit fleet operations in Asian waters, both readily sacrificed funds for bases and storage tanks to get new battleships.[15]

Once authorization of new battleships seemed assured, Admiralty attitudes began to soften. Civilians felt they must at least listen to dominion arguments in preparation for the Imperial Conference. Reversing its earlier stand, the Admiralty agreed to hold a conference of flag officers whose purpose would be to silence Australian demands for development of Sydney as a major naval port. Admiral Duff worked hard to quash those demands. He got officers assembled at Penang to endorse deployment of submarines at Hong Kong, Singapore, and Borneo to slow any possible Japanese southward advance. He recommended that two British battle cruisers and lesser craft be stationed at Borneo to deter Japanese advances on that oil-rich island. He argued that the Japanese were unlikely to attempt an invasion of Australia. Even if they did try, local naval forces could slow their advance until the Royal Navy arrived from Europe. To support them, Duff and the conferees recommended strengthening Singapore's land and naval defenses.[16]

In May 1921 this same idea of strengthening Singapore appealed to civilians on the C.I.D. The full committee commissioned its Overseas Defence Subcommittee to develop arguments on why Singapore rather than Hong Kong or Sydney should have priority in future base development programs. The discussion coincided with fresh Admiralty interest in Singapore. Having gotten approval to resume battleship building, the Board of Admiralty felt strong enough to revive schemes to construct a string of fuel oil depots from Suez to Singapore. Early in June, the Overseas Defence Subcommittee, despite departmental differences over its details, proposed building a Singapore base, and on the tenth of the month the full C.I.D. recommended that the scheme be put before the Imperial Conference. With surprising ease, proponents of the plan disregarded the illogic of launching so colossal a project at the very moment when Treasury officials sought cuts of 115 million to balance the national budget. Those in favor of the plan argued that the value of Singapore as a symbol of imperial unity and arguments of duty and obligation could overcome possible opposition at home.[17]

This decision to broach the question of a Singapore base set the stage for Balfour's exposition to the cabinet of a middle way out of naval and imperial problems. As its meeting of June 16, in Lloyd George's absence, Balfour outlined an ingenious solution. British representatives would propose to dominion prime ministers that the Anglo-Japanese alliance be renewed for a period of four to five, rather than ten, years. London's spokesmen would also stress their commitment to fortify Singapore—but explain that present financial circumstances made it impossible for Britain to do the work alone. Balfour argued that this would serve two purposes: it would permit concentration of British naval forces in the Southwest Pacific—effectively decoying those of Japan from any attack on Canada, and more importantly, it would deflate American claims of defending the white race in the Pacific. But its main advantage, Balfour insisted, was that London would "be in a position to say that we had a practical plan. This was even more important than actually commencing the work of developing Singapore at the moment." Although Balfour said nothing of the scheme's domestic political merits or costs, cabinet members readily endorsed his negotiating strategy.[18]

One suspects they did so for intensely political reasons. On one level, the plan suited Admiralty bureaucratic interests. It provided support for Lee's renewed appeals for fuel oil storage along the route to Singapore.[19] It was consistent with Beatty's vision of the peacetime role of the Royal Navy. It sidestepped the old, tangled quarrels over command and financing of an imperial fleet. Balfour, a shrewd veteran of Whitehall's bureaucratic wars, may also have seen the promise of a base as possible compensation to the Admiralty for eventual limitation of capital ships by international agreement.

On another level, the scheme appealed to the cabinet because it placed the burden of choice on other men's shoulders. Chamberlain and Churchill wanted to avoid having to choose between Washington and Tokyo. The Singapore stratagem seemed to promise help in reducing sharp differences between Canada and Australia over both the Anglo-Japanese alliance and naval defense. The plan called upon the dominions to demonstrate their loyalty to the empire by providing financial support for imperial naval defense. Hankey was certain that Lloyd George could persuade the Canadian prime minister, Arthur Meighen, to come around to London's point of view on naval and diplomatic issues. If he could not convince Meighen, then, as Balfour probably surmised, the blame for shattering imperial harmony would fall upon the Canadians.[20]

Harmony, indeed, was what Lloyd George sought in opening the Imperial Conference. He said Britain wanted to retain friendship with Japan, yet recognized that American and Japanese interests clashed in China. The empire, as broker between East and West, had a distinct interest in preventing international division along racial lines. "Friendly cooperation" with Washington was a cardinal principle. "We desire," the prime minister said, "to avoid the growth of armaments, whether in the Pacific or elsewhere [and] ... are ready to discuss with American statesmen any proposal for the limitation of armament which they wish to set out." But then in tones worthy of the staunchest prewar Tory, Lloyd George insisted that "the very life of ... the whole Empire has been built upon sea power.... We have ... to look to the measures which our security requires; we aim at nothing more; we cannot possibly be content with less."[21]

Then, while domestic political intrigues were seething everywhere, Lloyd George left the imperial conferees to themselves. Sharp differences between them emerged over the next ten days. Australia's Billy Hughes urged renewal of the Anglo-Japanese alliance and offered to contribute funds, on a per capita basis, for naval defense. He favored calling a Pacific conference and consideration of naval arms limitation with one or both of the other Pacific maritime powers. The New Zealand prime minister agreed with Hughes but was less sanguine about reaching an accord with the United States. Smuts of South Africa insisted that the Americans were difficult but essential friends. On June 28, Curzon built his case for renewal of the Anglo-Japanese alliance. The notion that it provoked friction with Washington was "tendencious," according to him. Then, after Lloyd George had left the meeting, Curzon insisted that there were only two real alternatives: renewal in significantly modified form for a four year term or temporary extension that would precede a conference on Pacific problems.[22]

Balfour then introduced the Singapore scheme. He insisted that ties with Tokyo were a strategic necessity—until Singapore could be greatly strengthened. He suggested that the Anglo-Japanese alliance might be transformed into a kind of western Pacific Monroe Doctrine, something consistent with the League of Nations Covenant. An arrangement of this kind, Balfour said, would allay American suspicions and quiet Canadian fears about the alliance's impact on relations between Washington and Ottawa. But the Canadian prime minister rejected both Curzon's and Balfour's arguments. As Meighen interpreted the latest cables from Washington, Harding might agree to a conference to limit naval armaments but firmly opposed continuation of the Anglo-Japanese alliance. Hughes quickly objected to Meighen's reading, and Smuts unsuccessfully tried to make peace between the Canadians and Australians. The meeting then degenerated into an inconclusive discussion of Washington's intentions.[23]

This deadlock over renewal or abrogation of the alliance demanded that the cabinet consider what to do next. Curzon wanted to bypass the Imperial Conference and begin talks with the American and Japanese ambassadors on modification of the pact. But Lloyd George preferred another, more evasive, tactic: the lord chancellor might say that, upon reexamination, he found that the alliance would continue automatically until specifically denounced by one of its parties. Such a ploy would buy time for exploratory talks with Washington and cast Meighen of Canada in the role of disrupter of imperial harmony. The cabinet readily agreed to this approach, and that afternoon the prime minister explained it to the Imperial Conference. The following day—after news of this stunning policy switch was leaked to the press—dominion prime ministers agreed that London should approach Washington and Tokyo about a Pacific conference.[24]

This proposal simply suspended differences temporarily. Meighen distrusted Curzon and feared Lloyd George would overlook Canadian objections to continuing the Anglo-Japanese alliance. Curzon's initial exchanges about a conference created confusion and disagreement over negotiating priorities. While the foreign secretary wanted to make Pacific problems the focal point of any gathering, Secretary of State Hughes wanted talks on naval limitation alone. But Lloyd George was untroubled by differences of this sort. He bubbled with enthusiasm when he broke news of Harding's invitation to a conference to dominion leaders. Later, when he made public Britain's acceptance of the American offer as amended, he simply glossed over differences among the dominions by speaking of two conferences—one on Pacific problems, the other on naval arms limitation.[25]

This inconsistency might have troubled some, but it suited the domestic political milieu perfectly. Lloyd George appeared to have preserved the harmony which journals as politically different as the *Times*, the *Nation*, and the *Round Table* wanted. His remarks pointed the way toward what the *Times*'s Washington correspondent termed the "middle road" between friendship for America and Japan alike. The prime minister's comments satisfied the Navy League's call for a three-power conference on naval limitation as the first step toward security with economy. His remarks picked up threads in Ambassador Harvey's July 4 address, which was concerned with the elimination of Atlantic naval tensions and the reduction of Pacific political problems as well as eventual arms limitation by international agreement. Editorial writers praised the decision to take part in a conference, but the *Times* felt compelled to add a warning: Assurance of Anglo-American amity must be the main object of any meeting. Even though that "goal is clear ... the means of approach to it need to be carefully chosen."[26]

Over the next four months, the British government found it both impossible and politically inexpedient to make clear-cut choices. Pursuit of the elusive middle way proved incompatible with definition of a coherent strategy for achieving arms limitation by international agreement. Lloyd George discovered that old differences of opinion persisted even after Harding's invitation to Washington. Late in July the prime minister made yet another effort to get dominion leaders to agree on naval standards and imperial defense. Arguing that new capital ships were necessary regardless of possible outcomes at Washington, he asked the dominions to help pay for them. Australia and New Zealand offered their support—provided the other dominions agreed. But Meighen of Canada rejected Billy Hughes's plan for contributions on a per capita basis. The conferees also declined to provide fuel oil storage facilities, essential if the fleet were ever to move east to the Singapore base. The Imperial Conference barely agreed on a weak resolution that defined "equality in fighting strength" as the standard for imperial naval security. As the conference drew to a close, the prime ministers simply glossed over their differences and postponed defining what equality meant.[27]

Lloyd George also found it impossible to overcome differences of opinion with his own foreign secretary and with Washington on the timing, location, and agenda for the forthcoming conference. Curzon wanted to hold a preliminary meeting in London—with dominion prime ministers present— that would focus on Pacific problems. He pressed this idea on Washington even after the Americans expressed hostility to it. Lloyd George then shifted ground on negotiating priorities. The prime minister told Churchill he feared the French and Italians would conspire to restrict British sea power in a conference such as Washington had proposed. Perhaps it would be better, Lloyd George suggested, to hold a preliminary conference at Bar Harbor, Maine, where the Americans might be persuaded to stop naval construction before formal meetings with all the major naval powers at Washington. Yet at the very same time that Maine was proposed as a conference site, Foreign Office officials were sounding the Japanese ambassador about the possibility of holding preliminary talks in London. Curzon persisted in his plan for a London meeeting until Ambassador Geddes and Harvey made clear Washington's opposition to anything other than a single meeting at the American capital city. The result of these maneuvers over the conference site was to intensify differences abroad and at home. Washington suspected London, and the *Times* attacked an embittered Curzon. He and Lloyd George finally concluded that it would be best to "leave exclusive responsibility for the Conference to the Government who initiated it."[28]

Inconsistencies of a similar sort persisted in naval building policies, with Lloyd George's government endorsing expansion and economy almost in the same breath. On July 15, the Admiralty urged the cabinet to override Treasury objections to funding the construction of four new capital ships. Lee offered an ambiguous personal defense for the proposal. Repeating Beatty's arguments, he insisted that without the ships Britain would fall to second or third place in naval standings and be unable to unite and defend her empire properly. But he also said that the authorization of the ships would strengthen London's hand in negotiations with Washington and Tokyo. Churchill repeated publicly in August what he had said privately earlier in the year: the ships could be bargaining counters in arms control negotiations. But when Lloyd George met with the cabinet, it was decided that the new ships should be begun regardless of the outcome of talks at Washington. This decision was made just as the dominion prime ministers refused financial support to the Royal Navy and was followed, barely three weeks later, by the cabinet's decision that economy should be the principle objective in preliminary C.I.D. and Admiralty studies of naval limitation.[29]

In addition to the differences which plagued official London, there was trouble within Admiralty House. Beatty, perhaps overconfident at the resumption of battleship construction, challenged Lee and, indirectly, the prime minister. The first sea lord rejected reforms which would make Sir Oswyn

Murray, permanent secretary of the Admiralty, a full voting member of the Board of Admiralty. Lee took the issue to Crown Law Officers, and in October they returned a verdict against Beatty. But in the interim, drift and indecision, not to mention rising civil-naval antagonism, were rife. Beatty left London for a long holiday, and Lee underwent surgery. Lloyd George did nothing to fill the gap in Admiralty leadership, resolve bureaucratic infighting, or otherwise insure that the navy was on course toward arms limitation.[30]

Lloyd George had good reason to believe that he could and should live with these continuing differences over naval policy. Disarmament in London was not the issue it had become in Washington. When the prime minister told Parliament that he had accepted Harding's invitation to a conference, Lloyd George prefaced his remarks with the even more significant announcement that Eamon DeValera, leader of the Irish independence movement, would come to London to begin negotiations on the Irish question. The latter news brought cheers from Parliament and served as a reminder that Ireland was still the greatest issue facing Britain. The prospect of resolving this problem revived Lloyd George's spirits in July. It brought immediate dividends, for old Liberals, like C. P. Scott, formerly estranged from the prime minister, now supported him. But the solution of the Irish problem also entailed the risk that enemies and supposed allies might coalesce against policies made by Lloyd George's government. Ireland was thus the great challenge, the issue that demanded Lloyd George's leadership and promised him a place in history.[31]

The prime minister also felt that he could manage the domestic politics of arms control in the House of Commons. His government had suffered setbacks and steady criticism of its financial policies. A leading "Coalie Lib" turned independent in June and argued that cutting defense expenditures was the only way to economize. The coalition lost by-elections and even lost a vote on a provision of the Finance Bill, a defeat which in the past had brought immediate resignation of the cabinet. But Lloyd George ignored this loss and got Parliament to approve funds for four new battleships. Then, meeting the demand for economy head on and out-flanking M.P.'s who wanted to introduce American-style parliamentary committee control over estimates, the prime minister named Sir Eric Geddes chairman of a special "axe" committee to cut away fat in departmental budgets.[32]

Lloyd George initiated such policies with a confidence that even his worst enemies admitted was justified. Scoffing at antiwaste leaders, he said that even with all the offices of government in hand these economy advocates could not change the spending habits of the Admiralty and other departments. Unperturbed by claims that the country was in revolt against his leadership, the prime minister had ample reason to believe that opinion leaders rejected mere budget cutting as the best solution to Britain's problems. Indeed, even the harshly critical *Times* had come around to Lloyd

George's point of view. Dropping its earlier insistence on setting limits to government expenditure, the newspaper agreed with the prime minister's assertion that only "increased production and trade" could solve the real problem, Britain's war debt. The *Times* conceded in October that while "Discontent is wide and deep ... it is not yet fully informed and clearly concentrated." Indeed, "the present government have reduced Parliament to a shadow." Other editors sharply criticized big budgets, but their words failed to excite a public more worried about jobs and housing than about naval estimates and the total national budget.[33]

These domestic concerns point to another reason why Lloyd George failed to assert himself on behalf of naval arms limitation. The public was no longer as passionately involved with questions of expansion or limitation as it had been in prewar days. The *Manchester Guardian*, the voice of Radical Liberal opposition to naval expansion before 1914, simply lamented the decision to go ahead with four new battleships. Without powerful party leadership committed to disarmament, the public seemed unwilling to rally to appeals to challenge the government. As the *Nation* pointed out early in October, "our public opinion is still indifferent" toward naval limitation. It was also true that Britons had drifted away from strident naval patriotism. With the exception of Archibald Hurd writing in the *Fortnightly Review*, no major naval commentator opposed a limitation agreement. Occasions like Trafalgar Day which in the past had evoked loud editorial support for the Royal Navy passed with little or no notice in 1921.[34]

Lloyd George's inattention to naval matters did not bother major political commentators. Indeed, to many his passive stance seemed diplomatically desirable. As these observers perceived the situation, Washington offered a chance to recoup the losses in Paris of two years earlier. To them, Lloyd George, linked in American minds with the supposed intrigues of the peace conference, was hardly the man likely to resolve Anglo-American naval and diplomatic differences. Success in the coming conference would not mean striking a preset naval balance or attaining specific naval budget cuts; the real objective would be "placing our relations with America upon a new, permanent foundation." Pro-American editors saw this as the goal of "the great adventure" ahead, and even those with more nationalistic inclinations felt that London would do best to avoid making specific proposals at the conference that might provoke American hostility. As British editors saw it, then, success would be defined more in broadly diplomatic terms than in narrowly naval ones.[35]

The absence of strong and specific public pressures for arms limitation together with the dearth of prime ministerial involvement in the issue all but assured the continuation of drift and indecision during the final stages of London's preparations for the Washington conference. The Admiralty approached the talks in a leisurely fashion, convinced that its interests could be protected even in the limitation of naval strength. Beatty took little interest in his subordinates' preliminary discussions and gave no response when Plans Division officers suggested that the coming conference might threaten the navy's protective role in the Pacific. Perhaps overconfident at parliamentary approval of funds for his new battleships, perhaps tired and embittered by his fight over civilian influence on the Board of Admiralty, Beatty left it to his assistant chief of the Naval Staff, Rear Admiral A. E. Chatfield, to prepare a disarmament proposal that would leave the navy strong enough to protect the empire's minimum strategic needs.[36]

Chatfield had already taken a more positive attitude toward naval limitation than his colleagues. In contrast to Plans and Intelligence officers who had insisted earlier in the year that neither Washington nor Tokyo would abandon fleet expansion programs, Chatfield felt that reduction in the numbers and size of capital ships was possible. As he saw it, the key to an agreement lay in guaranteeing Japan's regional security—perhaps through a tripartite Pacific maritime league. But when it came to drawing up specific arms limitation proposals, Chatfield wanted to protect the Royal Navy's interests. He concluded that the fleet must remain superior in European waters even if a force superior to Japan's were sent to the Pacific. This strength might be achieved through a short-term agreement limiting the tonnage of capital ships held by each of the five largest naval powers. Since the Royal Navy had already suffered from unilateral disarmament, that is, a five year moratorium on capital ship construction, Chatfield felt that the navy must not be bound for too long a term in the future. Security would demand parity with Washington and a two to one superiority over Tokyo. Chatfield concluded that an agreement which left Britain with a seven ship margin over Japan, a three ship superiority over America, and parity in capital ship tonnage with the United States would be acceptable.[37]

Nearly a month passed before Beatty read Chatfield's proposals and modified them for presentation to the C.I.D. The admiral, as always, thought first of service interests. His standard for limitation, as for expansion, was numbers of post-Jutland capital ships—not tonnage. Beatty felt that the Royal Navy must retain   eacetime fleet of sixteen capital ships, assuring parity with America and leaving Britain with a three to two margin of superiority over Japan. Beatty's reduction of the Pacific ratio that Chatfield proposed may have reflected the first sea lord's tendency to define security primarily in Atlantic terms and may also have represented compensation to Tokyo for his determination to develop Singapore while other powers preserved the status quo of their Pacific bases. The admiral rejected inspection to assure compliance with any limitation agreements and refused to divulge information on new weapons to other navies. Finally and most importantly, Beatty assumed that his four replacement post-Jutland battleships would be built even if a short-term limitation agreement was reached. In the admiral's view, the boost to service morale and stimulus to public support for the navy brought by continued construction should not be thrown away in any naval holiday.[38]

The C.I.D. began its discussion of Beatty's proposal on October 14, 1921—nearly two months after the cabinet's decision that the committee should shape arms limitation policies. No major political figure wanted to assume leadership within the group. Lloyd George did not take part in its discussions and had not yet decided who would represent Britain in Washington. Curzon, doubtful of the conference's success and fearing that its failure would be blamed on the government, proposed sending members of the opposition to Washington. Men of power outside the government, Bonar Law foremost among them, refused to go to the conference. When the C.I.D. began its preparations, even Balfour was loathe to undertake the mission.[39]

Consequently the C.I.D. found it easy to agree on technical specifics of naval limitation but difficult to concur on its broader terms. Committee members agreed that post-Jutland capital ships should be the standard of comparing naval strength. Members hoped to preserve the political and strategic status quo in East Asia, without abandoning naval commitments in the Pacific. They thought it desirable and essential to the preservation of Britain's European naval hegemony to seek abolition of submarine warfare and also felt it would be wise to avoid discussing rules of maritime warfare. Confident of Britain's technological strength, they overrode Admiralty objections to a weak inspection system designed to assure compliance with any limitation agreement.

But there was no agreement on the issues that had divided the cabinet throughout the postwar years. Some C.I.D. members opposed allowing Japan two-thirds as many battleships as Britain, for this would burden taxpayers with an unnecessary sixteen capital-ship fleet. Admiralty defenders retorted that there was no need to agree upon a set ratio before the conference and insisted that no power would be obliged to build up to the maximum strength permitted. The old debate over the purpose of continued building recurred: while Churchill insisted that it was the stick that would beat others into cutting their own fleets, others insisted that Britain would either have to build or have her program exposed as mere bluff. It proved impossible for the committee to agree on limitations for branches of the military other than the navy. Balfour met strong Air Ministry objections when he proposed consideration of air as well as naval reductions. This bureaucratic clash, together with the old Admiralty-Treasury feud, made it impossible for the C.I.D. to agree on negotiating priorities. Instead, the group postponed basic issues and concluded only that "we should maintain a fleet at least equal to any other."[40]

The events of the next week undermined the meaning of this shibboleth. Lloyd George's selection of delegates reinforced London's tendency to search for a diplomatically harmonious and politically risk-free middle way. With

Admiral Beatty conveniently on his way to the American Legion Convention at Kansas City, the prime minister named Lee, Auckland Geddes, and Balfour delegates to the Washington conference. Balfour, former prime minister and first lord, defender of empire, alliance, and friendship with Washington, personified the middle way. At ceremonies at Westminster Abbey honoring Britain's Unknown Soldier, Lloyd George joined other civilian leaders and General Pershing in calling for international harmony. Then on October 21, Trafalgar Day, Lee, anxious as both first lord and delegate to assure the success of the coming talks, proposed dropping even the C.I.D.'s vague guidelines. There was no need to define post-Jutland ships as the standard of naval security, as Beatty had wanted to do. Pre-Jutland vessels, if properly concentrated and maneuvered, could match ships of the American 1916 program. Even more importantly, Lee convinced the C.I.D. that the British delegation ought not to be committed by the terms of Beatty's earlier memorandum.[41]

Balfour picked up where Lee had left off. On October 24 he and members of the delegation agreed that their primary objectives were to preserve the Far Eastern status quo and conclude a naval limitation agreement. But rather than trying to agree on a specific limit for capital ships before the conference, the delegation concluded that it would be preferable to wait and react to other powers' proposals. "For the present," Balfour argued, the standard of naval strength should be equality to any other power. The qualifying phrase undermined Admiralty notions of the strategic minimum and, with Balfour's backing, won full cabinet approval. Balfour also got the cabinet to agree that Britain's general goal was to limit and lower the naval strength of all powers and to seek both air and land limitations as well. But beyond that the government failed to specify how these goals might be pursued at Washington.[42]

Contemporaries offered various explanations for the vagueness of London's intentions. The London *Times* asserted that imprecision cloaked diplomatic wisdom. The "circumspection displayed by British official circles" was not due to "indifference to the immense issues at stake, but rather to a sense of their intricacy and their transcendant importance." The patriotic editor of the *National Review* disagreed: the Americans were so obtuse that anything Britain proposed would certainly be rejected. Those close to the prime minister discerned domestic political reasons for diplomatic uncertainty. Lord Riddell sensed that Lloyd George had little interest in the Washington conference and felt its proceedings would be devoid of personal political profit. In the last days of October and the first of November, the Irish negotiations threatened to collapse and bring down the Lloyd George cabinet. Bonar Law came out of retirement to announce his support for the Orangemen of Ulster, and Lloyd George feared his old ally might be conspiring to succeed him if the government fell.[43]

London's course toward Washington was erratic, however, for reasons that transcended these immediate diplomatic and political circumstances. The conviction that a middle way out of diplomatic, imperial, and naval problems existed fundamentally affected the behavior of statesmen and admirals. That belief suited Lloyd George's style of leadership. It enabled him to sidestep the hard choices presented by the Anglo-Japanese alliance problem, overlook the inconsistencies of the Singapore stratagem, and reverse course on renewed battleship building. Belief in a middle way also suited the bureaucratic interests of the Royal Navy. Beatty used it to defend battleship building on the eve of an arms limitation conference and may have seen in it the rationale for future construction programs. Finally, the notion of the middle way appealed to the temperament, the sense of political realism, and the diplomatic talents of the man who sought it most consistently, Arthur Balfour.

The weakness of this approach to arms limitation is obvious in retrospect. Britain's statesmen and admirals were so used to shaping consenses that they failed to recognize the need for clear-cut decisions. The pursuit of the middle way blinded them to bureaucratic resistance to arms limitation and to inconsistencies in their own solutions to problems. But in spite of the vagueness and indecision that this approach produced, it had one great advantage: the government was uncommitted except in a most general way, and the prime minister was free. The hard decisions, the risks that might be reduced once the Washington conference got underway, had been postponed.

One suspects Lloyd George prized the advantage of indecision. On November 2, 1921, when official London bade Balfour and the delegation godspeed on the journey to Washington at the station, the prime minister was not there.[44]

11 Tokyo: Statesmen and Admirals, Risks and Opportunities

On November 3, 1921, the day after Arthur Balfour left London for Washington, Major General Leonard Wood prepared to leave Tokyo for Manila. President Harding had sent Wood to the Far East to report on attitudes toward the coming Washington conference and to assume the governor generalship of the Philippines. As he prepared to depart, Wood drafted a long cable for the secretary of war which he suspected would go to the president. Wood had seen Prime Minister Hara, Admiral Katō Tomosaburō, and former Minister of War Tanaka Giichi. He came away with the impression that they were looking for "a face-saving way of getting out" of continental Asian military commitments and avoiding diplomatic isolation. Wood was impressed by General Tanaka. He sensed that the former minister of war might be willing to drop schemes for fortifying Japanese-held Pacific islands. Struck by the high costs of the eight-eight fleet expansion program, Wood was also "inclined to think [that] they would be willing to discuss modification of the building plan" at the Washington conference.[1]

Contemporary observers like General Wood bequeathed hypotheses about Japan which historians have been loath to question. Despite differences in nationality and attitudes toward arms control, observers generally concluded that Japan had few choices in 1921. They assumed that as the weakest of the three great naval powers, Tokyo could not resist pressures for naval limitation that came from Washington and London, nor could Japan endure the heavy costs of competitive naval expansion in the post-World War I era.[2]

While this traditional approach has illuminated important facets of the Japanese decision for arms limitation, it has obscured the most significant of all: the choices for naval disarmament were quintessentially political. While those who made them had to think of the strategic and diplomatic consequences of arms limitation, they were even more concerned with its domestic political implications. Their choices flowed less from a sense of external compulsion than from an awareness of internal opportunities. The latter entailed both risks and rewards. It was the desire to minimize the risks and attain the rewards, to rearrange the balance of forces within the domestic politics of national defense, and to assure the survival of the Hara government, that determined Tokyo's response to arms limitation in 1921.

During the last months of 1920 and the first of 1921, a major change in Japanese defense policies seemed unlikely. When army, navy, and foreign ministry officials met in the late summer to prepare for the League of Nations meeting scheduled for December, they discussed disarmament. While the diplomats may have held hopes for progress on arms limitation, the admirals and generals were not about to disrupt past compromises or destroy recent achievements on arms expansion. Army spokesmen did not want to modify force level goals agreed on in 1918. Navy officials, having just secured Diet approval of the eight-eight fleet, could hardly be expected to embrace naval limitation. But rather than acknowledge that fact, navy spokesmen argued that League talks would prove fruitless without American participation.[3]

Prime Minister Hara used the same argument to build a consensus against any fundamental shifts in arms policies. The cabinet and Foreign Affairs Advisory Council readily approved instructions for Ambassador Ishii at Geneva that would not risk a Japanese initiative in arms limitation. Even if Hara had been tempted to take risks, he could not afford them. Having just strained his party's loyalty to achieve naval expansion, could he so suddenly reverse himself? In addition, army grumblings about withdrawal from advanced positions on the Asian mainland warned Hara against tampering with arms level authorizations. It would be far easier—and wiser—to let Ambassador Ishii argue that arms limitation initiatives should come not from Tokyo, but from Washington. This tactic proved correct, for while the

ambassador's remarks touched off sparks that ignited Borah's disarmament
campaign, they won widespread approval in the Tokyo press.[4]

Hara then set out to secure approval of an immense arms expansion
budget. Nearly half of the total expenditures proposed for the coming year
would be for national defense. Following guidelines agreed upon in 1918, the
navy would get nearly a half billion yen, almost twice the sum officially listed
for the army. The soldiers, however, would secure funds to complete coast
defenses on outlying islands. While Hara knew the total size of the budget
would draw criticism, he and Admiral Katō were confident of its approval.
Intracabinet opposition was ineffective or nonexistent. While Finance
Minister Takahashi had qualms about funding such huge expenditures, he
could not argue that they demanded new taxation. His criticism, such as it
was, was reserved for the army. Foreign Minister Uchida had neither the
personal stature nor the bureaucratic strength to object. Busy with purely
diplomatic problems and reluctant to engage in another clash with the
military, the diplomats had no stomach for a battle over arms policy. Most
importantly, Admiral Katō, borrowing budgeting tactics of old Jackie
Fisher, employed by Beatty and Long at the same time, prepared a sound
defense for his requests. Administrative economies, more rigorous cost
controls, and reduction of the number of older ships in commission could
free funds for new naval building.[5]

Admiral Katō repeated these arguments in the Diet while Hara and
Uchida strengthened the case for naval expansion. The prime minister
reminded Seiyūkai faithful of the party's commitment to a strong national
defense. He argued that prudent use of limited resources would enable Japan
to increase her arms, defend herself against disorder in the East Asian
region, and simultaneously maintain good relations with the great powers.
Uchida pointed out the inherent difficulties in League efforts toward arms
control and emphasized the need to resolve other issues that troubled
Tokyo's relations with Washington and London. Both men, without mentioning the domestic bureaucratic and political obstacles to any fundamental
shift in national defense policies, built diplomatic cases against Japanese
initiatives for arms limitation. Washington's torpor during the transition to
the Harding administration and London's postponement of naval decisions
during the captial ships controversy strengthened the Hara cabinet's argument that late January 1921 was not a time for change.[6]

Tokyo editors and politicians generally agreed with the government's
arguments. While editors criticized the total size of the budget and attacked
its revenue assumptions as unrealistic, they did not attack naval expansion
per se. They tended to blame the army rather than the navy for the high cost
of defense. With Hara, they accepted the notion of disarmament in
principle, but found it hard to agree on its policy consequences. It was easy
to report on the American crusade for arms control but extremely difficult,

as *Jiji* naval correspondent Itō Masanori recalled, to reconcile traditional support for a strong fleet with the idea of arms limitation by international agreement.[7]

Opposition politicians, with one exception, were not about to fight Hara on defense issues. The prime minister had an absolute majority in the lower house and numerous alliances in the upper. His opponents, weak and divided, were unwilling to challenge the admirals and generals. Katō Kōmei, barely able to keep his Kenseikai together on the explosive universal suffrage issue, endorsed the idea of arms limitation but insisted that nothing be done to halt progress on the eight-eight fleet program. Kokumintō leader Inukai Ki called for "industrialism, not imperialism," a phrase which could be interpreted to mean subsidies for private shipbuilders whose services would be needed to complete the eight-eight program. Neither of these party leaders nor any of the factional chieftains in the House of Peers saw naval limitation as an issue likely to promote his political fortune.[8]

But Ozaki Yukio, former minister of justice and a temperamental political maverick, disagreed with Hara and with other opposition party leaders. This man, whose statue now looks out over the city of Tokyo from a position of honor near the Diet Building, championed arms limitation by international agreement. He had opposed army expansion in 1912, and a trip to Europe in 1919 revived his old antimilitary feelings. Ozaki was shocked by a visit to Verdun, astounded at London's confused social mores, and incredulous at the size of Britain's first postwar budget deficit. When he first returned to Tokyo, he championed universal suffrage, but realizing that the Kenseikai party was hopelessly divided on this issue, Ozaki turned to disarmament. His efforts to get fellow party members to endorse the principle ended in failure—and his own expulsion from the party.[9]

Undaunted by this defeat, Ozaki on February 10, 1921, delivered an impassioned, two-and-one-half-hour speech on behalf of arms limitation by international agreement before the Diet. Following Senator Borah's tactic, he introduced a resolution that called upon Hara to seek a naval limitation agreement with Washington and London. Ozaki also urged the government to "readjust" army force levels in accordance with the principles of the League of Nations Covenant. Eloquent, courageous, and passionate though he may have been, Ozaki could not save his resolution. It was met with a chorus of nays shouted by members of the Seiyūkai and Kenseikai parties.[10]

On February 12, 1921, those same voices approved Hara's proposed budget. A month later the House of Peers, which included malcontents eager to oust Hara from the premiership, concurred with the budget decision. This victory, coming only a few days after Borah's first defeat of Harding and shortly after the president's inauguration, elated the prime minister. Once again he had managed arms expansion, thus preserving both cabinet solidarity and stability in the politics of national defense.[11]

The events of the next four months, however, gave Hara reason to doubt
that success would come so easily in the future. Arms limitation emerged as
an issue certain to affect not only Japan's role in international politics but
also the prime minister's position in domestic affairs. Its growth in political
significance was in no small measure due to Ozaki Yukio. Stung by his
defeat in the Diet, Ozaki launched a campaign to create a popular
nonpartisan disarmament movement. Borrowing the organizational techniques of William Jennings Bryan, he got unprecedented numbers of
students, businessmen, and ordinary citizens to listen to his message and
express their reactions to it. At the end of his speech-making tour, Ozaki had
over 30,000 postcard replies, of which over 90 percent supported arms
limitation by international agreement.[12]

Ozaki took old arguments and gave them new twists. He claimed that arms
expansion was counterproductive, in that it took limited resources needed for
educational reform and industrial development and wasted them on
weapons. Arms expansion, he asserted, was backward; contrary to admirals'
and generals' claims that more strength meant more international prowess,
more weapons meant lower prestige. Ozaki pointed out that the civilized
peoples of the West were demanding arms limitation as a step in the
progressive development of humanity. Why should Japan block such progress? Finally and most importantly, Ozaki revived prewar arguments about
the impact of arms expansion on domestic political development. Expansion
fed the power of conservative militarists and political oligarchs willing to
curry their favor, he said. If Japan were to keep in step with the rest of
humanity, she must reject their militarist control for greater democracy and
arms limitation.[13]

Despite the limited success of his campaign for arms control, Ozaki verged
on despair. He told Sir Charles Eliot that popular attitudes toward national
security remained unchanged. The people believed that "Japan had a certain
destiny to work out; that this must be done cheaply if possible, but if not,
then, though with considerable reluctance, at whatever price it might cost."
The British ambassador, however, sensed that Ozaki had done something
quite remarkable. While he had not attracted as many followers as Borah
and had not evoked the same degree of moral fervor that prewar British
"economists" had, the former minister had awakened intellectuals and
journalists, businessmen, and even opposition party leaders to the importance of arms limitation.[14]

Intellectuals and journalists began by emphasizing the international
implications of the arms control issue but soon discovered its domestic
political importance. Many argued that patriotism was compatible with
international cooperation, the wave of the future. Miyake Setsurei, a leader
of the older generation deeply concerned about Japan's national identity,
rejected the argument that the empire had no choice but to follow the lead of

stronger Anglo-Saxon nations, but he agreed with banker Soeda Juichi that Japan should pursue arms limitation to advance both her own welfare and that of all humanity. Shiga Tsurutarō could not accept Christian leader Kagawa Toyohiko's faith that international organization would replace armed force in world affairs. Shiga insisted, however, along with the editor of the *Osaka Mainichi*, that the people should have more direct control over the size and character of national defense programs. Yoshino Sakuzō, perhaps the most articulate of all these opinion leaders, emphasized the domestic political implications of arms control. As he saw it, Ozaki's appeal to college youth and his rejection by party politicians symbolized the generation gap in national political life. Men like Hara, tied to the elder statesmen and military leaders of a bygone era, could never understand arms limitation. To overcome such men, to breathe new life into national politics, and to put the empire in harmony with world developments, Yoshino argued, Japan must actively seek arms limitation.[15]

In April 1921 Yoshino looked to the business community for fresh leadership. He heaped praise on Mutō Sanji, president of the Kanegafuchi Spinning Company. Mutō, echoing the thoughts of men like Finance Minister Takahashi, Education Minister (and former Osaka Shōsen Kaisha president) Nakahashi Tokugorō, and Bank of Japan Governor Inoue Junnosuke, organized a campaign among Osaka businessmen to check spending on armaments. Drawing initial support from those among them who had pledged to oppose Diet candidates who favored the eight-eight fleet program in 1920, he originally planned to get the House of Peers to set absolute limits on government spending. By June he had shifted his efforts to Hara. Mutō got the Osaka Chamber of Commerce to pass a resolution which attacked the government's failure to pursue negotiations with Britain and America for arms limitation. He then succeeded in getting the National Association of Chambers of Commerce to endorse limitation by international agreement and urged Hara to pursue negotiations toward that end.[16]

Yoshino and foreign journalists undoubtedly exaggerated the political potency of Mutō's efforts. The ties between business, military, and naval leaders were by no means broken. As spring turned into summer, however, unmistakable signs of changed attitudes within the parties began to appear. While senior politicians were reluctant to talk about arms control and vague when they did so, younger men began to demonstrate great interest in exercising more effective control over national defense spending. Late in June 1921, Egi Tasuku of the Kenseikai made unprecedented proposals for greater civilian influence in the timing and substance of naval shipbuilding programs. Within the Seiyūkai, a special committee was set up. Its members visited the army and navy ministries in search of economies in the coming year's estimates.[17]

These changes coincided with the growth of doubts about the efficacy of

Tokyo's diplomatic strategy concerning arms limitation. The Hara government, like the Lloyd George cabinet, assumed that it could sanction naval expansion yet leave the door ajar for possible limitation talks. In February, for example, representatives of the Navy and Foreign Ministries hastily assured American and British officials that rejection of the Ozaki resolution did not mean official opposition to arms limitation per se. In March, when the *Japan Advertiser* printed a series of articles, syndicated in American newspapers, which claimed that "the most militaristic of peacetime budgets of modern times" was a deliberate attempt to equal or surpass American naval strength, government spokesmen hotly denied the charge, and the naval journalist Itō Masanori wrote a series of counter articles for the newspaper. Admiral Katō himself, in a March 24 interview with Associated Press representatives, amplified a hint naval spokesmen had dropped weeks earlier: Japan harbored no enmity toward America and was "prepared to carry out the limitation of armaments to a certain extent if any reliable agreement is concluded among the leading Powers. Japan does not want," he argued, "to insist on the maintenance of her eight-eight fleet under all circumstances." A few days later, Hara's party newspaper repeated claims made earlier: the government by no means opposed arms limitation by international agreement.[18]

Hara and Katō hoped that their words would convey feelings of friendship and flexibility rather than aggressiveness to the Americans. Apparently their hope was in vain. The air was rife with rumors that Washington was going to concentrate its fleet in the Pacific—against Japan. Secretary of State Hughes lectured Ambassador Shidehara on the Yap island issue. By late April, the ambassador's staff was forwarding translations of *New York Tribune* editorials which said Washington believed Tokyo was forging naval weapons against the United States. By early May, there were even unofficial reports to the effect that Harding had insisted that all diplomatic disputes between America and Japan be resolved before progress could be made on arms limitation.[19]

Under these circumstances, some change in Japan's national defense politics began to seem inevitable. But as Tokyo's leaders searched for new policies, they discovered change was anything but easy. Admiral Katō was the first to learn this lesson. He toured naval bases in search of economies, met for eight hours with naval elder statesmen upon his return, ordered the establishment of special intraservice economy committees, and met again with senior naval advisors, this time at the Imperial Palace, to sanction decisions for arms limitation.[20]

While Katō was in a far better position than Coontz or Beatty to make such decisions, doing so hurt. His service was by no means an emotional tinderbox like the Royal Navy. His life-long rival, Admiral Shimamura Hayao having just retired as chief of the Naval Staff, Katō was the senior officer on active duty. He hoped to lead, in the manner of a good Japanese bureaucrat, by defining a widely acceptable consensus. But this goal proved elusive. The admirals found it difficult to agree on the fate of the eight-eight fleet: Should it be given priority in the coming year's budget? Might it be abandoned in any possible arms control negotiations? Given that the ways were already filled with ships from earlier programs, that officials were worried about the fleet's ultimate cost, and that Katō had warned that the program faced setbacks, should it be postponed? The admirals apparently sidestepped answers to these questions by making a decision for new, intensive studies of arms limitation by international agreement. They then made cuts certain to hurt the morale and unity of any navy: all of one fleet and a major portion of another would go into reserve status, while overage ships would be sunk and the term of service for conscripts and reserves reduced. Eventually, nearly 100 million yen was pared from the coming year's proposed estimates.[21]

Admiral Katō was unusually touchy when reporters pressed him for details of these budgetary changes. His sensitivity and caution probably reflected an awareness that the actions proposed would undermine still further the tenuous interservice agreement on strategic priorities made in 1918. The fleet hardest hit by the reductions was in Siberian waters—where the army wanted to keep troops. All of the bases proposed for closing fronted the Japan Sea. While Katō rejected abandoning Maibara on the home island of Honshu, he hinted that the navy would have to pull out of Chinhai in Korea and Dairen in Manchuria—two areas the generals thought vital to national security. The admiral also disregarded army interests when he opened talks with the Foreign Ministry for the possible withdrawal of naval forces from the Pacific Islands mandate. Such withdrawal might well provide precedent and ammunition for those who wanted to pull army troops out of another war-occupied territory, Shantung.[22]

Changes in naval policies were bound to affect the army, but in the spring of 1921 internal developments within the military service magnified their politico-bureaucratic significance. While Katō convinced his subordinates to take cautious first steps toward arms limitation, the army's leaders determined to resist it. More moderate leaders, who were inclined to pull back from extended war-born continental commitments, found their influence on the wane. War Minister Tanaka hinted early in April that he would have to resign for reasons of health but proposed to delay his departure until the chief of the Army General Staff, Uehara Yūsaku, had been promoted into virtual retirement. Uehara, who championed continental expansion, was promoted—but declined to abandon his position of great influence within the army. Late in June Tanaka's doctors ordered him to resign. His amiable but weak vice minister, General Yamanashi Hanzō, succeeded him.[23]

Yamanashi was no match for Uehara, nor could he equal men like General Ugaki Kazushige. A factional rival to Uehara, Ugaki nonetheless shared the chief of the general staff's opposition to arms limitation, whether it be achieved by domestic budget cutting or diplomatic agreement. In April 1921 Ugaki publicly doubted the other powers' sincerity in pursuing arms limitation. Convinced that Japan must preserve her leadership in East Asia, he believed that determined, enlightened leadership at home could win the public away from the likes of Ozaki. While Yamanashi did not think in precisely these terms, he shared Ugaki's purpose. Early in July the war minister announced that the army most certainly could not be limited or cut. In what may have been an attempt to patch over interservice frictions, he appealed on behalf of the navy against reductions in service budgets.[24]

While the generals and admirals grappled with the problems of arms limitation, Hara Kei was preoccupied with other issues, specifically with the struggle for influence in and around the imperial family. Hara had created problems by naming Makino Nobuaki, a Satsuma man, to succeed a Chōshū adherent as imperial household minister. This supposedly apolitical post was of critical importance in the spring of 1921. Hara and Makino used it to resist efforts attributed to Marshal Yamagata to break the crown prince's engagement to a princess with Satsuma ties. The engagement issue momentarily lapsed when the prince, despite ultranationalist protests, left with Hara's blessing on an unprecedented journey to Western Europe. But the prime minister and those who knew court politics realized that the engagement was of supreme importance. It seemed that it would not be long before the crown prince would have to be named regent (the first in modern Japanese history) for his mentally defective father.[25]

If Hara's diary can be taken as evidence, the prime minister was far more concerned with these court problems than with frictions in American-Japanese relations or the fate of the Anglo-Japanese alliance. Consequently, he was extremely wary of taking positions on other issues likely to increase tensions within his government. Proposals from London and Washington for talks on nonnaval questions seemed certain to raise such feelings. Thus Hara, having heard of Curzon's overtures to the Japanese ambassador in London for a Pacific conference, told Marshal Yamagata that the British proposal was too vague. This was an oblique way of saying he would not participate in negotiations certain to generate frictions within the army and between it and the Foreign Ministry.[26]

A similar caution marked the Hara cabinet's discussion on July 12, 1921, of President Harding's invitation to Washington. While Hara's colleagues had warmed to the idea of arms talks, they were cool at the very mention of "Pacific and Far Eastern questions." That phrase, as pregnant with possibilities of bureaucratic conflict as Curzon's proposal, prompted each minister to protect his own special interests. Hara and Katō, perhaps drawing on British notions of holding two conferences, initially favored separating naval from diplomatic issues. Foreign Minister Uchida, perhaps fearing that the Anglo-Saxons would use naval issues to force concessions on diplomatic ones, took an even more cautious stand. Would it not be better, the foreign minister asked, to express agreement on arms limitation and ask Washington to clarify the scope of other issues it proposed to discuss? Uchida's suggestion readily won cabinet approval.[27]

The cabinet's cautious response was well taken. Editors and politicians welcomed the prospect of arms limitation talks, but succumbed to a profound sense of uneasiness about diplomatic issues just as they had in 1918–19. Katō Kōmei said he thought it was a mistake to agree to combine the discussion of naval and Far Eastern issues. A worried delegation from the House of Peers sought reassurances from the Foreign Ministry. The *Kokumin shinbun* editorialized that at any conference Japan would be "drubbed and mauled by the Powers" for supposed past misdeeds in China. In short, Harding's invitation awakened nationalistic impulses and fears of inferiority that could very well serve to strengthen Hara's domestic enemies and weaken his leadership.[28]

The call to Washington increased mounting interservice tensions. The cabinet's decision of July 12 helped tip the balance of intranaval opinion in favor of an arms limitation agreement. The definite shift became obvious on July 21, when the Committee for the Study of League of Nations Affairs submitted its report. Its authors, quite unlike their American counterparts, detected real advantages for the navy in disarmament. The international environment, as officers returning from Europe and America had long since made clear, was changing. Borah had widespread support in America, and Great Britain simply could not afford competitive naval expansion. There was a real possibility that the two Anglo-Saxon giants would combine, agree on arms limitation, and then try to force their decisions on Japan. To head off that eventuality, and to dispel foreign suspicions of the empire and enhance its security, the naval experts advised that Tokyo make its own positive arms limitation proposals.[29]

But what ought these proposals to be? The experts suggested proceeding from a general agreement on the standards of limitation to specific relationships among the three greatest naval powers. They presented exhaustive data on the merits of limiting budgets, personnel, and specific construction programs. They concluded, however, that the numbers and size of capital ships, together with the total tonnage of auxiliary vessels, was the most advantageous yardstick of limitation for Japan to use. Limiting numbers of capital ships would permit agreement on comparative strength ratios. Setting limits on their dimensions would prevent drastic and expensive changes like those the *Dreadnought* had occasioned, yet permit competition in technological excellence, where Japanese naval architects would triumph. Imposing the broadest possible limit on the construction of other types, moreover, would diminish the significance of the Westerners' lead in aviation and submarine technology; yet it would also leave these newer weapons, considered by many as the "weapon of the weak," for use against possible naval invaders of the western Pacific.

The committee argued that international limitations would improve Japan's standing among the powers. If competition continued, the empire's present 8.3 to 10 ratio in capital ships with 13.5 inch or larger guns would only change to Japan's disadvantage. If, on the other hand, total tonnage of all types of vessels were taken as the standard of measurement, an agreement might be drawn that would lift Japan from her present ratio of approximately 6 to 10 vis à vis the United States Navy to nearly 7 to 10. The latter figure had been considered the ideal by strategists since the end of the Russo-Japanese War. Consequently the committee went even further than Admiral Katō had in his public statements. It said that the navy could safely abandon the eight-eight fleet building program and agree on the standard for limitation of ships already built and currently under construction. This would leave Tokyo with three post-Jutland capital ships, permit completion of ships already on the ways, and allow negotiators to bargain down to the level of the 1917 eight-four expansion program.

This proposal in itself demanded that Admiral Katō take positive steps within the navy for policy changes that went beyond the spring's decisions to economize and temporize in expansion. But it made an even more significant demand on his leadership—one that touched the broader politics of national defense. The naval experts argued that inferiority to Britain and America was acceptable only if fortifications in the Anglo-Saxons' western Pacific territories were limited or destroyed. The committee pointed out that

> the fact that the Imperial Navy today is readily able to maintain the national defense against the United States Navy depends principally upon the fact that the United States has insufficient advanced bases in the Pacific and the Far East. If . . . the [Americans] were to complete the necessary military facilities . . . our strategic relationship would take on a completely new aspect. The disadvantages [for] the Empire would most certainly be unendurable.

Japanese experts felt that the American Congress was unlikely to fund base development at Guam and the Philippine Islands. These experts knew something of Jellicoe's recommendations and, in all probability, knew about the Penang Conference discussions. To maximize the advantage to Japan, the committee favored the broadest of three limitation schemes, one which would hold Singapore and Hong Kong, as well as American bases, at no more than present levels of development. To make this proposal attractive to London and Washington, the naval experts suggested that Tokyo should stop work on army fortifications being built in the Ogasawara and Amami Ōshima islands and limit those on Taiwan and the Pescadores.

The authors of the report obviously regarded the proposed talks in Washington as a great opportunity for the Japanese navy, for now the service could escape the obloquy brought on by making ever larger budget demands, cooperate in reducing international tensions, and at the same time keep its newest ships and secure its strategic position. The committee's proposal turned, however, on two assumptions. First, it presumed that Admiral Katō could lead the navy from expansion to limitation without creating serious internal disruptions. This supposition appeared to be grounded in fact, for when senior admirals met at the Imperial Palace on August 4, they almost certainly approved the general outlines of the committee proposal.[30] Secondly, the July report assumed that Admiral Katō and Prime Minister Hara would be able to persuade army leaders to agree, at the very least, to changes in the coastal fortifications program. In short, the committee report presumed that Tokyo's leaders could define a consensus on arms limitation.

But while navy experts hoped for consensus, the army moved in precisely the opposite direction. The sailor's opportunity loomed as the soldiers' nightmare. General Uehara, suspecting a covert assault on Japan's continental beachheads in the American conference proposal, delayed his retirement. The very day the cabinet considered Harding's invitation, General Ugaki recorded his doubts in his diary. Even Tanaka Giichi, convalescing in retirement, advised Prime Minister Hara against making any troop withdrawals from the continent. General Ugaki harbored another fear, one which seemed to have some basis in realtiy: arms limitation talks might foster domestic attacks on Japan's military decision-making system. Early in August, General Miura Gorō, a behind-the-scenes political manipulator and member of the Privy Council, proposed that Tokyo abolish the general staff system. A few days later, newspapers carried reports that Prince Konoe, a young but influential member of the House of Peers (and future prime minister), favored drastic revisions in the national security decision-making system.[31]

With these fears in the darker recesses of their minds, army leaders had to answer more immediate questions. Might arms limitation require new internal national defense agreements? Or should the army, despite what the navy might do, insist on preserving force levels projected in the past (that is, by the national defense compromise of 1918) or those actually realized in postwar budgets? Gradually but unmistakably army opinion crystallized around the latter alternative. Late in July the British military attaché reported that War Minister Yamanashi looked on the Washington talks "with great disfavor." By mid-August the war minister had unofficially designated General Tanaka Kunishige as army representative in those negotiations. Tanaka proved anything but friendly to the navy when inter-ministry preparatory talks began on August 16. The two services deadlocked immediately over whether or not to insist on force levels agreed upon in 1920 discussions of arms limitation. The question was referred to a subcommittee, but that group agreed only on vague principles to guide subsequent discussions. According to the subcommittee's guidelines, the army would not interfere with navy efforts to define terms for naval limitation and would not object to putting naval before diplomatic issues on the Washington agenda. But these principles meant nothing in practice. General Tanaka Kunishige insisted that the standards of strength agreed upon in 1920 should not be jeopardized in any international negotiations. The deadlock on this point was complete—before navy spokesmen even raised the equally disturbing question of Pacific island fortifications.[32]

Prime Minister Hara moved subtly and boldly to deal with mounting interservice friction. Hoping to soften army resistance to change, he put off withdrawals from Shantung, Siberia, and Manchuria and directed Uchida to clear up uncertainties about the conference agenda with Washington. By late July, Tokyo announced a formula that relieved anxieties among the generals and the public. Tokyo's representatives would not discuss purely bilateral issues or questions touching on past bilateral agreements at Washington. That is, Hara would not allow the great powers to call Tokyo on the carpet over wartime China policies, as former Prime Minister Ōkuma had feared they would. Hara's announcement produced sighs of relief in the press and enabled him to persuade the cabinet to agree on a strategy for seeking solutions to the Yap, Siberian, and Shantung questions outside the framework of the formal Washington conference. Uchida, in the meantime, kept up the fight with Hughes over the specific agenda. By late August the foreign minister had made enough of a show to convince the cabinet to accept Harding's formal invitation to the conference.[33]

Hara acted far more boldly, and with a definite eye to domestic bureaucratic politics, in dealing with the navy. While the interservice quarrel brewed, he toured Hokkaido and his home province in northeastern Japan. The theme of strength recurred in his speeches. Although he spoke of Japan's need for strength to compete peacefully with the other powers, Hara thought of domestic power, too. It was during this journey that he made probably his single most important decision for arms limitation: Hara determined to ask Admiral Katō to go to Washington for the conference. This was a choice made in virtual defiance of diplomatic considerations. The very day Hara informed Uchida of his decision, Hughes told Shidehara it would be best to keep admirals and generals off the delegations. Yet despite knowledge of the American view, despite his concern to improve American-Japanese relations, and despite his interest in destroying Japan's militarist image abroad, Hara on August 24, 1921, asked Admiral Katō to become a delegate to the conference.[34]

The choice was a masterstroke in domestic political terms. The admiral was the man most likely to unite the navy behind whatever compromises might be negotiated. His professional prestige would help insulate the government from possible ultranationalist criticism. Katō had proven cooperative and loyal in past domestic political crises. With his support, Hara might find it easier to break army resistance to compromise on continental Asian diplomatic issues. Hara did not voice these arguments to Katō, but he did suggest that domestic political considerations were foremost in his thoughts. When the admiral protested that Vice Admiral Saitō Makoto, his predecessor, had greater experience and linguistic skills, Hara reminded him of that admiral's involvement in the explosive inter-service conflicts of the prewar years.[35]

Admiral Katō asked for time to consider Hara's offer, but he obviously saw advantages in it. He went immediately from the prime minister's villa to the Foreign Ministry, where he reemphasized his desire to keep naval issues free of diplomatic tangles. Brushing over his subordinates' disagreements, Katō told Uchida that he and War Minister Yamanashi could deal with disarmament questions. Uchida agreed with this assertion and said that diplomatic problems could be left to Ambassador Shidehara. While the admiral's biographers have interpreted this conversation as a sign of his humility, in fact it was a crucial step in securing virtually complete power to make arms limitation decisions. Having secured the approval of naval elders Tōgō and Inoue for his going to Washington, Katō then sought Hara's aid in overcoming army resistance to arms limitation. Once the prime minister promised to get Marshal Yamagata's help in overcoming the resistance, Katō formally accepted the offer to go to Washington.[36]

His acceptance profoundly influenced subsequent preparations for the conference and raised the possibility of broad changes in the politics of national defense. Katō was a brilliant, energetic, perhaps even politically ambitious man. As senior delegate to the Washington talks, he had an interest in their outcome that transcended the narrow professional concerns of General Board admirals or Beatty's nightmares about presiding over the demise of the Royal Navy. Arms limitation afforded Katō not only the opportunity to assure the strength of the Japanese navy, but also the chance to secure his own power and reputation within it. Carefully selecting those who would accompany him was one way of pursuing both goals. He weighted the experts' group with veterans of the Committee for the Study of League of Nations Affairs and officers with experience and friendly feeling toward the United States. Rejecting suggestions that Rear Admiral Moriyama Keisaburō, a general staff officer interested in continental expansion and fearful of American strategic encirclement, head the experts' group, Katō chose Rear Admiral Katō Kanji for the position. President of the Naval War College in 1921, Katō knew English well and had a record of cooperation with Americans and Britons during the Siberian intervention.[37]

The navy minister was prepared to take risks for arms limitation.

Gradually he maneuvered his colleagues away from the retention of a set ratio as the best definition of naval security. On August 25 his expert committee provided new figures which showed that the fleet would have a total tonnage equal to 52 percent of America's by the end of 1921 and would have only 10 percent more tonnage by 1925, when the American 1916 program would be completed. Moreover, if construction of the eight-eight fleet were continued until 1927, the Imperial Navy would still be 200,000 tons weaker than its American rival. These statistics suggested that Tokyo was far, and would remain far, from the 70 percent ideal championed by strategists. As if to confirm these findings, Rear Admiral Katō Kanji, the man who later made so much of specific ratios, wrote an article in September which argued against defining security in terms of any particular ratio. Instead, he asserted, possession of a strong fleet, solid strategic position, and adequate industrial and financial resources would assure the empire's safety.[38]

The navy minister also eased his colleagues away from continuing naval construction. In July navy experts had thought of limitation in terms of future expansion programs, but by late September they and Admiral Katō had reached the conclusion that something very close to "stop now" would be best. To prevent completion of the American 1916 program, a goal which from Tokyo's point of view seemed the essence of London's interest in arms limitation, Japan would have to stop work on her own eight-eight plan. The experts argued, in utter disregard of the figures they themselves had produced in late August, that there would be little difference in comparative strength terms in stopping in 1922, 1925, or 1927. They proposed, in the interests of demonstrating amity toward the United States, that it would be best to halt construction as early as January 1, 1922.[39]

The inconsistencies in this argument offer insights into the intraservice politics of limitation. Although detailed evidence is lacking, there can be little doubt that there were sharp differences among the admirals over limitation by international agreement. The British naval attaché in Tokyo suspected that the ratio of capital ship strength against the U.S. Navy was the major point of dispute. Unable to completely eliminate differences among the admirals, Katō sought to smoothe them over. Before he went to Washington, he indicated that cuts in the naval budget certain to divide the navy and lower its morale would not be acceptable.[40]

As a delegate, Katō could afford to gloss over other conflicts in the name of tactical flexibility and did so on two fundamental issues. While he mentioned the 10 to 7 strength ratio before the Foreign Affairs Advisory Council, final official instructions for the delegates stressed "adjusting to the circumstances of the conference." Neither these instructions nor final ones for naval representatives demanded preservation of a 70 percent ratio versus the American or British navy. The admiral used the same compromise technique to deal with Pacific island fortification limits. In September Foreign Ministry officials argued that naval issues must be quickly resolved to demonstrate Japan's sincerity in seeking solutions to diplomatic problems; yet Vice Minister Ide Kenji, reacting to army obstructionism, insisted that limits on Pacific island fortifications were the sine qua non of any possible agreement. When Foreign Ministry officials hinted that to insist on this point would be poor negotiating tactics, Admiral Katō used their arguments to conceal a major shift in the navy's position. The matter would be postponed, Katō said, and raised at the "appropriate" moment in the conference.[41]

Verbal compromises of this sort might have overcome second-level objections to particular arms limitation proposals, but they were useless when it came to fundamental principles. Try as he might, Hara could not break down army resistance to change. He visited Marshal Yamagata and urged him to quiet obstructionists on the general staff. Later Hara tried to remove General Tanaka Kunishige from the Washington delegation by suggesting that the general would not get along personally with Admiral Katō. But maneuvers and arguments of this sort had no effect on Yamagata, who had twice listened to General Uehara's objections to arms limitation. Tanaka Giichi would do nothing to remove his namesake, and War Minister Yamanashi told Hara that change was impossible. The prime minister had no more success in seeking substantive changes in army policies. Press reports to the contrary, War Minister Yamanashi simply could not overcome General Uehara's opposition. As finally written, instructions for army representatives offered cuts of up to 20 percent in projected eventual strength—precisely the position the generals had taken a year earlier. Adamancy on this point indicated that army representatives were not about to open negotiations in Tokyo on force levels and budget programs.[42]

Army resistance was not simply blind obstructionism, for Hara gave those who opposed him good reason to suspect that arms limitations in Washington might threaten their positions in Tokyo. The very day Katō agreed to go to the conference, Hara hinted that he would like to become acting navy minister in the admiral's absence, thus breaking the tradition of having only officers on active duty head service ministries. Admiral Katō did not express opposition, but merely indicated his desire not to allow a powerful rival to settle into the navy minister's chair while he was away. Hara let the issue lapse until the cabinet had approved Kato's designation as a delegate. The prime minister then announced that the Legal Affairs Bureau would examine the constitutional question of his serving as interim navy minister.[43]

Several motives lay behind Hara's decision. One, certainly, was the prime minister's often repeated desire to dispel the militarist image of Japan abroad, an impression which numerous editors claimed Katō's appointment confirmed. Another was to strengthen Hara's personal ties with the navy minister when those with the army were weakening. But it is difficult to avoid the conclusion that Hara had far broader political considerations in mind. A man as shrewd, fond of power, and sensitive to changes in the current of opinion around him as Hara could not have been blind to the possibilities of broad political change that arms limitation offered. Although he was outwardly indifferent to Ozaki's appeal and even brusque in reacting to the businessmen's arms limitation resolution, the prime minister could not have missed the shift in public attitudes that editors and diplomats noted in September and October 1921. There appeared to be overwhelming support for arms limitation. If Hara capitalized on it, he might weaken the influence of conservative generals and elder statesmen, his enemies in the struggle for influence in court politics. He might also make himself the symbol of progressive conservatism, ushering in changes in civil-military relations that men like Ozaki, Yoshino Sakuzō, and Prince Konoe championed. Indeed, Hara may well have thought of becoming a far more popular leader in an era when more and more politicians, journalists, and citizens championed democracy.[44]

The prime minister told Prince Saionji that he wanted to assert civilian primacy by serving as interim navy minister and fought hard to get the army to agree to his proposal. The best he could wring out of even progressive leaders like Tanaka Giichi was grudging concurrence—on the condition that what applied to the navy by no means be considered a precedent for the army. Yet Hara acted both privately and publicly to set precedents and establish his primacy. Summoning Rear Admiral Katō Kanji to his villa, he stressed the urgency of arms limitation. Hara told the younger Katō that he understood how difficult it was to give up cherished building programs and definitions of security but demanded that the admiral follow Katō Tomosaburō in doing so. Shortly before the delegates left Tokyo, Hara took part in a widely publicized ceremony at the Navy Ministry. There Admiral Katō publicly assented to the changes Hara had wrought. He instructed his subordinates to give Hara as interim navy minister their fullest cooperation and obedience.[45]

A few days later Hara Kei did something which David Lloyd George had avoided: he went to Tokyo Station to bid farewell to Admiral Katō and the other delegates as they began their journey to the Washington conference.[46] This gesture pointed, once again, to the fact that arms limitation had become an issue of great personal and political concern to the prime minister. That truth guided him, as it did Admiral Katō, in the decisions for arms limitation. Those choices, to be sure, turned on Hara's and Katō's assessments of changing international conditions. Both men sensed that the international system was shifting from tension and arms expansion to cooperation and arms limitation. Tokyo's decisions flowed, too, from these leaders' awareness of the high finance costs and heavy political burdens that continued naval building entailed.

But those imperatives became meaningful and prompted action only when Hara Kei and Katō Tomosaburō understood their domestic political significance. The admiral perceived positive gains for the navy in arms limitation by international agreement; and unlike his British and American counterparts, he tied his personal, professional, and political future to its attainment. Hara Kei likewise ran the risk of having to make compromises at Washington because he saw advantages in Tokyo to be gained through them. This common understanding of the domestic political advantages of naval limitation underlay Hara and Katō's willingness to accept the imprecisions and uncertainties of the formal instructions prepared for the Washington conference delegates. That willingness also rested on Hara and Katō's faith that they had the strength and wisdom to overcome the obstacles at home and abroad to a naval arms limitation agreement.

The Washington conference would subject that faith to the severest possible tests.

12 Washington Again: The Arms Limitation Achievement

The Washington conference opened a day late. The Harding administration delayed it to remind the world of a key fact: the limitation of armaments that millions hoped for was a direct consequence of the war that had just passed. The message was clear and its staging spectacular. The president had proclaimed November 11, 1921, the third anniversary of armistice, a national holiday. He and the conference delegates joined the throngs who streamed across the Potomac to Arlington National Cemetery for the burial of America's Unknown Soldier. There Harding set the tone for the talks to come. He reminded all that the conscience of humanity denounced armed conflict —in the past and in the future. With characteristic simplicity he insisted, "It must not be again."[1]

The next day Harding spoke again, this time to open the conference meeting in Constitution Hall. After the president formally convened the conference, Secretary of State Hughes stepped to the rostrum. Hughes began what sounded like the typical address of welcome and introduction, but then in words which overwhelmed his audience, the secretary dropped the bomb he had been preparing over the preceding weeks. He announced that the United States was willing to scrap most of the ships in its 1916 program and to abandon its 1918 expansion scheme. In return, Washington would expect London and Tokyo to cut their fleets to attain a 5-5-3 ratio in capital ship strength. The secretary continued by suggesting corresponding reductions in the auxiliary surface ship strength of the three greatest naval powers and proposing limits on submarine strength. Then, as the galleries gasped surprise and applauded approval, Hughes listed the specific ships—American, British, and Japanese —to be scrapped. These proposed reductions, as an American journalist recalled, brought British admirals to the edge of their chairs as if they were dozing bulldogs suddenly kicked by a traveling salesman.[2]

Historians from that moment on have been fascinated by Hughes's address. They have looked upon the bombshell speech as the first in a series of negotiating pyrotechnics that determined the outcome of the Washington talks; in so doing they have narrowed and possibly misdirected the spotlight of historical inquiry. What happened at Washington did depend on the negotiating skills of individual delegates, but the conference results also turned on the outcome of critical debates within governments. These intragovernmental debates considered how reduction of international political tensions and establishment of a new naval order might affect particular national interests. To an even greater degree, however, the discussions focused on another, related question: What impact would an international arms limitation agreement have on the domestic politics of national defense? Put another way, the statesmen and admirals of 1921 had to consider how agreements proposed at Washington might enhance, protect, or harm their particular interests at home. The actions of their representatives and, indeed, the fate of the conference depended on their answers to that question. The conference would succeed only to the degree that its agreements suited the particular domestic political interests of Japanese, British, and American leaders.

No two statesmen were more keenly aware of that fact than Warren G. Harding and Charles Evans Hughes. The secretary's speech was the opening gun in a campaign to transform the politics of arms control and assure the domestic political success of the administration. The gun's report echoed the next morning in the Sunday editions of newspapers. The *New York Times*, for example, devoted thirteen pages to the conference opening, making it impossible for readers to miss the importance of events at Washington. Senator Hiram Johnson, progressive and irreconcilable though he was, sensed what his political enemies had done. The conference, he wrote, "obscures everything else." Hughes's speech, said Johnson, was "one of the most clever things that has ever been done in world politics," but Harding,

"a Child of Destiny," was ultimately responsible for it. The California
senator predicted that the president's luck and the fact that the conference
blotted out the domestic failures of his administration would "save him from
Wilson's fate." Former senator Sutherland of Utah, now chairman of the
American delegation's Advisory Committee, crowed that the conference
would enable Republicans to roll back recent Democratic victories in his
state's off-year elections. Even Borah had to admit that the talks had begun
in "splendid fashion." The senator's role had shrunk to pressuring the
administration not to conclude an entangling alliance in the Pacific or to
backslide before expected British and Japanese objections to Hughes's
proposals.[3]

The secretary of state intended his speech to diminish the force of
objections like Borah's. By dramatizing Washington's will to change,
Hughes hoped to capture the enthusiasm of ordinary citizens in Tokyo and
London and make it more difficult for their leaders to object to his scheme.
Immediate reactions in London suggested that his hopes were not completely
in vain. Leading politicians of every persuasion praised his efforts. Labour's
G. N. Barnes said that while the League had "nibbled" at disarmament,
Hughes had "tackled" it. Former Liberal prime minister Asquith said more
had been accomplished in a week at Washington than in the preceding three
years. Even the normally taciturn Unionist Bonar Law, now drawn out of
semiretirement by the Irish question, called Washington "a flash of sunlight." But the mood in Britain was not as expectant and euphoric as it was
in Washington. The *Times* noted this difference and attributed it to recent
history: after the hopes and disappointments created by international
conferences since the armistice, Britons were not able to expect very much of
this one. *The Nation*, by contrast, pointed to the absence of strong objections
to the anticipated outcome of the Washington talks as proof that the people
would accept the passing of British sea supremacy "without a murmur."[4]

Their leaders most certainly would not. Hughes's "really magnificent and
stunning" proposals demanded a British response. Balfour gave it in a very
general way in his speech accepting the American idea "in principle" on
November 15. His vagueness hid the fact that considerable differences
existed within his delegation and within the Lloyd George government over
priorities in arms limitation. The poles of opinion were clearest within the
delegation at Washington. Canada's Sir Robert Borden represented one
extreme. He pointed out that the Americans had been extraordinarily
generous in offering to scrap most of their 1916 program; their capacity to
outstrip Britain in competition of any kind was obvious. Consequently,
Borden advised, London ought to agree with Washington as rapidly and
completely as possible. By doing so, British leaders would escape the danger
that "the sailors" would divert them from the proper course and reach the
safe harbor of firm Anglo-American friendship.[5]

David Beatty reacted instinctively against this kind of thinking. Although he exuded optimism in public, he privately feared that Hughes's proposal had "for its object the extinction of naval power." It smacked of that in two ways. First, it left unacceptably vague the post-limitation balance of naval power in Europe. Beatty was ready to accept parity with Washington, but his experts wanted 60 percent superiority over any European power or combination of powers. Beatty also worried about extending any ratio to auxiliary as well as to capital ships. Such an extension might denude the empire of cruisers needed to protect its sea lanes. But the admiral concentrated his heaviest fire on the "stop now" feature of Hughes's proposal. Beatty talked about the risks of dangerous, destabilizing competition after so prolonged a holiday and openly worried about the waste of Britain's industrial and technological lead in naval construction. His arguments were strong enough to command a consensus within the British delegation about proceeding slowly on this "stop now" aspect of arms limitation. [6]

Assistant Secretary of the Navy Theodore Roosevelt, Jr., picked up tidbits of Beatty's arguments and quickly concluded that the admiral was "not intelligent" and was deliberately stalling in talks among naval experts. But in fact Beatty was extraordinarily shrewd—and anxious to protect his service's domestic political interests. The admiral correctly surmised that other naval men, Americans or Japanese, would discern and object to the flaws in Hughes's proposal. For this reason, opposing "stop now" need not affront the Americans. Beatty was also keenly aware of the psychological importance of continued building—even if, as Lee suggested, it was deemed "replacement" building. Ships on the ways on the Clyde and the Tyne were that very ocular demonstration of naval power so essential to Admiralty victories in the budget battles of Whitehall and Westminster. New ships, the need to excel, the pride of technological excellence—all were necessary to good naval morale. For this reason, shortly before he left Washington, Beatty told his chief deputy, Rear Admiral Chatfield, that it would be best to oppose limitations on auxiliary craft. The progress of such craft—and the challenge they posed—would insure the continued need to build capital ships. Finally, the admiral believed that continued construction was economically feasible and politically desirable in the fight against unemployment. [7]

The admiral's arguments appealed to Balfour's innate sense of balance and, perhaps, to the old diplomat's latent concern about the political fate of those who would yield Britain's traditional sea supremacy. They ran, however, against the drift of feeling in London. There Lloyd George acted with deceptive decisiveness impossible in Washington or Tokyo. When buttonholed and asked for his opinion on Beatty's arguments as cabled from Washington, the prime minister replied snappishly: Britain simply could not afford continued capital ship construction or competition in battleship armament and design. The Board of Trade was no less abrupt: the broad economic and industrial gains from arms limitation far outweighed the temporary costs of unemployment in the shipyards. On November 18 the government acted on these conclusions and ordered contractors to stop work on the four battleships approved in August. Moreover even those threatened by unemployment through this decision looked philosophically upon it. A *Times* reporter at Newcastle found those out of jobs feeling that the change was necessary for the progress of humanity.[8]

But in fact the significance of the decision to stop work was more limited. London was changing its negotiating strategy rather than fundamental assumptions about national security. Admiralty representatives recoiled in alarm as king, cabinet, and C.I.D. moved toward the conclusion that more, rather than less, limitation was in Britain's best interest. The debate took place within the C.I.D., where Churchill proposed an elaborate ruse to quiet Admiral Beatty's fears of the French and reduce threats to Britain's European naval hegemony. He recommended that London strongly object to the absence of restraints on French land and air power; Curzon proceeded to do just that in a published luncheon address. Churchill suggested that the French, as Premier Briand demonstrated, would reject military limitations. London would then offer to accept this rejection if Paris agreed to abolish the submarine. In this way the external threat, another continental challenge to the capital ship, would be removed, and the internal danger—continued, expensive, and increasingly unpopular battleship construction—would be eliminated.[9]

This scheme for broader naval limitation had definite political appeal in London. It would please nationalists by preserving British maritime hegemony in Europe and Royal Naval pride; yet by eliminating the need for building or modifying capital ships to match submarine technological advances, Churchill's plan would cut budgets and win Liberal arms control advocates' support. Little wonder that civilian members of the C.I.D. favored the plan and even succeeded in persuading Vice Admiral H. F. Oliver, the second sea lord, to put aside his objections to it. But what appealed to London appalled in Washington. When Balfour received instructions based on C.I.D. conclusions, the old diplomat "threatened to chuck the whole show." With biting sarcasm he complained that the scheme was jejeune and dangerous. In their pursuit of the will-of-the-wisp of submarine abolition (and with it domestic popularity), he asserted, the government ran the risk of letting Paris wreck the Washington talks. Balfour said he would try to carry out London's orders but insisted that the government respect priorities implicit in previous discussions of arms limitation policy, namely, that it was imperative to conclude a capital ship limitation agreement and to reduce Pacific international political tensions. To achieve these fundamental objectives, he preferred not to dally with the French but to support the Americans in their efforts to overcome Japanese objections to Hughes's proposals.[10]

Those objections did not come from Katō Tomosaburō. Immediately after Hughes's speech the admiral rode back in silence to the Shoreham Hotel, musing, as an aide surmised, that the fate of the eight-eight fleet was sealed. But if this was his thought, he made no mention of it in an interview with the *Jiji* naval correspondent. Katō simply expressed approval "in principle" of the American proposals and repeated that thought in his formal reply to Hughes. Then he waited silently and let others voice objections to the American proposals. From the Navy Ministry came the demand that Japan retain twelve capital ships instead of the ten Hughes proposed. The ministry insisted that the newest and largest of these ships, the *Mutsu*, should be among them. In Washington Katō Tomosaburō proposed to try to hold to the 10-7 capital ship ratio that had long been the standard of naval security. But it was the younger Katō who bristled at Theodore Roosevelt, Jr., and objected to the tonnage basis on which Hughes had based his calculations. In the experts' discussions Katō Kanji opposed the technical basis of Hughes's naval arithmetic, the 5-5-3 ratio, and the scrapping of the *Mutsu*. Meanwhile Japanese journalists at Washington split on the ratio question, and rifts developed within the delegation itself. Katō Kanji insisted on the 10-10-7 ratio one evening, only to have Prince Tokugawa imply the next day that that ratio was not the official Japanese position. News of such differences worried official Tokyo, and spokesmen for the Navy Ministry were quick to explain the rifts as a natural conflict between experts and generalists. But coupled with Katō Tomosaburō's silence, Japanese differences raised doubts in Washington. Was Tokyo toying with negotiating tactics, or did something larger loom behind Japanese objections?[11]

Changes that swept over Tokyo after the delegates' departure for the Washington conference made that question difficult to answer. On November 4, 1921, an assassin struck down Hara Kei at Tokyo Station. The prime minister's death shook the Japanese political world and opened a Pandora's box of troubles for Katō Tomosaburō. It took the elder statesmen nearly a week to agree on Hara's successor, Finance Minister Takahashi Korekiyo. Takahashi was a weak compromise candidate whom many observers did not expect to stay in office for long. His demands for economy and his opposition to the Siberian expedition had long since alienated him from army leaders. His weak ties with the Seiyūkai made party chieftains, especially Education Minister Nakahashi, suspicious and jealous. Even Foreign Minister Uchida harbored bitter feelings toward the new prime minister, for Uchida had dreamed of succeeding Hara himself.[12]

In Washington Katō Tomosaburō did not know what the balance of forces and clashes of ambition within the new government were. But one point was clear: Hara's loss was of immense significance. Takahashi lacked the prestige and finesse necessary to negotiate bureaucratic compromises important to diplomatic accommodation at Washington. The signs of weakness appeared immediately after his accession. The new prime minister reaffirmed his commitment to Hara's arms limitation policies but told the American ambassador that Katō Tomosaburō was the one to decide on specific issues in dispute. This autonomy might have been acceptable to the admiral, but in fact Tokyo showed signs of taking the issues out of his hands. On November 22 the Foreign Affairs Advisory Council, which had previously endorsed a policy of flexibility, instructed the Japanese delegation to stand firm on a 10-10-7 ratio. This stand may have reflected politicians' fears of the public, for many newspapers had championed the 10-10-7 ratio, and members of the cabinet were well aware of the outbursts of public anger that followed the Shantung compromise in 1919 and those that marked the end of the Russo-Japanese and Sino-Japanese wars. But from Admiral Katō's point of view this apparent new adamancy may have signified something much more ominous: the beginnings of internal political and bureaucratic maneuvering that might block a naval limitation compromise.[13]

This new situation demanded caution—and strong leadership. Admiral Katō's admirers have explained his behavior as a response to the calls of statesmanship, rather than mere naval leadership. But in fact Katō maneuvered at Washington to protect both Japan's national interests and his personal political positions within and outside the navy. The critical question before him and the home government was not whether or not to compromise with the Americans and British on naval issues, but rather how to arrange that compromise to maximize gains and minimize damages to particular bureaucratic and political interests. On November 23 Katō cautiously outlined the alternatives open to Tokyo: he might stand firm against any compromise; he might fight for a 5-3.5 or 5-3 ratio and retention of the *Mutsu*; or he might accede to the American demand for a straight 5-3 ratio.[14]

Foreign Minister Uchida replied favoring either of the first two choices. He urged Katō to negotiate to preserve long-term harmony with the Americans, something hardly consistent with the first alternative of standing firm. Uchida then went on to direct that if it proved necessary to accept choices three or four, Katō should include Pacific island nonfortification in the bargain package. Such a condition would enable the weak Takahashi government to claim that losses on the ratio had been exchanged for greater geographic-strategic security. Uchida's directive reversed earlier Foreign Ministry arguments about the urgency of a naval accord; it also contradicted the logic of Katō's own naval experts' advice earlier in the year. Those advisors had given higher priority to island nonfortification than to achievement of a specific ratio. The foreign minister's instruction also reversed the balance of responsibilities that Katō had worked out with Hara. Instead of the prime minister's smoothing the way for compromise which the admiral considered necessary, Katō was now to negotiate with an eye toward shoring up the government's domestic prestige.[15]

The admiral may not have been fully aware of the ironies of this situation, but he saw intranavy advantages to be gained by taking a hard line on the *Mutsu*, even if compromise on the ratio subsequently proved necessary. Katō did not exactly follow the instructions Foreign Minister Uchida sent. To be sure, Katō's subordinates presented a memorandum on November 30 firmly restating the Japanese position in the naval experts committee. The tactic proclaimed the existence of a deadlock and forced naval questions on the heads of delegations for resolution. Katō, bolstered the following day by news of Admiral Tōgō's support, laid some of his cards on the table. The admiral told Balfour of the domestic political situation in Tokyo and explained the importance of avoiding a concession on the ratio issue "apparently forced on him by [the] United States government." Katō also mentioned the importance of keeping the *Mutsu*. But his chief concern was to propose compromise on the ratio issue if the United States would agree to preserve the status quo in fortifications on Hawaii, Guam, and the Philippines. Japan, in return, would not proceed with army coast defense programs on Formosa, the Pescadores, and Amami Ōshima island. Disregarding Foreign Minister Uchida's advice, the admiral made no mention of possible specific ratio figures under 10-7.[16]

Later that afternoon, Balfour told Hughes of his conversation with Admiral Katō. The secretary of state expressed surprise at the Pacific island fortification limit plan and reservations about Senate attitudes toward it. He then sketched his own ideas for a consultative mechanism to prevent violations of an agreement and promised to discuss the matter with President Harding. But Hughes was not surprised by Katō's proposal; months earlier State Department experts had predicted Tokyo would make it. In addition, the department was intercepting and decoding cables exchanged between Tokyo and its Washington delegates. These cables revealed a willingness to compromise on island fortification and other issues. Thus Hughes could more confidently maneuver in any agreements to protect the success which Harding sought. While naval experts drifted toward deadlock, Hughes steered the British and Japanese toward agreement on ending the Anglo-Japanese alliance. He guided the Chinese and Japanese into parallel talks on the explosive Shantung issue. Both problems had troubled the Senate in the past, and Hughes did not want to face them again. The secretary pressed Tokyo to yield on outstanding issues and, following Harding's earlier suggestion, he repeatedly warned the Japanese about the dangers of wrecking the conference. Finally Hughes and the American delegation had agreed that a specific naval ratio in the Pacific was of less importance than "stop now." In a moment of overstatement, the secretary of state had spoken of allowing Japan a 10-8 ratio if that would assure cessation of capital ship construction.[17]

Consequently Hughes and Harding found it easy to accept the essence of

Katō's proposal. Penurious congresses had time and again refused to fund fortifications for western Pacific island possessions, and the public reckoned security in capital ship terms anyway. If Hawaii were excluded from the scheme, the pain of breaking earlier pledges to General Board officers not to accept nonfortification would be softened. That afternoon Hughes engaged in some sharp horsetrading with Admiral Katō. He accepted the nonfortification idea, excluded Hawaii from it, and made clear his belief that nonfortification should extend to British possessions outside Australia and New Zealand as well. In return he stood firm on the 10-10-6 ratio. Nothing was said of the *Mutsu*. Instead Hughes let the burden of accepting or rejecting compromise fall upon Tokyo.[18]

Admiral Katō shrewdly increased the weight of that burden. He excluded the *Mutsu* from the compromise package and agreed to proceed with talks with the French on the proposed Four Power Pact substitute for the Anglo-Japanese alliance, even though Tokyo had not yet considered it. Katō then sent a series of cables to Tokyo that supplemented the pressures Hughes applied. Their message was clear: Naval limitation was a prize of great worth which Washington and London were determined to win; Tokyo must not lose the opportunity to share it. While Katō's arguments prevailed within the navy, they were accepted only with considerable difficulty by civilian political leaders. Until December 7 the feud between Prime Minister Takahashi and Education Minister Nakahashi threatened to destroy the cabinet. Weakened by this struggle, its members temporized before nationalist protests from within the Seiyūkai and the House of Peers. But Admiral Katō made his arguments prevail with the prime minister and Seiyūkai leaders. Reassured of the navy position by Vice Minister Ide Kenji, the Foreign Affairs Advisory Council accepted compromise on the naval ratio, provided that the *Mutsu* was retained and Pacific island fortification limits agreed on. Yet in agreeing to compromise, Privy Councillor Itō Miyoji, Army Minister Yamanashi, and Kokumintō leader Inukai Ki made no attempt to hide either their fears of further compromise or their scorn for Takahashi and Uchida.[19]

These Japanese decisions confronted Americans and Britons with difficult choices. Hughes was well aware of this. The *Mutsu* threatened the aspect of his arms limitation proposal that had aroused the widest support. If Japan kept her, Britain and America would have to seek compensation—and continue to build capital ships. Concession on this point would be a highly visible departure from Hughes's original proposal, one likely to stir the suspicions and energies of Senator Borah. Anxious for counsel, Hughes turned to Admiral Coontz: Was the Japanese claim that the ship was complete and thus exempt from scrapping correct? The chief of naval operations replied affirmatively. American experts had erred in listing the *Mutsu* as incomplete. This error gave Hughes an excuse for modifying his original proposal, Admiral Katō the retention of the newest and largest ship in the fleet, and the Takahashi cabinet the symbol of resistance to American demands it coveted.[20]

While Tokyo wanted to exploit this compromise for domestic political purposes, Washington wanted to play it down and minimize its effect on the overall limitation agreement. Admiral Katō sensed this and offered to scrap the *Settsu*, an older battleship, in order to keep the *Mutsu*. Hughes seized this opportunity to resolve what Assistant Secretary of the Navy Theodore Roosevelt, Jr., had predicted would be "a real crisis" with the British. The secretary made two specific proposals to Balfour. The first would have allowed London to build two capital ships of nearly 50,000 tons and scrap five others in return; the second, which Hughes strongly favored, would have limited the ships built in compensation for the *Mutsu* to 35,000 tons and required the destruction of only four others. Here again the secretary was following the strategy of putting the burden of choice—and the blame for change—on his negotiating partners.[21]

The bases for making a choice between the proposals differed greatly in Washington and London. The notion that specific naval interests could be protected in an arms limitation agreement died hard within the British Empire Delegation at Washington. Balfour accepted Rear Admiral Chatfield's arguments about the advantages of building smaller capital ships; to build them would leave Britain a larger number of battleships. Moreover, despite Japanese and American opposition, Balfour tried even after the last formal negotiating session to further London's advantage by making legend tonnage the standard for defining the size of ships to be built in compensation for the *Mutsu*. The old diplomat claimed that his independent decision to yield on this point was necessary to minimize "ill effects," that is, American doubts about British sincerity in arms limitation. One suspects that Balfour still hoped to find that middle way between traditional British sea supremacy and equality with the Americans.[22]

In London statesmen realized that the conference agreements were in fact that middle way. Lloyd George had long since directed that Balfour oppose Japanese retention of the *Mutsu* and stand firm on "moral ground" for the ten year holiday. When he heard rumors that British naval experts were conspiring with their American and Japanese counterparts to frustrate an agreement, Curzon pointedly reminded the delegation of the adverse reactions in the House of Commons and the financial consequences certain to come if the naval holiday scheme failed. The suggestion of professional disloyalty incensed Beatty, and he was quick to deny it upon returning to London. But the first sea lord found even Churchill cool toward him and Lloyd George unwilling to hear his arguments. Flush with success in his negotiations for an Irish settlement, the prime minister had no reason to credit Beatty's claims that "stop now" would cost twenty million pounds more per year than building and pose "grave dangers" to the security of empire.[23]

Instead, London congratulated its negotiators and shared in the momentary euphoria that followed the public announcement of success in Washington. Hughes called a plenary session of the conference to allow Henry Cabot Lodge to bury the Anglo-Japanese alliance in tons of rhetorical praise for the new Four Power Pact. The subsequent announcement of agreement on capital ship ratios and Pacific island fortification limits evoked ecstatic press reactions. The *St. Louis Globe Democrat* pointed out that despite compromise, Hughes had won the essence of his original proposal. One eager *New York Tribune* Washington bureau reporter claimed that the agreements would save one hundred million dollars a year, or about three dollars per taxpayer. Those on the inside of the talks shared this sense of accomplishment and the feeling that they had neared the limits of agreement. Balfour had argued in late November that a capital ship limitation agreement was the most that could be hoped for. Sir Maurice Hankey came to the same conclusion early in December, and Lee was extremely doubtful of progress in limiting other types of ships. At the White House, Hughes had spoken to Harding and Theodore Roosevelt, Jr. about future conferences, indicating that he did not expect the Washington meeting to resolve everything.[24]

Yet despite their sense of achievement and recognition that they had neared the limits of agreement, the negotiators were still far from a final accord. Six weeks and several bitter battles would pass before they could leave the conference table. While the issues that remained ostensibly concerned broadening and completing the naval accords, they were something more than troublesome details. The capital ship ratio had to be extended to the French and Italian navies, and, if possible, expanded to limit surface and submarine auxiliary vessels. The details of Pacific island fortification limits had yet to be worked out. But in fact these remaining issues affected not so much the technical and international political dimensions of arms control as the particular domestic political and bureaucratic interests of statesmen and admirals. To win success, to protect those interests, remained the most important objective of the negotiators in Washington.

That intention was clearest in the American case. When news of the capital ship and Pacific island nonfortification agreements was released, there were shouts of joy and sighs of disappointment in the press. Senator Borah was quick to point out that the accords were imperfect and incomplete; whatever occurred at the conference, "however promising," was "only the first step." The senator called for the abolition of the submarine and limitation of other weapons. He also charged that "the Conference has not touched a single weapon of war with which the next war will be fought."

Then, twisting the British lion's tail just as he had in 1919, the Idahoan backed French claims for a capital ship ratio—parity with the Japanese—that would destroy Britain's European naval hegemony. Arguments of this sort, coming from Borah, were hardly likely to foster the image of success the Harding administration needed.[25]

Indeed the administration faced extremely delicate diplomatic and domestic political tasks as 1921 drew to a close. Harding wanted to protect the image of forceful leadership he hoped the conference presented. He and Hughes tried to convince the American public that the administration had gone as far as foreign negotiators would permit in pursuit of comprehensive naval limitation. The secretary of state had relatively little difficulty in convincing Americans of that fact when it came to extending the capital ship ratio agreement to France and Italy. Rome was agreeable, but Paris objected vehemently to the 1.75-1 ratio of battleship strength that Hughes proposed. The secretary then made the most of Wilsonian "open diplomacy." He tried to persuade Premier Brand to overrule French admirals at Washington on the capital ship issue and intimated that their resistance might wreck the conference. Hughes wanted the French to accept the proposed capital ship ratio without demanding freedom to build auxiliary craft in return. He appealed to the premier in a personal message, coached Ambassador Harvey to second his (Hughes's) arguments in London, and let the press know of his efforts. Yet Briand barely succeeded in persuading his cabinet colleagues to accept the capital ship ratio.[26]

Washington had extended the capital ship ratio to the lesser powers, but Harding and Hughes could not allow Paris to block progress in abolishing or limiting the submarine. They might well have said that in this case it was necessary to sacrifice principle to diplomatic reality, but such an argument would have laid the administration open to charges of hypocrisy like those Republican irreconcilables made against Wilson in 1919. Such a course would also "prove" Borah's charges of administration insincerity. To avoid these dangers, Hughes had the American Advisory Commission endorse General Board arguments against the abolition of the submarine. The commission concluded that subs were legitimate weapons and an inexpensive means of defending outlying island possessions. Hughes then went to Balfour in an attempt to work out a quiet settlement of the submarine issue. The secretary argued that the events of 1919 at Paris were likely to repeat themselves in 1921 at Washington. France, Italy, and Japan were certain to oppose submarine abolition. Would it not be wiser, Hughes suggested, to set a tonnage limit lower than that which he had originally proposed and agree on general rules governing the use of submarines? Here was precisely the right mix of pragmatism and morality needed to please American public opinion.[27]

Balfour could not accept so discreet a solution for the submarine problem, even though Hughes's proposal resembled his own suggestions of mid-November. While Balfour was personally inclined to finesse the submarine issue, he had to take account of sharp differences of opinion on it in London. There, a curious combination championed abolition: Labour and old-line pacifists favored it as a drastic measure against arms expansion; nationalists and those anxious to escape repetition of the submarine crisis of the recent war endorsed it; the king favored it; and Churchill backed it as a means of assuring Britain's hegemony in European waters—precisely the specific national naval interest that the editor of the *Saturday Review* wished the Washington negotiators would do more to protect. But the Admiralty opposed abolition. Naval advisors at Washington scorned the threat that hapless Frenchmen and Italians might pose against the Royal Navy. In London, Second Sea Lord Oliver had only with great reluctance yielded to Churchill's arguments in the C.I.D., and Beatty stood firm against them. Mindful always of the interests of his service, the admiral opposed abolition as an unnatural check on progress in surface and submarine weaponry essential to the morale and financial health of the naval service.[28]

In Washington Balfour planned to escalate discussions of the submarine issue from quiet colloquy to public debate only if the French refused both abolition and limits that left them inferior to the Royal Navy. Even before Admiral F. J. J. DeBon obliged by refusing, however, the first lord made the British case public: On December 22 he attacked the immorality of submarine warfare. Lee told Theodore Roosevelt, Jr., that his only interest was in strengthening the principle of abolition so that future conferences might agree on it, but in fact he acted for the benefit of London's arms control advocates and at the same time protected the Admiralty's particular interests. When Paris rejected abolition and limitation short of parity with Britain, Lee strengthened his admirals' case for continued submarine building. He delivered a scorching attack in which he quoted French Captain Castex's defense of the submarine as the sole means of bringing British naval hegemony to an end. This bit of open diplomacy buried abolition and left London free, as the Admiralty had hoped, of limits on antisubmarine surface auxiliary craft.[29]

At this point London might well have abandoned all efforts to limit submarines and other auxiliary vessels. Washington could not do so. Hughes admitted that he was "perplexed" about submarines. He toyed with further tonnage restrictions only to discover that Admiral Pratt, an "enlightened" naval advisor, strongly objected to anything short of the 10-10-6 ratio originally proposed. Yet mail condemning the Advisory Commission's defense of the submarine poured in. Hughes then seized upon a solution offered by Elihu Root. If it was impossible to abolish submarines or limit their construction, Root asked, why not control their uses? The Republican elder statesman proposed that unwarned submarine attacks on merchant vessels be deemed an act of piracy, "something," as he put it, "striking and vivid that could be easily grasped by the man in the street."[30]

Hughes fought for Root's proposals for the next ten days. But however sincere, legal, and moral they might have appeared to the American public, they were anathema to the negotiators at Washington. The Admiralty, as always, was wary of imposing artificial limits on the use of British sea power. Japanese naval experts, who had quietly opposed abolition from the very beginning of the conference, wanted to keep subs to attack an advancing enemy and to break blockades. Supported by the French and Italians, the Japanese raised the knotty problems posed by armed merchant ships. When the issue ran aground on this technical issue, the negotiators simply decided to leave the language on disputed points vague in what eventually became a separate treaty on submarine usage.[31]

This imprecise agreement was by no means the last to be written at Washington in January 1922. With one exception, the others concerned technical aspects of arms control that have been described elsewhere. But the dispute over article 19 of the naval treaty was different. The effort to write a Pacific island fortification limit agreement demonstrated how sensitive statesmen and admirals were to the domestic political consequences of arms control by international agreement. The controversy, aptly termed a squall by one historian, arose suddenly and unexpectedly; for a time it threatened to obscure the "flash of sunlight" at Washington. In December 1921 the negotiators had not been very precise about fortification limits. Hughes had excluded Hawaii from consideration, and Balfour had avoided mentioning Singapore. Admiral Katō had rejoiced that the American guns at Guam, which Tokyo cartoonists pointed at Mt. Fuji, would never be fired. Civilians in the Takahashi cabinet regarded controls on American bases as one more compensation for compromise on naval ratios.[32]

When the negotiators tried to make their agreement more precise, however, they found limitation of fortifications very difficult. Balfour, in a scheme which reflected intraimperial and bureaucratic desires, first proposed clarifications of the area in which bases were to be limited. The large parallelogram which he drew on the map of the Pacific conveniently exempted Singapore and the former German islands south of the equator from the terms of the agreement. In this way Balfour hoped to quiet Australasian fears for security against Japan and to protect the navy's imperial role and dreams of a Singapore base. But Balfour included the Ryūkyū and Bonin islands close to the Japanese homeland and the former German islands north of the equator in the fortification limitation zone. Tokyo was hardly likely to accept this inequity, and Katō Tomosaburō raised questions about the status of the Aleutian Islands. He did not do so for purely naval reasons. The younger Admiral Katō told Theodore Roosevelt, Jr., that the details of fortification limitation were of no great concern to the navy, but the elder Katō sensed that it had become an extremely important domestic political issue in Tokyo.[33]

A combination of nationalist pride, bureaucratic uncertainty, and political weakness made it important. Nationalists were already unhappy over the imprecise wording of the Four Power Pact. Did it guarantee the home islands' security or not? If it did, was this not humiliating for a power of the first rank? Ambassador Shidehara thought imprecision on this point wise, but Foreign Minister Uchida disagreed. Premature leaking of the terms of the pact already worried him. President Harding added to Uchida's woes by saying that he thought the agreement included the Japanese home islands. When Senators Lodge and Underwood warned Harding of possible Senate opposition to that interpretation, the president quickly reversed himself. This reversal alarmed Japanese nationalists already uneasy at the pact's imprecisions. They agreed with the cartoonist who depicted the United States as a wise old grandmother who took a big stick labeled "70% ratio" from the sleeping child Katō Tomosaburō and replaced it with a worthless bauble labeled "Four Power Pact." Late in December General Tanaka Kunishige cabled his objections to an agreement that might limit the empire's future southward expansion.[34]

The general's message reflected mounting army concern at developments in Washington and Tokyo. The fear that the Washington treaties portended major shifts in the climate of domestic political opinion could not be exorcised. General Ugaki, for one, thought the Takahashi regime spineless and unlikely to check the wave of antimilitary sentiment sweeping over the people. The size and power of that wave appeared to be growing daily. Back in September Ozaki Yukio had formed a league of journalists and intellectuals to promote arms limitation. In November the *Taiyō,* a leading journal of opinion, published a long article which demanded the abolition of separate service ministries and the establishment of a single ministry of defense. In January the same journal printed an assessment of the Washington agreements by Mizuno Hironori, a leading naval critic and former general staff member, that subtley endorsed army budget cuts. Shortly thereafter the Tokyo *Asahi shinbun* and the Kenseikai party conference called for military reductions. To prevent the politics of national defense from becoming dangerously unstable and to protect army interests, it seemed only reasonable to demand precise wording in the Four Power Pact and in the fortification limitations clause and to resist compromise on the Shantung issue.[35]

The Takahashi cabinet weakened before these military and nationalist pressures. Foreign Minister Uchida insisted that the negotiators exclude the home islands from the terms of the Four Power Pact. Then he supported General Tanaka Kunishige's arguments. Most alarming from a naval point of view was the foreign minister's expression of particular concern about the defenses of the Liaotung peninsula in Southern Manchuria, a key army position. Specific military needs on the peninsula, Uchida insisted, must be protected in any fortification limitation agreement. Moreover, the once docile Foreign Affairs Advisory Council demanded that the government take a strong line on these issues.[36]

These developments worried Admiral Katō in Washington. At first he tried to strengthen the government's case. He wrote Vice Minister Ide that the Seiyūkai, bereft of Hara's strong leadership, appeared to be having difficulty in shifting from strong support for arms expansion to acceptance of limitation and inferiority to the other two major naval powers. Katō told Ide to stand by Takahashi and Uchida in the coming Diet and evade precise statements about future naval policy. But after the first of the new year the admiral began to have second thoughts about the wisdom of this approach. He had repeatedly insisted that fortification limits on the islands in question had no real effect on national security; yet Tokyo refused to compromise. To test the government's intentions in the politico-bureaucratic struggle taking shape in Tokyo, the admiral asked if the cabinet was prepared to forego island fortification limitation and seek an upward revision of the naval ratio. Uchida evaded that question and insisted that public opinion would not allow acquiescence in Anglo-Saxon demands. Katō retorted that the Harding administration had to conclude the conference quickly to assure public support and Senate ratification of its agreements. Finally, his doubts about the cabinet's will to fight at home for those accords unresolved, Katō resorted to a direct challenge: if Tokyo could not agree quickly on a compromise on island fortification limits, he and the entire delegation would have no choice but to resign.[37]

Four days later, the admiral told Theodore Roosevelt, Jr. that the Japanese delegation was "in really serious trouble" at home. The next day he learned that three members of the Foreign Affairs Advisory Council had threatened to resign if a settlement that recognized Japan's sovereignty over islands whose fortifications were limited could not be reached. Katō then sensed that army bureaucratic interests were engaged and for the first time hinted that he thought railways in Shantung were the real bone of contention. He insisted that the cabinet agree to a compromise on that point, and Ambassador Shidehara supported him. Shortly thereafter Katō persuaded even General Tanaka Kunishige to drop his opposition to compromise on the island fortification problem. The navy minister defied Takahashi and Uchida for sound domestic political reasons. If the two statesmen were so weak and unwilling to crush opposition to compromise on the wording and form of fortification limitation and Shantung agreements, he felt, how could they be expected to secure Privy Council approval of the Washington treaties? If the government were so swayed by army pressures, what hope was there for the navy in the new, post-Washington politics of arms reduction for both services?[38]

The challenge was clear. Tokyo's response, at long last, was decided.

Takahashi and Uchida gave way before Katō's demands. They fended off Diet critics and postponed discussion of the Washington agreements until the admiral's return. They got cabinet and Foreign Affairs Advisory Council to compromise on Shantung railways and yet another version of Pacific island fortification limitation. The final text of article 19 did include southern islands over which the army had protested, and a separate instrument covered the Kurile and Aleutian islands in the north.[39]

With these last obstacles cleared away, the delegates made rapid progress in completing the draft treaties. The stage was set for a brief but brilliant ceremony to bring the Washington conference to a close. On February 6, 1922, after the naval limitation and four other treaties had been signed, there was a sudden burst of flashbulbs and clicking of shutters as Warren G. Harding entered the room. Once again the president spoke of "war's utter futility" but he went on to assert that the agreements signed will mark the beginning of a new and better epoch in human progress." Then compliments were handed round from all sides. Secretary Hughes and Ambassador Shidehara agreed that the competition in naval armaments had been ended. Balfour claimed that the conference had not only reduced arms but also "removed long-standing causes of offense" in Pacific international politics. Even the normally taciturn Katō Tomosaburō was moved to assert that "Japan is ready for the new order of thought—the spirit of international friendship and cooperation for the greater good of humanity—which the Conference has brought about." Those who negotiated the Washington agreements might well believe that they had indeed shaped "a new order of seapower."[40]

But the men who gloried in the achievements at Washington in 1922 had not acted on the basis of altruistic motives, strategic calculations, or economic imperatives alone. To be sure, they had sought a more stable, less tension-filled international political and naval system than that they had known before 1914. They did shape an international naval order which no single power might dominate. They limited capital ships in the belief that, despite the doubts raised about their long-range importance, battleships were the major implement of naval power. But an abiding concern for domestic political power underlay their actions. The realization that an international agreement for naval limitation could help them pursue and protect particular domestic political interests brought them to Washington and set bounds to their achievement.

No one knew this better than Warren G. Harding. The president had his success. Republicans had completed their international conference in less than half the time Democrats had taken at Paris two years earlier. Harding was "not so much of a duffer as a good many people expected me to be." He was confident that his quiet style of leadership would prevail in the Senate, where Wilson's had failed. The president was ready to confront and triumph over his domestic enemies. As he told California Senator Hiram Johnson, "the Disarmament Conference was the greatest of Republican achievements," and it demanded the senator's support. Johnson had to admit that this was true. Harding had turned the public demand for disarmament to his own advantage, united the Republican party behind it, and isolated Senator Borah. That the Senate approved all of the Washington treaties with but one vote against naval limitation was hardly surprising.[41]

The links between domestic political success and international naval agreement were less obvious but no less important in London. Through the Washington conference Balfour, Lloyd George, and even Beatty found that middle way which each had been seeking throughout the postwar years. Balfour played peacemaker in the Pacific while Beatty preserved the navy's role as protector of empire. The admiral did not preside, as he had once feared he would, over the demise of British naval power but stayed on as first sea lord for another five years to protect and promote it. The prime minister and journalists of every persuasion heaped praise on Balfour. The London *Times* went so far as to say that no British envoy had every enjoyed such widespread support. But that support was no accident. Lloyd George had deliberately put the former Unionist prime minister forward at a moment of weakness and tension in his cabinet. Now that he had succeeded, the prime minister was willing to make peace and limitation of expenditures as achieved at Washington the glue to hold his coalition together even longer. He knew, he taunted Labour critics, the "arithmetic of peace": reduced government expenditures, a smaller navy, and restored Anglo-American friendship added up to renewed British greatness and prosperity. This arithmetic, he hinted in a speech to a new association of "Lloyd George Liberals," enabled him to stand firmly for naval limitation during the Washington talks.[42]

Finally, as the last stages of those talks so clearly demonstrated, considerations of domestic politics deeply influenced Tokyo's decisions for naval limitation. Hara Kei and Katō Tomosaburō first grasped "the gift from the gods" that Washington offered; then the admiral went on not only to make the most of the opportunity of capital ship limitation, but also to assure his personal success in the future. By saving the *Mutsu*, getting Pacific island fortification limitation, and leaving the navy free to build submarines, airplanes, and aircraft carriers the admiral, as even Katō Kanji later admitted, had left the empire more secure on the seas after Washington than it had been before the conference. Katō Tomosaburō acted from an awareness of the need to protect his own interests in the new, post-Washington politics of national defense that was emerging in Tokyo. Showered with praise upon his return to Japan, scarcely three months later he became the logical choice of the elder statesmen as prime minister.[43]

The statesmen and admirals at Washington did indeed establish a new disposition of power in the Pacific. But they did so strong in the conviction that the new order would assure them a favorable disposition of power in Washington, London, and Tokyo.

Conclusion

The conclusion of the Washington conference marked the end of one order of seapower and the beginning of another. For the next fifteen years mutual limitation rather than competitive expansion would characterize the international naval system. But the Washington agreements also marked the beginning of a debate over disarmament that continues to this day. During the course of this debate, men have offered radically different answers to the question this book set out to answer: Why did statesmen and admirals limit their navies by international agreement in 1921–1922? In the 1920s a majority agreed with Walter Lippmann: men limited naval growth to stop "the drift into a ruinous and indecisive war." But in the tension-filled 1930s and more particularly during the holocaust of World War II, the verdict on the Washington conference changed: naval limitation by international agreement seemed the result of political leaders' myopic folly. In Dean Acheson's pithy phrase, "the Washington Conference of 1921 was a disaster."[1] That view can still be found in many writings on arms limitation today.

The arguments presented in this book, however, suggest a different set of conclusions, both about the origins of the Washington naval agreements and about the arms limitation process. The statesmen and admirals who hammered out the Washington treaties were not fools, nor were they adrift on the seas of historical inevitability. They were political realists struggling to master the forces for change in the international and domestic environments.

These leaders knew that the international system of 1921 was not what it had been seven years earlier. The Great War had shattered the old structure of alliances and destroyed one of the engines of naval expansion, Imperial Germany. The war had spawned and given life to Woodrow Wilson's vision of a new international order—one of peace, harmony, and progress toward a better life for all men. But the statesmen of the postwar era were not visionary idealists. Wilson himself appreciated the relationship between naval power and successful diplomacy. While Harding, Lloyd George, and Hara Kei shared his belief that imminent war was unlikely, none stood ready to modify basic assumptions about the need for sound naval defense. All three recognized that nations would continue to seek first their particular self interests. All three sensed that differences among the wartime allies, the discontents of the vanquished, and new nationalistic and revolutionary forces might yet disrupt what order there was in the world. To preserve that order and individual national interests, an adequate navy would continue to be necessary.

But what was "adequate"? In trying to answer that question, statesmen and admirals were guided in part by economic considerations, but those considerations were not primary. Politicians and naval officers found it easy to defy the laws of economics. In periods of economic recession they refused to abandon older expensive naval building programs and authorized even more costly new ones. Hara's getting Diet approval of the eight-eight fleet and Lloyd George's securing Parliament's authorization for four new capital ships testified to that fact. Moreover, experience suggested that trying to define the adequate in absolute dollar, pound, or yen sums would not work.

Technology also offered guidance in the determination of the adequate. Some commentators have suggested that the negotiators in Washington limited capital ship fleets because they believed battleships were already obsolete. This study suggests that precisely the opposite was true. While disarmament advocates might insist with greater force after the war than before it that battleships were worthless, and while advances in submarine and aviation technology threatened their supremacy, the case against the behemoths of the sea was far from proven. Political leaders might want, at times, to consign battleships to oblivion, but in their more reflective moments they recognized that capital ships remained the standard of naval power. That fact helped assure the success of the Washington negotiations. Had there been no prior consensus that the battleship was the yardstick for measuring comparative naval strength, difficulties over defining a standard, such as those that disrupted the later Geneva and London naval conferences, might well have made agreement at Washington more difficult to obtain.

Technological change, economics, and shifting diplomatic realities helped guide statesmen and admirals in their search for adequate naval power, but in the last analysis considerations of domestic politics were far more important. Those considerations were complex. Political and naval leaders were guided by something more than the axiom that successful defense policies must have solid legislative and popular support. They sought above all else to protect their personal and organizational power. Gradually they came to the realization that that power might be enhanced, or at the very least, perpetuated, by the limitation of their nations' instruments of naval power.

The paths to that truth were many and varied. One can see three distinct patterns of change at work in postwar Washington, London, and Tokyo. In the American capital, something more than a wave of popular disarmament sentiment propelled Warren G. Harding to seize the initiative for naval arms limitation by international agreement. The new president, regarded as weak, yet elected by a huge majority, wanted to lead. Senator Borah's "guerilla warfare,"[2] not only for naval limitation but also on a wide range of domestic and foreign policy issues, reinforced the president's determination. The need to prove his leadership capability and to consolidate his hold over the Republican party brought Harding to the realization that success could be achieved through conclusion of a naval arms limitation agreement. That domestic political imperative, far more than Hughes's negotiating tactics, assured the favorable outcome of the Washington negotiations.

Different domestic political imperatives guided statesmen and admirals in London. There no one wanted a confrontation over naval issues. There, too, a long tradition of rule by compromise and consensus shaped statesmen's and admirals' behavior. Lloyd George, as the leader of a coalition and as one preoccupied with the more urgent and divisive Irish question, could not afford to let questions on naval policy shatter the tenuous harmony of his government. Unlike Harding, he was not troubled and was by no means constrained by editorial criticism. Indeed, in contrast to the wave of concern for disarmament in the United States press, there was scarcely a ripple in the British press. Instead, Lloyd George had to respect his Conservative colleagues' contention that sea power was a vital symbol of security to the British people. That sensitivity made him, and them, eager to place the burden of blame for its possible diminution elsewhere—if not on the penurious dominions, then on the Americans. Similar shrewdness and concern for the long-term domestic political well-being of the naval service brought David Beatty to accept decisions which would reduce Britain's sea power. The result was the pursuit of a middle way, one which spelled compromise at Washington but preserved coalition and consensus in London.

Yet another pattern emerged in Tokyo. There Hara Kei sought not only to preserve consensus but also to restructure the politics of national defense through naval limitation. He and Katō Tomosaburō, while sensitive to changes abroad, to the call for naval limitation by particular domestic interest groups, and to the increasing economic costs of naval expansion, were far more concerned with the bureaucratic political opportunities that naval limitation presented. The prime minister discovered in the invitation to Washington the chance to consolidate his ties with the navy, reduce the foreign policy influence of the army, and enhance civilian influence over the military. The admiral, on the other hand, saw in limitation the chance to render credible a defensive strategy which helped preserve harmony within the navy, to avoid friction with party politicians over naval expansion costs, and, above all, to conclude an alliance with Hara that would reduce the generals' power. These gains, like the domestic benefits Hara hoped to achieve, far outweighed the possible risks of seeking naval limitation through negotiations.

For domestic political reasons that varied from capital to capital, then, statesmen and admirals decided to limit the size of their navies by international agreement. Their definition of the adequate in naval power abroad reflected their understanding of the essential, the possible, and the desirable in politics at home. The men responsible for the conclusion of the Washington naval limitation agreements were not masterful strategists. They were not starry-eyed idealists. They most certainly were not weak reeds bending before the winds of historical inevitability. They were, on the contrary, men of power trying simply to retain their hold on it. In 1921–22, concluding a naval arms limitation agreement seemed one way to strengthen that grasp.

To ask why these men acted as they did is to seek an answer to a particular question concerning a specific moment in time. But that fact should not obscure the more general implications of this episode. The Washington naval treaties symbolize an important truth, one that transcends the particulars of a half century ago. That truth is this: Arms limitation is, above all else, a political process. Whether it is wisdom or folly to seek limitation, and indeed whether or not it can be achieved, do not depend on one's possession of qualitative or numerical superiority, or even parity, of weapons. It does not depend on the congruence of one's objectives with universal principles of strategy, diplomacy, or morality. Nor do the decisions and prospects for arms limitation turn simply on the correctness of one's assessment of other nations' diplomatic and military intentions or their production capabilities. The success or failure, wisdom or folly of arms limitation by international agreement depends, above all else, on careful, constantly changing, and correct estimates of the domestic political risks and opportunities it presents to one's own leaders and to their prospective negotiating partners.

If those who read this book become sensitive to that truth, then it will have served its purpose.

Appendix

Principal Statesmen and Admirals, Politicians and Officials

Asquith, Herbert Henry
1852–1928
Chancellor of the Exchequer, 1905–8; Prime Minister, 1908–16; Earl of Oxford and Asquith, 1925.

Balfour, Arthur James
1848–1930
Prime Minister, 1902–1905; member, War Council, 1914–15; First Lord of Admiralty, 1915–16; Secretary of State for Foreign Affairs, 1916–19; Lord President of the Council, 1919–22; Earl of Balfour, 1922.

Beatty, Admiral of the Fleet David
1871–1936
Commander, battlecruiser squadron, 1913–16; Commander in Chief, Grand Fleet, 1916–19; First Sea Lord, 1919–27; Earl Beatty, 1919.

Benson, Admiral William Shepherd
1855–1932
U.S. Naval Academy, class of 1877; Chief of Naval Operations, 1915–19.

Bonar Law, Andrew
1858–1923
Secretary of State for Colonies, 1915–16; Chancellor of the Exchequer, 1916–18; Lord Privy Seal, 1918–21; Prime Minister, 1922–23.

Borah, William Edgar
1865–1940.
U.S. Senator from Idaho, 1907–40.

Borden, Sir Robert Laird
1854–1937
Prime Minister of Canada, 1911–20; member, British Empire Delegation, Washington conference, 1921–22.

Carson, Sir Edward Henry
1854–1935
Attorney General, 1915–16; First Lord of Admiralty, 1916–17; mem-

ber, War Cabinet, 1917–18; Baron
Carson of Duncairn, 1921.

Cecil, Edgar Algernon Robert
1864–1958

Under-Secretary of State for Foreign Affairs, 1915–18; Minister of Blockade, 1916–18; Assistant Secretary of State for Foreign Affairs, 1918–19; later Viscount Cecil of Chelwood.

Chamberlain, Sir Joseph Austen
1863–1937

Secretary of State for India, 1915–17; member, War Cabinet, 1918; Chancellor of Exchequer, 1919–21; Leader, Unionist party, 1921–22; Secretary of State for Foreign Affairs, 1924–29.

Chatfield, Admiral of the Fleet
A. Ernle
1873–1967

Flag Captain to Admiral Beatty, 1914–19; Fourth Sea Lord, 1919; Assistant Chief of Naval Staff, 1920–22; Commander in Chief, Atlantic Fleet, 1929–30, Mediterranean Fleet, 1930–33; First Sea Lord 1933–38; Minister for Coordination of Defense, 1939–40; Baron Chatfield, 1937.

Churchill, Sir Winston Spencer
1874–1965

President Board of Trade, 1908–10; Home Secretary, 1910–11; First Lord of the Admiralty, 1911–15; Chancellor of Duchy of Lancaster, 1915–16; Minister of Munitions, 1917; Secretary of State for War and Air, 1919–32; Secretary of State for Colonies, 1921–22; Chancellor of the Exchequer, 1924–29; First Lord of the Admiralty, 1939–40; Prime Minister, 1940–45, 1951–55.

Curzon, George Nathaniel
1859–1925

Lord Privy Seal, 1915–16; member, War Cabinet, 1916–19; Secretary of State for Foreign Affairs, 1919–22; Marquess Curzon of Kedleston, 1921.

Daniels, Josephus
1862–1948

Editor of Raleigh *News and Observer,* 1894–1933; Secretary of the Navy, 1913–21; Ambassador to Mexico, 1933–41.

Denby, Edwin
1870–1929

Member of House of Representatives, 1905–11; Secretary of the Navy, 1921–24.

Fisher, Admiral of the Fleet John Arbuthnot 1841–1920	Second Sea Lord, 1901–3; First Sea Lord, 1904–10, 1914–15; Baron Fisher of Kilverstone, 1909.
Geddes, Sir Auckland Campbell 1879–1954	M. D., 1903; professor, McGill University, 1913–14; Minister of National Service, 1917–19; President, Local Government Board, 1908–19; Minister of Reconstruction, 1919; President of Board of Trade, 1919–20; Ambassador to the United States, 1920–24; Baron, 1942.
Geddes, Sir Eric Campbell 1875–1937	Admiralty Controller, 1917; First Lord of Admiralty, 1917–19; Minister of Transport, 1919–21.
Grey, Sir Edward 1862–1933	Secretary of State for Foreign Affairs, 1905–16; Ambassador on special mission to the United States, 1919; Viscount Grey of Fallodon, 1916.
Hankey, Sir Maurice Paschal Alers 1877–1963	Secretary, Committee of Imperial Defense, 1912–38; Secretary of the Cabinet, 1916–38; Chancellor of Duchy of Lancaster, 1940–41; Baron, 1939.
Hara Kei (Takashi) 原 敬 1856–1921	Journalist; Vice Minister of Foreign Affairs, 1895; founder of Seiyūkai, 1900; Home Minister, 1911–12, 1913–14; president of Seiyukai, 1914–21; Prime Minister, 1918–21.
Harding, Warren Gamaliel 1865–1923	Newspaper editor and publisher, 1884–1921; member, Ohio State Senate, 1899–1903; Lieutenant Governor of Ohio, 1904–5; U.S. Senator from Ohio, 1915–21; President of the U.S., 1921–23.
House, Edward Mandell 1858–1938	Friend and confidant of Woodrow Wilson; U.S. representative, pre-armistice negotiations; member, U.S. delegation, Paris Peace Conference, 1919.
Hughes, Charles Evans 1862–1948	Associate Justice of U.S. Supreme Court, 1910–16; Republican Presidential Candidate, 1916; Secretary of State, 1921–25; Judge, Permanent Court of International Justice,

	1928–30; Chief Justice, U.S. Supreme Court, 1930–41.
Hughes, William Morris 1862–1952	Prime Minister of Australia, 1915–23.
Inukai Ki (Tsuyoshi) 犬養 毅 1855–1932	Journalist; member of Diet, 1890–1932; Leader of Kokumintō; Prime Minister, 1931–32.
Ishii Kikujirō 石井菊次郎 1866–1945	Ambassador to France, 1912–15, 1920–27; Minister of Foreign Affairs, 1915–16; Viscount, 1916; special envoy to U.S., 1917; President of Council and Assembly of League of Nations, 1923, 1926.
Jellicoe, Admiral of the Fleet John Rushworth 1859–1935	Commander in Chief, Grand Fleet, 1914–1916; First Sea Lord, 1916–17; Governor-General of New Zealand, 1920–24; Viscount Jellicoe of Scapa, 1918; Earl Jellicoe, 1925.
Katō Rear Admiral Kanji 加藤寛治 1870–1939	Commander, Fifth Fleet, 1918; member of inspection tour of Europe, 1919–20; President of Naval War College, 1920–22; Senior naval expert, Washington conference delegation, 1921–22; Vice-chief, Chief of Naval General Staff.
Katō Kōmei 加藤高明 1859–1926	Minister, Ambassador to Great Britain, 1898–1900, 1906–13; Minister of Foreign Affairs, 1900–1901, 1905–6, 1913, 1914–15; founder and leader of Kenseikai; Prime Minister, 1924–26; Viscount.
Katō Admiral Tomosaburō 加藤友三郎 1859–1923	Chief of Staff, Combined Fleet, 1905; Vice Minister of the Navy, 1906–9; Commanding Officer, Kure, 1909–14; Minister of the Navy, 1915–23; delegate to Washington conference, 1921–22; Prime Minister, 1922–23; Baron, 1920, Admiral of the Fleet, 1923.
Lee, Arthur 1868–1947	President, Board of Agriculture and Fisheries, 1919–21; First Lord of Admiralty, 1921–22; Baron, 1918; Viscount Lee of Fareham, 1922.
Lloyd George, David 1863–1945	M.P. 1890–1945; President, Board of Trade, 1905–8; Chancellor of Ex-

	chequer, 1908–15; Minister of Munitions, 1915–16; Secretary of State for War, 1916; Prime Minister, 1916–22; Earl Lloyd George of Dwyfor, 1945.
Lodge, Henry Cabot 1850–1924	Member, House of Representatives, 1887–93; U.S. Senator from Massachusetts, 1893–1924.
Long, Walter Hume 1854–1924	President of Local Government Board, 1915–16; Secretary of State for Colonies, 1916–18; First Lord of Admiralty, 1918–21; Viscount Long of Wraxall, 1921.
Makino Nobuaki 牧野伸顕 1861–1949	Foreign Minister, 1913–14; delegate to Paris Peace Conference, 1918–19; Minister of Imperial Household, 1921–24; Lord Keeper of the Privy Seal, 1924–35; Count, 1920.
McCormick, Joseph Medill 1877–1925	Member of House of Representatives, 1917–19; U.S. Senator from Illinois, 1919–25.
Morris, Roland Sletor 1874–1945	U.S. Ambassador to Japan, 1917–21.
Nakahashi Tokugorō 中橋徳五郎 1861–1934	President, Osaka Shōsen kaisha, 1898–1914; Minister of Education, 1918–22; Minister of Commerce and Industry, 1927–29; Home Minister, 1932.
Ōkuma Shigenobu 大隈重信 1838–1922.	Prime Minister, 1898, 1914–16.
Ozaki Yukio 尾崎行雄 1859–1954	Member of Diet, 1890–1954; Minister of Education, 1898; Mayor of Tokyo, 1913–14; Minister of Justice, 1914–16.
Poindexter, Miles 1868–1946	Member of House of Representatives, 1909–10; U.S. Senator from Washington, 1911–23; Ambassador to Peru, 1923–28.
Pratt, Admiral William Veazie 1869–1957	U.S. Naval Academy, class of 1889; Assistant Chief of Naval Operations, 1917–19; Commanding Officer, U.S.S. *New York*, 1919–20; member, General Board, 1921–22;

President, U.S. Naval War College,
1925–27; Commander in Chief,
U.S. Fleet, 1929–30; Chief of Naval
Operations, 1930–33.

Richmond, Admiral Sir Herbert
William
1871–1946

Assistant Director of Operations,
Naval War Staff, 1914; Commanding Officer, H.M.S. *Common-
wealth*, 1915–17, *Conqueror*, 1917–
18; Director, Training Division,
1918–20; Commanding Officer,
Naval War College, Greenwich,
1920–23.

Roosevelt, Franklin Delano
1882–1945

Assistant Secretary of the Navy,
1913–20; Democratic candidate for
vice president of the U.S., 1920;
Governor of New York, 1929–33;
President of the U.S., 1933–45.

Roosevelt, Theodore, Jr.
1887–1944

Organizer of American Legion,
1919; Assistant Secretary of the
Navy, 1921–24; Governor-General
of the Philippines, 1932–33.

Root, Elihu
1845–1937

Secretary of War, 1899–1904; Secretary of State, 1905–9; delegate,
Washington conference, 1921–22.

Shidehara Kijūrō
幣原喜重郎
1872–1951

Minister at the Hague, 1914; Vice
Minister for Foreign Affairs, 1915–
16; Ambassador to the U.S., 1919–
22; Minister of Foreign Affairs,
1924–27, 1929–31; Prime Minister,
1945–46; Baron, 1920.

Shimamura Admiral Hayao
島村速雄
1858–1923

Chief of Staff, Combined Fleet,
1904–5; Chief of Naval General
Staff, 1915–21; Admiral of the
Fleet, 1923; Baron, 1916.

Sims, Admiral William Snowden
1856–1936

U.S. Naval Academy, class of 1880;
naval aide to President Theodore
Roosevelt, 1907–9; Commander of
U.S. naval operations in European
waters, 1917–19; President of U.S.
Naval War College, 1920–22.

Smuts, Field Marshal Jan C.
1870–1950

Member, War Cabinet, 1918; Prime
Minister of South Africa, 1919–24.

Takahashi Korekiyo
高橋是清
1854–1936

Governor, Bank of Japan, 1912–13;
Minister of Finance, 1913–14, 1918–
22, 1927, 1931–34; Prime Minister,
1921–22; Viscount.

Takeshita Admiral Isamu
竹下 勇
1869–1949

Naval member, special mission to Washington, 1917; Senior naval representative, Paris Peace Conference delegation, 1918–19; tutor to crown prince, 1921; Vice Chief of Naval General Staff, 1921–22.

Tanaka General Giichi
田中義一
1863–1929

Chief of Military Affairs Bureau, Ministry of War, 1910–13; Vice Chief of Army General Staff, 1915–18; Minister for War, 1918–21, 1923–24; Prime Minister and Foreign Minister, 1927–29; Baron, 1920.

Tanaka General Kunishige
重国本氏
1869–1941

Former military attaché, embassies at Washington and London; Senior army delegate to Washington conference, 1921–22.

Terauchi Field Marshal Masatake
寺内正毅
1852–1919

Minister of War, 1902–11; Governor General of Korea, 1911–16; Prime Minister 1916–18; Viscount, 1907; Count, 1911.

Uchida Yasuya
内田康哉
1865–1936

Minister to China, 1901–6; Ambassador to Austria-Hungary, 1907–9; to the United States, 1909–11, to Russia, 1916–17; Minister of Foreign Affairs, 1911–12, 1918–23, 1932; President of South Manchurian Railway Company, 1931–32.

Uehara Field Marshal Yūsaku
上原勇作
1856–1933

Minister of War, 1912–13; Inspector-General of Military Education, 1914–15; Chief of Army General Staff, 1915–23; Viscount.

Wemyss, Admiral of the Fleet
Rosslyn Erskine
1864–1933

Commander, 12th Cruiser Squadron, 1914; Governor of Lemnos, 1915–16; Commander in Chief, East Indies and Egypt Station, 1916–17; Deputy First Sea Lord, 1917; First Sea Lord, 1918–19; Baron Wester Wemyss, 1919.

Wilson, Thomas Woodrow
1856–1924

Ph.D., Johns Hopkins, 1886; President of Princeton University, 1902–10; Governor of New Jersey, 1911–13; President of the U.S., 1913–21.

Yamagata Field Marshal Aritomo
山縣有朋
1838–1922

Chōshū elder statesman; Former Minister of War, Chief of Army General Staff; Home Minister;

Prime Minister, 1889–91, 1898–1900.

Yamamoto Admiral Gombei
山本権兵衛
1852–1933

Minister of the Navy, 1898–1906; Prime Minister, 1913–14, 1923–24; Count.

Yamanashi General Hanzō
山梨半造
1865–1944

Vice Minister of War, 1917–21; Minister of War, 1921–22.

Yashiro Admiral Rokurō
八代六郎
1861–1930

President of Naval War College, 1912–13; Commanding Officer, Maizuru, 1913–14; Minister of the Navy, 1914–15; Admiral, 1916.

ADM	Admiralty papers
CAB	Cabinet papers
CID	Committee of Imperial Defence
EMHP	Edward Mandell House papers
DBFP	Great Britain, Foreign Office, *Documents on British Foreign Policy*
FO	Foreign Office papers
FRUS	Department of State, *Foreign Relations of the United States*
GBP	General Board papers
GSSJN	Sangiin and Shūgiin, ed., *Gikai seido shichijūnen shi*
HKN	Hara Keiichirō, ed., *Hara Kei nikki*
JDA	Japan Defense Agency, Office of War History archives
JFMA	Japan Ministry of Foreign Affairs archives
LGP	Lloyd George papers
LT	London *Times*
NGKB	Gaimushō, ed., *Nihon gaikō bunsho*
NYT	*New York Times*
RG	National Archives record group
SN	Komura Tatsuo, ed., *Suiusō nikki: Itō ke monjo*
TRJD	Theodore Roosevelt, Jr. diary
WSSP	William Snowden Sims papers
WGHP	Warren Gamaliel Harding papers

Notes

Chapter 1

1. Jonathan Steinberg, *Yesterday's Deterrent* (New York, 1965), especially pp. 17–29; Gerhard Ritter, *The Sword and the Scepter*, trans. Heinz Norden, vol. 2 (Coral Gables, Florida, 1970), pp. 137–38.

2. Ian Nish, *The Anglo-Japanese Alliance: The Diplomacy of Two Island Empires, 1894–1907* (London, 1966), pp. 1–2, 371–77; Samuel R. Williamson, Jr., *The Politics of Grand Strategy* (Cambridge, Mass., 1969), chap. 1.

3. Arthur J. Marder, *From the Dreadnought to Scapa Flow: The Royal Navy in the Fisher Era, 1904–1919,* vol. 1 (London, 1951), pp. 43–45, 119–24, 214–32; Gordon C. O'Gara, *Theodore Roosevelt and the Rise of the Modern Navy* (Princeton, 1943), pp. 65–69; Bōeichō bōei kenshūjo senshi shitsu, *Kaigun gunsenbi I Shōwa jūrokunen jūichigatsu made* (Tokyo, 1969), pp. 60–63; financial data herein is based on sources indicated for its chart 1, p. 5.

4. Marder, *From the Dreadnought*, 1:14–27, 204–7, 264–71, and Arthur J. Marder, ed., *Fear God and Dread Nought: The Correspondence of Admiral of the Fleet Lord Fisher of Kilverstone*, volume 2, *The Years of Power, 1904–14* (London, 1956), chap. 11; Paul Haggie, "The Royal Navy and War Planning in the Fisher Era," *Journal of Contemporary History* 8 (July 1973): 113; Randolph S. Churchill, *Winston S. Churchill*, vol. 2, *Young Statesman, 1901–1914* (Boston, 1967), pp. 545–46, 681.

5. Donald M. Schurman, *The Education of a Navy* (Chicago, 1965), pp. 50–51, 78–79; Peter Karsten, *The Naval Aristocracy* (New York, 1972). Chapter 7 offers a revisionist assessment of Mahan and his influence.

6. Marder, *From the Dreadnought*, 1: 344–57, 367–76; Williamson, *The Politics of Grand Strategy*, pp. 227–48, 320–27.

7. Arthur J. Marder, *The Anatomy of British Sea Power* (New York, 1940), p. 516; Ruddock F. Mackay, *Fisher of Kilverstone* (Oxford, 1973), pp. 203, 403, 445–53; Randolph S. Churchill, *Churchill*, 2: 673–81; ed., "Capital Ships of the Future, Admiral Sir Percy Scott's Views," *Journal of the Royal United Service Institution* 58 (August 1914): 238–47; Admiral Sir Percy Scott, *Fifty Years in the Royal Navy* (London, 1919), pp. 261, 263; Peter Padfield, *Aim Straight: A Biography of Admiral Sir Percy Scott* (London, 1966), pp. 223–25; Marder, *Fear God*, 2:491, 498–99; A. Temple Patterson, ed., *The Jellicoe Papers: Selections from the Private and Official Correspondence of Admiral of the Fleet Earl Jellicoe of Scapa*, vol. 1 (London, 1966), pp. 31–35.

8. Fisher to A. G. Gardiner, March 7, 1913, A. G. Gardiner papers, cited by Stephen Koss in *Fleet Street Radical: A. G. Gardiner and the Daily News* (Hamden, Conn., 1973), pp. 143–44, Nicholas d'Ombrain, *War Machinery and High Policy: Defence Administration in Peacetime Britain, 1902–14* (London, 1973), pp. 11–12.

9. Nish, *The Anglo-Japanese Alliance*, pp. 353–58; Williamson, *The Politics of Grand Strategy*, chaps. 10–11, 13; Grey to Asquith and Churchill, May 25, 1914, Churchill papers, in Martin Gilbert, *Winston S. Churchill: The Challenge of War, 1914–16* (Boston, 1971), p. 2.

10. Zara S. Steiner, *The Foreign Office and Foreign Policy, 1898–1914* (Cambridge, 1969), p. 168; Henry Weinroth, "Left Wing Opposition to Naval Armaments in Britain before 1914," *Journal of Contemporary History* 6 (1971): 98.

11. Marder, *Fear God*, vol. 2, chap. 11; Marder, *From the Dreadnought*, 1: 216–17, 219, 311–13.

12. Mackay, *Fisher*, p. 394; Koss, *Fleet Street Radical*, p. 124; Scott to Lloyd George, January 25, 1914, in Trevor Wilson, ed., *The Political Diaries of C. P. Scott, 1911–1928* (Ithaca, N.Y., 1970), p. 79.

13. Weinroth, "Left Wing Opposition," pp. 119–20; Koss, *Fleet Street Radical*, p. 145; Stephen E. Koss, *Sir John Brunner: Radical Plutocrat, 1842–1919* (Cambridge, 1970), pp. 215–35; A. J. Anthony Morris, *Radicalism against War, 1906–1914* (Totowa, N.J., 1972), chaps. 4, 8.

14. Marder, *From the Dreadnought,* 1: 219–21; Ernest Llewellyn Wood-ward, *Great Britain and the German Navy* (Oxford, 1935) pp. 495–98; CAB 41/34/5 Asquith to the King, November 18, 1913; CAB 41/34/39 Asquith to the King, December 20, 1913; Wilson, ed., *Political Diaries,* p. 78; *The Economist* 77 (October 8, November 1, 15, 22, 29, 1913), pp. 898, 939, 1065, 1116, 1170–71; *LT,* December 17–18, 1913, January 17, March 18, 1914; *The Nation* 14 (November 25, 1913): 162; Koss, *Fleet Street Radical,* p. 144.

15. Koss, *Fleet Street Radical,* p. 126; Weinroth, "Left Wing Opposition," pp. 114–17.

16. *The Spectator* 111 (November 22, 29, 1913): 851, 902–3; *The Spectator* 112 (January 10, 1914): 44–45; *Fortnightly Review* 101 (January 1914): 238–52; Oron J. Hale, *Publicity and Diplomacy: With Special Reference to England and Germany, 1890–1914* (Gloucester, Mass., 1964; originally published 1940), pp. 349–59; Roy Jenkins, *Asquith: Portrait of a Man and an Era* (New York, 1964), pp. 231, 242; Peter Gretton, *Former Naval Person: Winston Churchill and the Royal Navy* (London, 1969), pp. 23–31.

17. "Armaments and Votes," *The Nation* 14 (November 22, 1913): p. 345; Jenkins, *Asquith,* pp. 298–300; Randolph S. Churchill, *Churchill,* vol. 2, chap. 17; Marder, *From the Dreadnought,* 1: 296–324; Friedrich Wilhelm Wiemann, "Lloyd George and the Struggle for the Navy Estimates of 1914," in A. J. P. Taylor, ed., *Lloyd George: Twelve Essays* (New York, 1971), pp. 71–91; Peter Rowland, *The Last Liberal Governments: Unfinished Business, 1911–14* (New York, 1971), pp. 269–88 chronicles the 1913–14 crisis.

18. David H. Burton, *Theodore Roosevelt: Confident Imperialist* (Philadelphia, 1969), chap. 2; William R. Braisted, *The United States Navy in the Pacific, 1897–1909* (Austin, 1958), pp. 172–73, 192–96; Charles E. Neu, *An Uncertain Friendship: Theodore Roosevelt and Japan, 1906–1909* (Cambridge, Mass., 1967), pp. 226–37.

19. Ronald Spector, *Admiral of the New Empire: The Life and Career of George Dewey* (Baton Rouge, 1974), pp. 137, 178, 204; Richard D. Challener, *Admirals, Generals, and American Foreign Policy, 1898–1914* (Princeton, 1973), pp. 56, 61, 268–69, 402; Bradley A. Fiske, *From Midshipman to Rear Admiral* (New York, 1919), pp. 479, 526–28.

20. John A. S. Grenville and George Berkeley Young, *Politics, Strategy, and Diplomacy* (New Haven, Conn., 1966), pp. 299–300; General Board to Secretary of the Navy, October 17, 1903, serial 420–2, cited in *Report of Secretary of the Navy for the Fiscal Year 1914* (Washington, D.C., 1915), p. 59; U.S. Congress, House, Committee on Naval Affairs, "Estimates Submitted by the Secretary of the Navy 1914," *Hearings,* 63d Congress, 2d session, (Washington, 1914), pp. 571–86, 794–95; Washington I. Chambers, "Aviation and Aeroplanes," *U.S. Naval Institute Proceedings,* 37 (March 1911): pp. 163–203; Chester W. Nimitz, "The Military Value and Tactics of Modern Submarines," *U.S. Naval Institute Proceedings,* 38 (December 1912): pp. 1193–1211.

21. Warner R. Schilling, "Admirals and Foreign Policy" (Ph. D. diss., Yale University, 1953), chap. 1; Willis Edward Snowbarger, "The Development of Pearl Harbor" (Ph.D. diss., University of California, Berkeley, 1950), pp. 142–43; Fiske, *From Midshipman to Rear Admiral*, pp. 526–29; Braisted, *U.S. Navy in the Pacific, 1897–1909*, pp. 216–23, 237–38; William R. Braisted, *The United States Navy in the Pacific, 1909–1922* (Austin, 1971), chaps. 3–5 (which will be cited subsequently as Braisted, *The U.S. Navy in the Pacific*), Challener, *Admirals, Generals and American Foreign Policy, 1898–1914*, pp. 225–64 discuss prewar strategy and base problems; Russell F. Weigley, *The American Way of War* (New York, 1973), pp. 188–91 points out Mahan's baleful influence on naval strategic thinking.

22. *Congressional Record*, 62d Congress, 2d sess., p. 7337.

23. Ibid., 63d Congress, pp. 7028, 7339–341; ibid., 63d Congress, 1st sess., pp. 7216–218; 63d Congress, 2d sess., pp. 6853–858, 6871–872; U.S. Department of Commerce, *Historical Statistics of the United States*, p. 711.

24. Taft to Nelson W. Aldrich, May 21, 1910, William H. Taft papers, cited by Braisted in *The U.S. Navy in the Pacific*, p. 22; Ibid., pp. 23–24; U.S. Congress, House, Naval Affairs Committee, "Estimates submitted by the Secretary of the Navy," *Hearings*, 62d Congress, 2d sess., 1912 (Washington, 1912), pp. 702, 890.

25. *LT*, February 13, March 28, 1912; *NYT*, August 21, 1912, March 2, December 5, 1913, January 30, 1914; Braisted, *The U.S. Navy in the Pacific*, pp. 142–44.

26. Arthur S. Link, *Wilson*, vol. 2 (Princeton, 1956): pp. 15–16, 122–24; Joseph L. Morrison, *Josephus Daniels: The Small-d Democrat* (Chapel Hill, 1966), p. 139; Report of the Secretary of the Navy for the Fiscal Year 1913 (Washington, 1914), pp. 10–11; U.S. Congress, House, Committee on Naval Affairs, "Estimates submitted by the Secretary of the Navy, 1914," *Hearings*, 63d Congress, 2d sess., (Washington, 1914), pp. 609–11, 613–15.

27. Report of the Secretary of the Navy for the Fiscal Year 1913 (Washington, 1914), p. 9; Daniels to Bryan, March 7, and Wilson to Bryan, March 16, 1914, RG 59, cited by Braisted in *The U.S. Navy in the Pacific*, p. 146; *NYT*, January 30, May 8, June 3, 30, 1914.

28. Sterling Tatsuji Takeuchi, *War and Diplomacy in the Japanese Empire* (Chicago, 1935), pp. 14–17, 52–59; George Akita, *Foundations of Constitutional Government in Modern Japan, 1868–1900* (Cambridge, 1967), p. 143; Okamoto Shumpei, *The Japanese Oligarchy and the Russo-Japanese War* (New York, 1970), pp. 11–40.

29. Yamamoto Eisuke, *Yamamoto Gombei* (Tokyo, 1958), p. 158, summarizes his early career; Kaigun shō hen, *Yamamoto Gombei to Kaigun* (Tokyo, 1966), and Asai Masahide, *Hakushaku Yamamoto Gombei*, 2 vols. (Tokyo, 1938) richly detail it; Tsunoda Jun, *Manshū*

mondai to kokubō hōshin (Tokyo, 1967), p. 648; Somei Gyoshi, "Rekidai no kaishō oyobi kono uyoku," *Taiyō* 20 (July 1914), p. 51.

30. Tsunoda, *Manshū mondai,* pp. 640–47, 657–58; Shimada Kinji, *Amerika ni okeru Akiyama Saneyuki* (Tokyo, 1969), pp. 34–61; Satō Tetsutarō, *Teikoku kokubō shi ron* (Tokyo, 1908). This was the text used at the Naval Academy, pp. 67–80 discussed Mahan; Symposium: On Expansion: North vs. South, *Taiyō,* 19 (November 15, 1913): pp. 2–96. Morita Akatsuki, *Kokubō to kaigun jūjitsu* (Tokyo, 1914); the author is grateful to Dr. Tsunoda Jun for making available a copy of Kokubō mondai no kenkyū, a primary defense of the strategic need for arms expansion written by members of the Naval General Staff.

31. Shimanuki Takeji, "Nihon no kokubō hōshin yohei kōryo," *Kokubō* (November, 1961), pp. 69–71; Hata Ikuhiko, "Meiji ki irkō ni okeru NichiBei Taiheiyō senryaku no hensen," *Kokusai seiji,* no. 2 (1967), pp. 96–104; Tsunoda, *Manshū mondai,* pp. 700–12, 719–28, 732; Bōeichō Bōei kenshū jo senshi shitsu, *Dai honei rikugun bu I Showa jūgo nen gogatsu made* (Tokyo, 1967), pp. 129–82; Bōeicho Bōei kenshūjo senshi shitsu, *Hitō kōryaku sakusen* (Tokyo, 1966), p. 6.

32. John K. Fairbank, Edwin O. Reischauer, and Albert M. Craig, *East Asia: The Modern Transformation* (Boston, 1965), pp. 555–58; Matsushita Yoshio, *Nihon gunsei to seiji* (Tokyo, 1960), p. 48; Kaigun Yūshū Kai, *Kinsei Teikoku kaigun shiyō* (Tokyo, 1938), pp. 45–47; Bōeichō, *Kaigun gunsenbi I,* 1:1–6, 15–19; Najita Tetsuo, *Hara Kei in the Politics of Compromise, 1904–1915* (Cambridge, 1967), pp. 7–8, 10; Peter Duus, *Party Rivalry and Political Change in Taishō Japan* (Cambridge, 1968), pp. 30–34.

33. Okawa Masazō, "The Armaments Expansion Budgets and the Japanese Economy after the Russo-Japanese War," *Hitotsubashi Journal of Economics* 5 (January 1965): 65–83; Megata Tanetarō, "Kokubō to zaisei," *Taiyō* 20 (May 1914): 65–69; Ukita Kazutami, "*Kokubō* mondai no komponteki kaisetsu," *Taiyō* 20 (July 1914): 2–16; Takekoshi Yosaburō, "Kyokan no jidai o owaru," *Taiyō* 20 (July 1914): 70–79; Tsunoda, *Manshū mondai,* pp. 775–804; *GSSJN,* 9:745; Suzuki Shogo, ed., *Ozaki Gakudō zenshu* (Tokyo, 1955–1956), 5:404–24, 467–78.

34. Masumi Junnosuke, *Nihon seito shi ron* (Tokyo, 1967), vol. 3, chap. 7; Yamamoto Shiro, *Taishō seihen no kisoteki kenkyū* (Tokyo, 1970) offers an exhaustive account of the 1911–13 crisis; Saitō shishaku kinen kai, *Shishaku Saitō Makoto den* (Tokyo, 1941) 2:271–340 provides the most detailed account of the Siemens incident; A. Morgan Young, *Japan under Taishō Tenno, 1912–1926* (London, 1928), pp. 43–48; *Taiyō,* 20 (February, 1914): 19–25; (March 1914), pp. 145–53; (April 1914), pp. 19–24.

35. U.S. Congress, House, Committee on Naval Affairs, "Estimates Sub-

mitted by the Secretary of the Navy 1914," *Hearings*, 63d Congress, 2d sess., p. 586.

Chapter 2

1. Winston S. Churchill, *The World Crisis, 1911–14* (New York, 1924), pp. 245–46.

2. *LT*, November 12–13, 1918; Lady Wester Wemyss, *The Life and Letters of Lord Wester Wemyss, Admiral of the Fleet* (London, 1935), p. 394; Beatty to "a friend," November 12, 1918, cited by W. S. Chalmers in *The Life and Letters of David, Earl Beatty* (London, 1941), p. 341.

3. Cameron Hazelhurst, *Politicians at War: July 1914 to May 1915* (New York, 1971), pp. 32, 128; Bernard Mallet and C. Oswald George, *British Budgets, Second Series 1913–1914 to 1920–21* (London, 1929), p. 352.

4. Angell to Dennis Robertson, Angell papers, C. P. Scott to E. D. Morel, Morel papers, cited in Marvin Swartz, *The Union of Democratic Control in British Politics during the First World War* (Oxford, 1971), pp. 23, 36; Hazelhurst, *Politicians at War*, pp. 140–42, 156; Walter Runciman to Sir Robert Chalmers, February 7, 1915, Runciman papers, cited in Hazelhurst, *Politicians at War*, p. 156.

5. Winston S. Churchill, *The World Crisis* (New York, 1924), 1:431–34; ibid., 2:199–200; Jenkins, *Asquith*, p. 339.

6. John P. Mackintosh, *The British Cabinet* 2d ed. (London, 1968), pp. 365–69; Hazelhurst, *Politicians at War*, p. 147.

7. Marder, *From the Dreadnought*, vol. 2., chapters 2–4 describe these events in detail; Churchill, *World Crisis*, 1: 257–60.

8. Churchill, *World Crisis*, 1: 432–38; CAB 41/34/57, Asquith to the King, November 4, 1914; Wilson ed., *Political Diaries*, November 27, 1914, pp. 110–112; Earl of Oxford and Asquith, *Memories and Reflections, 1852–1927* (Boston 1928), 2: 56; Gilbert, *Winston S. Churchill*, pp. 134–54.

9. Churchill, *World Crisis*, vol. 1, chaps. 18–19; Marder, *From the Dreadnought*, vol. 2, chap. 6; A. J. P. Taylor, ed., *Lloyd George: A Diary by Frances Stevenson* (New York, 1971), December 16, 23, 1914, pp. 17, 19; CAB 41/35/64, Asquith to the King, December 18, 1914.

10. CAB 41/35/64, Asquith to the King, December 16, 1914, p. 17; Gilbert, *Winston S. Churchill*, pp. 238–40, 261–62.

11. Beatty to Ethel Beatty, Beatty papers, in Gilbert, *Winston S. Churchill*, pp. 187, 258; Fisher to Jellicoe, November 19, December 20, 1914; Fisher to Churchill, January 18, 1915, in Marder, ed., *Fear God*, 3:76, 99, 133; CAB 42/1/11, 12, 16, War Council meetings, January 11–13, 1915; Mackay, *Fisher*, p. 468.

12. CAB 42/1/16, War Council meeting of January 13, 1915; Fisher to Churchill, January 18, Fisher to Jellicoe, January 19, Jellicoe to Fisher, January 23, Fisher to Asquith, January 28, 1915, in Marder, ed., *Fear God*, 3:133, 144–45; Gilbert, *Winston S. Churchill*, pp. 248–53.

13. Earl Oxford and Asquith, *Memories*, pp. 70–71; CAB 42/1/26, War Council meeting of January 28, 1915; Gilbert, *Winston S. Churchill*, pp. 268–73.

14. CAB 42/2/19 War Council meeting, May 14, 1915.; The Dardanelles debate from Churchill's viewpoint is described in Churchill, *World Crisis*, vol. 2, chaps. 8–15, and Gilbert, *Winston S. Churchill*, pp. 276–436.; Martin S. Gilbert, *Winston S. Churchill, Companion Vol. III Part 2 May 1915–December 1916,* pp. 839–974, documents the cabinet crisis. A detailed account of operations can be found in Marder, *From the Dreadnought*, vol. 2, chaps. 9–10, and Arthur J. Marder, *From the Dardanelles to Oran* (London, 1974), chap. 1.

15. Marder, *From the Dreadnought*, 2: 277–86; Hazlehurst, *Politicians at War,* p. 261–68; Gilbert, *Winston S. Churchill*, pp. 436–47.

16. Austen Chamberlain to Bonar Law, May 17, 1915, cited in Robert Blake, *The Unknown Prime Minister: The Life and Times of Andrew Bonar Law, 1858–1923* (London, 1955), p. 249; Churchill, *The World Crisis*, 2: 364–89; Marder, *From the Dreadnought*, 2: 280–90; Gilbert, *Winston S. Churchill*, chap. 14 and pp. xxiii–xxiv; Hazlehurst, *Politicians at War*, p. 263.

17. Taylor, ed., *Stevenson Diary*, May 15, 1915, p. 50; Gilbert, *Winston S. Churchill*, pp. 480–81, 778–91.

18. Wilson, ed., *Political Diaries,* March 6–8, 1916, p. 189; George Riddell, *Lord Riddell's War Diary* (London, 1933), March 10, 1916, p. 163; Jellicoe to Fisher, May 29, 1915, Fisher papers, in Mackay, *Fisher*, p. 505.

19. Winston S. Churchill, *The World Crisis, 1916–18* (New York, 1927), 1: 131.

20. I have relied upon the superb account of Jutland in Marder, *From the Dreadnought*, vol. 3, chaps. 1–4, for the details of the battle.

21. Ibid, pp. 195–96; Violet Bonham-Carter, *Winston Churchill as I Knew Him* (London, 1965), pp. 458–59; Patterson, ed., *Jellicoe Papers,* 1: 262; Hankey, *The Supreme Command* (London, 1961), 2:491–92; Riddell, *War Diary,* p. 186; Wilson, ed., *Political Diaries,* June 6–8, 1916, p. 214; *LT,* June 3, 1916.

22. CAB 42/15/4 War Council meeting of June 6, 1916; Balfour to Bonar Law, June 10, 1916, Balfour papers; on Churchill's proposal for seeking Japanese capital ships, see, Churchill to Grey, August 29, 1914, Churchill papers, cited in Gilbert, *Winston S. Churchill*, p. 202.

23. Beatty to Jellicoe, June 6, 9, 1916, in Patterson, ed., *Jellicoe Papers,* 1: 288–90; Jellicoe to Jackson, June 6, 1916, and Beatty to Mrs.

Beatty, August 8, 1916, in Marder, *From the Dreadnought*, 3: 191, 199; Admiral Sir Frederick T. Hamilton Diary, June 7, 1916, Hamilton Papers.

24. Riddell, *War Diary*, pp. 188, 204; Marder, *From the Dreadnought*, 3: 196–98, summarizes press commentary; Fisher to Leyland, June 9, H. W. Wilson to Fisher, June 19, Fisher to C. P. Scott, June 19, Fisher to Lady Jellicoe, June 15, 1915, in Marder, *Fear God*, 3: 354–58; *New Statesmen* (June 10, 1916), p. 218.

25. CAB 42/22/13, War Committee meeting, October 31, 1916; CAB 42/22/14, M. P. A. Hankey memorandum, October 31, 1916; Taylor, ed., *Stevenson Diary*, November 10, 1916, p. 121; Marder, *From the Dreadnought*, 3: 257–65; *New Statesman* (October 14, November 4, 1916), pp. 26, 100–101; *The Nation* (November 4, 11, 1916), pp. 151, 164, 170, 194.

26. Marder, *From the Dreadnought*, 3:279–85 analyzes Admiralty responses to the crisis; CAB 42/22/13, 42/23/3, and 37/159/33 record War Council discussions of the problem on October 31, November 2, 13, 1916; Blanche Dugdale, *Arthur James Balfour* (New York, 1937), 2: 116; Asquith to Balfour, November 20, 1916 Balfour papers; Fisher to Jellicoe, November 20, 28, 1916, in Marder, *Fear God*, 3: 388, 395; Stephen Roskill, *Hankey, Man of Secrets* (London, 1970), I: 314–15: *LT,* November 30, 1916.

27. The detailed, classic account of Lloyd George's rise to the premiership is to be found in Lord Beaverbrook, *Politicians and the War, 1914–1916* (London, 1928), chaps. 14–15; I have accepted the revisionist account briefly expounded by Cameron Hazlehurst, "The Conspiracy Myth," in Martin Gilbert, ed., *Lloyd George* (Englewood Cliffs, N.J., 1968), pp. 148–57, and developed further by Peter Lowe, "The Rise to the Premiership, 1914–1916," in Taylor, ed., *Lloyd George*, pp. 95–136.

28. John Grigg, *The Young Lloyd George* (Berkeley, 1974), traces Lloyd George's career down to 1902 and notes the early appearance of characteristics singled out later by his contemporaries; Taylor, ed., *Stevenson Diary*, December 7, 1916, p. 134; J. M. Keynes, *Essays in Biography*, 2d ed. (London, 1951), pp. 32–33; Frances Lloyd George, *The Years That Are Past* (London, 1967), p. 182.

29. Taylor, ed., *Stevenson Diary*, January 17, 1915, November 22, 1916, pp. 21–22, 127.

30. Wilson, ed., *Political Diaries*, December 2–5, 1916, pp. 243–48; Memorandum, The Government Crisis, December 7, 1916, A. J. Balfour papers; Ian Colvin, *The Life of Lord Carson* (New York, 1937), 3: 217–18, 252; Riddell, *War Diaries*, April 5, 1917, p. 249; Carson to Beatty, March 26, 1917, Beatty papers, cited by Marder in *From the Dreadnought*, 4: 113.

31. For an illustration of the Admiralty's and Jellicoe's views before the admiral came to Whitehall, see Patterson, *Jellicoe*, p. 154; Marder,

From the Dreadnought, 4:58–61; CAB 42/24/9, H. J. Jackson memorandum, Combined Strategy in Connection with Submarines, November 15, 1916; CAB 42/23/3, 42/24/13, War Committee meetings of
November 2, 13, 1916; Jellicoe to Duff, November 27, 1916, Admiral Sir
Alexander L. Duff papers. The debate over antisubmarine measures
can be followed in the minutes of War Cabinet meetings from December 12, 1916, through April 2, 1917, see especially CAB 23/1/3, 12, 32,
38–39, 44, 58, 63, 65 and 110; ADM 116/1702 details the effort to get
Japanese naval assistance; ADM 167/51, Board of Admiralty meetings, January 3, 31 and February 9, 1917, memorandums describe
changes in the building program; Christopher Addison, *Four and a
Half Years* (London, 1934), 2:316.

32. Marder, *Fear God*, 3: 438–44; Wilson, ed., *Political Diaries*, February
26–March 1, 1917, p. 263; Hankey, *The Supreme Command*, 2: 583,
645–49; Roskill, *Hankey*, 1: 356, 373; Lloyd George's arguments on
the submarine problem can be traced in War Cabinet discussions,
especially CAB 23/1/1, 5, 8, 46, 57, 62, 70, 73, 91, 104, and 107;
Riddell, *War Diaries*, April 1, 1917, p. 247.

33. Addison, *Four and a Half Years*, 2: 351; Roskill, *Hankey*, p. 356;
Arthur J. Marder, *Portrait of an Admiral* (London, 1952), pp. 233–35,
246; Marder, *From the Dreadnought*, 4: 152–59, 172–73; David Lloyd
George, *War Memoirs, 1916–1917* (Boston, 1934), 3:105; CAB 23/2/
111, 123, 124–26, War Cabinet meetings of April 17, 20, 23, and 25,
1917.

34. Dewar to Richmond, April 27, 1917, Vice Admiral K. G. B. Dewar
papers; Hankey, *Supreme Command*, 2:650; CAB 23/2/130/136, War
Cabinet meetings May 2, 11 1917; Carson to Lloyd George, May 5,
1917, LGP; Jellicoe to Beatty, May 10, 1917, Beatty papers, in Marder,
From the Dreadnought, 4: 175; Riddell, *War Diaries*, May 12, 1917,
p. 249.

35. Lord Beaverbrook, *Men and Power, 1917–1918* (London, 1956), pp.
159–68; Marder, *From the Dreadnought*, 4: 203–4, 206–7; Hankey,
Supreme Command, 2: 625–55; Milner to Lloyd George, June 25,
1917, LGP.

36. Hankey, *Supreme Command*, 2: 654–56; Beaverbrook, *Men and
Power*, p. 171; Addison, *Four and a Half Years*, 2: 406–11; Beatty to
Mrs. Beatty, June 4, 1917, in Chalmers, *Beatty*, p. 318; Hankey to
Lloyd George, July 9, Lloyd George to Carson, July 6, 7, Carson to
Lloyd George, July 7, Milner to Lloyd George, July 16, 1917, LGP;
Marder, *From the Dreadnought*, 4: 209.

37. Geddes to Lloyd George, August 2, 16, Churchill to Lloyd George,
August 20, Bonar Law to Lloyd George, August 24, 1917 LGP; Dewar
to Richmond, August 19, 1917, Vice Admiral K. G. B. Dewar papers;
"The Naval Staff of the Admiralty: Its Work and Development," Naval
Staff Monograph 29, chap. 16, Naval Historical Branch, Ministry of
Defense, London; Marder, *Portrait of an Admiral*, p. 277.

38. ADM 167/53 Board of Admiralty meetings, August 30, Sept. 6, 1917; "The Naval Staff of the Admiralty," chap. 16; ADM 167/54, draft memorandum on Admiralty Board reorganization n.d.; ADM 116/ 1805, Geddes to Lloyd George, September 10, 1917; CAB 24/26, gt 2003, Geddes to War Cabinet, September 11, 1917; Marder, *From the Dreadnought*, 4: 222.

39. Marder, *From the Dreadnought*, vol. 4, chap. 9, recounts these operations; Marder, *Portrait of an Admiral*, p. 266; ADM 167/53, Admiralty Board meetings of September 20, 27, October 26, 1917.

40. Jellicoe to Browning, July 7, 1917, Jellicoe papers; Wemyss, *Life and Letters*, pp. 362–63; Stephen Roskill, *Naval Policy Between the Wars* vol. 1 (London, 1968), pp. 337–38, summarizes Admiralty reactions to the air decision; Roskill, *Hankey*, 1: 447; A. M. Gollin, *Proconsul in Politics: A Study of Lord Milner in Opposition and in Power* (London, 1964), pp. 453–55.

41. Wemyss, *Life and Letters*, p. 364; Roskill, *Hankey*, 1:472–73; Marder, *From the Dreadnought*, 4: 335–38; ADM 116/1806, Geddes to Lloyd George, December 20, 1917.

42. Milner made clear his preference that Geddes remain at the Admiralty in Milner to Lloyd George, November 23, 1917, LGP; Lloyd George, *War Memoirs*, 3:122; Author's interview with Sir Reay Geddes, September 10, 1969; for details of Geddes' actions, cf. ADM 116/1807, correspondence December 24, 1917, to January 4, 1918; Stephen Roskill, "The Dismissal of Admiral Jellicoe," *Journal of Contemporary History* 1 (October 1966): pp. 69–94, first presented a detailed secondary account of the Jellicoe affair.

43. Marder, *From the Dreadnought,* 4: 342, summarizes press comment on the Jellicoe resignation; Fisher to Hankey, Fisher to G. Lambert, January 3, 1918, Marder, *Fear God*, 3: 502–4; Admiral Sir Reginald Bacon, *The Life of John Rushworth Earl Jellicoe* (London, 1936), pp. 384, 286–387; Gollin, *Proconsul in Politics*, p. 464; ADM 116/1807, Carson to Lloyd George, December 31, 1917, Notes for Naval Estimates Debate, March 6, 1918; Balfour to Geddes, March 8, 1918; Balfour to Carson, January 3, 1918, Balfour papers.

44. These generalizations are based upon my reading of Marder, *From the Dreadnought*, vol. 5, chaps. 3, 4, and 6.

45. *LT*, January 7, 1918.

Chapter 3

1. *NYT*, February 1916; Link, *Wilson*, 4:48, fn. 111.

2. Theodore Roosevelt, *The Outlook* (August 22, 1914), cited in Mark Sullivan, *Our Times* (New York, 1933), 5:202; General Board Proceedings, September 18, November 6, 10–11, 1914, General Board papers, cited in Braisted, *The U.S. Navy in the Pacific*, pp. 174, 178; Braisted,

The U.S. Navy in the Pacific, p. 183; Dewey to Daniels, November 14, 1914, Report of the Secretary of the Navy for the Fiscal Year 1914 (Washington, 1915), pp. 59–67; Report of the Secretary of the Navy for the Fiscal Year 1914, p. 8; Fiske, *From Midshipman to Rear Admiral*, pp. 563–70; Josephus Daniels, *The Wilson Era: Years of Peace, 1910–1917* (Chapel Hill, N.C., 1944), pp. 242–43; *NYT*, March 3, 1915.

3. Ernest R. May, *The World War and American Isolation, 1914–1917* (Cambridge, 1959), pp. 307–8, reconstructs the British decision; ibid., pp. 122–32, 149–50, 152–53, deals with the German submarine policy and American post-*Lusitania* decisions; Thomas A. Bailey and Paul B. Ryan, *The Lusitania Disaster* (New York, 1975) offers a detailed account of this episode; Henry Cabot Lodge to J. F. Williams, June 1, 1915, Henry Cabot Lodge papers.

4. A. P. Gardner to Henry Cabot Lodge, May 18, F. D. Roosevelt to A. P. Gardner, n.d. May 1915, Henry Cabot Lodge papers; Wilson to Daniels, July 21, 1915, Woodrow Wilson papers, ser. 4; Link, *Wilson*, 3:591–92.

5. General Board Proceedings, July 23–August 31; General Board to Secretary of the Navy, July 30, General Board confidential memorandum, August 5, file 420-2, General Board to Secretary of the Navy, August 10, file 420-15, GBP; W. S. Benson to Daniels, September 25, 1915, William S. Benson papers.

6. Link, *Wilson*, 4:33–34; Operations memorandum, October 6, 1915, file 420, General Board Proceedings, October 6–9, Secretary of the Navy to General Board, October 7, General Board to Secretary of the Navy, October 12, 1915, serial 415, GBP; *NYT*, October 5, 15, 20, 1915; Report of the Secretary of the Navy for the Fiscal Year 1915 (Washington, 1916), pp. 6–9.

7. U.S. Congress, House, Committee on Naval Affairs, "Estimates submitted by the Secretary of the Navy, 1916," *Hearings*, 64th Congress, 1st sess., pp. 378, 1956, 2021, 2078, 2111, 2116, 3775–776; Report of the Secretary of the Navy for the Fiscal Year 1915, pp. 58–59.

8. Link, *Wilson*, 4: 327–34; "Naval Appropriation Bill," *House Report*, 64th Congress, 1st sess., no. 743, May 24, 1916; *House Report*, 64th Congress, 1st sess., no. 743, (May 31, June, 1916).

9. Lodge to Theodore Roosevelt, July 10, 1916, Henry Cabot Lodge papers; Lansing to Wilson, September 11, 1915, Lansing papers, cited in May, *The World War*, pp. 157–58; House to Wilson, January 15, May 16, June 1, 1916, EMHP.

10. Link, *Wilson*, 4:20; Ray Stannard Baker and William E. Dodd, eds., *The Public Papers of Woodrow Wilson* (New York, 1925–27), 3:332, 374, 4:36, 228–30; Patrick Devlin, *Too Proud to Fight Woodrow Wilson's Neutrality* (New York, 1975), p. ix.

11. *NYT*, July 22, August 7, 9, 16, 30, 1916; Wilson to Daniels, Daniels-Wilson correspondence, Josephus Daniels papers.

12. John Milton Cooper, Jr., *The Vanity of Power* (Westport, Conn., 1969), pp. 220–29, analyzes the new coalition; "Naval Appropriation Bill," *House Report*, 64th Congress, 1st sess., no. 743 (May 24, 1916).

13. Arthur S. Link, *Wilson the Diplomatist* (Baltimore, 1957), chap. 3; May, *American Isolation*, chaps. 16, 19; General Board Proceedings, September 28–October 16, 1916; General Board to Secretary of the Navy, October 16, 1916, file 420, GBP; Annual Report of the Secretary of the Navy for the Fiscal Year 1916 (Washington, 1917), pp. 6–9; *NYT*, February 3–5, 7, 14–15, 1917.

14. *NYT*, February 9, March 2–5, July 22, August 30, September 7, 1917; E. David Cronon, ed., *The Cabinet Diaries of Josephus Daniels, 1913–1921* (Lincoln, Nebraska, 1963), May 1, 1917, p. 145.

15. Cronon, ed., *Daniels Diaries*, March 20, April 11, 21, 30, July 30, August 11, 1917, pp. 117, 131, 133, 144, 183, 190; Sims to Daniels, April 19, 1917, WSSP, cited by Elting E. Morison in *Admiral Sims and the Modern American Navy* (Boston, 1942), p. 342; Pratt to Chief of Naval Operations, June 7, 1917, file td, RG 45; Schilling, "Admirals and Foreign Policy," first explored the intra-Navy Department debate on priorities; Braisted, *The U.S. Navy in the Pacific*, pp. 295–96, 299–300, also chronicles it.

16. Chief of Naval Operations to Secretary of the Navy, n.d. February 1917, "Estimate of the Situation," Josephus Daniels papers; Diary, March 11, 1917, Franklin D. Roosevelt papers, cited in Braisted, *The U.S. Navy in the Pacific*, p. 291; Braisted, *The U.S. Navy in the Pacific*, pp. 291–92, summarizes anti-Japanese rumors; General Board to Secretary of the Navy, April 20, 1917, file 420; General Board Hearings, September 6, 1917, GBP; Badger to Secretary of the Navy, April 5, July 13, 1917, in U.S. Congress, Senate, "Naval Investigation, Hearings before the Subcommittee of the Committee on Naval Affairs," *Hearings*, 66th Congress, 2d sess., (Washington, 1921), 1: 1144, 1218–19.

17. Wilson to Daniels, July 2, August 2, 1917, Wilson-Daniels correspondence file, Daniels papers; Cronon, ed., *Daniels Diaries*, July 20, 1917, p. 179; Frank Friedel, *Franklin D. Roosevelt: The Apprenticeship* (Boston, 1952), chap. 17.

18. Cronon, ed., *Daniels Diaries*, April 21, 1917, p. 139; House diary, May 13, 14, July 7, 1917; Balfour to House, July 5, 1917; House to Wilson, July 7, 1917, EMHP; Balfour memorandum, May 24, 1917, *FRUS, 1917, Supplement 1*, pp. 70–71; David Trask, *Captains and Cabinets: Anglo-American Naval Relations 1917–1918* (Columbia, Missouri, 1972), chap. 3, provides a detailed discussion of the abortive treaty; CAB 23/2/142, Minutes of War Cabinet meeting, May 22, Balfour to Lloyd George, May 14, 1917.

19. Cronon, ed., *Daniels Diaries*, April 21, 1917, p. 139; Notes on Interview with the President, July 13, 1917, Sir William Wiseman papers, printed in Wilton B. Fowler, *British-American Relations, 1917-1918* (Princeton, 1969), pp. 243-46.

20. Cronon, ed., *Daniels Diaries*, March 20, July 30, August 11, 1917, pp. 117, 184, 190; Secretary of State to Page (for Admiral Sims from the President), July 4, *FRUS, 1917, Supplement II*, 1:117-18; Wilson to Daniels, July 2, Winston Churchill (American novelist and Naval Academy graduate) to Wilson, October 22, forwarded with Wilson to Daniels, November 12, 1917, Wilson-Daniels correspondence file, Daniels papers.

21. *NYT*, July 4, 1917; samples of wartime favorable comment appear in *Times* editorials, May 18, September 8, October 10, and December 3, 1917, and in numerous articles; Daniels, *The Wilson Era: Years of War, 1917-1923*, chaps. 8-17, record naval achievements and reflect positive feelings recorded in the author's diary; William S. Sims, *The Victory at Sea* (Garden City, N.Y., 1921), fills out the story of naval accomplishments. It is significant that Congress for all its probing into army operations, made no effort to examine naval operations. See Seward W. Livermore, *Politics is Adjourned* (Middletown, Conn., 1966), chaps. 5-7.

22. General Board to Secretary of the Navy, August 29, 1917, file 420-2; Sims to Secretary of the Navy, November 14, 1918, serial 889, GBP; Benson to House, February 28, 1918, EMHP; Pratt to Sims, May 27, 1917, April 21, 1918, Sims to Pratt, June 7, 15, 1917, August 30, 1918, file td, RG 80.

23. General Board to Secretary of the Navy, August 29, 1917, June 15, September 10, 1918, file 420-2, Sims to Secretary of the Navy, May 21, 1918, serial 890, file 420, GBP; Pratt n.d. 1918 memorandum, Planning Committee to Benson, October 7, 1918, pd 100-23, RG 80.

24. *NYT*, March 15, 20, May 23, June 12, July 2, 1918; France to Wilson, March 28, 1918, Wilson papers, cited by Cooper in *Vanity of Power*, p. 199.

25. Warren F. Kuehl, *Hamilton Holt* (Gainesville, Fla., 1960), pp. 119-32; Ruhl. J. Bartlett, *The League to Enforce Peace* (Chapel Hill, 1944), chaps. 2-3; Sandra R. Herman, *Eleven against War* (Stanford, 1969), pp. 68-79; C. Roland Marchand, *The American Peace Movement and Social Reform, 1898-1918* (Princeton, 1972), pp. 156-60.

26. Paolo E. Coletta, *William Jennings Bryan* (Lincoln, Nebraska, 1969), 3:44-45; *NYT*, February 9, 18, 1918; Bartlett, *League to Enforce Peace*, pp. 92, 100-101, 111; Charles Forcey, *The Crossroads of Liberalism* (New York, 1961), pp. 265; 283-84; Charles Chatfield, *For Peace and Justice: Pacifism in America, 1914-1941*, (Knoxville, Tenn., 1971), pp. 25, 31; Norris to J. A. Kees, George W. Norris papers, cited by Richard Lowitt in *George W. Norris: The Persistence of a Progressive, 1913-1933* (Urbana, Ill., 1971), p. 107; Annual

Report of the Secretary of the Navy for the Fiscal Year 1917 (Washington, 1918), pp. 82–83; "Police of the Sea," *The League Bulletin*, no. 65 (December 14, 1917), pp. 109–10, cited in Kuehl, *Seeking World Order*, p. 252.

27. Albert Shaw, ed., *The Messages and Papers of Woodrow Wilson* (New York, 1924), p. 381; Arno Mayer, *Political Origins of the New Diplomacy* (New Haven, 1959), chap. 9 analyzes the origins and drafting of the Fourteen Points address.

28. Baker and Dodd, *The Public Papers of Woodrow Wilson*, 5:159–61.

29. *NYT*, January 9, February 18, 1918; Bryan to Wilson, January 15, 1918, Wilson papers, cited by Coletta in *Bryan*, 3:84.

30. ADM 116/1809, Geddes to Lloyd George, August 26, Geddes to F. D. Roosevelt, August 28, notes for speech before members, House Naval Affairs Committee, August 2; Roosevelt to Daniels, October 16, 1918, Franklin D. Roosevelt papers; Schilling, "Admirals and Foreign Policy," p. 136; Daniels to Wilson, September 26, Wilson to Daniels, October 2, 1918, Woodrow Wilson papers.

31. ADM 116/1809, memorandum, September 5, meeting of First Lord with members of Board; memorandum of meeting in First Lord's cabin, October 5; n.d. notes for guidance as to the line to be adopted in conversations with the U.S. Navy Department and in informal conversations; minutes of meeting at Navy Department, October 8; Balfour to Geddes, October 12; Geddes to Lloyd George, October 13; notes on October 16, 1918 Geddes-Wilson interview; Trask, *Captains and Cabinets*, chap. 8 chronicles the Geddes mission.

32. Cronon, ed., *Daniels Diaries*, October 14–17, 1918, pp. 349–52.

Chapter 4

1. Kaigun daijin kanbō, *Kaigun gunbi enkaku*, 2d ed. (Tokyo, 1970), 1:241.

2. Aritake Shūji, *Saitō Makoto* (Tokyo, 1958), pp. 62–63; Ōkuma kō hachijū go nen shi hensan iinkai, *Ōkuma kō hachijū go nen shi*, 2d ed. (Tokyo, 1970), 3:150; Matsushita, *Nihon gunsei to seiji*, p. 51; Maeda Renzan, *Rekidai naikaku monogatari* (Tokyo, 1961), 2:43–51, 56–59; Duus, *Party Rivalry*, pp. 86–89.

3. Gaimushō hyakunen shi hensan iinkai, *Gaimushō no hyakunen* (Tokyo, 1969), 1:605–8.

4. Masumi, *Nihon seitō shi ron*, 3:271–75, 281; Roger F. Hackett, *Yamagata Aritomo in the Rise of Modern Japan, 1838–1922* (Cambridge, 1971), pp. 275–300; *HKN*, 6, August 14, 1914; Peter Lowe, *Great Britain and Japan, 1911–1915* (New York, 1969), chaps. 6–7; Kwanha Yim, "Japanese Policy toward China during World War I" (Ph.D. diss., Fletcher School of Law and Diplomacy, 1968), chapter 2 analyzes the origins of the Twenty-one Demands; Madelaine Chi, *China Diplomacy, 1914–1918* (Cambridge, 1970), pp. 33–53.

5. Ogasawara Chōsei, *Kyojin Yashiro Rokurō* (Tokyo, 1931), pp. 196–98; Kiba Hirosuke, *Nomura Kichisaburō* (Tokyo, 1961), pp. 152–53; Itō Masanori, *Katō Kōmei* (Tokyo, 1929), 2:7–9; Suzuki Hajime, ed., *Suzuki Kantarō jiden* (Tokyo, 1949), pp. 189–92; *HKN*, 6, June 8, 1914, pp. 52–54.

6. Kiba, *Nomura*, pp. 156–58; Nihon kaigun kōkū shi hensan iinkai, *Nihon Kaigun kōkū shi*, I:66–68; "Operation of Japanese Squadrons during the War, 1914–1919," U.S. Naval Intelligence report, file wa-5, RG 45; Itō, *Katō Kōmei*, 2:126–27.

7. Suzuki, ed., *Suzuki Kantarō jiden*, p. 205; Nakagawa, *Gensui Shima-mura Hayao den* (Tokyo, 1933), pp. 3–12, 239–40; Arai Tatsuo, *Katō Tomosaburō* (Tokyo, 1958), p. 198; Lt. Comdr. Lyman A. Cotton Naval War College lecture, February 26, 1915, Naval Intelligence file c-10-h, RG 45.

8. Arai, *Katō*, pp. 188, 191–92, 198–99; Abo Kiyokazu, *Katō Kanji taishō den* (Tokyo, 1941), p. 703; Ozaki Yukio, "Jiden," in Suzuki Shogo, ed., *Ozaki Gakudō zenshū*, 11: 629–30; author's interviews with Admiral Yamanashi Katsunoshin, member of Japan's Washington Conference delegation, July 12, 1966, and with Enamoto Jūji, senior civilian secretary in the Navy Ministry, June 1, 1966.

9. Ogasawara Chōsei, ed., *Kaigun hen*, vol. 13, in *Denki Dai Nippon shi,* edited by Nagasaka Kaneo (Tokyo, 1936), pp. 158–59; Kaigun daijin kanbō, *Kaigun gunbi enkaku,* 1: 199–201.

10. Arai, *Katō*, pp. 126–28; Suzuki, ed., *Suzuki Kantarō jiden*, p. 205; 37th Diet, Shūgiin, *Yosan iinkai giroku*, December 10, 24, 1915, pp. 8, 9; 37th Diet, Shūgiin, *Dai yon bunryōkai giroku,* December 20, 1915, p. 14; Itō Masanori, *Shinbun seikatsu nijūnen* (Tokyo, 1933), pp. 250–54; 259–63; Satō Tetsutarō "Kaikoku no shimei," *Kaigun* 10 (April 1915): 6–7; Akiyama Saneyuki, "Rekkoku to Nippon kaigun ryoku," *Kaigun* 10 (October 1915): 7–10; Anonymous, "Kokubō no jūjitsu to shōrai no seikan keikaku," *Kaigun* 10 (November 1915): 23–24; Anonymous, "Kaigun hojū keikaku ni tsuite," *Taiyō* 22 (September 1915), 81–88; Anonymous, Kaisenjutsu no shin keikō to zōkan seisaku," *Taiyō* 22 (July 1916): 129–34; Matsumoto Chujirō, "Genka no zaisei jōtai to kaigun jūjitsu mondai," *Chūō Kōron* 30 (September 1915): 63–68; Tomizu Hirōto, "Kinsei sekai no keisei o ronjite: Kosaku naru kaigun hojūan o nan zu," *Chūō Kōron* 30 (December 1915): 18–27; Suzuki Kantarō statement, *Hochi shinbun,* October 6, quoted in Naval Attaché Tokyo to Secretary of State, October 8, 1915, 894.34/10, Department of State files, reel 20, National Archives Microfilm Publication 422.

11. Kaigun daijin kanbō, *Kaigun gunbi enkaku*, 1: 194–208; Arai, Katō, p. 132. Katō did express a pro-forma desire to resign at Ōkuma's fall but readily acceded to Terauchi's requests and the device of an Imperial command to remain in office, Suzuki. *Suzuki Kantarō jiden*, pp. 205–6, demonstrates that the internal healing of the service was far

enough along for Katō to appoint former Minister Yashiro to a major fleet command; *HKN*, 6, August 15, 20, 1915, pp. 301–2, 308–9.

12. Kaigun daijin kanbō, *Kaigun gunbi enkaku*, 1: 185–86; *HKN* 6, September 1, 1914, p. 121.

13. Ōkurasho Shōwa zaisei shi henshu shitsu hen, *Shōwa zaisei shi* (Tokyo, 1965), 1:26–31; Yamasaki Kakujirō and Ogawa Gotarō, *The Effect of the World War upon the Commerce and Industry of Japan* (New Haven, 1929), pp. 8–10, 33–34; *GSSJN*, 9:818, 845; Shibuya Sakudō, *Taketomi Tokitoshi* (Tokyo, 1934), p. 41.

14. Kaigun daijin kanbō, *Kaigun gunbi enkaku*, 1: 180–83; Ōkuma kō hachijūgo nen shi hensan iinkai, *Ōkuma kō*, 3:148–50; Bōeichō, *Dai honei rikugun bu I*, pp. 192–94.

15. *HKN*, 6, December 2, 1914, June, December 25–27, 1915, pp. 190, 261, 366–67; Wakatsuki Reijirō, *Kofuan Kaiko roku* (Tokyo, 1950), pp. 211–12, 256–57; Shibuya, *Taketomi*, pp. 39–40; Suzuki, ed., *Suzuki Kantarō jiden*, pp. 195–96; *GSSJN*, 9:793.

16. *HKN*, 6, May 21, 24, 30, June 6, 13, 24, 30, July 1, 1916, pp. 413–43, passim.

17. Lawrence Olson, Jr., "Hara Kei: A Political Biography" (Ph.D diss., Harvard University, 1953); Robert A. Scalapino, *Democracy and the Party Movement in Prewar Japan: The Failure of the First Attempt* (Berkeley and Los Angeles, 1953), p. 213; Najita, *Hara Kei in the Politics of Compromise, 1905–1915*, pp. 14–16, 219–22, and Duus, *Party Rivalry*, pp. 68–82, are the best English language sources on Hara; Maeda Renzan, *Hara Kei* (Tokyo, 1958), is the best Japanese language biography; my assessment of Hara's character is also drawn from close reading of the *Hara nikki* and from an interview with Hara's adopted son, July 5, 1969.

18. *HKN*, 6, July 21, September 4–6, November 1, December 20–25, 1914, pp. 90–91, 123–25, 166–67, 209–15; *GSSJN*, 9:776; Itō, *Katō Kōmei*, 2:35–36.

19. Itō, *Katō Kōmei*, pp. 843–45, 857; *HKN*, 6, 7, April 22, May 26, 1916, January 12, 1917, pp. 406, 418, 105–6; Makino Ryōzō, *Nakahashi Tokugorō* (Tokyo, 1944), 1:301.

20. *GSSJN*, 9, p. 878; *HKN*, 7, December 6, 10, 21, 1917, January 14, 1918, pp. 287, 289–91, 299, 310.

21. *HKN*, 7, November 17, December 1, 26, 28, 1917, February 3–4, 12, 1918, pp. 271, 279–280, 302, 306–7, 320–22, 328; Editorial, March 30, 1918, *Tokyo Asahi Shinbun*.

22. *HKN*, 7, June 2–6, 1917, pp. 179–85; *Gaimushō no hyakunen*, 1: 614–17, 621–30, surveys Japan's wartime foreign policies; Shinobu Seizaburō, *Taishō seiji shi* (Tokyo, 1951), 1: 230–50, and Masumi, *Nihon seitō shi ron*, 3:322–51, offer interpretive accounts of China policy developments; Peter Berton, "The Secret Russo-Japanese Alliance of 1916" (Ph.D. diss., Columbia University, 1956), and Yoshimura Michio, *Nihon to Roshia* (Tokyo, 1968), analyze Russo-

Japanese relations; Francis C. Prescott, "The Lansing-Ishii Agreement" (Ph.D. diss., Yale University, 1949), and Shigemitsu Osami, "Ishii Ranshingu kyōtei," *Kikan kokusai seiji* (Summer 1958), pp. 66–78, Nagaoka Shinjirō, "Ishii Ransingu kyōtei no seiritsu," *Kikan kokusai seiji* (1967, no. 2), pp. 54–71, and Kurobane Shigeru, *Taiheiyō o meguru NichiBei sensō shi* (Tokyo, 1968), chap. 10, deal with the 1917 talks; Kajima Morinosuke, *Nihon gaikō shi* (Tokyo, 1965), pp. 808–15, reviews the decision to dispatch ships to Europe; ADM 116/1702, Japanese Naval Assistance, 1916–1919, compiles official correspondence on the subject; Bōeichō, *Dai honei rikugun bu*, 1:208–10 reviews army debates on a European expedition.

23. This change can best be followed in the *Hara nikki* from January through June 1918, and in Komura Tatsuo, ed, *Suiusō nikki Itō ke monjo* (Tokyo, 1966), pp. 125–87; James Morley, *The Japanese Thrust into Siberia, 1918* (New York, 1957), Hosoya Chihiro, *Shiberia shuppei no shiteki kenkyū* (Tokyo, 1955), Kurobane, *Taiheiyō o meguru NichBei senso shi*, pp. 275–81, and Masumi, *Nihon seitō shi ron*, 3:352–83, analyze the Siberian debates; *HKN*, 7, June 5–19, 1918, pp. 409–21, chronicles the final decision.

24. "Teikoku sansen no mokuteki ikaga," *Taiyō* 24 (March 1918): 71–125; Ibid., (April 1918); for similar private doubts as to American war aims, see Ugaki Kazushige, *Ugaki Kazushige nikki* (Tokyo, 1968), 1:155; Tanaka Giichi, "Kokubō no seirian," item 58, microfilm reel 2, Tanaka Giichi papers; Araki Sadao, *Gensui Uehara Yūsaku den* (Tokyo, 1937), 2:115; Takakura Tetsuichi, *Tanaka Giichi denki* (Tokyo, 1963), 2:168.

25. Araki, *Uehara*, 2:114; Funakoshi to Shimamura, June 16, October 20, 1916, Ewatari to Suzuki Kantarō, January 20, 1917, Chūzaiin hōkoku, Japan Defense Agency archives; 40th Diet, Shūgiin, *Yosan iinkai giroku*, January 25, 1918.

26. Akiyama Saneyuki, "Ōshū taisen to kōgyō," in Murakami Kakuichi, ed., *Gundan Kaigun* (Tokyo, 1918), pp. 249–73; Notes for speech at Yokohama, July 25, 1916, item 58, Gotō Shinpei papers; Horie Kiichi, "Gunkoku shugi to keizai seisaku," *Taiyō* 22 (July, 1916): 49–56; Makino, *Nakahashi Tokugorō*, 2:544–45.

27. Shimamura memorandum, November 1914, *NGKB, 1914*, 3:648–51; *NGKB, 1917, 3: 115–16*; Anonymous naval officer, "Ōshū shuppei ron o homuru," *Taiyō* 21 (February 1915): 129–34; Yamakawa Tadao, Teikoku ga gunji jo shutoku rieki to suru Dokuryo Nanyō Shotō no hani, Nichi Doku seneki kōwa junbi chōsa fuzoku sankō choso, pp. 142–50; Nichi Doku seneki kōwa junbi iinkai giroku, February 9, 1916, JFMA; Katō Tomosaburō to Takeshita Isamu, June 10, 1917, UD-15, reel UD-16. These and similar firm designations used hereinafter are those developed in Cecil Uyehara, *Checklist of Archives in the Japanese Ministry of Foreign Affairs, Tokyo, 1868–1945* (Washington, 1954).

28. Abo Kiyokazu memorandum, January 6, 1918, Kiyokawa Junichi

memorandum, February 25, 1918, Dai roppen, pp. 70, 72–75, 78–84, JDA; *Tokyo Asahi Shimbun*, November 9, 1919, recalled Yoshida's earlier efforts.

29. Morley, *The Japanese Thrust*, pp. 214–15.

30. Yamagata memorandum, June 1918, in Ōyama Azusa, ed., *Yamagata Aritomo ikensho* (Tokyo, 1967), pp. 361–75.

31. Bōeichō, *Kaigun gunsenbi I*, pp. 65–67. The two general staffs began drafting revision schemes in May, but not until Yamagata came to Tokyo in early June and the Siberian decision was imminent did a concrete proposal work its way through the routines of official approval; Ōyama, *Yamagata*, pp. 33–34; Takakura, *Tanaka*, 2:168.

32. Morley, *The Japanese Thrust*, p. 309; Bōeichō, *Hitō kōryaku sakusen*, pp. 8, 10–11.

33. Shinobu, *Taishō seiji shi* (Tokyo, 1951), 2:539–693, surveys the rice riots and cabinet crisis, as does Maeda Renzan, *Rekidai naikaku monogatari*, 2:206–19, and Masumi, *Nihon seitō shi ron*, 4:314–34; Duus, *Party Rivalry*, pp. 101–6; An "inside" account of these events is drawn in *HKN*, 8, September 12–18, 1918, pp. 4–10, and Hayashi Shigeru and Oka Yoshitake, eds., *Taishō demokurashii ki no seiji: Matsumoto Gokichi seiji nisshi* (Tokyo, 1959), September 12–27, 1918, pp. 27–33; Bōeichō, *Kaigun gunsenbi I*, p. 67; Araki, *Uehara*, p. 116.

34. Maeda Renzan, *Rekidai naikaku monogatari*, 2:219–29; Anonymous, "Hara naikaku shutsugen no jijō oyobi igi," *Taiyō* 24 (November 1918): 19–28; Yoshino Sakuzō, "Hara naikaku ni taisuru yobō," *Chūō Kōron* 33 (October 1918): 80–85.

35. *HKN*, 7, September 28, October 11, 14, .1918, pp. 35, 52, 56; *Ugaki nikki*, 1:178–79.

36. Kaigun daijin kanbō, *Kaigun gunbi enkaku*, p. 241; *HKN*, 8, October 18, 1918, pp. 63–64.

37. *HKN*, 8, October 18, 1918, pp. 63–64.

38. Takakura, *Tanaka*, 2:181; Imamura Takeo, *Hyōden: Takahashi Korekiyo* (Tokyo, 1950), p. 111; *HKN*, 8, October 23, 1918, p. 68.

39. Takakura, *Tanaka*, 2:182–84.

40. *HKN*, 8, October 23, 1918, p. 68.

Chapter 5

1. Cronon, ed., *Daniels Diaries*, October 8, 17, 26, 1918, pp. 339, 342, 345; Wilson to Lansing, September 2, 1918, *FRUS, The Lansing Papers*, 2:380, cited in Roy Watson Curry, *Woodrow Wilson and Far Eastern Policy, 1913–1921* (New York, 1957), p. 237; House diary, October 13, 1918, EMHP; Notes of Wilson-Wiseman interview, October 16, 1918, Wiseman papers, cited in Fowler, *British-American Relations, 1917–1918*, pp. 286–87.

2. *NYT*, October 9, 13, 1918; Livermore, *Politics is Adjourned*, pp. 185–223; Cronon, ed., *Daniels Diaries*, October 21, 23, 1918, pp. 342–44; Secretary of State to Charge in Great Britain, October 14, 1918, *FRUS, 1918*, Supplement, 1, p. 361.

3. Wilson, ed., *Political Diaries*, August 7–8, 1918, pp. 351–52; D. D. Cuthbert, "Lloyd George and the Conservative Central Office, 1918–1922," in Taylor, ed., *Lloyd George*, pp. 169–76; Arno J. Mayer, *Politics and Diplomacy of Peacemaking*, 2d ed. (New York, 1969), pp. 135–39; V. H. Rothwell, *British War Aims and Peace Diplomacy 1914–1918* (London, 1971), pp. 254–62.

4. CAB 23/8/484, /17/29, /14/489A, War Cabinet meetings, October 11, 19, 21, 1918; ADM 167/53, Board meeting October 18, 1918; Fisher to Archibald Hurd, October 16, 1918, in Marder, *Fear God*, 3:554; CAB 24/67, gt 6042, gt 6065, Wemyss memorandum October 19, Hankey memorandum, October 22, 1918.

5. CAB 23/17/29, /14/489, 489A War Cabinet meetings, October 19, 21, 26, 1918.

6. Richmond diary, October 19, 24, 1918, Richmond papers; Thomas Jones, *Whitehall Diary*, vol. 1, 1916–1925, ed. Keith Middlemas (London, 1969), October 15, 1918, p. 69; CAB 23/14/491A, War Cabinet meeting, October 25, 1918.

7. CAB 23/14/491b, War Cabinet meeting, October 26, 1918.

8. House diary, October 28–31, House to Wilson, cable and letter, October 29, 30, Wilson to House, October 30, 1918, EMHP; Hankey diary, October 29–30, 1918, in Roskill, *Hankey*, 1:623–24.

9. Hankey diary, November 3–4, 1918, in Roskill, *Hankey*, 1:627; House diary, November 1–4, 1918, EMHP.

10. CAB 23/8/496, War Cabinet meeting, November 5, 1918; House diary, November 1–4, 1918, EMHP; Wemyss, *Life and Letters*, pp. 387–88; "Armistice 1918," item AI 43, Admiral Baron Rosslyn Erskine Wester Wemyss papers, January 1918–October 1919, microfilm copy, University of California, Irvine; Hankey diary, November 4, 1918, in Roskill, *Hankey*, 1:627; Marder, *From the Dreadnought*, 5:180–84 and Trask, *Captains and Cabinets*, pp. 331–42, summarize the negotiations.

11. Cronon, ed., *Cabinet Diaries*, November 6, 1918, p. 347; House to Wilson, November 5, House diary, December 11, 1918, EMHP; Benson to Daniels, November 21, 1918, file vm, RG 45; Daniels to Wilson, November 14, Wilson to Daniels, November 18, 1918, Daniels papers; Daniels to Wilson, November 23, cited by Schilling in "Admirals and Foreign Policy, 1913–1919," p. 223; *NYT*, December 3, 1918.

12. ADM 116/1809, Geddes to Lloyd George, October 13, 1918; notes of interview with President Wilson, October 16, 1918, Sir William Wiseman papers, cited by Fowler in *British-American Relations, 1917–1918*, p. 220; Proposed Plans for Establishment of League of Nations Army and Navy, November 11, 1918, file vl, RG 45; Records of Charles

250 Notes to Chapter Five

L. Swem, Princeton University Library, cited by Arthur Walworth in *Woodrow Wilson* (New York, 1958), 2:217.

13. Mayer, *Politics and Diplomacy*, chap. 5; George Riddell, *Lord Riddell's Intimate Diary of the Peace Conference and After, 1918–1923* (London, 1934), December 15, 26, 1918, pp. 4, 8; CAB 23/44, 23/42, Imperial War Cabinet meetings, November 6, 20, 26, 28, December 12, 18, 20, 23–24, 1918; CAB 29/2, Smuts memorandum, "Our Policy at the Peace Conference," December 3, 1918; Swartz, *The Union of Democratic Control*, p. 138; Henry R. Winkler, *The League of Nations Movement in Great Britain, 1914–1919* (New Brunswick, N.J., 1952), describes the growth of pro-league sentiment.

14. ADM 116/1772, Admiralty memoranda for War Cabinet, Freedom of the Seas, December 21, Naval Aspects of a League of Nations and Limitations of Armaments, n.d. but forwarded to Sir Maurice Hankey, December 23, 1918; CAB 23/42, Imperial War Cabinet meeting, December 24, 1918.

15. CAB 23/42, Imperial War Cabinet December 30, 31, 1918; David Lloyd George, *Memoirs of the Peace Conference* (New Haven, 1939), 1:94, 110, 114.

16. Generalizations on the Tokyo atmosphere are based on my reading of the *Japan Advertiser* and *Asahi Shimbun* for October 15–December 1, 1918, and on American Embassy Tokyo staff reports, n.d. October 1918, "On the preponderance of imperialistic forces in Japan," K. A. Baldwin memorandum, October 24, 1918, Roland S. Morris papers; Chinda to Uchida, November 7, 8, Ishii to Uchida, November 9, Matsui to Uchida, November 13, 1918, *NGKB, 1918*, 3:498–99, 594, 605–6, 614–15; *Gaimushō no hyakunen*, 1:701–2, 705; *HKN*, 7, 8, December 6, 1917, November 1, 17, 1918, pp. 72, 86, 341.

17. *Gaimushō no hyakunen*, 1:714; *SN*, Foreign Affairs Advisory Council meetings, November 13, 19, December 2, 1918, pp. 285–86, 297–310, passim; Usui Katsumi, "Berusaiyu-Washington taisei to Nihon no shihaisō," in Miyazawa Toshiyoshi and Ōkōchi Kazuo, eds., *Kindai Nihon seiji shisō shi* (Tokyo, 1970), 2:109–12; my "Nihon to Wuisuronteki sekai chitsujo," in Satō Seizaburō and Roger Dingman, eds., *Kindai Nihon no taigai taido* (Tokyo, 1974), pp. 93–123, treats the more general debate in Tokyo over the League.

18. Uchida to Chinda, December 26, *NGKB, 1918*, 3:665–78; *Gaimushō no hyakunen*, 1:711–13; *HKN*, 8, December 8, 18–19, 1918, pp. 106, 114–15.

19. Miller diary, November 25, 1918; London Planning Staff memorandum, November 7, 1918; Miller to House, December 13, 1918, all in David Hunter Miller, *My Diary at the Conference of Paris* (New York, 1924), 1:13; 2:94, 262–64; House to Grey, December 25, House diary, December 31, 1918, EMHP.

20. ADM 167/53, Board minutes, December 5, 1918; ADM 116/1772, Wemyss memorandum for War Cabinet, December 21, 1918; ADM

116/1861, "Peace Terms," 1918–1920 chronicles the Admiralty Peace Committee's drafting of "Admiralty Policy in relation to the Peace Settlement," completed in January 1919; ADM 116/1863, Cecil to Wemyss, January 30, 31, Wemyss to Cecil, January 31, 1919; Miller, *My Diary*, 1:62, 84–105; 3:85–88, 259, 431.

21. Naval Advisory Staff memorandum 10, December 25, 1918, RG 45; cited by Schilling in "Admirals and Foreign Policy," p. 164; ADM 116/1861, Wemyss memorandum, December 18, 1918; CAB 23/42, Imperial War Cabinet meeting, December 24, 1918; Gerda Richards Crosby, *Disarmament and Peace in British Politics* (Cambridge, 1957), p. 137; Miller, *My Diary*, 1:368, 4:350–57.

22. Winkler, *The League of Nations Movement*, pp. 43, 87; Miller, *My Diary*, 3:75–85; ADM 116/1772, Proceedings of Peace Committee of Admiralty, January 3, 1918; Long memorandum for War Cabinet, March 3, 1919, later protested the ban on private arms manufacture. *SN*, Foreign Affairs Advisory Council meeting, January 26, March 30, 1919, pp. 349–81, 447–48; Seth Tillman, *Anglo-American Relations at the Paris Peace Conference, 1919* (Princeton, 1961), pp. 120–22.

23. Miller, *My Diary*, 3:75–85; U.S. Naval Advisory Staff memorandum for Chief of Naval Operations, n.d., in Miller, *My Diary*, 2:101–7; ADM 116/1861, Draft Plans Division "Limitation of Armaments," December 1918; ADM 116/1772, Admiralty memorandum on Naval Aspects of a League of Nations and Limitation of Armaments, n.d. forwarded to Sir Maurice Hankey, December 23, for cabinet consideration December 24, 1918; Takeshita to Katō Tomosaburō and Shimamura Hayao, February 7, 1919, Inin tōchi mondai, JFMA.

24. *SN*, Foreign Affairs Advisory Council meetings, February 19, 22, 1919, pp. 411, 414, 426; *HKN*, 8, February 15, 19, 1919, pp. 160–61, 163; ADM 167/56, Board meetings, February 27, March 1, 1919; ADM 116/1772, "League of Nations Covenant" memorandum for War Cabinet, March 3, 1919; Crosby, *Disarmament and Peace in British Politics*, chap. 6, offers a detailed account of the drafting of article 8.

25. CAB 29/28, British Empire Delegation meetings, March 13, April 21, 1919; ADM 115/1772, Long memorandum, the League of Nations Covenant, April 30, 1919; Takeshita to Katō Tomosaburō and Shimamura Hayao, March 26, April 29, House to Wilson, May 22, 1919, EMHP.

26. *HKN*, 7, November 22, 1918, p. 91; *SN*, Foreign Affairs Advisory Council, December 2, 1918, p. 325; *Gaimushō no hyakunen*, 1:701; *Tokyo nichi nichi* editorial, December 2, 1918. translated in *Japan Advertiser*, December 3, 1918; Kamikawa Hikomatsu, "Doitsu shokuminchi no shobun mondai," *Taiyō*, 24 (June 15, 1918): 257; CAB 23/42, Imperial War Cabinet, December 31, 1918; CAB 29/1, note on possible terms of peace by the First Sea Lord, October 12, 1916; ADM 116/1861, November 22, 1918 draft, Naval Terms of Peace; CAB 29/7, summary of Admiralty policy for information of British Delegation, January 22,

1919; William Roger Louis, *Great Britain and Germany's Lost Colonies, 1914–1919* (London, 1967), chap. 3; April 5, 1917, draft General Board to Secretary of the Navy, file 414-3; A. P. Niblack to Secretary of the Navy (Operations), October 18, 1917, Badger to Benson, December 2, 1918, file 438, GBP; Naval Advisory Staff memorandum 20, February 26, 1919, E. T. Williams and S. K. Hornbeck memorandum, January 20, 1919, RG 256; Lawrence E. Gelfand, *The Inquiry: American Preparations for Peace, 1917–1919* (New Haven, 1963), pp. 270–72.

27.   Council of Ten, secretary notes, January 24, 27–28, 30, *FRUS, Paris Peace Conference 1919*, 3:738–55, 785–86; House to Wilson, January 26, 1919, EMHP; CAB 29/28, British Empire Delegation meeting, January 28, 1919; Louis, *Great Britain and Germany's Lost Colonies*, pp. 130–32, 136–37.

28.   House diary, January 28, 1919, EMHP; Miller, *My Diary*, 1:100; *SN*, Foreign Affairs Advisory Council meeting, February 3, 1919, p. 387; Takeshita to Kato Tomosaburo and Shimamura Hayao, January 31, 1919, Inin tōchi mondai, JFMA; Yamakawa Tadao memorandum, Nichi Doku seneki kōwa junbi iinkai chōsa shiryō, pp. 142–50.

29.   Yamanashi to Secretary, Ministry of Foreign Affairs, Inin tōchi mondai, Japan Foreign Ministry archives; *HKN*, 8, February 3, 1919, pp. 149–50; Shimei kai memorandum, December 7, 1918, Kokumin Gaikō Dōmei kai memorandum, December 6, 1918, Foreign Affairs Advisory Council, February 3, 1919, in *SN*, pp. 785–90, 389–400; "Saito Man" column, December 6, 1918, journal summaries, January 16, 28, 1919, *Japan Advertiser*; Yoshino Sakuzō, "Kōwa kaigi ni teigen subeki wagakuni no nanyō shotō shobun an," *Chūō Kōron* 34 (January 1919): 146a–147a.

30.   Miller, *My Diary*, 1:100; W. S. Rogers memorandum, January 30, *FRUS, Paris Peace Conference, 1919*, 7:512–15; Council of Four Minutes, April 21, 30, May 7, 1919, *FRUS, Paris Peace Conference, 1919*, 5:109, 363, 500, 506–8; Plenary Session minutes, April 28, 1919, *FRUS, Paris Peace Conference, 1919*, 3:289–91; House to Wilson, July 9, 1919, in Miller, *My Diary*, 20:348–49; House to Wilson, July 11, 1919, Wilson papers; Polk to House, July 18, 1919, cited in Braisted, *The U.S. Navy in the Pacific*, pp. 451–52; Braisted, chap. 25, summarizes the Pacific Islands debate. For differing views of Wilson's motives, see Russell H. Fifield, *Woodrow Wilson and the Far East* (New York, 1952), pp. 134–35, and Schilling, "Admirals and Foreign Policy, 1913–1919," pp. 218–26.

31.   CAB 23/14/491B, War Cabinet meeting, October 26, 1918; ADM 116/1861, December 1918 draft, January 1919 final version of Admiralty Policy in relation to the Peace Settlement; Beatty to Wemyss, November 5, Beatty to "a friend," November 12, 1918, cited in Chalmers, *Beatty*, pp. 338, 341–42; *NYT*, November 23, 1918; Navy Minister's Private Secretary to Foreign Minister's Private Secretary, December 10, 1918, *NGKB*, 1918, 3:623–25; Benson to Daniels, November 27, 1918,

film vm, Benson to Daniels, December 4, 1918, Rand diary, file ub, RG 45; Naval Advisory Staff memorandum 18, February 20, 1919, William S. Benson papers; Naval Advisory Staff memorandum 20 and 21, February 26, March 5; Benson to American Commission to Negotiate Peace, February 21; Herter to Grew, February 22, Meeting of Commissioners Plentipotentiary of American Delegation, February 24, 1919, RG 256; House diary, March 6, 1919; Benson to House, March 18, 1919, EMHP.

32. CAB 23/14/489a, War Cabinet meeting, October 21, 1918; ADM 116/1861, notes of Staff meeting, November 9, 1918; n.d. draft memorandum, Limitation of Armaments; ADM 116/1772 draft memorandum for War Cabinet, Limitation of Armaments, circulated to First Lord December 18, 1918; Takeshita to Katō Tomosaburō and Shimamura Hayao, February 25, March 9, 1919, Inin tōchi mondai, JFMA; *FRUS, Paris Peace Conference, 1919,* 13:334–50; Ray Stannard Baker, *Woodrow Wilson and the World Settlement* (Garden City, N.Y., 1923), 1:338.

33. London Planning Staff memorandum 68, November 7, 1918, file tx; Naval Advisory Staff memorandum, February 18, 1919, file vp, RG 45; Planning Committee (Washington) to Benson, January 18, 1919, file 420-15; General Board to Secretary of the Navy, December 2, 1918, RG 45, cited by Warner R. Schilling in "Weapons, Doctrine, and Arms Control: A Case from the Good Old Days," in Robert J. Art and Kenneth N. Waltz, *The Use of Force* (Boston, 1971), p. 464; Hart to Benson, January 6, 1919, pd-169-1, RG 80.

34. CAB 23/14/491B, October 26, 1918; ADM 116/1861, Peace terms November 22, 1918, draft; ADM 116/1861, First Proof, Notes on matters affecting naval interests connected with the Peace Settlement, December 1918; E. S. Land to Sims, January 6, 1919, file 420-15, GBP; ADM 116/1772, Memorandum to First Lord, January 18, 1919, Admiralty memorandum for War Cabinet, January 21, 1919; Navy Minister's Private Secretary to Foreign Minister's Private Secretary, December 10, 1918, *NGKB, 1918,* 3:623–25; *SN,* Foreign Affairs Advisory Council meeting, December 22, 1918, pp. 356–57.

35. Takeshita to Katō Tomosaburō and Shimamura Hayao, February 6, 22, March 12, April 29, Inin toji mondai, JFMA; Takeshita to Shimamura Hayao, March 14, May 22, 1919, cited in Enamoto Jūji, comp., Kōwa gunbi seigen kankei shorui: buhin, Shiryō chōsakai (Historical Research Institute), Tokyo; ADM 116/1863, Memorandum: Abolition of Submarines, December 14, 1918; Fuller to McNamee, June 17, 1919, pd 169-1, RG 80; House to Wilson, May 22, 1919, EMHP.

36. Supreme War Council meeting, March 17, *FRUS, Paris Peace Conference, 1919,* 4:364; Benson to Wilson, January 24, 1919, Wilson papers, cited by Braisted in *The U.S. Navy in the Pacific,* p. 430; House diary, March 17, 1919; Benson diary, March 15, 16, file ub, RG

45; CAB 24/73, Wemyss memorandum for War Cabinet, January 14, 1919; Takeshita to Kato, February 5, 15, 1919, Inin tōchi mondai, JFMA; Memorandum: Views of Admiral Takeshita, April 28, 1919, William S. Benson papers.

37. *NYT*, December 20, 1918, January 5, February 25, 1919; Wilson to Tumulty, December 22, 1918, Wilson papers, cited in Tillman, *Anglo-American Relations*, p. 167; Cronon, ed., *Daniels Diaries*, November 3, 1918; CAB 24/73, Wemyss memorandum for War Cabinet, January 14, 1919; ADM 167/56, Board meeting, March 6, 1919; CAB 27/76, Long memorandum for War Cabinet, March 13, 1919.

38. Naval Advisory Staff memorandum 21, March 5, 1919, RG 256; Benson to Operations, March 8, file vm, RG 45; House diary, March 6–8, 10, 1919, EMHP; *NYT*, March 7, 1919; Supreme War Council meeting, March 6, 1919, *FRUS, Paris Peace Conference, 1919*, 4:222–28.

39. Wemyss to Hope, June 22, 1919, item AI 61, Wemyss papers microfilm; Council of Four meeting, April 25, *FRUS, Paris Peace Conference, 1919*, 5:238–329; Marder, *From the Dreadnought*, vol. 5, chap. 11, analyzes Scapa and its immediate consequences; Benson to Wilson, April 28, May 6, 1919, Josephus Daniels papers; Sims to Daniels, February 5, 1919, Josephus Daniels papers; Pratt to Benson, November 12, 1918, Pratt papers; Naval Advisory Staff memorandum 24, March 13, 1919, Woodrow Wilson papers, cited in Braisted, *The U.S. Navy in the Pacific, 1909–1922*, p. 433; Naval Advisory Staff memorandum 25, April 7, 1919, file va, RG 45.

40. ADM 116/3242, Fuller memorandum, February 24, 1919; ADM 116/1772, Long to War Cabinet, March 14, 1919; CAB 24/76 gt 6987, gt 6979, Grant memorandum, March 14, 1919; Long memorandum for War Cabinet, March 13, 1919; CAB 23/9, War Cabinet meeting, January 17, 1919; Long to Lloyd George, March 19, 1919, LGP.

41. Daniels, *The Wilson Era*, 2:367; Cronon, ed., *Daniels Diaries*, March 25–29, 1919, pp. 379–80; Wemyss to Lloyd George, March 29, 1919, LGP.

42. House diary, March 27, 1919, EMHP; Cronon, ed., *Daniels Diaries*, March 30–April 1, 1919, pp. 380–81; Cecil to Balfour, Robert Cecil papers; Wemyss to Long, April 3, 1919, Wemyss papers microfilm.

43. Long to Lloyd George, April 3, 6, 8, 1919, LGP; Benson to House, n.d. April 1919, House diary, April 3, 1919, EMHP; Cronon, ed., *Daniels Diaries*, April 7, 1919, pp. 384–85; *NYT*, April 7, 1919.

44. Cecil to Lloyd George, April 4, Cecil to House, April 8, House to Cecil, April 9, LGP; House diary, April 8, House to Wilson, April 9, 1919, EMHP.

45. Cecil to House, April 10, EMHP; Cecil to Lloyd George, April 10, 1919, LGP; Tillman, *Anglo-American Relations*, pp. 295–97.

46. Takeshita to Katō Tomosaburō and Shimamura Hayao, June 3, 1919, Inin tōchi mondai, JFMA.
47. *NYT*, May 4, 1919; Cronon, ed., *Daniels Diaries*, April 12, May 1, 1919, pp. 389, 405; House diary, April 12, 1919, EMHP; Long to Lloyd George, May 2, 8, 1919, LGP; Takeshita to Katō Tomosaburō and Shimamura Hayao, April 16, May 27, 1919, Inin tōchi mondai, JFMA.

Chapter 6

1. *NYT*, September 14, 1919; Cronon, ed., *Daniels Diaries*, August 9–September 11, 1919, pp. 429–42; Daniels, *The Wilson Era: Years of War and After*, p. 479.
2. U.S. Congress, House, Committee on Naval Affairs, "Estimates Submitted by the Secretary of the Navy, 1919," *Hearings*, 65th Congress, 3d sess., pp. 947–48; Chief of Naval Operations Council minutes, June 17, 1919, file 100, RG 80.
3. Daniels to Wilson, January 4, 25, 1919, Daniels papers; Wilson to Daniels, January 27, 1919, file vm, RG 45; *Congressional Record*, 65th Congress, 3d sess., pp. 2862, 2908, 3076–102; Lodge to Brooks Adams, December 28, 1918, Lodge to D. L. Pickman, December 30, 1918, January 2, 1919, Lodge papers; *NYT*, February 27, 1919.
4. *NYT*, March 4, May 28–29, June 1, 7, 1919; Cronon, ed., *Daniels Diaries*, June 2–7, 1919, p. 417; U.S. Congress, House, Committee on Naval Affairs, "Estimates Submitted by the Secretary of the Navy, 1920," *Hearings*, 66th Congress, 2d sess., 2:2216.
5. "Naval Appropriations," House Report, 66th Congress, 1st sess., no. 35 (June 12, 1919); *Congressional Record*, 66th Congress, 1st sess., p. 1086; *NYT*, May 14, June 7, 12–14, 17, 1919; Poindexter to Fullam, June 2, 1919, William F. Fullam papers; Ralph Stone, *The Irreconcilables* (Lexington, Ky., 1970), pp. 1–13, 39–40, 57, 95–98.
6. Cronon, ed., *Daniels Diaries*, June 19, 28, 1919, pp. 421–22; U.S. Congress, Senate, Committee on Naval Affairs, "Naval Appropriations Bill," *Hearings*, 66th Congress, 1st sess., pp. 62–71, 92; "Naval Appropriations Bill, Fiscal 1920, Conference Report," *House Reports*, 66th Congress, 1st sess., no. 89 (June 28, 1919); *Congressional Record*, 66th Congress, 1st sess., pp. 1816–17, 2081, 2129; Thomas A. Bailey, *Woodrow Wilson and the Great Betrayal* (New York, 1945), pp. 84–85, 99–103; *NYT*, June 27, July 12, September 4–27, 1919.
7. Bailey, *Wilson*, pp. 72–87, 149–66, first analyzed Wilson's opponents' strategy; ibid., pp. 390–91, reproduces the arms limitation reservation; Stone, *The Irreconcilables*, chaps. 3–5, offers the most thorough recent examination of their position.
8. Bailey, *Wilson*, pp. 136, 177–86; Cronon, ed., *Daniels Diaries*, Octo-

ber 6, 8, 27, November 11, 26, 1919, pp. 445–47, 453, 459, 464; Navy Department, Annual Reports for the Fiscal Year 1919. Report of the Secretary of the Navy (Washington, 1920), pp. 62, 70, 107.

9. Stone, *The Irreconcilables*, pp. 148–49, 156–57, 170.

10. House diary, July 14, 28, August 7; House to Wilson, July 30, EMHP; House to Wilson, August 8, 1919, *FRUS, 1919 Paris Peace Conference*, 11:630–31; For British discussions of the Grey mission, see chap. 7, p. 109; Stone, *The Irreconcilables*, p. 160; Grey to Curzon, November 26, December 12, 1919, *DBFP*, ser. i, 5:1039, 1062.

11. Bailey, *Wilson*, pp. 290–310; Stone, *The Irreconcilables*, pp. 171–72.

12. *NYT*, March 16, 1920; London Planning Staff memoranda, May 1918, November 23, 1918; Chiefs Bureaus of Ordinance, Construction and Repair, and Steam Engineering to Secretary of the Navy, June 3, 1918; General Board to Secretary of the Navy, June 15, July 6, 1918; Sims to Daniels, November 14, 1918; W. S. Pye memorandum, January 20, 1919, file 420-6; Pratt memorandum, July 1, 1918, GBP; Pratt memorandum, 1918, pd 137-1; Commander in Chief Atlantic Fleet to Secretary of the Navy, January 20, 1919, pd 137-5, RG 80; Benson to Pratt, October 21, 1918, Pratt papers.

13. F. F. Fletcher to Secretary of the Navy, February 23, 1916, file 420, General Board proceedings 1916; Earle to Badger, May 27, 1919, Chief Bureau of Ordinance to Secretary of the Navy, May 24, 1919, Sims to Daniels, November 14, 1918, file 420-6, GBP; Daniels, *The Wilson Era*, 2:367; Cronon, ed., *Daniels Diaries*, May 16, 1919, p. 416.

14. General Board Executive Committee proceedings, May 23–24, 26–27, Acting Chief of Naval Operations memorandum, May 27, 1919; General Board to Secretary of the Navy, May 28, June 24, 1919, file 420-6; Badger to Secretary of the Navy, May 27, 1919, file 420-2, GBP.

15. Navy Department, Annual Reports for the Fiscal Year 1919, Report of the Secretary of the Navy (Washington, 1920), pp. 28–41; Archibald D. Turnbull and Clifford L. Lord, *History of United States Naval Aviation* (New Haven, 1949), pp. 142–63, recounts the growth of naval aviation; General Board to Secretary of the Navy, September 10, 1918, file 420-2; General Board to Secretary of the Navy, September 10, 1918, file 420-2; General Board Hearings, September 4, 23, 1918; General Board to Secretary of the Navy, October 16, 1919, McKean to Pratt, October 13, 1918, file 420-7; General Board to Secretary of the Navy, November 14, 1918, Secretary of the Navy to General Board, December 18, 1918, quoted in General Board to Secretary of the Navy, April 15, 1919, file 449, GBP.

16. General Board Hearings, March 27–May 23, 1919; General Board to Secretary of the Navy, April 15, May 24, June 23, 1919, file 449;

General Board to Secretary of the Navy, September 22, 1919, file 420-2, GBP; Lansing to Yarnell, July 13, 1919, pd 138-6, Director War Plans to Chief of Naval Operations, September 22, 1919, pd 198-2, November 10, 1919, pd 100-94, RG 80.

17. Comments of Captain N. E. Irwin, December 1, 1919, file 449; Craven to Chief of Naval Operations, May 6, 1920, file 420-7, General Board papers; Operations Council minutes, November 10, 1919, May 25, 1920, file 100, GBP; Turnbull and Lord, *History of U.S. Naval Aviation*, p. 98.

18. Operations Council minutes, May 4, June 1, 24, 1920, file 100, RG 80; G. W. Steele to commander in chief of Atlantic Fleet, March 28, 1919, H. H. Bartlett to William Leahy, September 23, 1919, file 449, Chief of Naval Operations to General Board, June 7, 1920, Chief of Bureau of Construction and Repair to Secretary of the Navy, May 24, 1920, General Board to Secretary of the Navy, December 16, 1920, Sims to General Board, December 23, 1920, file 420-7, GBP.

19. Secretary of the Navy to General Board, January 9, Plans Committee to Chief of Naval Operations, January 18, Hart to Chief of Naval Operations, February 12, 1919, file 420-15, GBP; n.d. 1918 Plans Section, General Board, Submarine Force memoranda on submarine building policy, pd 139-1; Hart to Chief of Naval Operations, January 6, Hart to Planning Section July 16, Hart to Evans, n.d. July 1919 memorandum, pd 169-1; Operations Council minutes, January 7, 14, 1919, RG 80.

20. Thomas C. Hart file, Biographies Branch, Department of the Navy; Charles A. Lockwood, *Down to the Sea in Subs* (New York, 1967), describes Hart's Philippine career; Director, Plans Division to Chief of Naval Operations, January 13, Chief of Naval Operations to General Board, January 15, 1920, file 420-15, GBP.

21. General Board hearings, February 7, 1919, January 30, February 4, 1920; G. A. Rood memorandum, February 3, 1920, file 420–14, GBP.

22. General Board to Secretary of the Navy, February 26, June 17, 1920; Hart to Chief of Naval Operations, May 29, 1920; Stirling to Secretary of the Navy, March 28, 1921; Chief Bureau of Construction and Repair to Secretary of the Navy, May 18, 1921, file 420-15; General Board to Secretary of the Navy, file 420-2, GBP.

23. Sims to Secretary of the Navy, May 21, November 14, 23, 1918, file 420-6; General Board to Secretary of the Navy, September 10, 1918, September 22, 1919, file 420-2, GBP; Sims to Pratt, August 30, 1918, Pratt to Sims, May 27, 1917, file td; Benson to Daniels, November 27, 1918, file vm; U.S. Naval Advisory Staff memorandum 25, April 7, 1919, file vp, RG 45; n.d. March 1918 Pratt memorandum, referenced in Pratt to Sims, April 2, 1918, Sims papers; Pratt to Benson, November 12, 1918, Pratt papers; Benson to Daniels, May 6, 1919, Daniels papers.

24. Benson to McKean, May 21, 1919, Benson papers, cited by Braisted in *The U.S. Navy in the Pacific*, p. 469; Revised Organization Orders of the Office of Naval Operations, August 1, 1919, file 446, Commander in Chief Asiatic Fleet to CNO, July 1, 1919, file 405, GBP; James H. Oliver, Harry E. Yarnell, William S. Pye, Holloway H. Frost, Biographies Branch, Department of the Navy; Yarnell Diary, August 12, 1919, September 20, 1920, pd 100-115, Naval attaché Tokyo to ONI, May 14, 1919, W. F. Willoughby to ONI, June 13, 1919, intelligence reports made available by Director of Naval History.

25. Harry E. Yarnell, "Strategy of the Pacific," September 8, 1919, file 425, GBP; for a detailed analysis of the postwar development of American naval intelligence in Japan, see my "Power in the Pacific: The Evolution of American and Japanese Naval Policies, 1918-1921" (Ph.D. diss., Harvard University, 1968), pp. 84–85.

26. Yarnell, "Strategy of the Pacific," September 8, 1919, file 425, GBP; Director Plans Division to Chief of Naval Operations, October 22, 1919, pd 198-2, RG 80.

27. Sims to Pratt, February 7, 1919, Sims to Gardiner, August 13, 1920, Sims papers; William V. Pratt, Critique of Naval War College Strategic Problem, 1919, Pratt papers; General Board Executive Committee meting, September 4, 1919, Proceedings, February 4, March 5, 1920; Baum to Sims, May 25, June 4, 1920, Sims papers, cited by Braisted in *The U.S. Navy in the Pacific*, p. 481; Director Plans Division to Chief of Naval Operations, October 22, 1919, pd 198-2, RG 80.

28. Operations Council minutes, May 13, 1919, file 100; Coontz to Secretary of the Navy, February 27, 1920, pd 198-2, RG 80; General Board hearing, March 5, 1920, GBP.

29. Yarnell diary, October 21, November 1, 22, 1919, January 19, 1920, pd 100-115, RG 80; Secretary of the Navy to General Board, June 14, 1920, cited by Braisted in *The U.S. Navy in the Pacific,* p. 480. Braisted argues in chapter 28 for a stronger consensus on Pacific naval policy than I perceive; General Board to Secretary of the Navy, May 25, August 10, 13, 1920; Sims to President, General Board, August 13, 1920; Report of Special Board of Inspection of Naval Bases on the Pacific Coast, October 20, 1919, file 404, GBP.

30. Louis Morton, "War Plan Orange: Evolution of a Strategy," *World Politics* 11 (January 1959): 221–50, credited the army with initiatives for coordination of war plans; Op 56 to Roosevelt, April 26, 1919, in Frank Friedel, *Franklin D. Roosevelt* (Boston, 1954), 2:19, demonstrates navy planners' prior interest in the subject; Ernest R. May, "The Development of Political-Military Consultation in the United States," *Political Science Quarterly* 70 (June 1955): 167; Joint Board 325, serial 28-d, December 18, serial 87, December 22, 1919; serial 107, August 5, 1920; Joint Board 304, Joint Planning Committee to Joint Board, serial 90, April 27, and July 15, 1920, Joint Board

papers, RG 225; Yarnell diary, March 4, April 12, 27, 29, May 22, July 6, 1920, pd 100–115; Chief of Naval Operations to Major General Commandant of Marines, January 28, Major General Commandant of Marines to Chief of Naval Operations, April 29, 1920, pd 198-7, RG 80.

31. Cronon, ed., *Daniels Diaries*, March 18, April 1–2, 1920, pp. 507–12; *NYT*, April 3, June 7, 1920; Naval Appropriation Bill, *House Report*, 66th Congress, 2d sess., no. 1067 (May 31, 1920); *Congressional Record*, 22 Congress, 2d sess., pp. 8099, 8162–63; Coontz to Secretary of the Navy, August 12, Cole memorandum, September 13, Oliver to Secretary of the Navy, September 18, 1920, no. 11158/83, RG 80, cited by Braisted in *The U.S. Navy in the Pacific*, p. 484; Chief of Naval Operations to War Portfolio Distribution List, January 10, 1921, file 425, GBP; Navy Department, Annual Reports for the Fiscal Year 1920, Report of the Secretary of the Navy (Washington, 1921), pp. 10–13.

32. Sims to Pratt, August 13, 1918, Pratt papers; Sims to Daniels, February 5, 1919, Sims to Pratt, February 7, 1919, Sims to Fullam, October 1, November 8, 1919, WSSP; Sims to Fullam, May 15, 1919, Miles Poindexter papers; Sims to Pratt, January 28, 1919, reprinted in U.S. Congress, Senate, Subcommittee on Naval Affairs, "Naval Investigation," *Hearings*, 66th Congress, 2d sess., 2:3288; Sims to F. D. Roosevelt, August 26, November 8, 1919, Franklin D. Roosevelt papers.

33. Cronon, ed., *Daniels Diaries*, December 15–26, 1919, pp. 470–74, Sims's charges of January 7, 1920, are reproduced in full in "Naval Investigation," 1:1–9; *NYT*, December 24, 1919, January 21, 1920.

34. Sims to N. C. Twining, February 13, 1920, WSSP; *NYT*, December 24, 1919, January 20–23, 30, 1920.

35. Fullam to Sims, June 19, 1919, January 7, 1920; T. T. Craven to Sims, January 23, 1920; Sims to Fullam, February 7, 1920; Sims to Twining, February 13, 1920; Yarnell to Sims, June 7, 1920, WSSP; Fiske, *From Midshipman to Rear Admiral*, pp. 629–34; Fullam to James Wadsworth, August 3, 1919, Poindexter papers; Poindexter to Fullam, June 2, 1919, William F. Fullam papers; Pratt to Mrs. Pratt, January 20, 1920, Pratt papers.

36. "Naval Investigation," 1:203–85, 613–14, 759, 852, 1021–22, 1262, 1265–356, 1578, 1765; 2:3410; Cronon, ed., *Daniels Diaries*, March 15, 19, April 21, 1920, pp. 507, 521.

37. "Naval Investigation," 2:1981–3178, especially pp. 1981, 1984, 1992–94; 2286, 3367; Cronon, ed., *Daniels Diaries*, May 10–24, 1920, pp. 529–34.

38. Fullam to Sims, May 16, 1920, Gardiner to Sims, August 13, 1920, Sims to Fullam, July 20, 1919, WSSP; *NYT*, January 21, 23, February 2, March 23–24, April 25, May 13, 1920; Cronon, ed., *Daniels*

Diaries, January 19, April 22, June 10, 15, 1920, pp. 486, 521, 539–40; Jonathan Daniels, *The End of Innocence* (Philadelphia, 1954), p. 306; Hale to Fullam, October 14, 1920, Fullam papers.

39. *NYT*, April 8, 28–29, May 23, 28, June 3, 1920; Poindexter to Fullam, June 2, 1919, Fullam papers; Sims to Fullam, July 20, 1920.

Chapter 7

1. ADM 116/1604, Oswyn Murray to First Lord, November 21, 1918, Geddes to Murray, November 22, 1918; Riddell, *Intimate Diary*, August 14, 1919, p. 111.

2. Generalizations in this and the following paragraph derive from my reading of the War Cabinet minutes from January to October 1919; Pierre Renouvin, *War and Aftermath, 1914–1929*, trans. Remy Inglis Hall, (New York, 1968), pp. 134, 136; Richard H. Ullman, *Anglo-Soviet Relations, 1917–1920*, vol. 2, *Britain and the Russian Civil War* (Princeton, 1968), analyzes the Russian problem; Roskill, *Naval Policy Between the Wars*, vol. 1, chap. 3, describes its naval dimensions.

3. Kenneth O. Morgan, "Lloyd George's Stage Army: The Coalition Liberals, 1918–1922," in Taylor, ed., *Lloyd George*, p. 236; Robert Rhodes James, *Churchill: A Study in Failure, 1900–1939* (New York, 1970), p. 111; CAB 23/15, 596A War Cabinet meeting, July 21, 1919.

4. Churchill to Lloyd George, marked "W to P.M.," December 26, 1918, May 1, July 14, 1919, LGP; C. E. Callwell, *Field-Marshall Sir Henry Wilson: His Life and Diaries* (London, 1927), 2:368; Mallet and George, *British Budgets Second Series 1913–1921*, p. 391.

5. Long to Lloyd George, March 2, May 8, 1919, LGP; Long subsequently described his role as that of an advocate subordinate to the cabinet. Cf. Walter Long, *Memories* (London, 1923), p. 270; Mackintosh, *The British Cabinet*, chap. 15; Roskill, *Hankey*, 2:125; CAB 21/5, Hankey to Lloyd George, "Towards a National Policy, July 1919," cited by J. Kenneth MacDonald, "Lloyd George and the Search for a Postwar Naval Policy, 1919," in Taylor, ed., *Lloyd George*, pp. 199–201. This essay provides an excellent review of the naval problems of 1919; my differences from its interpretations will be made clear in the following paragraphs.

6. John Ehrman, *Cabinet Government and War, 1890–1940* (Cambridge, 1958), p. 101; Henry Roseveare, *The Treasury* (London, 1969), pp. 248–52; CAB 23/11, Cabinet meeting, August 12, 1919; CAB 27/71, Cabinet meeting, August 20, 1919; Bonar Law to Lloyd George, August 21, 1919, LGP.

7. Wemyss to Calthorpe, March 18, 1919, Wemyss papers microfilm; CAB 24/76, /82, /83, Long memoranda for War Cabinet, March 13, June 19, July 5, 1919; ADM 24/76, Long memorandum for War Cabinet, March 13, 1919; ADM 167/56, Board meetings, May 29,

June 5, 1919; ADM 167/58, memorandum 809 for June 5, 1919 Board meeting.

8. CAB 24/83, /5, Chamberlain memorandum, "Navy Votes," July 8, 1919, Treasury memorandum, "The Financial Position and Future Prospects of this Country," July 18, 1919; Jones to Hankey, July 11, 1919, in Middlemas, ed., *Whitehall Diary*, 1:89.

9. CAB 21/5, Hankey memorandum, "Towards a National Policy," July 17, 1919, cited by MacDonald, "Lloyd George and the Search for a Postwar Naval Policy, 1919," in Taylor, ed., *Lloyd George*, pp. 199–201.

10. ADM 167/59, Board meetings June 19, July 16, 17, 31, 1919.

11. House diary, July 14, 27, House to Wilson, July 30, 1919, EMHP; Grey memorandum, July 29, in Curzon to Lloyd George, July 30; Grey memorandum, August 5, forwarded by Curzon to Lloyd George, August 6, 1919, LGP.

12. CAB 24/5, Treasury memorandum, "The Financial Position and Future Prospects of this Country," circulated to War Cabinet, July 18, 1919; CAB 23/15/606A, War Cabinet meeting, August 5, 1919.

13. CAB 27/71, War Cabinet Finance Committee meeting, August 11, 1919.

14. CAB 24/86, Long memorandum for War Cabinet, August 12, 1919; CAB 23/15/690A, 610A, 616A, War Cabinet meetings, August 8, 15, 1919; CAB 23/12/618, Cabinet meeting, August 19, 1919.

15. CAB 23/15/609A, 610A, 616A, War Cabinet meetings, August 8, 15, 1919; CAB 23/12/618, Cabinet meeting, August 19, 1919.

16. CAB 27/71, Cabinet Finance Committee meeting, September 23, 1919; Treasury memorandum, October 8, 1919, "Staffs of Government Department"; ADM 167/56, Board meetings, August 8, September 22, 1919; Draft Admiralty memorandum for War Cabinet, August 16, 1919; *LT*, December 5, 11, 1919.

17. Wemyss, *Life and Letters*, pp. 438–45; Wemyss to Long, August 28, September 19, Long to Beatty, September 24, Beatty to Long, September 26, Long to Wemyss, October 11, 1919, in Charles Petrie, *Walter Long and His Times* (London, 1936), pp. 225–28; Wemyss memorandum for First Lord, Wemyss to Beatty, February 28, 1919, and "Admiralty" in Wemyss memoirs, Wemyss papers microfilm; Long to Lloyd George, April 20, 29, May 8, June 3, 15, 1919, LGP; Marder, *From the Dreadnought*, pp. 203–12; Chalmers, *Beatty*, p. 364.

18. *LT*, March 31, June 13, September 23, 29, October 24, 1919; Beatty to Lady Beatty, in Chalmers, *Beatty*, p. 365.

19. Long to Beatty, September 24, 1919, in Petrie, *Walter Long*, p. 226; ADM 167/56, Board meetings of September 22, 30, October 2, 8, 16, 23, 1919; ADM 167/58, Draft memorandum for War Cabinet, October 2, 1919; ADM 167/59, Beatty memorandum to Board, January 1,

Board meeting, January 14, 1920; ADM 116/1774, Long memorandum for War Cabinet, October 24, 1919; CAB 24/98, Long memorandum for cabinet, February 13, 1920; John W. Davis diary, February 11, 1920, John W. Davis papers.

20. ADM 167/59, Murray memorandum, January 24, Board meetings, February 11, 18, Long memorandum for Cabinet, February 20, 1920. Long defended his request for fuel oil depots and stockpiling as a way of avoiding dependence on American fuel sources; CAB 27/72, Long memorandum, February 20, 1920; CAB 23/27/26, Conference of ministers, February 25, 1920; Long to Bonar Law, February 8, 18, 20, 1920. A second version of Long's last letter is in ADM 116/1677.

21. CAB 23/20/13-20, Cabinet meeting, March 4, 1920; *LT*, March 16, 18–19, 24, 1920; Hankey to Lloyd George, February 3, Auckland Geddes to Lloyd George, June 4, 8, 1920, LGP; Middlemas. ed Whitehall Diary, February 9, 1920, 1:104; Taylor, ed., *Stevenson Diary*, January 23–March 15, 1920, pp. 199–205; Morgan, "Lloyd George's Stage Army," in Taylor, ed., *Lloyd George*, pp. 247–55.

22. Chalmers, *Beatty*, pp. 381–82; Petrie, *Long*, p. 235; ADM 116/1803, Instructions for Naval Staff, August 2, 1919; ADM 116/1799, Operations Committee meeting, July 14, and ADM 157/56, Board meetings, March 27, July 10, 1919, chronicle submariners' fights to survive; Roskill, *Naval Policy between the Wars*, 1:570–71; *LT*, March 13, 1919; Admiral Sir William James, *The Sky Was Always Blue* (London, 1951), pp. 112, 118.

23. ADM 167/71, Murray memorandum, May 1; Chatfield memorandums, May 6, 15; ADM 116/1775, Beatty draft memorandum for cabinet, May 7, Long endorsement, May 8, 1920; ADM 167/59, Long to Financial Secretary, July 9, 1920; CAB 24/109, Long memorandum for cabinet, July 23, 1920.

24. ADM 167/59, Financial Secretary to Long, August 10, Board meeting, October 13, 1920; ADM 167/71, Long memorandum, October 7, 1920; ADM 116/1775, Beatty draft memorandum for cabinet, October 28, Long endorsement, October 29, Long memorandum for cabinet, November 22, 1920.

25. CAB 27/71, Cabinet Finance Committee meeting, November 29, 1920; ADM 167/59, Board meeting, December 8, 1920; Long, *Memories*, p. 305; *LT*, December 7, 1920.

26. House diary, August 2, 1919, EMHP; Wemyss memorandum for Long, January 23, 1919, Wemyss to Long, March 10, 1919, Wemyss papers, describe his efforts to dissuade Jellicoe from publishing and to head off the ensuing controversy; *LT,* February 12, March 18, 1919; *Times Literary Supplement*, February 20, 1919; Patterson, *Jellicoe*, p. 230; Richmond to Carlyon Bellairs, February 18, 25, March 12, 1919, Richmond papers, cited by Marder in *Portrait of an Admiral*, pp. 336–40; Patterson, *The Jellicoe Papers*, 2:399–411.

27. Patterson, *Jellicoe*, pp. 230–33; Richmond diary, January 12, 1920,

Richmond papers; Jellicoe to Long, July 5, 16, 1920, Long to Jelli-coe, August 15, 1920, Jellicoe papers, cited by Bacon in *Jellicoe*, pp. 448–49; Chalmers, *Beatty*, pp. 357–58.

28. *LT*, June 24, October 27, 29, 30, November 4, 9, 1920; Bacon, *Jellicoe*, pp. 449–50; Carlyon Bellairs, *The Battle of Jutland: The Sowing and the Reaping* (London, 1919).

29. *LT*, November 2, 1920; Richmond diary, November 10, 1920, Richmond papers; Patterson, *Jellicoe*, p. 236.

30. *LT*, November 9, December 16, 18, 1920; "The Jutland Dispatches," *The Spectator* 125 (December 25, 1920): 842–43.

31. *LT*, November 23, 27, December 10–14, 1920; Padfield, *Aim Straight*, pp. 262–74, reviews Scott's role in the controversy.

32. *LT*, December 3, 6, 7, 1920.

33. "Naval Hypotheses," *The New Statesman* 16 (December 18, 1920): 328–29; "The Naval Skin Game," *The Spectator* 125 (December 11, 1920): 765; *The Nation* 27 (December 11, 1920): 373–74; *The Nation* 27 (December 18, 1920): 409–10; *Manchester Guardian*, December 10, 15, 1920.

34. CAB 27/27, Chamberlain memorandum for Finance Committee, November 20, 1920; CAB 27/71, Economy committee, Cabinet Finance Committee meeting, November 29, 1920, Finance Committee meeting, December 7, 1920; CAB 23/23/65-20, Conference of ministers, November 25, 1920; Hankey diary, December 8, 1920, in Roskill, *Hankey*, 2:205.

35. CAB 23/23/67-20, Cabinet meeting, December 8, 1920; CAB 27/71, Cabinet Finance Committee meeting, December 7, 1920; *LT*, December 10, 1920.

36. Hankey diary, December 8, 1920, in Roskill, *Hankey*, 2:206; CAB 2/3, C.I.D. meeting, December 14, 1920; Long to Lloyd George, December 13, 17, 1920, LGP; ADM 116/1775, Beatty memorandum for cabinet, December 15, 1920.

37. Davis diary, memorandum of conversations with Prime Minister Lloyd George, November 13–15, 1920, John W. Davis papers; for a discussion of these international developments, see chap. 9; *NYT*, December 24, 1920; CAB 2/3, C.I.D. meetings, December 12, 23, 1920; Riddell, *Intimate Diary*, December 18, 1920, pp. 254–55.

38. CAB 2/3, C.I.D. meeting, December 14, 1920; Hankey diary, December 20, 1920, in Roskill, *Hankey*, 2:207; the Subcommittee on the Question of the Capital Ship in the Navy, 1920–1921, was chaired by Bonar Law and included Beatty, Long, Churchill, Sir

39. Beatty to Lady Beatty, January 23, 25, 1921, Beatty papers, cited by Chalmers in *Beatty*, p. 365; CAB 16/37, hearings of the Subcommittee on the Question of the Capital Ship in the Navy, 1920–1921, December 30, 1920, January 7, 11, 13–14, 27, 1921.

40. CAB 16/37, hearings of the Subcommittee on the Question of the

Capital Ship in the Navy, 1920–1921, January 3, 25–26, 1921; Richmond had already denounced prewar standards of naval security based on the capital ship as "unscientific," warned against axiomatically assuming battleship superiority, and predicted that future naval encounters were unlikely to be great fleet engagements. Cf. Ric 10/4 Lectures at Royal Naval War College, autumn 1920, Richmond papers.

41. CAB 16/37, Subcommittee hearings, January 7, 26, 27, 1921.

42. ADM 167/64, Second Sea Lord memorandum, January 10, Plans Division memorandum, January 17, Oswyn Murray memorandum, January 19, 1921; ADM 167/63, Board meetings, January 20, 31, 1921; ADM 116/1775, Long memorandum to Capital Ships Committee, January 30, 1921; Lloyd George to Bonar Law, n.d. 1921, Bonar Law papers; Bonar Law to Lloyd George, January 31, Long to Lloyd George, February 9, 1921, LGP; *NYT*, February 13, 1921.

43. Churchill was succeeded by Sir L. Worthington Evans. *NYT*, January 8, 18, February 13, 1921; Churchill to Lloyd George, January 30, Lee to Lloyd George, February 10, 1921, LGP.

44. CAB 27/71, Cabinet Finance Committee meetings, February 21, 25, 1921; ADM 167/63, Lee memorandum for cabinet, February 28, 1921.

45. CAB 27/71, Cabinet Finance Committee meeting, February 28, 1921.

46. *LT*, January 29, 1921; For analysis of the changing international climate, see chapter 10; Auckland Geddes to Lloyd George, January 3, 1921, LGP; Riddell, *Intimate Diary*, January 26, 1921, pp. 200–203; Hankey diary, January 13, 1921, in Roskill, *Hankey*, 2:215.

47. CAB 27/71, Cabinet Finance Committee meeting, February 28, 1921; CAB 16/37, Subcommittee meeting, February 28, 1921; Report of the Subcommittee on the Question of the Capital Ship in the Navy, 1920–1921, March 2, 1921.

48. Balfour to Bonar Law, March 3, Bonar Law to Balfour, March 4, 1921, Bonar Law papers.

Chapter 8

1. *HKN*, 9, July 28, 1920, p. 20; *Kaigun gunsenbi*, vol. 1, chart 5, Naval Expenditures since 1890.

2. This analysis is based on statistics presented in *Kaigun gunsenbi*, 1: 246–49 and chart 5; Kaigun daijin kanbō hen, *Kaigun gunbi enkaku furoku*, 2d ed. (Tokyo, 1970), chart 7.

3. Kaigun daijin kanbō hen, *Kaigun gunbi enkaku furoku*, chart 8.

4. *Kaigun gunsenbi*, 1:15–16, 25–30; Personnel data supplied by Japan Defense Agency, Office of War History; Ijiri Tsunekichi, *Rekidai kenkan roku*, 2d ed. (Tokyo, 1967), pp. 456–61; Kyoto Daigaku bungaku bu kokushi kenkyū shitsu, ed., *Nihon kindai shi jiten* (Tokyo, 1958), p. 722; Ide Kenji, "Waga kaigun no sūsei," *Kaigun* 10 (August 1915): 5–6.

5. Naval General Staff, March 1918 chart, item 192, Saitō Makoto papers; Rinji kaigun gunji chōsakai, Ōshū sensō kaigun gunji chōsa shiryō, no. 134, Statistics concerning the European War, part 5, report no. 81, June 1919, Shiryō chōsakai, Tokyo.

6. Rear Admiral Akiyama Saneyuki, "Ōshū taisen to kōgyō," in Murakami Kakuichi, ed., *Gundan kaigun* (Tokyo, 1917), pp. 249–53, 261; Mizuno Hironori, "Waga gunkoku shugi ron," *Chūō Kōron* 34 (January 1919): 123; Hikada Kinji, "Doitsu haisen no kyōkun to waga kokubō no shorai," in Kusai Sutetarō, ed., *Kokusan shōreikai shusai: Matsushima kōen shū* (Tokyo, 1919), pp. 172–74, 182–86; Anonymous admiral, "Sengō no kaigun jūjitsu mondai," *Taiyō* 24 (June 15, 1918): 153–50; Rinji kaigun gunji chōsakai, Ōshū sensō kaigun gunji chōsa shiryō, no. 129, Dōmei gawa hain kenkyū shiryō no. 2, April 1919, Shiryō chōsakai. This series of studies on the causes of German defeat continued through January 1922. For other accounts of Japanese naval observers in Germany in 1919, see Notes on Paymaster Admiral Utsunomiya lectures, December 1919, Rinji kaigun gunji chōsakai, Shiryō chōsakai; Ōsumi taishō denki kankō kai, ed., *Danshaku Ōsumi Mineo den* (Tokyo, 1943), pp. 474–75; Mizuno Hironori, *Kono issen*, 2d ed. (Tokyo, 1958), appendix, p. 332; Abo Kiyokazu, *Katō Kanji taishō den* (Tokyo, 1941), pp. 707–22.

7. Kaigun yūshūkai, ed., *Kinsei teikoku kaigun shiyō*, pp. 264–65, 382–89; Fukui Shizuo, *Nihon no gunkan* (Tokyo, 1956), pp. 162–63; Hatano Sadao, *Murakami Kakuichi den* (Tokyo, 1933), pp. 176–79; 40th Diet, Shūgiin yosan iinkai, *Dai yon bunryō kai giroku,* Remarks of Katō Tomosaburō, February 1, 6, 1918; *Asahi Shinbun*, February 1, 1918; *Kaigun gunsenbi*, 1:686–97, chronicles the fuel oil problem; Naval attaché Tokyo to Office of Naval Intelligence, August 19, 1920, March 3, 1921, documents made available by Director of Naval History, Washington; Suzuki Kantarō, *Suzuki Kantarō jiden* (Tokyo, 1949), p. 197; Jeffrey J. Safford, "Experiment in Containment: The United States Steel Embargo and Japan, 1917," *Pacific Historical Review* 39 (November, 1970), pp. 439–52, analyzes the steel problem from American sources; Japanese attitudes emerge in the Fukuda memorandum, June 28, 1917, Vice Minister of Foreign Affairs to Vice Minister of Communications, July 28, 1917, reel 71, JFMA; Satō Aimaro to Minister of Foreign Affairs, September 12, 1917, Ishii to Minister of Foreign Affairs, September 15, 1917, UD-15, reel UD-16, JFMA.

8. Yamakawa Tadao memorandum, Nichi Doku seneki kōwa junbi chōsa fuzoku sankō chosho, pp. 142–50; Nichi Doku seneki kōwa junbi iinkai giroku, February 9, 1919, JFMA; Hidaka Kinji *Osaka Asahi Shinbun* article, translated in Naval Attaché Tokyo to Office of Naval Intelligence, July 8, 1919, wa-5, RG 45; Katō Tomosaburō memorandum, July 26, 1919, *Kaigun gunbi enkaku*, 1:221; Bōeichō, *Hitō kōryaku sakusen*, pp. 8, 10–11.

9. Kambe Makoto, "Ōbei ni okeru senji keizai zaisei jōtai ni tsuite," *Kensei* 1 (October 1918): pp. 33–40; *Tokyo Asahi shinbun,* November

16, 25–29, December 22, 1919, January 3–7, 1920, February 6, 1920; Naval Attaché Washington to Chief of Naval General Staff, October 22, December 14, 1918, Taishō shichinen: Chūzaiin jōhō denpō; Taikōshi tsuke bukan, JDA: Consul Matsui to Vice Foreign Minister, April 2, 1919, mt 5.1.10-3, reel 464, JFMA; 41st Diet, Shūgiin, yosan iinkai, *Dai yon bunryōkai giroku*, February 5, 1919.

10. *Tokyo Asahi shinbun*, February 21, 1919; Director of Naval Intelligence to General Board, Operations, et al, May 24, October 13, 1919, wa-5, RG 45; Ley to Kobayashi, February 11, 1919, Kobayashi to Ley, February 15, 1919, Eikoku taishikan tsuke kaigun bukan ōfuku bunsho: Taishō hachinen, JDA; *Nippon kaigun kōkū shi* (Tokyo, 1969), 1:91; Kaigun yūshū kai, ed., *Kinsei teikoku kaigun shiyō*, pp. 229, 254; Desmond Young, *Rutland of Jutland* (London, 1963), pp. 77–81, describes the work of the British mission; Yamamoto Tosemaro, "Shin kōkūki bokan *Hosho* ni tsuite," *Kaigun* 16 (September 1920), n.p.

11. Katō Tomosaburō memorandum, June 2, 1919, Kaigun daijin kanbō hen, *Kaigun gunbi enkaku*, 1:236–39; *HKN*, 8, June 3, 1919, p. 234.

12. Makino, *Nakahashi Tokugorō*, 1:291; 2:544–45; *Tokyo Asahi shinbun*, January 20, 29, February 6, 11, 14, 1919; *HKN*, 8, February 13, March 26, 1919, pp. 158, 185.

13. *HKN*, 8, May 22, June 3, 1919, pp. 227, 234.

14. *HKN*, 8, June 3, 19, 1919, pp. 234, 250; Mitani Taichirō, "Tenkanki (1918–1921) no gaikō shidō," in Shinohara Hajime and Mitani Taichirō, eds. *Kindai Nihon no seiji shidō* (Tokyo, 1965), pp. 325–32, analyzes Hara's changing foreign policy assumptions.

15. *HKN*, 8, April 4, 29, May 15, June 20, July 10–11, 29, August 14, September 9, 1919, pp. 191, 216, 249, 262, 267, 320; *SN*, May 29–June 26, 1919, pp. 508–26.

16. *HKN*, 8, April 29, May 9, 15–16, 19, 22, August 8, September 13, 1919, pp. 202–320, passim; Alston to Curzon, March 19, 1920, citing report of April 1919; 711.94/292, Morris to Secretary of State, June 2, 1919, reel 3, National Archives microfilm publication 423; Hara Takashi, "Through Nationalism to Internationalism," *Outlook* 125 (June 16, 1920): 316.

17. *HKN*, 8, July 29, 1919, p. 279.

18. *HKN*, 8, August 4, 12, September 12, 30, 1919, pp. 287–88, 294, 322, 342–3; F.O. 410/67/19, Alston to Curzon, July 18, 1919; 894.00/154, Morris to Secretary of State, August 15, 1919, reel 4 National Archives microfilm publication 422; Oka and Hayashi, eds., *Taishō demokurashii ki no seiji*, pp. 36–40.

19. *HKN*, 8, September 19, October 3, 16, 1919, pp. 334, 342, 355; *Tokyo Asahi shinbun*, November 9, 1919.

20. *HKN*, 8, October 28, November 6, 1919, pp. 371, 379; *Jiji*, November 6, translated in *Japan Advertiser*, November 7, 1919; *Tokyo Asahi shin-*

bun, November 2, 4, 7, 9, December 21, 1919; Takakura, *Tanaka,* 2:186.

21. *HKN,* 8, October 28, November 11, 21, 25, December 16, 1919, pp. 371, 385, 396, 400; *Tokyo Asahi shinbun,* November 8, December 21, 1919.

22. HKN, 8, November 15, 18, 24–25, December 7, 1919, pp. 390–400, 420; *Japan Advertiser,* January 18, 23, 1920; *Tokyo Asahi shinbun,* November 2, 4, 7, 9, 1919.

23. *Jiji,* October 29, November 7–10, 1919, January 29, 1920; *Hōchi,* November 10, 12, 1919; *Tokyo Nichi nichi,* January 24, 1920, all translated in *Japan Advertiser,* October 30, November 8–11, 13, 1919, January 30, 1920; *Tokyo Asahi shinbun,* November 8, December 22, 1919; *HKN,* 8, February 12, 1920, pp. 478–80, 483; 42nd Diet, Shūgiin, *Yosan sokai giroku,* January 26, 1920, remarks of Katō Tomosaburō; 42nd Diet, Shūgiin, Yosan iinkai, *Dai yon bunryōkai giroku,* February 2, 4, 1920.

24. *Japan Advertiser,* February 6, 1920; *HKN,* 8, February 11, 14–15, 26, 29, 1920, pp. 482, 485, 492, 497.

25. *HKN,* 8, November 14, December 8, 1919, January 24, February 19, 23–24, 26, May 10–15, 1920, pp. 389, 421, 467, 492–97, 540–46; Oka and Hayashi, eds., *Taishō demokurashii ki no seiji,* p. 45; *Japan Advertiser,* May 1–6, 1920; *GSSJN,* 9:961; 894.00/161, Morris to Secretary of State, March 18, 1920, reel 4, National Archives microfilm publication 422.

26. 894.00/171, Bell to Secretary of State, September 1, 1920, reel 4, National Archives microfilm publication 422; *HKN,* 8, April 9–June 28, 1920, pp. 523–27 passim.

27. 894.00/166, Morris to Secretary of State, May 14, 1920, 894.00/171, Bell to Secretary of State, September 1, 1920, reel 4, National Archives microfilm publication 422; *HKN,* 8, May 21, June 26–27, 1920, pp. 547, 576–77; Hara Takashi, "Through Nationalism to Internationalism," *Outlook* 125 (June 16, 1920): 316; Mitani Taichirō, "Nihon no kokusai kinyūka to kokusai seiji," in Satō and Dingman, eds., *Kindai Nihon no taigai taido,* pp. 142–44.

28. *HKN,* 8, June 29, 1920, p. 580; *Tokyo Asahi shinbun,* June 29, July 5, *Yorodzu,* June 29, *Hōchi,* June 29, July 6, *Nichi nichi shinbun,* July 8, translated in *Japan Advertiser,* June 30, July 6–9, 1920; *GSSJN,* 11:963.

29. *HKN,* 8, 9, July 7–15, 23–27, 1920, pp. 484–587, 10–19; *Japan Advertiser,* July 11, 13, 15, 1920.

30. *NYT,* July 19, 1920; *Literary Digest* 66 (August 14, 21, 1920): 13, 52–54; *LT,* July 20, 1920; 711.94/306, Morris to Secretary of State, November 19, 1919, reel 3, National Archives microfilm publication 423.

31. Satō Tetsutarō, "NichiBei kankei to waga tachiba," *Taiyō* 26 (August 1920): 83–89.

32. Robert M. Spaulding, "The Bureaucracy as a Political Force, 1920–

1945," in James William Morley, ed., *Dilemmas of Growth in Prewar Japan* (Princeton, 1971), p. 35, develops the "transitional bureaucrat" category.

Chapter 9

1. Raymond Leslie Buell, *The Washington Conference* (Garden City, N.Y., 1922); A. Whitney Griswold, *The Far Eastern Policy of the United States* (New York, 1938), chap. 7; Harold and Margaret Sprout, *Toward a New Order of Sea Power* (Princeton, 1940), chaps. 6–8, argued that both internal and external factors shaped the American approach to arms control but stressed the latter; Leonard C. Hoag, *Preface to Preparedness: The Washington Disarmament Conference and Public Opinion* (Washington, 1941), stressed public opinion; John Chalmers Vinson, *The Parchment Peace* (Athens, Ga., 1955), claimed that "the fortunate coincidence of the divergent aims of all these indispensable factors" brought about an arms limitation conference (pp. 97, 114) but emphasized the institutional conflict between president and Senate; Thomas A. Buckley, *The United States and the Washington Conference, 1921–1922* (Knoxville, Tenn., 1970), argued that "the conference was precipitated by events taking place not in Washington, but in London" (pp. 10–19); William R. Braisted, *The United States Navy in the Pacific, 1909–1922*, chaps. 30–33, offers an exhaustive review of the strategic and naval technical origins of the conference. British and Japanese historiography on the conference will be reviewed in chapters 10 and 11.

2. *Literary Digest* 67 (December 24, 1920): 10; Department of the Navy, *Annual Reports for the Fiscal Year 1920. Report of the Secretary of the Navy* (Washington, 1921), pp. 2–4.

3. Lodge to Harding, November 10, George Sutherland to Harding, November 10, 1920, WGHP; *Literary Digest* 68 (March 5, 1921): 8.

4. Andrew Sinclair, *The Available Man* (New York, 1965), pp. 57–83, summarizes Harding's senate career; William Allen White, *The Autobiography of William Allen White*, p. 522, cited in Sinclair, *The Available Man*, p. 69; Francis Russell, *The Shadow of Blooming Grove: Warren G. Harding in His Times* (New York, 1968), chaps. 12–13, and Randolph C. Downes, *The Rise of Warren Gamaliel Harding, 1865–1920* (Columbus, Ohio, 1970), chaps. 11–13, 15, detail his Senate experience. Downes, chaps. 21–25, offers a detailed account of the campaign of 1920, as does Wesley M. Bagby, *The Road to Normalcy*, 2d ed. (Baltimore, 1968); Harding to Hiram Johnson, July 27, August 15, 1920, WGHP.

5. Ray Stannard Baker, *American Chronicle* (New York, 1945), p. 485, cited by Sinclair in *Available Man*, p. 177; Harding to Borah, November 13, 1920, WGHP; Russell, *The Shadow of Blooming Grove*, pp. 420–23, gives details of his journey; *NYT*, December 5, 1920.

6. *NYT*, December 7–8, 1920; Harding to Malcolm Jennings, December 14, 1920, WGHP.

7. The "best minds" conferences can be followed in reports of the *New York Times*, December 10, 1920–January 20, 1921; *NYT*, November 25, 1920–February 27, 1921, details controversies over cabinet choices. Robert K. Murray, *The Harding Era* (Minneapolis, 1969), pp. 95–109, analyzes Harding's cabinetmaking; *Literary Digest* 68 (March 5, 1921): 7.

8. *NYT*, December 10, 15, 1920; Vinson, *The Parchment Peace*, pp. 48–49.

9. *NYT*, December 12, 15, 1920; Robert James Maddox, *William E. Borah and American Foreign Policy* (Baton Rouge, 1969), pp. xii–xx, 88–90; Borah to David K. Egbert, February 26, 1916, Borah to L. R. Thomas, December 22, 1920, William E. Borah papers; Stone, *The Irreconcilables*, pp. 12, 16; LeRoy Ashby, *The Spearless Leader* (Urbana, Ill., 1972), p. 21.

10. *Literary Digest* 67 (January 15, 1921): 7–9; ibid., (February 5, 1921), p. 15, reviews immediate reactions to Borah's proposal, as does Vinson, *Parchment Peace*, pp. 51–57; Borah-Fullam correspondence, January 20–31, 1921, Borah papers; *NYT*, December 15, 17, 1920, January 4, 1921.

11. Borah to F. L. Allen, published in *NYT*, March 10, 1921; *NYT*, December 8, 22, 1920, January 14, February 12, 1921; Harding to Borah, November 13, 1920, WGHP.

12. *NYT*, January 21–23, 26, 28, February 4–5, 10, 12, 1921; Harding to Lodge, February 13, 1921, WGHP. This letter in the version sent House Leader Mondell was published in the *New York Times*, February 15, 1921; Vinson, *Parchment Peace*, pp. 58–68, summarizes legislative maneuvering over Borah's resolutions.

13. For a sampling of press commentary on Borah's proposals, see *Literary Digest* 68 (January 15, 1921): 7–9; and ibid., (February 13, 1921), pp. 14–15; *NYT*, January 1, 7, 15, 18, February 5, 1921.

14. *The New Republic* 25 (February 23, 1921): 354; *Literary Digest* 48 (March 5, 1921): 10–12; Harding to Lodge, February 20, 1921, Henry Cabot Lodge papers; Lodge to Harding, February 20, 25, 1921, WGHP.

15. *NYT*, February 7, 18, 26, March 1, 2, 5, 1921. The *Times* report said Harding had written a "prominent Republican senator" that he wanted approval of the naval appropriations bill, but I have been unable to locate any letter appropriately dated in the papers of the most likely recipients, Lodge and Poindexter; Harding to A. E. Seibert, February 20, 1921, Harding to James Reed, February 25, 1921, WGHP.

16. Harding to Theodore Roosevelt, Jr., November 13, January 10, 1921; Harding to Lowden, February 14, 1921; Lowden to Harding, January 27, February 12, 14, 1921, WGHP; *NYT*, February 27, 1921.

17. Lodge to Harding, February 25, 1920, Lodge papers; Murray, *The*

Harding Era, p. 128; *Literary Digest* 68 (February 12, 1921): 11; (March 5, 1921), pp. 7–10; (March 12, 1921), pp. 10–12.

18. *NYT*, March 5, 1921; McCormick's journey can be followed in *NYT*, November 25, December 1, 16, 25, 1920, January 13, February 14, 1921. McCormick conferred with Harding, presumably on his diplomatic and naval policy recommendations, on February 13, 1920. Harding to Root, November 5, Harding to Lodge, December 29, Harding to Frank Brandegee, December 30, McCormick to Harding, n.d., but from internal evidence after November 22, McCormick to Harding, December 22, 1920, WGHP.

19. Lodge to Harding, December 24, 1920, February 25, 1921, WGHP; Sims to Gardiner, June 14, 1920, Gardiner to Sims, June 17, August 13, 19, n.d. August 1920, WSSP; Gardiner to Allan Dawson, September 22, 1920, William Howard Gardiner papers. For a detailed account of Gardiner's maneuvers in the spring of 1921, see my doctoral dissertation, pp. 269–75, and M. G. Fry, "The North Atlantic Triangle and the Abrogation of the Anglo-Japanese Alliance," *Journal of Modern History* 39 (March, 1967): 52–53.

20. *NYT*, April 13, 1921.

21. *NYT*, March 20, April 11, 13, 1921; Hughes to Charles Evans Hughes, Jr., Charles Evans Hughes papers; Hughes to George Wickersham, March 28, 1923, WGHP; John Chalmers Vinson, "Charles Evans Hughes," in Norman A. Graebner, ed., *An Uncertain Tradition: American Secretaries of State in the Twentieth Century* (New York, 1961), pp. 128–40; Betty M. Glad, *Charles Evans Hughes and the Illusions of Innocence* (Urbana, Ill., 1966), chaps. 8–10; Nelson E. Woodward, "Postwar Reconstruction and International Order: A Study of the Diplomacy of Charles Evans Hughes, 1921–1925" (Ph.D. diss., University of Wisconsin, 1970), all analyze Hughes's career as secretary of state.

22. *NYT*, April 19, 1921; Hughes to Charles Evans Hughes, Jr., August 27, 1921, Hughes papers; Hughes to Harding, April 4, 30, 1921, WGHP. It should be noted that William H. Gardiner met with Harding's Undersecretary of State-designate, Henry P. Fletcher, on February 24, 1921 to expound his ideas and on April 13, 1921, proposed precisely the opposite strategy to that Harding selected, that is, putting resolution of the Anglo-Japanese alliance problem before a European peace. Cf. Gardiner to Fletcher, April 13, 1921, William Howard Gardiner papers.

23. Denby to Hughes, n.d. April 1921, 1921, WGHP; Denby to Hughes, April 15, 1921, Harding to Hughes, April 27, 1921, Department of State 811.30/131, 133, RG 59, cited by Braisted in *U.S. Navy in the Pacific*, p. 547; Hughes to Bell, April 2, 1921, *FRUS, 1921* (Washington, 1936), 2:283; memorandum of Fletcher-Shidehara conversation, April 13, 1921, Hughes papers; *NYT*, March 26, 1921, published one such "signal." For a full discussion of these indicators, see chapter 11.

24. *NYT*, April 14, 17, May 4, 7, 1921; memorandum of Hughes-Geddes conversation, April 12, 1921, Hughes papers; Geddes to Curzon, April 15, 1921, forwarded by Curzon to Lloyd George, April 28, 1921, LGP; for a review of London's signals, see Vinson, *Parchment Peace*, pp. 102–3 and chap. 10.

25. *NYT*, April 22, 26, 29, 1921; "Construction of an Airplane Carrier for the Navy," *House Report*, 67th Congress, 1st sess., no. 100; "Naval Appropriation Bill, Fiscal Year 1922," *House Report*, 67th Congress, 1st sess., no. 12; *Congressional Record*, 67th Congress, 1st sess., p. 618.

26. *NYT*, May 11, 14, 1921; Hoag, *Preface to Preparedness*, pp. 92–95; Hiram Johnson, Jr., and A. M. Johnson to Hiram Johnson, Hiram Johnson papers; Mark Sullivan diary, May 18, 1922, Mark Sullivan papers, Hoover Institution.

27. *NYT*, May 4–5, 10, 14, 1921.

28. Poindexter to Harding, May 11, Harding to Poindexter, May 14, Harding to H. H. Kohlsaat, May 16, 1921, WGHP; *NYT*, May 19, 24–26, 1921.

29. Frank Cobb to Borah, June 1, 1921, Borah papers, cited by Vinson, *Parchment Peace*, p. 92; Vinson, *Parchment Peace*, pp. 93–94, surveys Democratic criticisms; *NYT*, May 31, 1921; *Literary Digest* 69 (June 11, 1921): 8.

30. *NYT*, June 4–8, 12, 13, 17–18, 1921; Stephen G. Porter to Harding, June 4, 1921, WGHP.

31. *NYT*, June 15, 24–25, 29–30, July 1, 1921; memorandum of Hughes-Geddes conversation, June 23, 1921, Hughes papers.

32. CAB 32/2, Minutes of meetings, Imperial Conference, 1921, June 30, 1921; CAB 23/26/56-21, Cabinet meeting, June 30, 1921; Hughes to Harvey, July 8, 9, Hughes to Harding, July 9, 1921, *FRUS, 1921*, 1: 18, 23–24; Geddes to Curzon, July 7, Curzon to Geddes, July 9, 1921, *DBFP*, ser. 1, 14:328–29, 336–38; *NYT*, July 11, 1921; David J. Danelski and Joseph S. Tulchin, eds., *The Autobiographical Notes of Charles Evans Hughes* (Cambridge, 1973), p. 206.

33. *NYT*, July 12, 26, 1921; *Literary Digest* 70 (July 23, 1921): 5–7; Borah to S. O. Levinson, July 18, 1921, Borah papers.

34. Harding to Jennings, Malcolm Jennings papers; *NYT* July 6, 18, 26, 29, August 16, 1921.

35. *NYT*, July 15, 26, August 24, 1921.

36. Harding to Robert W. Lansing, March 28, 1921; Lodge to Harding, July 21, 1921; C. D. Hilles to Harding, August 17, 1921; Harding to Hilles, August 20, 1921; Harding to Malcolm Jennings, January 6, 1922, WGHP; *NYT*, September 9, 1921.

37. Hiram Johnson to Hiram Johnson, Jr., and A. M. Johnson, August 13, 1921, Hiram Johnson papers; Borah to Frank W. Borah, August 23, 1921, Borah papers; *NYT*, August 12, 1921.

38. *NYT*, August 12, October 4, 13, November 4, 1921; Harding to Hughes, October 10, 1921, WGHP.

39. *NYT*, June 24, 1921; U.S. Congress, House, Committee on Naval Affairs, "Disarmament" *Hearings*, 66th Congress, 3d sess., p. 763; for examples of Sims' attitude, see Sims to Fullam, March 24, Sims to Gardiner, August 3, 1921, WSSP.

40. Sims to Fiske, March 17, 1921, WSSP, made clear his despair at hope of internal reform of the Naval Department; Elting E. Morrison, Naval Administration: Selected Documents on Navy Department Organization (unpublished Navy Department manuscript, 1945), chap. 4; *NYT*, July 14, 19, 22, 28, 1921; Samuel F. Wells, Jr., "William Mitchell and the Ostfriesland," *The Historian* 26 (August 1964): 538–62.

41. General Board Proceedings, July 23, 25, August 3, 1921; Secretary of the Navy (Roosevelt, acting) to General Board, July 27, 1921, serial 1088; Schofield memorandum, August 22, 1921; General Board Limitation of Armaments, Policy and Discussion Book, GBP; Roosevelt to Denby, August 8, 1921, Edwin Denby papers, pointed out that Lodge and Hughes had urged him to begin explorations of arms limitation and concluded that Borah was isolated in opposing the building program.

42. August memoranda, especially W. L. Rodgers memorandum, August 20, 1921, General Board Limitation of Armaments, Policy and Discussion Book; Rodgers to Secretary of the Navy, September 12, 17, October 3, 1921, serial 1088, GBP.

43. Rodgers to Secretary of the Navy, September 12, 17, October 3, serial 1088, and General Board to Secretary of the Navy, October 22, 1921, GBP.

44. *NYT*, September 7–8, 1921; Theodore Roosevelt, Jr., to Hughes, October 3, 1921, Theodore Roosevelt, Jr. papers; Denby to Hughes, October 10, 1921, Denby papers.

45. Hughes to Denby, October 6, 1921, Denby papers; Colonel Lucas memorandum, May 20, 1924, William Howard Gardiner papers; General Board Proceedings, October 4, 6, 8, 1921; General Board to Secretary of the Navy, October 14, 1921, serial 1088-3; Explanatory of Navy Department, Plans I-III, October 20, 1921, General Board Advisory Book, GBP; Minutes of Secretary of the Navy's Council, October 13, 1921, RG 45; TRJD, October 21, 1921.

46. TRJD, October 20, 1921; Minutes of American Delegation meeting, October 21, 1921, Department of State 400.A41.12, RG 43, hereafter cited as Minutes of American Delegation; Harding to Walter B. Brown, October 24, 1921, WGHP, reconfirmed the essential domestic political dynamic behind his proposal; Sullivan diary, October 14, 1921, Mark Sullivan papers, Hoover Institution.

47. Minutes of American Delegation meetings, October 24, 31; TRJD,

October 24–31, 1921; William V. Pratt to Harold Sprout, October 24, 1939, Pratt papers.

48. Minutes of American Delegation meeting, November 2–3, 1921; J.V.A. MacMurray to Hughes, October 26, 1921, Washington Conference delegation papers, box 310, RG 43; Braisted, *The U.S. Navy in the Pacific*, pp. 587–95, reviews final preparations for the conference.

Chapter 10

1. The emphasis on the diplomatic and imperial aspects of naval limitation can be traced in R. A. Chaput, *Disarmament in British Foreign Policy* (London, 1935), pp. 99–106; Sprout and Sprout, *Toward a New Order of Sea Power*, pp. 123–26; Roskill, *Naval Policy Between the Wars*, vol. 1, chap. 7; Max Beloff, *Imperial Sunset I: Britain's Liberal Empire, 1897–1921* (New York, 1970), pp. 337–43; Malcolm D. Kennedy, *The Estrangement of Great Britain and Japan* (Berkeley, 1969), chap. 4; and, most recently and thoroughly, William Roger Louis, *British Strategy in the Far East, 1919–1939* (Oxford, 1971), chaps. 1–2; and Ian H. Nish, *Alliance in Decline* (London, 1972), chaps. 17–21.

2. *The Nation* 39 (May 14, 1921): 240.

3. *LT*, March 14, 15, 1921.

4. *LT*, March 17–18, April 1, 25–26, May 26, June 4, 9, 15, 17, 1921; *Manchester Guardian*, March 15, 1921; *The Nation* 38 (March 19, 1921): 861; *The Nation* 29 (April 30, 1921): 153; *The Nation* 29 (May 28, 1921): 309.

5. Generalizations herein are based on my reading of cabinet minutes and the London *Times*, March–June 1921; Wilson, ed., *Political Diaries*, p. 390; D. G. Boyce, *Englishmen and Irish Troubles* (Cambridge, 1972), p. 15.

6. *LT*, March 18–19, 1921; Taylor, ed., *Stevenson Diary*, April 26, May 14, 25, 1921, pp. 210, 215–16, 219; Riddell, *Intimate Diary*, April 24, 1921, p. 295; Hankey diary, March 16, 1921, in Roskill, *Hankey*, 2: 224; Lord Beaverbrook, *The Decline and Fall of Lloyd George* (New York, 1963), chap. 2.

7. Taylor, ed., *Stevenson Diary*, June 1, 5, 11, 18, 1921, pp. 219–21.

8. CAB 2/3, C.I.D. meeting, December 14, 1920; Geddes to Curzon, April 15, forwarded to Lloyd George April 28, 1921, LGP; Riddell, *Intimate Diary*, January 26, 1921, pp. 270–73; *LT*, May 27, 1921; *NYT*, May 20, 1921.

9. Loring Christie memorandum, February 1, 1921, cited by Beloff in *Imperial Sunset*, p. 339; CAB 23/24/14-21, February 18, 1921, conference of ministers; Lloyd George to Governor General of Canada, draft, February 22, Churchill to Lloyd George, April 25, Lee to Lloyd George, March 19, Sir Edward Grigg to Lloyd George, May 25, 1921,

LGP; M. W. Lampson memorandum on correspondence with the Canadian Government relating to the Anglo-Japanese Alliance, April 8, 1921, and explanatory minute and footnote, *DBFP*, ser. 1, 14: 271-76; CAB 24/123, Lee memorandum for cabinet, "Anglo-Japanese Alliance," May 21, 1921.

10. Nish, *Alliance in Decline*, pp. 303-4, 325.

11. CAB 23/25/43-21, Cabinet meeting, May 30, 1921.

12. ADM 116/1770, Admiralty memorandum, May 17, ADM 116/1603, Wemyss statement to Imperial War Cabinet, June 27, 1918, Wemyss to Geddes, July 25, 27, August 7, 1918; CAB 32/1, Imperial War Conference meeting, July 22, Sir Joseph Cook to Sir Eric Geddes, November 16, 1918, cited by Bacon in *Jellicoe*, p. 393; ADM 116/1815, Murray to Geddes, November 30, December 23, 1918, instructions to Lord Jellicoe. This Admiralty file contains the complete official correspondence on the Jellicoe tour; A. Temple Patterson, ed., *The Jellicoe Papers* 2 (London, 1968): 284-398, reprints selections from Jellicoe's reports.

13. ADM 116/1832, Jellicoe to Chelmsford, April 30, 1919; ADM 116/1834, Jellicoe to Admiralty, August 21, 1919; ADM 116/1831, Jellicoe to Admiralty, February 3, 1920, all cited by Roskill in *Naval Policy Between the Wars*, 1: 276-81. This volume offers the best secondary account of the Jellicoe mission, pp. 271-88; ADM 116/1815, Wemyss to Long, October 31, 1919; ADM 167/59, Notes by Chief of the Naval Staff to accompany Admiralty Memorandum on Imperial Naval Defence, August 4, 1919; ibid; Memorandum, Imperial Naval Defence, August 1919.

14. Sir Oswyn Murray to Foreign Office, February 12, 1920, *DBFP*, ser. 1, 6:1054; ADM 116/1677, Chief of Naval Staff memorandum for Board of Admiralty, January 1, 1920; Nish, *Alliance in Decline*, p. 297; Hankey to Chamberlain, June 16, 1921, enclosing Naval Staff memorandum "Empire naval policy and cooperation," Austen Chamberlain papers, cited in Nish, *Alliance in Decline*, p. 319.

15. ADM 116/3101, Commander in Chief China proposal, March 30, revised, October 1, 1920; Minutes by Director of Trade Division, December 18, 1920, and Director of Plans Division, January 8, 1921; ADM 116/3167, Secretary of State for Colonies to Governor General of Australia, December 21, 1920; CAB 24/79, Long memorandum for cabinet, May 6, 1919; CAB 24/98, Joint Admiralty and Petroleum Executive memorandum for cabinet, February 5, 1920; CAB 24/101, Long memorandum for cabinet, "Oil Supplies," March 18, 1920; ADM 116/1775, Beatty memorandum for cabinet, "Naval strategy as affected by the proposed future status of Egypt," October 27, 1920; CAB 2/3, Committee of Imperial Defense meeting, December 14, 1920; for Beatty's earlier remarks and the budget strategy, see chap. 7.

16. ADM 116/3167, Director, Plans Division draft invitation, January 20,

O. Murray (?) minute, January 18, 1921; Commander in Chief, China to Admiralty, February 4, 1921; ADM 116/3100, Report of the Penang Conference of Commanders in Chief East Indies, China, and Australian Fleets, March 23, 1921.

17. CAB 7/9, Overseas Defense Subcommittee of C.I.D. meetings, May 10, June 7, 1921; ADM 116/2100, Report of Overseas Defence Subcommittee of C.I.D. on Development of Singapore, June 7, 1921; CAB 2/3, C.I.D. Standing Defense Subcommittee meetings, May 2, 6, June 10, 13, 1921. The terms of the draft memorandum for the cabinet were agreed upon on June 10, the final text accepted June 13; ADM 116/3102, Beatty to Lee, May 21, 1921, urged that the full Board discuss fuel oil needs east of Suez; ADM 167/64, Board meeting, May 26, 1921, endorsed stockpiling 1.2 million tons at Singapore.

18. CAB 23/25/20-1, Cabinet meeting, June 16, 1921.

19. ADM 116/3102, Admiralty memorandum to C.I.D., June 21, 1921.

20. Hankey to Lloyd George, June 14, 15, 1921, LGP; LT, March 18, June 20–21, 1921.

21. CAB 32/2, Imperial Conference meeting, June 20, 1921.

22. Ibid., CAB 32/2, June 21–22, 24, 28, 1921; Taylor, ed., Stevenson Diary, June 20, 1921, p. 223.

23. CAB 32/2, Imperial Conference meetings, June 28, 29, 1921.

24. CAB 23/26/56-21, Cabinet meeting, June 30, 1921; CAB 32/2, Imperial Conference meeting, June 30, 1921.

25. Taylor, ed., Stevenson Diary, July 4, 1921, p. 224; CAB 32/2, Imperial Conference meeting, July 8, 1921; Curzon to Geddes, July 9, 1921, Curzon memorandum, July 8, 1921, DBFP, ser. 1, 14:331–33, 336–38; Riddell, Intimate Diary, July 10, 1921, pp. 304–5; LT, July 12, 1921.

26. LT, June 20–21, July 5, 9, 11, 15, 1921; Manchester Guardian, July 12, 1921; The Nation 29 (June 25): 459–60; The Nation 29 (July 16, 1921): 564; "The Meeting of the Imperial Cabinet," The Round Table 11 (June 1921): 544–49.

27. CAB 32/4, Imperial Conference meetings, July 19–20, 22, 27, 1921; LT, August 19, 1921.

28. Curzon memorandum, July 24, Curzon to Geddes, August 1, 1921, DBFP, ser. 1, 14:345–51, 363; Hayashi Gonsuke, Waga shichijūnen o kataru (Tokyo, 1935), pp. 379–82; Lloyd George to Churchill, July 18, 1921, LGP; CAB 32/2, Imperial Conference meetings, July 21, 26, 1921; CAB 23/26/68-21, Conference of ministers, July 25, 1921.

29. CAB 24/126, Lee memorandum for cabinet, July 15, 1921; Lee to Lloyd George, July 16, 1921, LGP; LT, August 4, 1921; CAB 23/26/60–21, Cabinet meeting, July 20, 1921; CAB 23/67-21, Cabinet meeting, August 15, 1921.

30. ADM 167/64, Memorandum 1390, draft Order-in-Council, August 10, 1921; ADM 167/63 Board meetings, August 13, October 13, 1921; ADM 116/3139, Law Officers' report, August 17, Lee minute, August 18, 1921; Riddell, *Intimate Diary*, August 19, 1921, p. 313.

31. *LT*, July 12, October 11, 1921; Taylor, ed., *Stevenson Diary*, July 11, 1921, p. 221; Wilson, ed., *Political Diaries*, July 28, October 27–29, 1921, pp. 396–98, 402–5; Boyce, *Englishmen and Irish Troubles*, pp. 140–55.

32. *LT*, June 9, 15, 17, July 20–21, August 3–4, 1921; M. Epstein, ed., *The Annual Register, Volume 163, 1921* (London, 1922), pp. 60, 82–85.

33. Taylor, ed., *Stevenson Diary*, July 29, 1921, p. 233; *LT*, July 20, 30, October 15, 1921; *The Nation* 29 (August 6, 1921): 671.

34. *Manchester Guardian*, July 22, August 4, 1921; *Nation* 30 (October 1, 1921), p. 6; Archibald Hurd, "The Navy League's Renunciation," *Fortnightly Review* 110 (August 1921): 278–91; "A Policy of National Suicide," *Fortnightly Review* 110 (October 1921): 663–76; generalizations on journalistic opinion are based upon my reading of the *Fortnightly Review, Nation, New Statesman, Nineteenth Century and After, National Review, Saturday Review,* and *Spectator* for July–November 1921; *LT*, October 21, 1921.

35. *LT*, July 13, October 24, 1921; "Mr. Lloyd George and Washington," *Spectator* 127 (October 22, 1921): 516–17; "The Washington Conference," *Nineteenth Century and After* 90 (October 1921): pp. 563–70; *National Review* 78 (September 1921): 13.

36. ADM 116/3447, Director of Plans memoranda, March 1, 31, June 25, 1921; Brock memorandum, April 11, Chatfield memorandum April 12, Beatty to Lee, April 14, 1921; Plans Division memorandum, September 1, 1921.

37. Plans Division memorandum, September 1, 1921; Director of Naval Intelligence memorandums, March 14, April 7, Chatfield to Lee, September 15, 1921.

38. CAB 2/3, Admiralty memorandum on limitation of naval armaments, October 14, 1921, CID. 277b.

39. Curzon to Lloyd George, September 20, 28, Hankey to Sir Edward Grigg (Lloyd George's personal secretary) enclosing Balfour cables, September 29, 1921, LGP; *LT*, October 13, 1921.

40. CAB 2/3, C.I.D. Standing Defence Subcommittee meeting, October 14, 1921.

41. *LT*, October 18, 1921; CAB 2/3, C.I.D. Standing Defence Subcommittee meeting, October 21, 1921; CAB 23/27/80-21, Cabinet meeting, October 17, 1921.

42. CAB 30/1a, CID 280b, Memorandum by Standing Defence Subcommittee, October 24, 1921; CAB 2/3, C.I.D. Standing Defence Sub-

committee meeting, October 31, 1921; CAB 23/27/83-21, Cabinet meeting, November 1, 1921.

43. *LT*, October 24, 1921; *National Review* 78 (October 1921): 147; Curzon to Geddes, September 18, 1921, *DBFP*, ser. 1, 14:398; Riddell, *Intimate Diary*, October 16, 30, November 3, 1921, pp. 326, 330–31; Taylor, ed., *Stevenson Diary*, October 28, November 6, 8, 1921, pp. 234–36.

44. *Manchester Guardian*, November 3, 1921.

Chapter 11

1. Wood to Secretary of War, November 3, 1921, Department of State file 711.94/431, reel 4, National Archives microfilm publication 423; Wood to Harding, February 25, Harding to Weeks (Secretary of War), March 20, 1921, WGHP.

2. The theme of compulsion runs through English-language literature on the Washington Conference, previously cited, and emerges with special force in James B. Crowley, *Japan's Quest for Autonomy, National Security and Foreign Policy* (Princeton, 1966), pp. 26–27. It also appears, in varying forms, in Ichihashi Yamato, *The Washington Conference and After* (Stanford, 1928); Itō Masanori, *Washington kaigi to sono go* (Tokyo, 1928); Matsushita Yoshio, *Nihon gunji hattatsu shi* (Tokyo, 1938), p. 376; Shinobu Seizaburō, *Taishō seiji shi* (Tokyo, 1954), 1:318–20; Kobayashi Tatsuo, "Kaigun gunshuku jōyaku (1921-1936)," in Tsunoda, ed., *Taiheiyō sensō e no michi*, 1: 25–30; Asada Sadao, "Japan and the United States, 1915–1925" (Ph.D. diss., Yale University, 1963); Mitani Taichirō, "Tenkanki (1918–1921) no gaikō shidō," in Mitani and Shinohara, eds., *Kindai Nihon no seiji shidō*, pp. 296–97, 326–31; Satō Seizaburō, "Kyōchō to jiritsu to no aida—Nihon," *Nenpō seiji gaku 1969* (Tokyo, 1970), pp. 108–14; Oka Yoshitake, *Tenkanki no Taishō*, vol. 5 in *Nihon kindai shi taikei* (Tokyo, 1969), pp. 176–81. Royama Masamichi, *Foreign Policy of Japan, 1914–1939* (Tokyo, 1941), pp. 33–35.

3. Kokusai Renmei kankei jikō kenkyūkai ni okeru gunbi seigen mondai ni kansuru kenkyū narabi ni ketsugi, August 5, 1920; Kokusai Remmei kakugun daihyōsha ni ataeru kunrei no ken, September 16, 1920, reel 130, JFMA.

4. *Japan Advertiser*, August 12, September 24, 1920; *HKN*, 9, September 21–22, 1920, pp. 74–75; S 15.1.3.0.1, Cabinet decision Instructions to League of Nations Conference Delegation, November 9, 1920, reel 427, JFMA; *NYT*, December 12, 1920; *Osaka Asahi* editorials, December 14, 23, *Chūgai shōgyō* editorial, December 23, 1920, translated in *Japan Advertiser*, December 16, 25, 1920.

5. *Jiji* budget analysis, November 26, 1920, translated in *Japan Advertiser*, November 27, 1920; Imamura Takeo, *Hyōden: Takahashi*

Korekiyo (Tokyo, 1950), pp. 82, 102, 113–14; *HKN*, 9, November 25–28, 1920, pp. 139–41; *Tokyo Asahi shinbun*, December 18, 1920, January 8, 16, 1921.

6. *Tokyo Asahi shinbun*, February 12, 1921; *GSSJN*, 9: 998–1000; *Japan Advertiser*, January 23, 1921.

7. *Yomiuri* editorial, November 26, *Tokyo Asahi* editorial, *Jiji* editorials, December 24, 26–28, 30, January 1, 8–9, 1921, *Kokumin* and *Hōchi* editorials, December 24, 1920, translated in *Japan Advertiser*, November 27, December 2, 11, 25, 27–29, 31, 1920, January 6, 9, 1921; Itō Masanori, *Shinbun seikatsu nijūnen*, pp. 323–25,

8. *Japan Advertiser*, January 21, 1921.

9. Suzuki, ed., *Ozaki zenshū*, 11: 578–93; Scalapino, *Democracy and the Party Movement in Prewar Japan*, p. 193; *Tokyo Asahi shinbun*, January 26, 29, 31, 1921; *Japan Advertiser*, February 5, 1921.

10. Suzuki, ed., *Ozaki zenshū*, 11: 608–11; *Japan Advertiser*, February 11–13, 1921.

11. *Japan Advertiser*, March 24, 1921; *HKN*, 8, March 22, 27, pp. 253, 256; F.O. 410/70/22, Eliot to Curzon, February 14, 1921.

12. Suzuki, ed., *Ozaki zenshū*, 11: 591, 612; *Osaka Mainichi*, February 22, translated in *Japan Advertiser*, February 24, 1921; *Japan Advertiser*, February 17, May 21, 1921.

13. Suzuki, ed., *Ozaki zenshū*, 6: 391–440, compiled his answers to questions on his tour; Ozaki Yukio, *Gunbi seigen ron* (Tokyo, 1921), presented basic arguments for arms limitation.

14. F.O. 410/70/99, Eliot to Curzon, April 16, 1921; F.O. 410/71/74, Eliot to Curzon, June 28, 1921.

15. Kenneth Pyle, *The New Generation of Meiji Japan* (Stanford, 1969), pp. 150–56, describes Miyake's earlier ideas; Yoshino Sakuzō, et al., "Jikoku honchi shugi tai kokusai kyōdō shugi hihan," *Chūō Kōron* 36 (February 1921): 39–72; Miyake Setsurei, "Kyōsō ni makeru to kagiranu," *Taiyō* 27 (March 1921): 58–60; Kagawa Toyohiko, "Seigen yori mo teppatsu," *Taiyō* 27 (March 1921): 60–64; Ukita Kazutami, "Ketsugi an no hikentsu o oshimu," *Taiyō* 27 (March 1921): 67–68; Shiga Tsurutarō, "Gunbi seigen mondai ni tsuite," *Taiyō* 27 (April 1921): 18–23; Yoshino Sakuzō, "Nijū seifu yori nijū Nippon," *Chūō Kōron* 36 (March 1921): pp. 93–101; *Osaka Mainichi*, February 10, 25, translated in *Japan Advertiser*, February 12, 26, 1921.

16. Yoshino Sakuzō, "Jitsugyōka no dassanteki gunbi seigen undō," *Chūō Kōron* 36 (April 1921): 218–20; *Japan Advertiser*, February 26, March 10, June 12, 28, 1921; *Osaka Mainichi*, May 4, translated in *Japan Advertiser*, May 6, 1920.

17. *Tokyo Asahi shinbun*, May 25–26, June 3, 25–26, July 10, 1921.

18. Naval Attaché Tokyo to Office of Naval Intelligence, February 18, 1921; documents supplied by Director of Naval History, Washington, D.C.; F.O. 410/70/22, Eliot to Curzon, February 14, 1920 [sic]; *Japan*

Advertiser, March 11–13, 20–21, 31, April 7, 1921; *Chūō*, April 12, translated in *Japan Advertiser*, April 13, 1921; *NYT*, March 24, 1921.

19. *Tokyo Asahi shinbun*, April 10, 1921; MT 5.1.10.5, reel 464, JFMA; *Japan Advertiser*, May 3, 1921.

20. *Tokyo Asahi shinbun*, April 7, 24, 29, May 5, 1921; F.O. 410/70/22, Eliot to Curzon, February 14, 1920 [sic] reported naval officials giving "serious attention" to arms limitation.

21. *Tokyo Asahi shinbun*, January 8, March 31, May 3, 8, 29, June 1–2, 29, July 2, 1921; Nakagawa, *Shimamura*, p. 13; Matsuoka Masao, *Kaigun taishō Yamashita Gentarō den* (Tokyo, 1941), p. 224; F.O. 410/70/164, Eliot to Curzon, May 25, 1921; the massive, basic arms limitation study within the navy submitted July 21 was so sizeable and different from its predecessors as to have had to been undertaken sometime in the late spring at the latest. For details, see below, pp. 187–89; *HKN*, 9, August 24, 1921, p. 402.

22. *Tokyo Asahi shinbun*, April 14, July 21, 1921.

23. *HKN*, 9, April 11, 27, June 4, 7, 1921, pp. 272, 287, 329, 332; Takakura, *Tanaka*, 2:203–10.

24. Ugaki, *Ugaki Kazushige nikki* 1, April–May 1921, pp. vii, 343–45; *Tokyo Asahi shinbun*, July 2, 1921.

25. *HKN*, 9, February 4, 15, 17, April 9, May 4, 7, 11, 20, 31, June 7, 1921, pp. 210–11, 222, 225, 271, 294–333, passim.

26. Ibid., 9, July 7, 1921, p. 362.

27. Ibid., 9, July 8, 12, 1921, pp. 363, 368–69.

28. *Japan Chronicle*, July 15–23, 1921; F.O. 410/71/44, Eliot to Curzon, July 14, 1921; Naval Attaché Tokyo to Office of Naval Intelligence received July 18, 1921, file QY c-10-1, RG 38.

29. Hidaka Kinji interview, translated in *Japan Advertiser*, March 11, 1921; Mizuno Hironori, *Nami no uneri* (Tokyo 1922). The latter was a series of articles written during 1921 that stressed changes abroad. Mizuno had been the official naval historian of the Russo-Japanese war, and had written an enormously popular novel based upon that history. In January 1921 he was dismissed from active duty for publishing unauthorized criticism of navy conservatism in weapons technology and definitions of fleet adequacy. See Matsushita Yoshio, "Mizuno Hironori to *Kono issen*," in Mizuno, *Kono issen* 2d ed. (Tokyo, 1958), pp. 342–44; Kokusai renmei kankei jikō kenkyū kai, NichiBeiEi kaigun seigen mondai ni kansuru kenkyū, July 21, 1921, in Gunbi seigen taisaku kenkyū, 9, Enamoto Jūji papers, JDA. Material on this report in the following paragraphs is taken from this source.

30. Naval Attaché Tokyo to Office of Naval Intelligence, August 26, 1921, file c-10-1, RG 38.

31. Ugaki, *Ugaki nikki*, 1, July 12, 1921, p. 350; *NYT*, August 6, 1921; *Japan Chronicle*, August 10, 1921.

32. *Japan Chronicle*, August 20, 1921; F.O. 410/71-89, Eliot to Curzon, July 27, 1921; F.O. 410/110, Eliot to Curzon, August 14, 1921; Washington kaigi ikken: junbi, 2: 011308, 011310–011320, JFMA.

33. *HKN*, 9, July 12, 19, 22, August 23, 1921, pp. 368–69, 373, 377–78, 401; *Japan Chronicle*, July 24, August 2, 1921; F.O. 410/71/103, Eliot to Curzon, August 7, 1921.

34. *Japan Chronicle*, August 12, 1921; *HKN*, 9, August 19, pp. 397–98; Memorandum of Hughes-Shidehara meeting, August 18, 1921, 793.94/1191½, RG 59, cited by Braisted in *The U.S. Navy in the Pacific*, p. 572.

35. *HKN*, 9, August 24, 1921, pp. 402–3.

36. Ibid. (August 25, 1921), pp. 403–5; Uchida Yasuya denki hensan iinkai, ed., *Uchida Yasuya*, (Tokyo, 1969), pp. 256–57.

37. Admiral Yamanashi Katsunoshin, then head of the Naval Affairs Bureau and an author of the Committee for the Study of League of Nations Affairs report, later recalled that Admiral Katō looked upon the invitation to Washington as a "gift from the gods" that would extricate him from the multiple difficulties surrounding construction of the eight-eight fleet. Author's interview with Yamanashi Katsunoshin, July 12, 1966; *Yamanashi Katsunoshin sensei ihō roku*, pp. 69–70; author's interview with Enamoto Jūji, Secretary to the Navy Ministry, June 3, 1966. Other ranking members of the naval experts included Captains Nomura Kichisaburō and Suetsugu Nobumasa, both members of the Committee for the Study of League of Nations Affairs, Captains Nagano Osami and Ueda Yoshitake, both attached to the Embassy in Washington. Nomura was also a former naval attaché in the United States. For a full listing and brief biographical sketch of the Japanese naval experts, see F.O. 410/71/224, Eliot to Curzon, October 13, and Naval Attaché Tokyo to Office of Naval Intelligence, October 10, 1921, file qy, RG 38.

38. *HKN*, 9, August 25, 1921, p. 405; Kafu kaigi gunbi seigen mondai ni kansuru kenkyū, September 28, 1921, in Gunbi seigen taisaku kenkyū, vol. 11, Enamoto Jūji papers, JDA. The August report was appended to this later study; Katō Kanji, "Gunbi seigen no taisei to sono teido," *Taiyō* 27 (October 1921): 18–22.

39. Gunbi seigen mondai ni kansuru kenkyū, September 28, 1921, in Gunbi seigen taisaku kenkyū, vol. 11, Enamoto Jūji papers, JDA.

40. F.O. 410/70/164, Eliot to Curzon, May 25, 1921; F.O. 410/71/122, Eliot to Curzon, August 18, 1921; *HKN*, 9, August 24, 1921, p. 402.

41. Washington kaigi ikken: junbi, p. 011353; NichiEiBei kaigun kyōtei no kyūmu, *ibid.*, pp. 011358-011364; Kunrei, October 1921, Washington kaigi keika: Choron: kaigi zenki, reel ud 20, UD 22, JFMA; Uchida to delegation, November 22, 1921, no. 44, m.t. 2.4.3.48, reel 312.

42. *HKN*, 9, August 26, September 2, 6, 13, 20, 1921, pp. 407, 415, 423, 438, 447; Oka Yoshitake and Hayashi Shigeo eds., *Taishō demo-*

kurashii ki no seiji: Matsumoto Gōkichi seiji nisshi, p. 114; *Japan Chronicle*, September 14, 1921; Kunrei, October 1921, Washington kaigi keika: Choron: Kaigi zenki, reel ud 20, UD 22, JFMA.

43. *HKN*, 9, August 25, September 6, 22, 1921, pp. 404, 423, 454–55.

44. *HKN*, 9, June 25, p. 348; *Japan Chronicle*, August 10, 17, September 10–15, 1921; F.O. 410/71/155, Eliot to Curzon, August 25, 1921; F.O. 410/71/228, Eliot to Curzon, October 21, 1921.

45. *HKN*, 9, September 22, October 5–7, 10–13, 1921, pp. 454, 455, 465–68, 470, 473; *Tokyo Asahi shinbun* seijibu hen, *Sono goro o kataru* (Tokyo 1928), p. 378, cited by Satō Seizaburō in Kyōchō to jiritsu to no aida—Nihon, *"Nenpō seiji gaku 1969,"* p. 131.

46. *HKN*, 9, October 15, 1921, p. 474.

Chapter 12

1. *NYT*, November 12, 1921; *LT*, November 12, 1921.

2. *NYT*, November 13, 1921; Mark Sullivan, *The Great Adventure at Washington* (New York, 1922), pp. 23–24; Vinson, *Parchment Peace*, pp. 138–39 surveys immediate reactions to Hughes's speech.

3. *NYT*, November 13, 1921; Borah to John Spargo, November 16, Borah to C. E. Ellicott, November 21, Borah to E. H. Powell, November 28, 1921, Borah papers; Hiram Johnson to Hiram Johnson, Jr., and A. M. Johnson, November 16, 1921, Hiram Johnson papers; George Sutherland to Arthur Thomas, November 16, 1921, George Sutherland papers.

4. *NYT*, November 12, 16, 18, 1921; *The Nation* 30 (November 19, 1921): 297; *Nineteenth Century and After* 90 (December 1921): 932; Hankey to Lady Hankey, n.d. November 1921, in Roskill, *Hankey*, 2:241.

5. *NYT*, November 16, 1921; Sir Robert Borden to Sir James Lougheed, November 15, 17, Borden to Balfour, November 25, 1921, Sir Robert Borden papers, microfilm OC 611, reel c-287, Public Archives of Canada, Ottawa.

6. ADM 116/2149, Naval section memorandum 3, November 13, 1921; CAB 30/1a, Minutes of British Empire Delegation meeting, November 13, 1921; Balfour to Curzon, n.d. (but from preceding minutes sent November 13, 1921), *DBFP*, ser. 1, 14:472.

7. TRJD, November 16; CAB 30/1a, Minutes of British Empire Delegation, November 15–16; ADM 116/2149, Chatfield to Beatty, November 16, 21, Beatty Answers to ACNS's agenda, November 22, 1921.

8. Thomas Jones, *Whitehall Diary*, 1, November 15, 1921, p. 178; CAB 2/3, C.I.D. Standing Defence Subcommittee meeting, November 14, 1921; Lloyd George to Balfour, November 15, President, Board of Trade, to Sir Llewellyn Smith, November 18, 1921, *DBFP*, ser. 1, 14: 475–76, 485; *LT*, November 19, 1921.

9. ADM 116/1776, H. F. Oliver memorandum for cabinet, November 21,

1921; CAB 2/3, C.I.D. meeting, November 23, 1921; Curzon to Balfour, November 23, 1921, *DBFP*, ser. 1, 14:497–500; *LT*, November 22, 24, 1921.

10. Balfour to Curzon, November 24, 1921, *DBFP*, ser. 1, 14:503–5; ADM 116/3445, Lloyd George to C.I.D., November 30, 1921. The prime minister may have acted in response to strong anti-capital ship arguments which reappeared in the *Times*, November 23–25, and to the king's views expressed in Stamfordham to Lloyd George, November 23 (?), 1921, RA GV E1739/7, in Roskill, *Naval Policy Between the Wars*, 1:315; Hankey to Lady Hankey, November 27, 1921, in Roskill, *Hankey*, 2:246; Louis, *British Strategy in the Far East, 1919–1939*, pp. 97–102, analyzes Balfour's differences with Curzon.

11. *Yamanashi Katsunoshin sensei ihō roku*, p. 79; Itō Masanori, *Shinbun seikatsu nijūnen*, pp. 328–31; Ide to Katō Tomosaburō, November 14, Delegation to Uchida, November 16, 1921, no. 28, Gunbi seigen taisaku kenkyū, vol. 11, JDA; Uchida to delegation, December 9, 1921, m.t. 2.4.3.48, reel 313; *Tokyo Asahi shimbun*, November 15, December 4, 1921; *NYT*, November 16, 1921; *LT*, November 16, 30, 1921; TRJD, November 17, 1921.

12. Maeda Renzan, *Rekidai naikaku monogatari*, 2:309–16; F.O. 410/71/271, Eliot to Curzon, November 18, 1921; Yoshino Sakuzō, "Kyōhen yori shin naikaku no seiritsu made," *Chūō Kōron* 36 (December 1921): 134–36.

13. *Yamanashi Katsunoshin sensei ihō roku*, p. 94; Warren to Hughes, November 17, 1921, *FRUS, 1922*, 1:61; *Tokyo Asahi shimbun*, November 18, 23–25, 30, 1921; Uchida to zenken, November 22, 1921, no. 44 m.t. 2.4.3.48, reel 312.

14. Arai, *Katō*, pp. 76–78; Zenken to Uchida, November 23, 1921, Gunbi seigen taisaku kenkyū, vol. 11, JDA; Author's interview with Yamanashi Katsunoshin, July 12, 1966; Author's interview with Enamoto Jūji, June 1, 1966.

15. Uchida to zenken, November 28, 1921, no. 73, m.t. 2.4.3.48, reel 313; Ide to Katō Tomosaburō, November 28, Katō daijin kaigun jikan ōfuku denpō tei, JDA.

16. Memorandum of Japanese naval experts, November 30, 1921, *FRUS, 1922*, 1:69; Balfour to Curzon, December 1, 1921, *DBFP*, ser. 1, 14: 529–30; Ide to Katō Tomosaburō, n.d. but received December 1, 1921, Gunbi seigen taisaku kenkyū, vol. 11, JDA.

17. Hankey memorandum of Balfour-Hughes conversation, December 1, 1921, Hughes to Warren, November 27, 1921, *FRUS, 1922*, 1:67, 74–75; John V. A. MacMurray to Hughes, October 26, 1921, Lodge materials, RG 43; American Delegation meeting, November 16, 1921, RG 43; TRJD, November 27, 1921; Stanley Jerome Granat, "Chinese Participation at the Washington Conference, 1921–1922" (Ph.D. diss., University of Indiana, 1969); Asada Sadao, "Japan and the

United States, 1915–1925," (Ph.D. diss., Yale University, 1963), analyze the discussion of nonnaval issues at Washington; Herbert O. Yardley, *The American Black Chamber* (London, 1931) chaps. 14–16, describes the code-breaking effort and reprints some of the cables.

18. American Delegation meetings, November 2, December 1–2, 1921, RG 43; Hankey memorandum of Hughes-Balfour-Katō meeting December 2, 1921, *FRUS, 1922*, 1:75–83.

19. Zenken to Uchida, December 1, 2, 3, 5, 9, 1921, nos. 119, 127, 131, 136, 151, m.t. 2.4.3.51, reel 317; Katō Tomosaburō to Ide, December 4, Ide to Katō Tomosaburō, December 7–10, Ide to Nomura, December 8, 1921, Katō daijin kaigun jikan ōfuku denpō tei, JDA: *Tokyo Asahi shinbun*, December 7, 11, 1921; Maeda Renzan, *Rekidai naikaku monogatari*, 2:336–37; Warren to Hughes, December 7, 1921, *FRUS, 1922*, 1:88.

20. TRJD, December 2, 12–13, 1921; Minutes of American Delegation meeting, December 13, 1921, RG 43.

21. Hankey memoranda of Balfour-Hughes-Katō meetings, December 13, 14, 1921, *FRUS, 1922*, 1:99–114; TRJD, December 1, 1921.

22. TRJD, December 14–15, 1921; Hankey memoranda of Balfour-Hughes-Katō meetings, December 14–15, *FRUS, 1922*, 1:115–27; Balfour to Curzon, December 15, 1921, *DBFP*, ser. 1, 14:558–61; ADM 116/2149, Chatfield to Balfour, December 16, 1921.

23. Lloyd George to Balfour, December 1, Curzon to Balfour, December 9, Balfour to Curzon, December 12, 1921, *DBFP*, ser. 1, 14:526–27, 544–45, 552; Hankey to Lloyd George, November 25, December 12, 1921, LGP; CAB 2/3, C.I.D. meeting, December 2, 1921; Beatty memorandum for cabinet and C.I.D., December 17, 1921.

24. CAB 23/27/92, Cabinet meeting, December 12, 1921; *Conference on Limitation of Armaments at Washington, November 12, 1921–February 6, 1922* (Washington, 1922), pp. 158–66; *NYT*, December 16, 1921; *Literary Digest* 71 (December 31, 1921): 10; Balfour to Curzon, November 24, 1921, *DBFP*, ser. 1, 14:503; Hankey to Lloyd George, December 2, 1921, LGP; TRJD, December 5–6, 1921; Hughes to Paul D. Cravath, December 19, 1921, Hughes papers.

25. *NYT*, December 12–13, 1921; Borah to Joseph Kaschmitter, December 10, Borah to Mrs. J. C. Saltzmann, December 18, 1921, Borah papers.

26. Hughes' efforts are recorded in *FRUS, 1922*, 1:132–43, and can be followed in *NYT*, December 16–20, 1921; TRJD, December 15–21, 1921.

27. TRJD, December 22, 1921; General Board to Secretary of the Navy, November 15, Report of Advisory Commission, December 1, 1921, Lodge materials, RG 43; Balfour to Curzon, December 19, 1921, *DBFP*, ser. 1, 14:567.

28. Resolution, November 18, 1921, in Labour Party of Great Britain, Report of the Executive Committee (Edinburgh, 1922), p. 39, cited by Donald S. Birn in "Open Diplomacy: The Washington Conference of 1921–1922," *Comparative Studies in Society and History* 12 (July 1970): 300. Birn's essay stresses British desires to use the submarine issue to escape other auxiliary craft limitation; D'Abernon record of interview with King George V, December 3, 1921, *DBFP*, ser. 1, 14:545; CAB 2/3, C.I.D. meeting, November 26, 1921; ADM 116/2149, Beatty answers to ACNS's agenda, November 22, 1921; ADM 116/3445, Plans Division memoranda for First Sea Lord, December 4, 23, Beatty to Chatfield, December 23, 1921; *Saturday Review* 132 (December 17, 1921): 681.

29. CAB 30/1a, British Empire Delegation meeting, December 20, 1921; TRJD, December 19, 22; *NYT*, December 29, 31, 1921.

30. TRJD, December 24, 1921; Pratt to Theodore Roosevelt, Jr., December 27, 1921, Rodgers to Root, December 31, 1921, GBP.

31. Kunrei, October 1921, reel UD 20, microfilm UD 22, JFMA; Uchida to zenken, January 2, 1922, no. 274, Ide to Katō Kanji, received December 28, 1921, no. 52, Gunbi seigen taisaku kenkyū, vol. 11, JDA; *Yamanashi Katsunoshin sensei ihō roku*, p. 96; TRJD, January 5, 1922; Treaty on Submarines and Poison Gasses, *FRUS, 1922*, 1: 267–70.

32. Harold Sprout and Margaret Sprout, *Toward a New Order of Sea Power*, pp. 204–36, and Thomas Buckley, *The United States and the Washington Conference of 1921–1922*, pp. 118–26, offer detailed accounts of negotiations on cruisers and destroyers, aircraft and the aircraft carriers, and poison gas; *Tokyo Asahi shinbun*, November 22, *NYT*, December 16, 1921.

33. TRJD, December 21, 1921, January 2, 8, 1922; CAB 30/1a, British Empire Delegation meeting, January 3, 1922; Notes on Balfour-Katō conversation, January 5, 1921, *DBFP*, ser. 1, 14:586.

34. Zenken to Uchida, December 8, 1921, no. 143, m.t. 2.4.3.48, reel 317; Uchida to zenken, December 12, 16, m.t. 2.4.3.48, reel 313; *NYT*, December 21, 1921; Ugaki, *Ugaki nikki*, December 15, 27, 1921, p. 364; *Tokyo Asahi shinbun*, December 6, 8, 1921; Tanaka Kunishige to War Minister, December 29, 1921, in Buckley, *The United States and the Washington Conference, 1921–1922*, p. 140. Harding's remarks on nonfortification led some contemporaries and historians to conclude that he had little involvement in the conference. Hughes insisted the opposite was true and argued that the president had merely forgotten what he said in his daily briefing at the White House. See Mark Sullivan diary, March 27, 1922, Hoover institution.

35. Ugaki, *Ugaki nikki*, n.d. January 1922, pp. 365–67; Kisaka Junichirō, "Gunbu to demokurashii," *Kokusai seiji* (1969), pp. 25–26; Hara Shōichirō, "Kokubō kaizō ron," *Taiyō* 27 (November 1921): 28–

48; Mizuno Hironori, "Kaigun seigen to sono zengosaku," *Taiyō* 38 (January 1922): 25; *Tokyo Asahi shinbun,* January 18, 1922; Uchida to zenken, December 10, no. 156, no number, received December 22, no. 263, December 29, 1921, Gunbi seigen taisaku kenkyū, vol.⁻11, XI, JDA.

36. Uchida to zenken, January 12, 1922, nos. 300, 301, 305, 306, m.t. 2.4.3.48, reel 313.

37. Katō to Ide, December 27, 1921, in Nihon kokusai seiji gakkai Taiheiyō sensō genin kenkyū bu, *Taiheiyō sensō e no michi,* 8 (Tokyo, 1963): 3–7; Katō to Uchida, December 16, no. 248, December 24, 1921, no. 281, January 12, Shidehara memorandum, January 10, Katō Tomosaburō to Ide Kenji, January 11, 16, 1922, nos. 34, 36; Zenken to Uchida, January 16, 1922, Gunbi seigen taisaku kenkyū, vol. 11, XI, JDA; Uchida to zenken, January 12, 1922, nos. 306–307, m.t. 2.4.3.48, reel 313.

38. TRJD, January 20, 1922; Ide to Katō Tomosaburō, January 20, 21, 1922, nos. 71, 72; Katō Tomosaburō to Ide, January 22, Shidehara to Uchida, January 23, 1922, Gunbi seigen taisaku kenkyū, vol. 11, JDA; Tanaka Kunishige to Minister of War, January 18, 1922, m.t. 2.4.3.9, cited by Braisted in *The U.S. Navy in the Pacific,* p. 644.

39. Uchida to zenken, January 25, 1922, no. 352, m.t. 2.4.3.48, reel 313; Uchida to zenken, January 28, 1922, no. 362, Gunbi seigen taisaku kenkyū, vol. 11, JDA; *FRUS, 1922,* 1:252–53.

40. *NYT,* February 7, 1922; *Literary Digest* 72 (February 18, 1922): 7–8; *Conference on Limitation of Armaments,* pp. 396–404.

41. *Conference on Limitation of Armaments,* p. 9; Harding to Malcolm Jennings, January 6, Malcolm Jennings papers; Hiram Johnson to Hiram Johnson, Jr., March 5, Hiram Johnson to Hiram Johnson, Jr., and A. M. Johnson, March 16, 26, 1922, Hiram Johnson papers.

42. *LT,* January 23, 1922; *NYT,* February 8, 1922.

43. *Tokyo Asahi shinbun,* ed., *Sono goro o kataru* (Tokyo, 1922), p. 383, cited by Satō Seizaburō in "Kyōchō to jiritsu to no aida—Nihon," *Nenpō seiji gaku 1969,* p. 117; Arai, *Katō,* p. 144; Maeda, *Rekidai naikaku,* 2:359–65.

Conclusion

1. Both quotations appear in Dean Acheson, *This Vast External Realm* (New York, 1973), p. 52.

2. The phrase is LeRoy Ashby's, *The Spearless Leader,* p. 24.

Bibliography

This book is based upon three kinds of sources: official and private archival materials, interviews, and printed biographical and secondary studies. They are to be found scattered across the United States, in London, and in Tokyo.

To understand American naval policy one must begin in Washington with the General Board papers and the various Department of the Navy materials in the National Archives, but the broader politics of national defense must be examined by sifting through the mass of congressional documents concerning naval affairs and by consulting the private papers of major political figures. Among those private manuscripts, the Harding, Hughes, Theodore Roosevelt, Jr., and Hiram Johnson papers proved particularly useful. The many biographies and secondary studies of American politics, diplomacy, and naval affairs during the Wilson and Harding years provide an essential supplement to archival materials. Among these studies, William R. Braisted's pioneering works on the U.S. Navy in the Pacific are of special importance.

Arthur J. Marder provided similarly vital assistance to the student of British naval policy in his magisterial volumes on the Royal Navy. His works presented an indispensable introduction to the complexities and personalities of the naval service which greatly facilitated archival research in London. There the Admiralty archives, in particular the 116 series of memorandums and the 137 series of Board minutes, together with various cabinet papers files at the Public Record Office (portions of which are now available on microfilm) yielded a wealth of data on the inner politics of naval policy. The most valuable source among the various political leaders' papers consulted remains the Lloyd George collection at the House of Lords Library.

The study of Japanese naval policy in Tokyo presented different problems. While the papers of the Imperial Japanese Navy, largely destroyed and scattered during World War II, have been reassembled at the Office of War History of the Japan Defense Agency and preserved at the Shiryō chōsakai (Historical Research Institute), they are far from complete. The Enamoto collection is the most valuable single source for the study of naval arms limitation. Large portions of the Ministry of Foreign Affairs archives were microfilmed by the Library of Congress and have been published in the *Nihon gaikō bunsho* series. But close reading of the original files concerning the Lansing–Ishii conversations of 1917, the Paris Peace Conference of 1919, and the Washington Conference of 1921–1922 revealed that items of major importance had been excluded from both. The *Hara nikki* has been ranked as one of the classics of Japanese literature and proved indispensable to this study. Finally, the volumes of the official World War II history series and once-scorned prewar biographies of leading naval, military, and political figures helped make Tokyo's politics of national defense come alive.

The following list includes all items mentioned in the text and footnotes, together with other materials of major use in the writing of this book.

Archival Sources

A. Official

Admiralty papers. Public Record Office, London.
Cabinet papers. Public Record Office, London.
Department of Navy papers. Record groups 38, 45, 80. National Archives, Washington, D.C.
Department of State papers. Record groups 43, 59, 256. National Archives, Washington, D.C.
General Board papers. Naval History Division. Department of the Navy, Washington, D.C.
Imperial Japanese Navy papers. Office of War History. Japan Defense Agency, Tokyo.

International Military Tribunal for the Far East, Transcripts of the Record. Vols. 2, 60. Harvard University Law School Archives, Cambridge, Massachusetts.
Joint Army and Navy Board papers. Record group 225. National Archives, Washington, D.C.
Ministry of Foreign Affairs papers, Tokyo.
Naval General Staff papers. Shiryō chōsakai [Historical Research Institute], Tokyo.
Naval Staff monographs. Naval Historical Branch. Ministry of Defense, London.

B. Private

Arthur James Balfour papers. British Library (formerly British Museum), London.
William S. Benson papers. Library of Congress, Washington, D.C.
Andrew Bonar Law papers. Beaverbrook Library, London.
William E. Borah papers. Library of Congress, Washington, D.C.
Sir Robert Borden papers. Microfilm OC611. Public Archives of Canada, Ottawa.
Edgard Algernon Robert Cecil (Viscount Cecil of Chelwood) papers. British Library, London.
Josephus Daniels papers. Library of Congress, Washington, D.C.
John W. Davis papers. Yale University Library, New Haven, Connecticut.
Edwin Denby papers. Detroit Public Library, Detroit, Michigan.
Vice Admiral Kenneth G. B. Dewar papers. National Maritime Museum, Greenwich.
Admiral Sir Alexander Duff papers. National Maritime Museum, Greenwich.
Enamoto Jūji 榎本重治 papers. Office of War History, Japan Defense Agency, Tokyo.
Admiral Sir Sydney Fremantle papers. National Maritime Museum, Greenwich.
William F. Fullam papers. Library of Congress, Washington, D.C.
William Howard Gardiner papers. Houghton Library, Harvard University, Cambridge, Massachusetts.
Gotō Shinpei 後藤新平 papers. National Diet Library, Tokyo.
Admiral Sir Frederick T. Hamilton papers. National Maritime Museum, Greenwich.
Warren G. Harding papers. Ohio Historical Society, Columbus, Ohio.
Stanley K. Hornbeck papers. Hoover Institution, Stanford University, Stanford, California.
Edward Mandell House papers. Yale University Library, New Haven, Connecticut.
Charles Evans Hughes papers. Library of Congress, Washington, D.C.
Admiral of the Fleet Earl Jellicoe (John Rushworth Jellicoe) papers.

British Library, London.
Malcolm Jennings papers. Ohio Historical Society, Columbus, Ohio.
Hiram Johnson papers. Bancroft Library, University of California, Berkeley.
David Lloyd George papers. House of Lords Library, London.
Henry Cabot Lodge papers. Massachusetts Historical Society, Boston.
Makino Nobuaki 牧野伸顕 papers. National Diet Library, Tokyo.
Joseph Medill McCormick papers. In Hanna-McCormick family papers, Library of Congress, Washington, D.C.
George VonLengerke Meyer papers. Massachusetts Historical Society, Boston.
Roland Sletor Morris papers. Library of Congress, Washington, D.C.
Admiral of the Fleet Sir Henry F. Oliver papers. National Maritime Museum, Greenwich.
Miles Poindexter papers. Alderman Library, University of Virginia, Charlottesville.
William Veazie Pratt papers. United States Naval War College, Newport, Rhode Island.
Admiral Sir Herbert Richmond papers. National Maritime Museum, Greenwich.
Franklin D. Roosevelt papers. Hyde Park, New York.
Theodore Roosevelt, Jr. papers. Library of Congress, Washington, D.C.
Elihu Root papers. Library of Congress, Washington, D.C.
Saitō Makoto 斎藤実 papers. National Diet Library, Tokyo.
Shōda Kazue 勝田主計 papers. Ministry of Finance, Tokyo.
William S. Sims papers. Naval Historical Collection, Library of Congress, Washington, D.C.
Mark Sullivan papers. Hoover Institution, Stanford University, Stanford, California.
George Sutherland papers. Library of Congress, Washington, D.C.
Tanaka Giichi 田中義一 papers. National Diet Library, Tokyo.
Terauchi Masatake 寺内正毅 papers. National Diet Library, Tokyo.
Charles Beecher Warren papers. Detroit Public Library, Detroit, Michigan.
Admiral Baron Rosslyn Eskine Wester Wemyss papers. Microfilm copy. University of California, Irvine.
Woodrow Wilson papers. Library of Congress, Washington, D.C.
Yamamoto Gombei 山本権兵衛 papers. National Diet Library, Tokyo.

Interviews

Enamoto Jūji, 榎本重治, June 1, 3, 1966.
Sir Reay Geddes, September 10, 1969.
Hara Mitsugi (Keichirō) 原奎一郎 , July 5, 1969.
Suzuki Hajime 鈴木一, July 28, 1969.
Takeshita Masahiko 竹下政彦, July 23, 1969.
Takarabe Minoru 財部實 , July 22, 1969.
Admiral Yamanashi Katsunoshin 山梨勝之進, July 12, 1966.

Printed Primary and Secondary Sources

Abo Kiyokazu 安保 清種. *Katō Kanji taishō den* 加藤寛治大将伝 [The Life of Admiral Katō Kanji]. Tokyo: Katō Kanji denki hensankai 加藤寛治伝記編纂会, 1941.

Acheson, Dean. *This Vast External Realm.* New York: Norton, 1973.

Addison, Christopher. *Four and a Half Years.* 2 vols. London: Hutchinson, 1934.

Akita, George. *Foundations of Constitutional Government in Modern Japan.* 1868–1900. Cambridge: Harvard University Press, 1967.

Akiyama Saneyuki kai 秋山真之会. *Akiyama Saneyuki* 秋山真之. Tokyo: Akiyama Saneyuki kai 秋山真之会, 1933.

Andrade, Ernest, Jr. "The United States Navy and the Washington Conference." *The Historian* 31 (May 1969): 345–63.

Arai Tatsuo 新井達夫. *Katō Tomosaburō* 加藤友三郎. Tokyo: Jiji tsūshinsha 時事通信社, 1958.

Araki Sadao 荒木貞夫. *Gensui Uehara Yūsaku den* 元帥上原勇作伝 [A Biography of Field Marshal Uehara Yūsaku]. 2 vols. Tokyo: Gensui Uehara Yūsaku denki kankōkai 元帥上原勇作伝記刊行会, 1937.

Aritake Shūji 有竹修二. *Saitō Makoto* 斉藤実. Tokyo: Jiji tsūshinsha 時事通信社, 1958.

Asada Sadao. "Japan and the United States, 1915–1925." Ph.D. dissertation, Yale University, 1963.

Asada Sadao. "Japan's 'Special Interests' and the Washington Conference, 1921–1922." *American Historical Review* (October 1961), pp. 62–70.

Asai Masahide 浅井政秀. *Hakushaku Yamamoto Gombei den* 伯爵山本権兵衛伝 [The Life of Count Yamamoto Gombei]. 2 vols. Tokyo: Hakushaku Yamamoto Gombei denki hensan iinkai 伯爵山本権兵衛伝記編纂委員会, 1938.

Ashby, LeRoy. *The Spearless Leader.* Urbana, Ill.: University of Illinois Press, 1972.

Bacon, Admiral Sir Reginald. *The Jutland Scandal.* 2d ed. London: Hutchinson, 1925.

Bacon, Admiral Sir Reginald. *The Life of John Rushworth, Earl Jellicoe.* London: Cassell, 1936.

Bagby, Wesley M. *The Road to Normalcy.* 2d ed. Baltimore: Johns Hopkins University Press, 1968.

Bailey, Thomas A., and Ryan, Paul B. *The Lusitania Disaster.* New York: The Free Press, 1975.

Bailey, Thomas A. *Woodrow Wilson and the Great Betrayal.* New York: Macmillan, 1945.

Baker, Ray Stannard, and Dodd, William E. *The Public Papers of Woodrow Wilson.* 6 vols. New York: Harper and Brothers, 1925–1926.

Baker, Ray Stannard. *Woodrow Wilson and the World Settlement.* 3 vols. Garden City, N.Y.: Doubleday, Page, and Co., 1923.

Bartlett, Ruhl J. *The League to Enforce Peace.* Chapel Hill: University of North Carolina Press, 1944.

Beaverbrook, Lord. *The Decline and Fall of Lloyd George.* New York: Duell, Sloan, and Pearce, 1963.

Beaverbrook, Lord. *Men and Power, 1917–1918.* London: Collins, 1956.

Beaverbrook, Lord (Max Aitken). *Politicians and the War, 1914–1916.* London: Thornton Butterworth, 1928.

Bellairs, Carlyon. *The Battle of Jutland: The Sowing and the Reaping.* London: Hodder and Stoughton, 1919.

Beloff, Max. *Imperial Sunset I: Britain's Liberal Empire, 1897–1921.* New York: Knopf, 1970.

Berton, Peter. "The Secret Russo-Japanese Alliance of 1916." Ph.D. dissertation, Columbia University, 1956.

Birn, Donald S. "Open Diplomacy: The Washington Conference of 1921–1922." *Comparative Studies in Society and History* 12 (July 1970): 297–319.

Blake, Robert. *The Unknown Prime Minister: The Life and Times of Andrew Bonar Law, 1858–1923.* London: Eyre and Spottiswoode, 1955.

Bōeichō bōei kenshūjo senshi shitsu 防衛庁防衛研修所戦史室 [Office of War History, Japan Defense Agency]. *Dai honei rikugunbu I Shōwa jūgonen gogatsu made* 大本營陸軍部〈 I 〉昭和十五年五月まで [Imperial Headquarters: Army Section, I: To May 1940]. Tokyo: Asagumo shinbunsha 朝雲新聞社, 1967.

——— 防衛庁防衛研修所戦史室 [Office of War History, Japan Defense Agency], *Hitō kōryaku sakusen* 比島攻略作戦 [Strategy for the Philippines Assault]. Tokyo: Asagumo shinbunsha 朝雲新聞社, 1966.

——— 防衛庁防衛研修所戦史室 [Office of War History, Japan Defense Agency], *Kaigun gunsenbi I Shōwa jūrokunen jūichigatsu made* 海軍軍戦備〈 I 〉昭和十六年十一月まで [Naval War Preparations I: To November 1941]. Tokyo: Asagumo shinbunsha 朝雲新聞社, 1969.

Bonham-Carter, Violet. *Winston Churchill as I Knew Him.* London: Eyre, Spottiswoode, and Collins, 1965.

Boyce, D. G. *Englishmen and Irish Troubles.* Cambridge: MIT Press, 1972.

Braisted, William R. *The United States Navy in the Pacific, 1897–1909.* Austin: University of Texas Press, 1958.

Braisted, William R. *The United States Navy in the Pacific, 1919–1922.* Austin: University of Texas Press, 1971.

Buckley, Thomas A. *The United States and the Washington Conference, 1921–1922.* Knoxville: University of Tennessee Press, 1970.

Buell, Raymond Leslie. *The Washington Conference.* New York: D. Appleton and Company, 1922.

Burton, David H. *Theodore Roosevelt: Confident Imperialist.* Philadelphia: University of Pennsylvania Press, 1969.

Bywater, Hector C. *Sea Power in the Pacific.* Boston: Houghton Mifflin, 1921.

Callwell, C. E. *Field-Marshall Sir Henry Wilson: His Life and Diaries.* 2 vols. London: Cassell, 1927.

Challener, Richard. *Admirals, Generals, and American Foreign Policy, 1898-1914*. Princeton: Princeton University Press, 1973.

Chalmers, William Scott. *The Life and Letters of David, Earl Beatty*. London: Hodder and Stoughton, 1951.

Chaput, Rolland A. *Disarmament in British Foreign Policy*. London: G. Allen and Unwin, 1935.

Chatfield, Charles. *For Peace and Justice: Pacifism in America, 1914-1941*. Boston: Beacon Press, 1973.

Chatfield, Lord. *It Might Happen Again*. London: William Heinemann, 1947.

Chatfield, Lord. *The Navy and Defence*. London: William Heinemann, 1942.

Chi, Madelaine. *China Diplomacy, 1914-1918*. Cambridge: Harvard University Press, 1970.

Chūō Kōron 中央公論 [The Central Review], 1911-1922.

Churchill, Randolph S. *Winston S. Churchill*. Vol. 2 and companion vols. Boston: Houghton Mifflin 1967, 1969.

Churchill, Winston S. *The World Crisis*. 6 vols. New York: Charles Scribner's Sons, 1923-31.

Clinard, Outen Jones. *Japan's Influence on American Naval Power, 1897-1917*. Berkeley: University of California Press, 1947.

Coletta, Paolo. *William Jennings Bryan*. 3 vols. Lincoln: University of Nebraska Press, 1964-1969.

Colvin, Ian. *The Life of Lord Carson*, vol. 3. New York: Macmillan, 1937.

Conference on the Limitation of Armament, Washington, November 12, 1921-February 6, 1922. Washington: Government Printing Office, 1922.

Congressional Record, 62nd through 67th Congresses, 1911-1922.

Coontz, Robert E. *From the Mississippi to the Sea*. Philadelphia: Dorrance, 1930.

Cooper, John Milton, Jr. *The Vanity of Power*. Westport, Conn.: Greenwood Publishing Company, 1969.

Cronon, E. David, ed. *The Cabinet Diaries of Josephus Daniels, 1913-1921*. Lincoln: University of Nebraska Press, 1963.

Crosby, Gerda Richards. *Disarmament and Peace in British Politics*. Cambridge: Harvard University Press, 1957.

Crowley, James. *Japan's Quest for Autonomy: National Security and Foreign Policy*. Princeton: Princeton University Press, 1966.

Curry, Roy Watson. *Woodrow Wilson and Far Eastern Policy, 1913-1921*. New York: Bookman Associates, 1957.

Danelski, David J., and Tulchin, Joseph S., eds. *The Autobiographical Notes of Charles Evans Hughes*. Cambridge: Harvard University Press, 1973.

Daniels, Jonathan. *The End of Innocence*. Philadelphia: Lippincott, 1954.

Daniels, Josephus. *The Wilson Era*. 2 vols. Chapel Hill: University of North Carolina Press, 1944-1946.

Date Genichirō, ed. 伊達源一郎. Teikoku no kokubō 帝国の国防 [The Empire's Defense]. Tokyo: Minyūsha 民友社, 1915.

Davies, Richard Bell. *Sailor in the Air: The Memoirs of Vice-Admiral Richard Bell Davies.* London: Peter Davies, 1967.

Davis, George T. *A Navy Second to None: The Development of the Modern American Navy.* New York: Harcourt, Brace and Company, 1940.

DeChair, Admiral Sir Dudley. *The Sea is Strong.* London: Harrap, 1961.

Department of the Navy. Annual Reports of the Department of the Navy, 1911–1922. Washington: Government Printing Office, 1911–1923.

Department of State. *Papers Relating to the Foreign Relations of the United States,* 1914 through 1922. Washington: Government Printing Office, 1922–1938.

Department of State. *Papers Relating to the Foreign Relations of the United States 1919: The Paris Peace Conference.* 13 vols. Washington: Government Printing Office, 1942–1947.

Devlin, Patrick. *Too Proud to Fight: Woodrow Wilson's Neutrality.* New York: Oxford University Press, 1975.

Dewar, K. G. B. *The Navy from Within.* London: Gollancz, 1939.

Dingman, Roger. "Nihon to Wuirusonteki sekai chitsujo" 日本と・ウィル゛ン的世界秩序 [Japan and the Wilsonian World Order]. In *Kindai Nihon no taigai taido* 近代日本カ対外態度 [Modern Japanese Attitudes towards the Outside World], edited by Satō Seizaburō and Roger Dingman. Tokyo: Tokyo daigaku shuppankai 東京大学出版会, 1974.

Dingman, Roger. "Power in the Pacific: The Evolution of American and Japanese Naval Policies, 1918–1921." Ph.D. dissertation, Harvard University, 1968.

D'Ombrain, Nicholas. *War Machinery and High Policy: Defence Administration in Peacetime Britain, 1902–1914.* London: Oxford University Press, 1973.

Domvile, Barry. *By and Large.* London: Hutchinson, 1936.

Downes, Randolph C. *The Rise of Warren Gamaliel Harding, 1865–1920.* Columbus: Ohio State University Press, 1970.

Dreyer, Admiral Sir Frederic. *The Sea Heritage.* London: Museum Press, 1955.

Dugdale, Blanche. *Arthur James Balfour.* New York: G. P. Putnam's Sons, 1937.

Duus, Peter. *Party Rivalry and Political Change in Taishō Japan.* Cambridge: Harvard University Press, 1968.

The Economist, 1911–1922.

Ehrman, John. *Cabinet Government and War, 1890–1940.* Cambridge: Cambridge University Press, 1958.

Epstein, M., ed. *The Annual Register,* 1911–1922, n.s. 12 vols. London: Longmans, Green and Co., 1912–1923.

Fairbank, John K.; Reischauer, Edwin O.; and Craig, Albert M. *East Asia: The Modern Transformation.* Boston: Houghton Mifflin, 1965.

Fifield, Russell H. *Woodrow Wilson and the Far East.* New York: Thomas Y. Crowell Co., 1952.

Fiske, Bradley A. *From Midshipman to Rear Admiral.* New York: The Century Company, 1919.

Forcey, Charles. *The Crossroads of Liberalism*. New York: Oxford University Press, 1961.

Fortnightly Review, 1914–1922.

Fowler, Wilton B. *British-American Relations, 1917–1918*. Princeton: Princeton University Press, 1969.

Friedel, Frank. *Franklin D. Roosevelt*, vols. 1, 2. Boston: Little, Brown, 1952–1954.

Fry, Michael G. *Illusions of Security: North Atlantic Diplomacy, 1918–1922*. Toronto: University of Toronto Press, 1972.

Fry, M. G., "The North Atlantic Triangle and the Abrogation of the Anglo-Japanese Alliance." *Journal of Modern History* 39 (March 1967): 353–62.

Fujiwara Akira 藤原 彰. *Gunji shi* 軍事史 [Military History]. Tokyo: Tōyō keizai shinpōsha 東洋経済新報社, 1961.

Fukai Eigo 深井英五. *Kaiko shichijūnen* 回顧七十年 [Memoirs of Seventy Years]. Tokyo: Iwanami shoten 岩波書店, 1941.

Fukudome Shigeru 福留 繁. *Kaigun no hansei* 海軍の反省 [Reflections on the Navy]. Tokyo: Nihon shuppan kyōdōsha 日本出版共同社, 1951.

Fukui Shizuo 福井静夫. *Nihon no gunkan* 日本の軍艦 [*Japan's Warships*]. Tokyo: Shuppan kyōdōsha 出版共同社, 1956.

Gaikō jihō 外交時報 [Diplomatic Review], 1914–1922.

Gaimushō 外務省 [Ministry of Foreign Affairs], ed. *Nihon gaikō bunsho, 1914–1920* 日本の外交文書 [Documents on Japanese Diplomacy]. 28 vols. Tokyo: Gaimushō 外務省, 1965–1974.

Gaimushō 外務省 [Ministry of Foreign Affairs] ed. *Nihon gaikō nenpyō narabi ni shuyō bunsho, 1840–1945* 日本外交年表並主要文書 [Japan Diplomatic Chronicle and Principal Documents, 1840–1945]. 2 vols. Tokyo: Hara shobō 原書房, 1965.

Gaimushō hyakunenshi hensan iinkai 外務省百年史編纂委員会 [Ministry of Foreign Affairs One Hundred Years History, Editorial Committee], ed. *Gaimushō no hyakunen* 外務省の百年 [One Hundred Years of the Ministry of Foreign Affairs]. 2 vols. Tokyo: Hara shobō 原書房, 1969.

Geddes, Auckland Campbell. *The Forging of a Family*. London: Faber and Faber, 1952.

Gelfand, Lawrence E. *The Inquiry: American Preparations for Peace, 1917–1919*. New Haven: Yale University Press, 1963.

Gilbert, Martin, ed. *Lloyd George*. Englewood Cliffs, N.J.: Prentice Hall, 1968.

Gilbert, Martin. *Winston S. Churchill: The Challenge of War, 1914–1916* and companion volumes. Boston: Houghton Mifflin, 1971, 1973.

Glad, Betty M. *Charles Evans Hughes and the Illusions of Innocence*. Urbana, Ill.: University of Illinois Press, 1966.

Gollin, A.M. *Proconsul in Politics: A Study of Lord Milner in Opposition and in Power*. London: Anthony Blond, 1964.

Graebner, Norman A. *An Uncertain Tradition: American Secretaries of State in the Twentieth Century*. New York: McGraw Hill, 1961.

Graham, Roger. *Arthur Meighen*. Toronto: Irwin and Co., 1963.

Granat, Stanley Jerome. "Chinese Participation at the Washington Conference, 1921–1922." Ph.D. dissertation, University of Indiana, 1969.

Great Britain, Foreign Office. *Documents on British Foreign Policy, 1919–1939,* edited by E. L. Woodward, Rohan Butler, and J. P. T. Bury. Ser. 1, vols. 5, 6, 14. London: H. M. Stationery Office, 1954–1966.

Grenville, John A. S., and Young, George Berkeley. *Politics, Strategy and Diplomacy.* New Haven: Yale University Press, 1966.

Gretton, Peter. *Former Naval Person: Winston Churchill and the Royal Navy.* London: Cassell, 1968.

Grigg, John. *The Young Lloyd George.* Berkeley: University of California Press, 1974.

Griswold, A. Whitney. *The Far Eastern Policy of the United States.* New York: Harcourt, Brace and Company, 1938.

Guinn, Paul. *British Strategy and Politics, 1914 to 1918.* Oxford: Clarendon Press, 1965.

Hackett, Roger. *Yamagata Aritomo in the Rise of Modern Japan, 1838–1922.* Cambridge: Harvard University Press, 1971.

Hagedorn, Hermann. *Leonard Wood: A Biography.* 2 vols. New York: Harper and Brothers, 1931.

Haggie, Paul. "The Royal Navy and War Planning in the Fisher Era." *Journal of Contemporary History* 8 (July 1973): 113–30.

Hale, Oron J. *Publicity and Diplomacy: With Special Reference to England and Germany 1890–1914.* 2d ed. Gloucester, Mass.: Peter Smith, 1964.

Hankey, Maurice P. A. *The Supreme Command 1914–1918.* 2 vols. London: George Allen and Unwin, 1961.

Hara Kei zenshū kankōkai 原敬全集刊行会 [Publication Committee for the Collected Works of Hara Kei]. *Hara Kei zenshū* 原敬全集 [The Collected Works of Hara Kei]. 2d ed. 2 vols. Tokyo: Hara shobō 原書房, 1969.

Hara Keichirō, ed. 原奎一郎. *Hara Kei nikki* 原敬日記. 9 vols. Tokyo: Kangensha 乾元社, 1950.

Harper, J. E. T. *The Truth about Jutland.* London: John Murray, 1927.

Harvin, Harry L., Jr. "The Far East in the Peace Conference of 1919." Ph.D. dissertation, Duke University, 1956.

Hata Ikuhiko 秦郁彦. "Meiji ki ikō ni okeru NichiBei Taiheiyō senryaku no hensen 明治期以降における日米太平洋戦略の変遷 [Changes in American and Japanese Pacific Strategies since the Meiji Era]. *Kokusai Seiji* 国際政治 [International Politics] (1967), pp. 96–115.

Hatano Sadao 波多野貞夫. *Kaigun taishō Murakami Kakuichi den* 海軍大将村上格一伝 [The Life of Admiral Murakami Kakuichi]. Hiratsuka, Kanagawa Prefecture 神奈川県平塚. Privately printed, 1933.

Hayashi Gonsuke 林権助. *Waga shichijūnen o kataru* わが七十年を語る [Speaking of My Seventy Years]. Tokyo: Daiichi shobō 第一書房, 1935.

Hayashi Katsuya 林克也. *Nihon gunji gijutsu shi* 日本軍事技術史 [A History of Japanese Military Technology]. Tokyo: Aogi shōten 青木商店, 1957.

Hayashi Shigeru and Oka Yoshitake, eds. 林茂, 岡義武. *Taishō demokurashii no seiji: Matsumoto Gōkichi seiji nisshi* 大正デモクラシー期の政治—松本剛吉政治日誌. [The Politics of Taishō Democracy: The Political

Diaries of Matsumoto Gōkichi]. Tokyo: Iwanami shoten, 岩波書店 1959.

Hazelhurst, Cameron. *Politicians at War, July 1914 to May 1915*. New York: Knopf, 1971.

Herman, Sondra R. *Eleven against War*. Stanford: Hoover Institution Press, 1969.

Hoag, Charles Leonard. *Preface to Preparedness: The Washington Disarmament Conference and Public Opinion*. Washington: American Council on Public Affairs, 1941.

Hosoya Chihiro 細谷千博 *Shiberia shuppei no shiteki kenkyū* シベリア出兵の 史的研究 [Historical Research on the Siberian Expedition]. Tokyo: Yūhikaku 有斐閣, 1955.

Hutchinson, William T. *Lowden of Illinois: The Life of Frank O. Lowden*. 2 vols. Chicago: University of Chicago Press, 1957.

Hyde, H. Montgomery. *Carson: The Life of Sir Edward Carson, Lord Carson of Duncairn*. London: William Heinemann, 1953.

Ichihashi Yamato. *The Washington Conference and After*. Stanford: Stanford University Press. 1928.

Ijiri Tsunekichi 井尻常吉. *Rekidai kenkan roku* 歴代顕官録 [Records of Successive High Officials]. 2d ed. Tokyo: Hara shobō 原書房, 1967.

Imai Seiichi 今井清一. "Taishō ki ni okeru gunbu no seijiteki chii" 大正紀における 軍部の政治的地位 [The Political Position of the Military in the Taishō Period]. *Shisō* 思想 [Thought] (September 1957), pp. 3–21; (December 1957), pp. 106–22.

Imamura Takeo 今村武雄. *Hyōden: Takahashi Korekiyo* 評伝高橋是清 [Takahashi Korekiyo: A Critical Biography]. Tokyo: Keizai zaisei kōhōsha 経済財政弘報社, 1950.

Iriye, Akira. *After Imperialism*. Cambridge: Harvard University Press, 1965.

Iriye, Akira. *Pacific Estrangement*. Cambridge: Harvard University Press, 1972.

Itō Masanori 伊藤正徳. *Dai kaigun o omou* 大海軍を思う [Recollections of a Great Navy]. Tokyo: Bungei shunjūsha 文芸春秋社, 1956.

Itō Masanori 伊藤正徳. *Gunbatsu kōbō shi* 軍閣興亡史 [A History of the Rise and Fall of Military Cliques]. Tokyo: Bungei shunjūsha 文芸春秋社, 1958.

Itō Masanori 伊藤正徳. *Katō Kōmei* 加藤高明. 2 vols. Tokyo: Katō denki hensan iinkai 加藤伝記編纂委員会, 1929.

Itō Masanori 伊藤正徳. *Shinbun seikatsu nijūnen* 新文生活二十年 Tokyo: Chūō kōronsha 中央公論社, 1933.

Itō Masanori 伊藤正徳. *Washington kaigi to sono go* ワシントン会議と其後 [The Washington Conference and Its Aftermath]. Tokyo: Tōhō jironsha 東方時論社, 1928.

James, Robert Rhodes. *Churchill: A Study in Failure, 1900–1939*. New York: World, 1970.

James, Admiral Sir William. *The Sky Was Always Blue*. London: Methuen, 1951.

Japan Advertiser, 1914–1922.

Japan Chronicle, 1914–1922.

Jellicoe, Viscount Admiral of the Fleet. *The Crisis of the Naval War.* London: Cassell, 1920.

Jellicoe, Admiral Viscount of Scapa. *The Grand Fleet, 1914–1916.* London: Cassell, 1919.

Jenkins, Roy. *Asquith: Portrait of a Man and an Era.* New York: Chilmark Press, 1964.

Jensen, Gustav. *Japans Seemacht: Der schelle Aufstieg im Kampf um Selbstbehauptung und Gleichberechtigung in den Jahren 1853–1937* [Japan's Seapower: Its Brilliant Rise in the Struggle for Autonomy and Equality of Rights in the 1853–1937 Period]. Berlin: Verlag Karl Siegismund, 1938.

Jessup, Philip D. *Elihu Root.* 2 vols. New York: Dodd, Mead and Company, 1938.

Johnson, Claudius O. *Borah of Idaho.* New York: Longmans, Green, and Co., 1936.

Jones, Thomas. *Lloyd George.* London: Oxford University Press, 1951.

Jones, Thomas. *Whitehall Diary. Vol. 1, 1916–1925.* Edited by Keith Middlemas. London: Oxford University Press, 1969.

Journal of the Royal United Service Institution, 1914–1922.

Kaigun 海軍 [The Navy], 1914–1920.

Kaigun daijin kanbō 海軍大臣官房 [Navy Minister's secretariat]. *Kaigun gunbi enkaku* 海軍軍備沿革 [The Development of Naval Armaments]. 2d ed. 2 vols. Tokyo: Gannandō shoten 巌南堂書店, 1970.

Kaigunshō 海軍省 [Navy Ministry]. *Yamamoto Gombei to kaigun* 山本権兵衛と海軍 [Yamamoto Gombei and the Navy]. Tokyo: Hara shobō 原書房, 1966.

Kaigun Yūshū Kai, 海軍有終会. *Kinsei teikoku kaigun shiyō* 近世帝国海軍史要 [Essential History of the Modern Imperial Navy]. Tokyo: Kaigun Yūshū Kai 海軍有終会, 1938.

Kajima Morinosuke 鹿島守之助. *Nihon gaikō shi* 日本外交史 [A History of Japanese Diplomacy]. Tokyo: Kajima kenkyūjo 鹿島研究所, 1965.

Kajima Morinosuke 鹿島守之助. *NichiBei gaikō shi* 日米外交史 [A History of Japanese-American Relations]. Tokyo: Kajima kenkyūjo 鹿島研究所, 1958.

Kajima Morinosuke 鹿島守之助. *Washinton kaigi oyobi imin mondai* ワシントン会議及移民問題 [The Washington Conference and the Emigration Problem]. Vol. 13 in Kajima Morinosuke, *Nihon gaikō shi* 日本外交史 [A History of Japanese Diplomacy]. Tokyo: Kajima kenkyūjo shuppankai 鹿島研究所出版会, 1971.

Karsten, Peter. *The Naval Aristocracy.* New York: The Free Press, 1972.

Kennedy, Malcolm D. *The Estrangement of Great Britain and Japan.* Berkeley and Los Angeles: University of California Press, 1969.

Kensei 憲政 [Constitutional Government], 1918–1922.

Kenworthy, J. M. (Baron Strabolgi). *Sailors, Statesmen—and Others: An Autobiography.* London: Rich and Cowan, 1933.

Keynes, Joseph M. *Essays in Biography*. London: Rupert Hall-Davis, 1951.

Kiba Hirosuke 木場 浩介. *Nomura Kichisaburō* 野村吉三郎. Tokyo: Nomura Kichisaburō denki kankōkai 野村吉三郎伝記刊行会 1961.

Kisaka Junichirō 木坂順一郎. "Gunbu to demokurashii" 軍部とデモクラシー [The Military and Democracy]. *Kokusai seiji* 国際政治 [International Politics] (Summer 1969), pp. 1–41.

Kizokuin giji sokkiroku 貴族院議事速記録 [Record of the Debates of the House of Peers] 27th through 46th Diets, 1911–1922.

Kizokuin iinkai giji sokkiroku 貴族院委員会議事速記録 [Record of House of Peers Committee Debates] 27th through 46th Diets, 1911–1922.

Klachko, Mary. "Anglo-American Naval Competition, 1918–1922." Ph.D. dissertation, Columbia University, 1962.

Klein, Ira. "Whitehall, Washington, and the Anglo-Japanese Alliance," *Pacific Historical Review* 41 (1972): 460–83.

Kobayashi Tatsuo 小林龍夫. "Kaigun gunshuku jōyaku" 海軍軍縮条約 [The Naval Limitation Treaties]. In Nihon kokusai seiji gakkai Taiheiyō sensō genin kenkyū bu, 日本国際政治学会太平洋戦争原因研究部 [Japan Association of International Relations, Study Group on the Origins of the Pacific War]. *Taiheiyō sensō e no michi* 太平洋戦争への道, vol. 1. Tokyo: Asahi shinbunsha 朝日新聞社, 1963.

Kobayashi Tatsuo 小林龍夫. *Suiusō nikki: Itō ke monjo* 翠雨荘日記伊藤家文書 [The Green Rain Diary: Itō Family Documents]. Tokyo: Hara shobō 原書房, 1966.

Koizumi Sakutarō 小泉策太郎. *Kai ō jidan* 懐往時談 [Memoirs]. Tokyo: Chūō kōronsha 中央公論社, 1935.

Koss, Stephen E. *Fleet Street Radical: A. G. Gardiner and the Daily News*. Hamden, Conn.: Archon Books, 1973.

Koss, Stephen E. *Sir John Brunner; Radical Plutocrat, 1842–1919*. Cambridge: Cambridge University Press, 1970.

Kuehl, Warren F. *Hamilton Holt*. Gainesville, Fla.: University of Florida Press, 1960.

Kuehl, Warren F. *Seeking World Order*. Nashville: Vanderbilt University Press, 1969.

Kuriya Kanichi 栗屋関一. Shōrai no kaigun: Daikan ka shokan ka hikōki 将来の海軍大艦か小艦か飛行機 [The Navy of the Future: Big Ships, Small Ships, or Aircraft?]. Tokyo: Kokusai renmei kyōkai 国際連盟協会, 1921.

Kuroha Shigeru 黒羽茂. *Taiheiyō o meguru NichiBei kōsō shi* 太平洋をめぐる日米抗争史 [A History of Japanese-American Rivalry over the Pacific]. Tokyo: Nansōsha 南窓社, 1968.

Kusai Sutetarō 小財捨太郎. *Hieizan kōen shū* 比叡山講演集 [A Collection of Speeches Given at Mount Hiei]. Tokyo: Kokusan shōrei kai 国産奨励会, 1918.

Kusai Sutetarō 小財捨太郎. Matsushima kōen shū 松島講演集 [A Collection of Speeches Given at Matsushima]. Tokyo: Kokusan shōreikai 国産奨励会, 1919.

Kyoto daigaku bungakubu kokushi kenkyū shitsu 京都大學文學部國史研究室 [Office for National Historical Research, Humanities Division, Kyoto University]. *Nihon kindai shi jiten* 日本近代史辞典 [A Dictionary of Modern Japanese History]. Tokyo: Tōyō keizai shinpōsha 東洋経済新報社, 1958.

Link, Arthur S. *Wilson.* 5 vols. Princeton: Princeton University Press, 1947–1965.

Link, Arthur S. *Wilson the Diplomatist.* Baltimore: Johns Hopkins University Press, 1957.

Literary Digest, 1918–1922.

Livermore, Seward W. *Politics Is Adjourned.* Middletown, Conn.: Wesleyan University Press, 1966.

Lloyd George, David. *Memoirs of the Peace Conference.* 2 vols. New Haven: Yale University Press, 1939.

Lloyd George, David. *War Memoirs.* 6 vols. Boston: Little, Brown and Co., 1933–1937.

Lloyd George, Frances. *The Years That Are Past.* London: Hutchinson, 1967.

Lockwood, Charles. *Down to the Sea in Subs.* New York: Norton, 1967.

Long, Walter. *Memories.* London: Hutchinson, 1923.

Louis, William Roger. *British Strategy in the Far East, 1919–1939.* Oxford: Clarendon Press, 1971.

Louis, William Roger. *Great Britain and Germany's Lost Colonies, 1914–1919.* Oxford: Clarendon Press, 1967.

Lowe, Peter. *Great Britain and Japan, 1911–1915.* New York: St. Martin's Press, 1969.

Lowitt, Richard. *George W. Norris: The Persistence of a Progressive, 1913–1933.* Urbana, Ill.: University of Illinois Press, 1971.

MacDonald, J. Kenneth. "Lloyd George and the Search for a Postwar Naval Policy, 1919." In *Lloyd George: Twelve Essays,* edited by A. J. P. Taylor. New York: Atheneum, 1971.

MacKay, Ruddock F. *Fisher of Kilverstone.* Oxford: Clarendon Press, 1973.

Mackintosh, John P., *The British Cabinet.* 2d ed., London: Stevens and Sons, 1968.

Maddox, Robert James. *William E. Borah and American Foreign Policy.* Baton Rouge: Louisiana State University Press, 1969.

Maeda Renzan 前田蓮山. *Hara Kei* 原敬. Tokyo: Jiji tsūshinsha 時事通信社, 1958.

Maeda Renzan 前田蓮山. *Rekidai naikaku monogatari* 歴代内閣物語 [Tales of Successive Cabinets]. 2 vols. Tokyo: Jiji tsūshinsha 時事通信社, 1961.

Makino Ryōzō 牧野良三. *Nakahashi Tokugorō* 中橋徳五郎. 2 vols. Tokyo: Nakahashi Tokugorō Ō denki hensankai 中橋徳五郎翁伝記編纂会, 1944.

Makino Nobuaki 牧野伸顕. *Kaisōroku* 回想録 [Memoirs]. 3 vols. Tokyo: Bungei shunjūsha 文芸春秋社, 1948–1951.

Mallet, Bernard, and George, C. Oswald. *British Budgets, Second Series 1913–1914 to 1920–21.* London: Macmillan, 1929.

Manchester Guardian, 1914–1922.

Marchand, C. Roland. *The American Peace Movement and Social Reform 1898–1918.* Princeton: Princeton University Press, 1972.

Marder, Arthur J. *The Anatomy of British Sea Power.* New York: 1940.

Marder, Arthur J., ed. *Fear God and Dread Nought: The Correspondence of Admiral of the Fleet Lord Fisher of Kilverstone.* 3 vols. London: Jonathan Cape, 1952–1959.

Marder, Arthur J. *From the Dardanelles to Oran.* London: Oxford University Press, 1974.

Marder, Arthur. *From the Dreadnought to Scapa Flow: The Royal Navy in the Fisher Era, 1904–1919.* 5 vols. London: Oxford University Press, 1961–1970.

Marder, Arthur J. *Portrait of an Admiral.* London: Jonathan Cape, 1952.

Masumi Junnosuke升味準之輔. *Nihon seitō shi ron* 日本政党史論 [A Historical Analysis of Japanese Political Parties]. 4 vols. Tokyo: Tokyo daigaku shuppankai東京大学出版会, 1965–68.

Matsuoka Masao 松岡正男. *Kaigun taishō Yamashita Gentarō den* 海軍大将山下原太郎伝 [The Life of Admiral Yamashita Gentarō]. Tokyo: Kaigun taishō Yamashita Gentarō denki hensan iinkai 海軍大将山下原太郎伝記編纂委員会, 1941.

Matsushita Yoshio, and Itō Kō, 松下芳男, 伊豆公夫. *Nihon gunji hattatsu shi*日本軍事発達史 [A History of Japan's Military Development]. Tokyo: Mikasa shobō 三笠書房, 1938.

Matsushita Yoshio 松下芳男. *Nihon gunsei to seiji* 日本軍制と政治 [Politics and the Japanese Military System]. Tokyo: Kuroshio shuppansha くろしお出版社, 1960.

Matsushita Yoshio 松下芳男. *Nihon rikkaigun sōdō shi* 日本陸海軍騒動史 [A History of Japanese Military and Naval Strife]. Tokyo: Tsuchiya shoten 土屋書店, 1965.

May, Ernest R. "The Development of Political-Military Consultation in the United States," *Political Science Quarterly* 70 (June 1955): 161–80.

May, Ernest R. *The World War and American Isolation, 1914–1917.* Cambridge: Harvard University Press, 1959.

Mayer, Arno. *Political Origins of the New Diplomacy.* New Haven: Yale University Press, 1959.

Mayer, Arno J. *Politics and Diplomacy of Peacemaking.* 2d ed. New York: Vintage Books, 1969.

Miller, David Hunter. *My Diary at the Conference of Paris.* 21 vols. New York: Privately printed, 1924.

Mitani Taichirō三谷太一郎. "Nihon no kokusai kinyūka to kokusai seiji" 日本の国際金融家と国際政治[Japan's International Financiers and International Politics]. In *Kindai Nihon no taigai taido*近代日本の対外態度 [Modern Japanese Attitudes towards the Outside World], edited by Satō Seizaburō and Roger Dingman. Tokyo: Tokyo daigaku shuppankai 東京大学出版会, 1974.

Mitani Taichirō 三谷太一郎. "Tenkanki (1918–1921) no gaikō shidō 転換期の外交指導 [The 1918–1921 Period of Change in Diplomatic Leadership]. In

Kindai Nihon no seiji shidō 近代日本の政治指導 [Political Leadership in Modern Japan], edited by Shinohara Hajime and Mitani Taichirō 篠原一, 三谷太一郎. Tokyo: Tokyo daigaku shuppankai, 1965.

Mitchell, Brian R. *Abstract of British Historical Statistics.* Cambridge: Cambridge University Press, 1962.

Miyata Mitsuo 宮田 光. *Gensui Katō Tomosaburō den* 元帥加藤友三郎伝 [The Life of Admiral of the Fleet Katō Tomosaburō]. Tokyo: Gensui Katō Tomosaburō denki hensan iinkai元帥加藤友三郎伝記編纂委員会, 1928.

Mizuno Hironori 水野広徳. *Kono issen* 此一戦 [This One War]. 2d ed. Tokyo: Shuppan kyōdōsha 出版協同社, 1958.

Mizuno Hironori 水野広徳. *Nami no uneri* 波のうねり[The Surging of the Seas]. Kinbi Bunendō 金尾文淵堂, 1922.

Mochizuki Kotarō望月小太郎. *Gunbi seigen to NichiBei kankei*軍備制限と日米関係 [Arms Limitation and Japanese-American Relations]. Tokyo: Hyōronsha 評論社, 1921.

Morgan, Kenneth O. *David Lloyd George: Welsh Radical as World Statesman.* Cardiff: University of Wales Press, 1963.

Morgan, Kenneth. "Lloyd George's Premiership: A Study in 'Prime Ministerial Government.' " *Historical Journal*, 13 (March 1970): 130–57.

Morgan, Kenneth O. "Lloyd George's Stage Army: The Coalition Liberals, 1918–1922." In *Lloyd George: Twelve Essays*, edited by A. J. P. Taylor. New York: Atheneum, 1971.

Morison, Elting E. *Admiral Sims and the Modern American Navy.* Boston: Houghton Mifflin, 1942.

Morita Akatsuki 盛田 暁月. *Kokubō to kaigun jūjitsu* 国防と海軍充実 [National Defense and Naval Replenishment]. Tokyo: Teikoku kaigun no kiki hakkōjo 帝国海軍之危機発行所, 1914.

Morley, James. *The Japanese Thrust into Siberia.* New York: Columbia University Press, 1957.

Morris, A. J. Anthony. *Radicalism against War 1906–1914.* Totowa, N.J.: Rowan and Littlefield, 1972.

Morrison, Joseph L. *Josephus Daniels: The Small-d Democrat.* Chapel Hill: University of North Carolina Press, 1966.

Morton, Louis. "War Plan Orange: Evolution of a Strategy." *World Politics* 11 (January 1959): 221–50.

Mowat, Charles L. *Lloyd George.* Oxford: Oxford University Press, 1964.

Murakami Kakuichi 村上格一, ed. *Gundan kaigun* 軍談海軍 [The Navy: Professional Talks]. Tokyo: Jitsugyō no Nihonsha実業之日本社, 1918.

Murray, Sir Oswyn A. R. "The Admiralty." *The Mariner's Mirror* 23 (1937): 13–35; 25 (1939): 89–111, 216–28, 328–38.

Murray, Robert K. *The Harding Era.* Minneapolis: University of Minnesota Press, 1969.

Nagaoka Shinjirō 長岡新次郎. "Ishii Ranshingu kyōtei no seiritsu" 石井ランシング協定の成立 [The Conclusion of the Ishii-Lansing Agreement]. *Kokusai seiji* 国際政治 [International Politics] (1967), pp. 54–71.

Najita Tetsuo, *Hara Kei in the Politics of Compromise, 1904–1915.* Cambridge: Harvard University Press, 1967.

Nakagawa Shigeo 中川 繁丑 . *Gensui Shimamura Hayao den* 元帥島村速
雄伝 [A Biography of Admiral of the Fleet Shimamura Hayao]. Tokyo:
Privately printed, 1933.
The Nation, 1911-1922.
National Review, 1918-1922.
Neu, Charles E. *An Uncertain Friendship: Theodore Roosevelt and Japan
1906-1909.* Cambridge: Harvard University Press, 1967.
The New Republic, 1918-1922.
New Statesman, 1911-1922.
New York Times, 1911-1922.
Nihon kaigun kōkū shi hensan iinkai 日本海軍航空史編纂委員会 [Editorial
Committee for the History of Japanese Aviation]. *Nihon kaigun
kōkū shi* 日本海軍航空史 [A History of Japanese Naval Aviation], vol. 1.
Tokyo: Jiji tsūshinsha, 時事通信社 1969.
Nihon kokusai seiji gakkai Taiheiyō sensō genin kenkyū bu 日本国際政治学会
太平洋戦争原因研究部 [Japan Association of International Relations, Pacific
War Origins Study Group]. *Taiheiyō sensō e no michi* 太平洋戦争への道
[The Road to the Pacific War] vols. 1, 8. Tokyo: Asahi shinbunsha
朝日新聞社 , 1963.
Nineteenth Century and After, 1914-1922.
Nish, Ian. *Alliance in Decline.* London: Athlone Press, 1972.
Nish, Ian. *The Anglo-Japanese Alliance: The Diplomacy of Two Island
Empires, 1894-1907.* London: University of London Press, 1966.
Northedge, F. S. *The Troubled Giant: Britain among the Great Powers
1916-1939.* New York: Praeger, 1966.
O'Gara, Gordon C. *Theodore Roosevelt and the Rise of the Modern Navy.*
Princeton: Princeton University Press, 1943.
Ogasawara Chōsei 小笠原長生 , ed. *Kaigun hen* 海軍篇 [The Navy]. Vol.
13 in *Denki Dai Nippon shi* 伝記大日本史 [A Biographical History of
Great Japan], edited by Nagasaka Kaneo, 長坂金雄 . Tokyo: Yūzankaku
雄山閣 , 1936.
Ogasawara Chōsei 小笠原長生 . *Kyōjō Yashiro Rokurō* 侠将八代六郎
[The Gallant Admiral Yashiro Rokurō]. Tokyo: Seikyōsha 政教社 ,
1931.
Ogata Taketora 緒方竹虎 . *Ichi gunjin no shōgai* 一軍人の生涯 [A
Sailor's Life]. Tokyo: Bungei shunjūsha 文芸春秋社 , 1955.
Oka Yoshitake 岡 義武 . *Tenkanki no Taishō* 転換期の大正 [Taishō: An
Era of Change]. Tokyo: Tokyo daigaku shuppankai 東京大学出版会,
1969.
Okada Keisuke 岡田啓介 . *Kaikoroku* 回顧録 [Memoirs]. Tokyo: Main-
ichi shinbunsha 毎日新聞社 , 1950.
Okamoto, Shumpei. *The Japanese Oligarchy and the Russo-Japanese
War.* New York: Columbia University Press, 1970.
Okawa Masazō. "The Armaments Expansion Budgets and the Japanese
Economy after the Russo-Japanese War." *Hitotsubashi Journal of Eco-
nomics* 5 (January 1965): 65-83.
Ōkuma kō hachijūgonen shi hensan iinkai 大隈侯八十五年史編纂委員会 [Edi-

torial Committee, Marquis Ōkuma's Eighty Five Years]. *Ōkuma kō hachijūgonen shi*大隈侯八十五年史 . Tokyo: Hara shobō 原書房, 1970.

Okurashō Showa zaisei shi henshūshitsu ; 大蔵省昭和財政史編集室 [Office of Shōwa Financial History , Ministry of Finance]. *Shōwa zaisei shi* 昭和財政史 [A Financial History of the Shōwa Era], vol. 1. Tokyo: Okurashō 大蔵省 , 1965.

Olson, Lawrence, Jr. "Hara Kei: a Political Biography." Ph.D. dissertation, Harvard University, 1953.

Ōsumi taishō denki kankōkai 大角大将伝記刊行会 [Committee for the Publication of the Biography of Admiral Ōsumi]. *Danshaku Ōsumi Mineo den* 男爵大角岑生伝 [The Life of Admiral Ōsumi Mineo]. Tokyo: Ōsumi taishō denki kankōkai 大角大将伝記刊行会 , 1943.

Outlook, 1914–1922.

Earl of Oxford and Asquith (Herbert Henry Asquith). *Memories and Reflections 1852-1927*. 2 vols. Boston: Little, Brown and Company, 1928.

Ōyama Azusa 大小梓 . Yamagata Aritomo ikensho 小縣 有朋意見書 [The Yamagata Aritomo Memoranda]. Tokyo: Hara shobō 原書房, 1966.

Padfield, Peter. *Aim Straight: A Biography of Admiral Sir Percy Scott*. London: Hodder and Stoughton, 1966.

Patterson, A. Temple. *Jellicoe: A Biography*. London: Macmillan, 1969.

Patterson, A. Temple, ed. *The Jellicoe Papers: Selections from the Private and Official Correspondence of Admiral of the Fleet Earl Jellicoe of Scapa*. 2 vols. London: Navy Records Society, 1966–1968.

Petrie, Charles. *The Life and Letters of the Right Hon. Sir Austen Chamberlain*. 2 vols. London: Cassell, 1940.

Petrie, Charles. *Walter Long and His Times*. London: Hutchinson, 1936.

Pomeroy, Earl S. *Pacific Outpost: American Strategy in Guam and Micronesia*. Stanford: Stanford University Press, 1951.

Prescott, Francis C. "The Lansing-Ishii Agreement." Ph.D. dissertation, Yale University, 1949.

Pusey, Merle J. *Charles Evans Hughes*. 2 vols. New York: Macmillan, 1951.

Pyle, Kenneth. *The New Generation of Meiji Japan*. Stanford: Stanford University Press, 1969.

Rapaport, Armin. *The Navy League of the United States*. Detroit: Wayne State University Press, 1962.

Renouvin, Pierre. *War and Aftermath 1914-1929*. Translated by Remy Inglis Hall. New York: Harper and Row, 1968.

Richardson, Alexander, and Hurd, Alexander, eds. *Brassey's Naval and Shipping Annual*, 1919–1920, 1920–1921, 1921–1922. 3 vols. London: William Clownes and Sons, 1920–1922.

Riddell, Lord (George). *Lord Riddell's Intimate Diary of the Peace Conference and After 1918-1923*. New York: Reynal and Hitchcock, 1934.

Riddell, Lord (George). *Lord Riddell's War Diary*. London: Ivor Nicholson and Watson, 1933.

Riddell, Lord. *More Pages from My Diary 1908-1914*. London: Country Life Press, 1934.

Ritter, Gerhard. *The Sword and the Scepter.* Translated by Heinz Norden. Coral Gables, Fla.: University of Miami Press, 1970.
Roosevelt, Eleanor B. *Day Before Yesterday.* Garden City, N.Y.: Doubleday, 1959.
Roseveare, Henry. *The Treasury.* London: Allen Lane, 1969.
Roskill, Stephen. "The Dismissal of Admiral Jellicoe." *Journal of Contemporary History* 1 (October 1966): 69–94.
Roskill, Stephen. *Hankey: Man of Secrets.* 2 vols. London: Collins, 1970-72.
Roskill, Stephen. *Naval Policy between the Wars.* London: Collins, 1968.
Rothwell, V. H. *British War Aims and Peace Diplomacy, 1914-1918.* London: Oxford University Press, 1971.
The Round Table, 1918-1922.
Rowland, Peter. *The Last Liberal Governments: Unfinished Business 1911-1914.* New York: St. Martin's Press, 1971.
Royama Masamichi.*Foreign Policy of Japan 1914-1939.* Tokyo: Japan Council Institute of Pacific Relations, 1941.
Russell, Francis. *The Shadow of Blooming Grove: Warren G. Harding in His Times.* New York: McGraw Hill, 1968.
Safford, Jeffrey J. "Experiment in Containment: The United States Steel Embargo and Japan, 1917." *Pacific Historical Review* 39 (November 1970): 439-52.
Saitō shishaku kinen kai 斎藤子爵記念会 [Viscount Saitō Memorial Society]. *Shishaku Saitō Makoto den* 子爵斎藤實伝 [The Life of Viscount Saitō Makoto]. Tokyo: Saitō Shishaku kinen kai 斎藤子爵記念会, 1941.
Satō Seizaburō 佐藤誠三郎. "Kyōchō to jiritsu to no aida—Nihon"協調と自立との間 一日本 [Japan: Between Association and Autonomy]. *Nenpō seiji gaku 1969*年報政治学[The Political Science Annual, 1969], pp. 99-144.
Satō Tetsutarō 佐藤鉄太郎. *Teikoku kokubō shi ron* 帝国国訪史論 [A Historical Study of Japanese Defense]. Tokyo: Tokyo insatsu東京印刷, 1908.
Saturday Review, 1921-1922.
Scalapino, Robert A. *Democracy and the Party Movement in Prewar Japan: The Failure of the First Attempt.* Berkeley and Los Angeles: University of California Press, 1953.
Schilling, Warner R. "Admirals and Foreign Policy." Ph.D. dissertation, Yale University, 1953.
Schilling, Warner R. "Weapons, Doctrine, and Arms Control: A Case from the Good Old Days." In *The Use of Force,* edited by Robert J. Art and Kenneth N. Waltz. Boston: Little, Brown and Co., 1971.
Schurman, Donald. *The Education of a Navy.* Chicago: University of Chicago Press, 1965.
Scott, Admiral Sir Percy. *Fifty Years in the Royal Navy.* London: John Murray, 1919.
Seymour, Charles, ed. *The Intimate Papers of Colonel House.* 4 vols. Boston: Houghton Mifflin, 1926-1928.

Shaw, Albert. *The Messages and Papers of Woodrow Wilson.* 2 vols. New York: Review of Reviews Company, 1924.

Shibuya Sakudō 渋谷作動. *Taketomi Tokitoshi* 武富時敏. Tokyo: Taketomi Tokitoshi Kankōkai 武富時敏刊行会, 1934.

Shigemitsu Osami 重光蔵. "Ishii Ranshingu kyōtei" 石井ランシング協定 [The Ishii-Lansing Agreement]. *Kokusai seiji* 国際政治 [International Politics] (Summer 1958), pp. 66–96.

Shimada Kinji 島田謹二. *Amerika ni okeru Akiyama Saneyuki* アメリカにおける秋山真之 [Akiyama Saneyuki in America]. Tokyo: Asahi shinbunsha 朝日新聞社, 1969.

Shimanuki Takeji 島貫武治. "Nihon no kokubō hōshin yōhei kōryō" 日本の国防方針用兵綱領 [Reflections on Japan's National Defense Policies and Tactics]. *Kokubō* 国防 [Defense] 10 (November 1961): 66–82.

Shinobu Seizaburō 信夫清三郎. *Taishō seiji shi* 大正政治史 [Political History of the Taishō Era]. 4 vols. Tokyo: Kawade shobō 河出書房, 1951–1952.

Shūgiin and Sangiin, comp., 衆議院, 参議院 [Houses of Representatives and of Councillors]. *Gikai seido shichijūnen shi* 議会制度七十年史 [Seventy Years' History of the Parliamentary System]. 12 vols. Tokyo: Shūgiin and Sangiin 衆議院, 参議院, 1960–1963.

Shūgiin, *Dai yon bunryōkai giroku, Yosan iinkai giroku* 衆議院 第四分量会議録, 予算委員会議録 [House of Representatives, 4th subcommittee and Budget Committee Hearings], 27th through 46th Diets, 1911–1922.

Shūgiin giji sokkiroku 衆議院議事速記録 [Records of Debates of the House of Representatives], 27th through 46th Diets, 1911–1922.

Shūgiin iinkai giji sokkiroku 衆議院委員会議事速記録 [Record of the Debates of House of Representatives Committees], 27th through 46th Diets, 1911–1922.

Sims, William S. *The Victory at Sea.* Garden City, New York: Doubleday, Page and Co., 1921.

Sinclair, Andrew. *The Available Man.* New York: Macmillan, 1965.

Snowbarger, Willis Edward. "The Development of Pearl Harbor." Ph.D. dissertation, University of California, Berkeley, 1950.

Spaulding, Robert M., "The Bureaucracy as a Political Force, 1920–1945." In *Dilemmas of Growth in Prewar Japan,* edited by James William Morley. Princeton: Princeton University Press, 1971.

The Spectator, 1911–1922.

Spector, Ronald. *Admiral of the New Empire: The Life and Career of George Dewey*. Baton Rouge: Louisiana State University Press, 1974.

Spender, J. A. and Asquith, Cyril. *Life of Lord Oxford and Asquith.* 2 vols. London: Hutchinson, 1932.

Sprout, Harold and Sprout, Margaret. *Toward a New Order of Sea Power.* Princeton: Princeton University Press, 1940.

Steinberg, Jonathan. *Yesterday's Deterrent.* New York: Macmillan, 1965.

Steiner, Zara S. *The Foreign Office and Foreign Policy, 1898–1914.* New York: Cambridge University Press, 1969.

Stirling, Yates. *Sea Duty: The Memoirs of a Fighting Admiral.* New York: G. P. Putnam's Sons, 1939.

Stone, Ralph. *The Irreconcilables.* Lexington: University Press of Kentucky, 1970.

Sullivan, Mark. *The Great Adventure at Washington.* Garden City, N.Y.: Doubleday, Page and Co., 1922.

Sullivan, Mark. *Our Times.* Vol. 5. New York: Charles Scribner's Sons, 1933.

Suzuki Hajime, ed. 鈴木一. *Suzuki Kantarō jiden* 鈴木貫太郎自伝 [The Autobiography of Suzuki Kantarō]. Tokyo: Ōgikukai shuppanbu, 櫻菊会出版部, 1949.

Suzuki Kantarō denki iinkai, 鈴木貫太郎伝記委員会 [Suzuki Kantarō Biographical Association]. *Suzuki Kantarō den* 鈴木貫太郎伝 [The Life of Suzuki Kantarō]. Tokyo: Suzuki Kantarō denki iinkai 鈴木貫太郎伝記委員会, 1961.

Suzuki Shinkichi 鈴木信吉. Yashiro kaigun taishō shokan shū 八代海軍大将書翰集 [The Collected Letters of Admiral Yashiro]. Tokyo: Ōgikukai shuppanbu 櫻菊会出版部, 1941.

Suzuki Shōgo 鈴木正吾 ed. *Ozaki Gakudō zenshū* 尾崎咢堂全集 [The Collected Works of Ozaki Yukio]. 12 vols. Tokyo: Kōronsha 公論社, 1955–1956.

Swartz, Marvin. *The Union of Democratic Control in British Politics during the First World War.* Oxford: Clarendon Press, 1971.

Sylvester, A. J. *The Real Lloyd George.* London: Cassell, 1947.

Taiyō 太陽 [The Sun], 1911–1922.

Takakura Tetsuichi 高倉徹一. *Tanaka Giichi denki* 田中義一伝記 (A Biography of Tanaka Giichi]. 2 vols. Tokyo: Tanaka Giichi denki kankōkai 田中義一伝記刊行会, 1963.

Takenobu, Y. *The Japan Year Book,* 1914–1922. Tokyo: Japan Year Book Office, 1914–1922.

Takeuchi, Sterling Tatsuji. *War and Diplomacy in the Japanese Empire.* Chicago: University of Chicago Press, 1935.

Tate, Merze. *The United States and Armaments.* Cambridge: Harvard University Press, 1948.

Taylor, A. J. P., ed. *Lloyd George: A Diary by Frances Stevenson.* New York: Harper and Row, 1971.

Taylor, A. J. P. *Politics in Wartime and Other Essays.* London: Hamish Hamilton, 1964.

Taylor, A. J. P., ed. *Lloyd George: Twelve Essays.* New York: 1971.

Teitoku Osawa Jizaburō den kankōkai 提督小沢治三郎伝刊行会 [Association for Publication of a Biography of Admiral Osawa Jizaburō]. *Teitoku Osawa Jizaburō den* 提督小沢治三郎伝 [The Life of Admiral Osawa Jizaburō]. Tokyo: Hara shobō 原書房, 1969.

Tillman, Seth. *Anglo-American Relations at the Paris Peace Conference, 1919.* Princeton: Princeton University Press, 1961.

The *Times* (London), 1911–1922.

Times Literary Supplement, 1918–1922.

Tokyo Asahi shinbun 東京朝日新聞, 1911–1922.

Tokyo Asahi shinbun, seijibu　東京朝日新聞政治部　[Political Desk, *Asahi shinbun*]. *Sono goro o kataru*　そのころを語る　[Speaking of Those Days]. Tokyo: Asahi shinbunsha 朝日新聞社, 1928.

Trask, David. *Captains and Cabinets: Anglo-American Naval Relations, 1917–1918.* Columbia: University of Missouri Press, 1972.

Tsunoda Jun 角田 順. *Manshū mondai to kokubō hōshin* 満州 問題と国防方針 [The Manchurian Problem and National Defense Policy]. Tokyo: Hara shobō 原 書房, 1967.

Tuleja, Thaddeus. *Statesmen and Admirals: Quest for a Far Eastern Policy.* New York: Norton, 1963.

Turnbull, Archibald, and Lord, Clifford L. *History of United States Naval Aviation.* New Haven: Yale University Press, 1949.

Uchida Yasuya denki hensan iinkai 内田康哉伝記編纂委員会 [Editorial Committee for a Biography of Uchida Yasuya]. *Uchida Yasuya* 内 田 康哉. Tokyo: Kajima shuppankai 鹿 島 出 版会, 1969.

Ugaki Kazushige 宇垣 一 成. *Ugaki Kazushige nikki* 宇垣一成日記 [The Diary of Ugaki Kazushige]. Tokyo: Asahi shinbunsha 朝日新聞社, 1968.

Ujita Naoyoshi 宇治田直義. *Shidehara Kijūrō* 幣原喜重郎. Tokyo: Jiji tsū-shinsha 時事通信社, 1958.

Ullman, Richard H. *Anglo-Soviet Relations, 1917–1920: II, Britain and the Russian Civil War.* Princeton: Princeton University Press, 1968.

U.S. Congress, House of Representatives, 62nd through 67th Congresses, *Hearings.* Washington: Government Printing Office, 1911–1922.

U.S. Congress, House of Representatives, 62nd through 67th Congresses, *House Reports.* Washington: Government Printing Office, 1911–1922.

U.S. Congress, Senate, 62nd through 67th Congresses, *Hearings.* Washington: Government Printing Office, 1911–1923.

U.S. Congress, Senate, 62nd through 67th Congresses, *Senate Reports.* Washington: Government Printing Office, 1911–1922.

U.S. Department of Commerce, *Historical Statistics of the United States 1789–1945.* Washington: Government Printing Office, 1949.

United States Naval Institute Proceedings, 1911–1922.

Unterberger, Betty Miller. *America's Siberian Expedition, 1918–1920: A Study of National Policy.* Durham: Duke University Press, 1956.

Usui Katsumi 臼井 勝美. "Berusaiyu-Washinton taisei to Nihon no shihaisō" ヴェルサイユ・ワシントン体制と日本の支配層 [Japan's leadership elite and the Versailles-Washington system]. In *Kindai Nihon seiji shisō shi* 近代日本政治思想史 [A History of Modern Japanese Political Thought] edited by Miyazawa Toshiyoshi and Ōkōchi Kazuo 宮沢俊義・大河 一男. 2 vols. Tokyo: Yūhihaku 有 斐 閣, 1970.

Utsunomiya Kan and Satō Tetsujirō 宇都宮鼎・佐藤鋼次郎. *Kokubōjō no shakai mondai* 国防上之社会問題 [Social Problems Relating to National Defense]. Tokyo: Tōshōsha 冬夏社, 1920.

Uyehara, Cecil. *Checklist of Archives in the Japanese Ministry of Foreign Affairs, Tokyo, 1868–1945.* Washington: Library of Congress, 1954.

Vinson, John Chalmers. *The Parchment Peace.* Athens: University of Georgia Press, 1955.

Wakatsuki Reijirō 若槻礼次郎. *Kofūan kaiko roku* 古風庵回顧録 [Memoirs].
Tokyo: Yomiuri shinbunsha 読売新聞社, 1950.
Walker, Sir Charles. *Thirty-Six Years at the Admiralty.* London: Lincoln
Williams, 1934.
Walworth, Arthur. *Woodrow Wilson.* 2 vols. New York: Longman's, Green,
1958.
Washington Post, 1918–1921.
Weigley, Russell F. *The American Way of War.* New York: Macmillan,
1973.
Weinroth, Henry. "Left Wing Opposition to Naval Armaments in Britain
before 1914." *Journal of Contemporary History* 6 (1971): 93–120.
Wells, Samuel F., Jr. "William Mitchell and the Ostfriesland." *The
Historian* 26 (August 1964): 538–62.
Wester Wemyss, Lady. *The Life and Letters of Lord Wester Wemyss,
Admiral of the Fleet.* London: Eyre and Spottiswoode, 1935.
Wheeler, Gerald E. *Admiral William Veazie Pratt, U.S. Navy: A Sailor's
Life.* Washington: Naval History Division, Department of the Navy, 1974.
Wheeler, Gerald E. *Prelude to Pearl Harbor: The United States Navy and
the Far East, 1921–1931.* Columbia: University of Missouri Press, 1963.
Williamson, Samuel R. Jr. *The Politics of Grand Strategy.* Cambridge:
Harvard University Press, 1969.
Wilson, Trevor, ed. *The Political Diaries of C. P. Scott, 1911–1928.* Ithaca,
N.Y.: Cornell University Press, 1970.
Winkler, Henry F. *The League of Nations Movement in Great Britain, 1914–
1919.* New Brunswick, New Jersey: Rutgers University Press, 1952.
Woodward, Ernest Llewellyn. *Great Britain and the German Navy.* Oxford:
Clarendon Press, 1935.
Woodward, Nelson E. "Postwar Reconstruction and International Order: A
Study of the Diplomacy of Charles Evans Hughes, 1921–1925." Ph.D.
dissertation, University of Wisconsin, 1970.
Yamamoto Eisuke 山本英輔. *Yamamoto Gombei* 山本権兵衛. Tokyo: Jiji
tsūshinsha 時事通信社, 1958.
Yamamoto Shirō 山本四郎. *Taishō seihen no kisoteki kenkyū* 大正政変の基礎
的研究 [Basic Research on the Taishō Political Change]. Tokyo: Ocha-
nomizu shobō 御茶水書房, 1970.
Yamanashi Katsunoshin sensei kinen shuppan iinkai 山梨勝之進先生 記念
出版委員会 [Committee for the Publication of a Memorial to Yamanashi
Katsunoshin]. *Yamanashi Katsunoshin sensei ihō roku* 山梨勝之進先生
遺芳録 [A Memorial Record of Yamanashi Katsunoshin]. Tokyo:
Privately printed, 1968.
Yamasaki Kakujirō and Ogawa Gotarō. *The Effect of the World War upon
the Commerce and Industry of Japan.* New Haven: Yale University
Press, 1929.
Yardley, Herbert. *The American Black Chamber.* Indianapolis: Bobbs-
Merrill. 1931.
Yim, Kwanha. "Japanese Policy Toward China During World War I." Ph.D.
dissertation, Fletcher School of Law and Diplomacy, 1968.

Yoshimura Michio 吉村 道男. *Nihon to Roshia* 日本とロシア [Japan and Russia]. Tokyo: Hara shobō 原書房 1968.

Young, A. Morgan. *Japan under Taishō Tenno.* London: George Allen and Unwin, 1928.

Young, Desmond. *Rutland of Jutland.* London: Cassell, 1963.

Young, Kenneth. *Arthur James Balfour.* London: G. Bell and Sons, 1963.

Zacharias, Ellis M. *Secret Missions.* The Story of an Intelligence Officer. New York: G. P. Putnam's Sons, 1946.

Zebel, Sidney H. *Balfour: A Political Biography.* Cambridge: Cambridge University Press, 1973.

Index

Abo, Rear Admiral Kiyokazu, 59
Admiralty, Board of: political power of,
6–8, 107–8, 115, 168; and naval estimates, 10, 108–14, 119–20, 161–62,
171, 262 n.20; leadership of, 20, 26,
119; and Jutland, 24–25, 115–16; and
war operations, 24–25, 42; organization of, 28–30, 171–72, 174; and arms
limitation, 78, 82–83, 110, 173–74, 208;
and terms of peace, 83–84; and standard of naval strength, 108, 110, 170,
173–77, 264 n.40; strategic views of,
165–67. *See also* Royal Navy
aircraft carrier, 95–96, 99, 123, 127, 150
Akiyama, Rear Admiral Saneyuki, 14,
58, 125
Amami, Ōshima, 189, 203
Angell, Norman, 19
Anglo-American naval rivalry, 4, 37, 78,
97, 161; efforts to end, 86–88,
109–11, 121
Anglo-German naval rivalry, 4–6, 81, 94
Anglo-Japanese alliance: origins of, 4,
7; renegotiation of, 8, 128, 164–65,
169–70, 177, 186; uses of, 14, 49;
termination of, 148, 152–53, 166, 204,
206, 270 n.22
arms control. *See* arms limitation
arms limitation: of armies, 74, 78, 82;
of capital ships, 150, 156–57, 174–75,
187–88, 192–93, 196–97, 201, 203; of
submarines, 158, 175, 200, 207–9; of
aircraft, 175–76
—prewar, discussion of, 8; advocates
of, 9–10, 12, 15; opponents of, 10;
wartime discussion of, 33, 39, 44–47;
postwar proposals for, 68, 74–75, 92–
93, 109, 143–46, 148, 150–52, 160,
164, 182–83; negotiations for, 76–79,
81–84, 88, 111–12, 201–12 passim

311

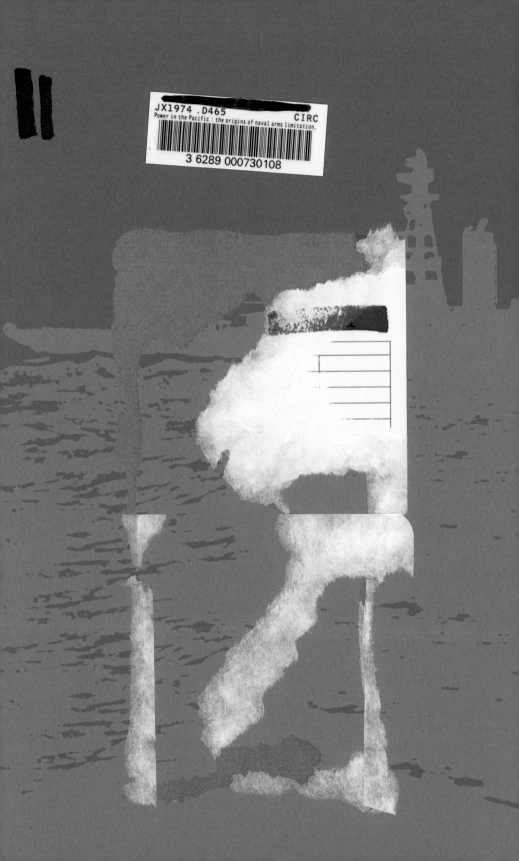